THE CHALLENGE
OF EFFECTIVE
SPEAKING

THE CHALLENGE
OF EFFECTIVE
SPEAKING

EIGHTH EDITION

Rudolph F. Verderber

University of Cincinnati

Wadsworth Publishing Company

Belmont, California

A Division of Wadsworth, Inc.

Communication Editor: Peggy Randall
Developmental Editor: John Bergez
Editorial Assistant: Sharon Yablon
Production Editor: Donna Linden
Designer: James Chadwick
Print Buyer: Barbara Britton
Permissions Editor: Peggy Meehan
Copy Editor: Steven Bailey
Photo Researcher: Stephen Forsling
Compositor: Thompson Type, San Diego, California
Cover Design: Vargas/Williams Design
Cover Photo: © Ian Berry/Magnum

Photo credits are listed on page 411.

Printed in the United States of America 34

1 2 3 4 5 6 7 8 9 10 — 95 94 93 92 91

Library of Congress Cataloging-in-Publication Data
Verderber, Rudolph F.
    The challenge of effective speaking / Rudolph F. Verderber. — 8th ed.
        p.   cm.
    Includes index.
    ISBN 0-534-13968-X
    1. Public speaking.   I. Title.
PN4121.V4   1991
808.5′1 — dc20   90-12626
                                                                     CIP

Brief Contents

Contents

Checklists

Preface

In 1970, with the publication of the first edition of *The Challenge of Effective Speaking*, I shared with my colleagues my solution to the speech teacher's dilemma of how students could master a great deal of basic information before they give their first speeches and at the same time be fully prepared to give speeches early in the term. The results have been gratifying. Not only has *Challenge* become a widely used text, but also the then-radically different approach that I have developed over the years has become the standard format for a significant number of successful speech texts.

The "Verderber Method": A Structured Approach

What some people now refer to as "the Verderber method" is a student-centered approach that organizes the principles of speechmaking in a hierarchical fashion and fosters student skill development through a structured four-step learning model. The first seven chapters present the most fundamental principles underlying all types of speechmaking, enabling students to develop the basic skills necessary to deliver a major speech within the first two weeks of the course. Subsequent sections of the book build on this foundation by focusing on increasingly more complex and more specific skills.

Because "skillfulness" has both cognitive and behavioral requirements, the four-step learning model begins with "skill learning." During this first step students read the text to understand the theory of preparation and presentation. The second step of the learning model is practice. The practice exercises embedded in each chapter are specifically designed so that students can apply the skills particular to that chapter while continuing to develop competence in the use of previously learned skills. Practice with skills culminates in speech assignments that give the students an opportunity to show mastery of a group of skills in oral presentations. The third step is learning by observation. Accordingly, students are provided a sample speech for each assignment with marginal notes pointing out examples of successful skill usage and making suggestions about where and how skills might have been used better. The fourth step in the learning model is providing critical feedback of students' speeches. Specific written and oral critiques of speeches show students how well they have met the specific assignments or how well they have mastered various skills necessary for accomplishing that assignment. Critiques are built into the chapter exercises and are facilitated by checklists that provide specific evaluative criteria for each type of speech.

Organization

Now let me explain the structure of *The Challenge of Effective Speaking* in greater detail. After an introductory chapter, which comprises Part I, the text is organized in four major parts: Fundamental Principles, Informative Speaking, Persuasive Speaking, and Adapting to Other Occasions and Formats. Fundamental Principles is a six-chapter unit with approximately 100 pages of the unit discussing the basic steps of preparing and presenting a sound speech. Although 100 pages may sound like a lot, the unit is not only written to be a relatively "fast read," but also to be "an easy learn." Information needed to prepare and deliver speeches is presented in a clear step-by-step fashion. Each step is reinforced with an exercise. As a result, when students have completed the 12 Speech Preparation Exercises in Chapters 2–6, they will be ready to deliver their first major speeches. For instance, Exercise 1 in Chapter 1 guides students through the process of generating a list of suitable topics and selecting three for possible use for their first speeches; Exercise 2 guides students in the process of writing three well-worded speech goals for the topics they selected from their brainstorming sheets and selecting one of the three for their first speeches. The sequence of exercises culminates in Exercise 12 in Chapter 6, in which students write diaries of their speech practice sessions (the final stage before actual delivery of the speeches to an audience) to indicate how their analyses of each practice led to the improvement of their speeches.

Part III focuses on informative speaking. Because effective informative speaking involves a learning process, Chapter 8, "Principles of Informative Speaking" is designed to help students move audiences through the three steps of learning: attending to information, understanding information, and remembering information.

Succeeding chapters in the informative speaking unit then focus on the skills of demonstrating (explaining processes), using visual aids, describing, defining, and reporting. To give students a chance to practice these skills, each of these chapters features an assignment emphasizing use of those skills, a critique sheet that encourages critical listening for those skills, and a sample speech that exemplifies those particular skills.

Part IV focuses on persuasive speaking. The persuasive speaking principles are an extension of both fundamental and informative speaking principles. For instance, although a persuasive speech may be designed to motivate a person to act, the student may use skills of demonstration, description, definition, or reporting within the speech. In Chapter 14, "Principles of Persuasive Speaking," students are introduced to specific goals that are designed to change beliefs and move to action, to analyzing audience attitude and making use of that analysis, to forming speech arguments that serve as the building blocks of the persuasive speech body, to organizing arguments to meet audience needs, to using language to gain emotional reaction to material, and to building credibility.

Succeeding chapters in the unit focus on the persuasive speaking skills of reasoning, motivating, and refuting. As was true of the unit on informative speaking, in the persuasive speaking unit students have a chance to practice these skills. Each of the individual chapters features an assignment, critique sheet, and sample speech.

Preceding each of the major parts of the book, an introductory statement helps students to understand the goals of the part and why the information in that part is written and organized as it is.

Although few courses are long enough to allow students practice time with all of the informative and persuasive speaking skills individually, most courses include at least three speeches, one as a culmination of learning the fundamental principles, another as a separate informative speech, and a third as a persuasive speech. This book is written to give focus to these three assignments. In addition, an instructor may have a chance to make one or more additional assignments that emphasize individual informative and persuasive speaking skills.

Regardless of what assignments are given, the instructor can approach each assignment with the knowledge that the students have developed an understanding of the skills necessary to complete that assignment.

Special Features and Changes in the Eighth Edition

Since the introduction of *The Challenge of Effective Speaking* in 1970, many other authors have adopted some or all of the Verderber method, including sections on specific informative and persuasive skills and the use of student speeches as models. As a result, what was once a novel approach to the pedagogical issues has now been "copied" by many other successful texts. Yet even though utilizing the general approach, other books lag behind in making improvements to this approach. In each edition I have incorporated improvements, some of them very subtle, some of them less so, that have refined both the hierarchical approach to content presentation and the learning model. With this eighth edition, I have undertaken a significant revision that I believe increases the soundness of the underlying pedagogy and thus the learning potential of your students.

In addition to the **exercises, assignments,** and **annotated student speeches** that continue to be an integral part of the text, three new or modified features of this edition are especially notable:

• The text now presents the 12 **speech preparation exercises** in Chapters 2–6 as a complete and coherent sequence that guides the student through the preparation of a speech.

• New to this edition are the 16 **checklists** that provide reminders of steps to perform as well as critique forms for different types of speeches. A listing of the checklists can be found following the table of contents.

• Also new to this edition are extended **case studies** that profile three quite different individuals who use public speaking in a variety of ways, both professionally and avocationally. The case studies vividly illustrate how the skills taught in a public speaking course may come to play a large and often surprising role in students' future lives.

A number of other substantive and organizational changes improve the clarity and comprehensiveness of the text. Part I, Orientation, continues to comprise a one-chapter introduction. In this chapter, in addition to giving greater emphasis to the importance of public speaking principles in both formal and informal speaking contexts, I have included a preview of the steps of preparation and delivery that form Part II, Fundamental Principles. The goal of this preview is to give students enough of a taste of the method that each can present a narrative speech, one of the traditional "warm-up" speeches that instructors often assign during the first week of the course.

Part II, Fundamental Principles, includes six chapters. The major changes in this part are designed to provide a more complete and cohesive overview of speech fundamentals. Chapter 2, "Selecting Your Topic and Refining Your Goal," considers brainstorming for topics, writing a speech goal, writing a thesis statement, analyzing the audience, and analyzing the occasion. This chapter now includes a much expanded section on audience analysis as well as a more detailed explanation of writing speech goals and thesis statements. Chapter 3, "Finding, Recording, and Using Information," covers sources and kinds of information that speakers need to build their speeches. After a now more complete explanation of sources of information, the chapter features a new section on the raw material of speeches: finding factual statements and expert opinion. The chapter concludes with an expanded section on methods of shaping information, including such forms as example, illustration, comparison, and contrast. Chapter 5, "Speech Language," puts much greater emphasis on the means of achieving clarity, vividness, emphasis, and appropriateness of language. Chapter 7, "Listening Critically to Speeches," has been entirely rewritten. The chapter now contains sections on attending, understanding, evaluating, and remembering, as well as a discussion of critical standards for speeches. This chapter, previously the second chapter, has been moved to the end of the Fundamental Principles unit to give students a better understanding of the criteria to use in evaluating speeches.

Each of the chapters in Part III, Informative Speaking, has been rewritten to more clearly emphasize the skill-development process. Chapter 8, "Principles of Informative Speaking," now includes a more detailed definition of informative speaking as well as a greater emphasis on the means of getting attention, creating understanding, and increasing retention. Chapter 9, "Using Visual Aids," has been rewritten and includes a more complete discussion on how to make overheads, use flipcharts, and use computer graphics. The next four chapters (Chapter 10, "Demonstrating Process"; Chapter 11, "Describing"; Chapter 12, "Defining"; and Chapter 13, "Reporting") have been revised completely to emphasize skill development. The chapters are written so that each skill can be made the focus of an informative speech or can be used in combination with others in a single informative speech assignment.

Part IV, Persuasive Speaking, also has been rewritten to better emphasize skill development. Chapter 14, "Principles of Persuasive Speaking," has a new section on the definition of persuasive speaking and a much more complete section on the importance of audience analysis in determining speech goals and speech material. The next four chapters (Chapter 15, "Reasoning with Audiences"; Chapter 16, "Motivating

Audiences"; and Chapter 17, "Critically Evaluating Arguments: Refuting") have been revised completely to emphasize skill development. The chapters are written so that each skill can either be made the focus of a persuasive speech or be used in combination with others in a longer persuasive speech assignment.

Part V, Adapting to Other Occasions and Formats, has been minimally revised.

Overall, this edition is designed not only to emphasize the Verderber method, but also to improve upon that method. I firmly believe that students who apply themselves to the learning of the material in this book will find themselves being able to give the very best speeches possible.

Acknowledgments

Although I am responsible for what appears in this book, the content reflects the thoughts of a great many people. I gratefully acknowledge the students who contributed speeches and outlines to this edition. I also thank the many instructors who offered feedback and insights gained through their use of the seventh edition: Carole Blair, University of California, Davis; Rodney M. Cole, University of Maine, Augusta; Patricia Comeaux, Murray State University; Ronald E. DeBacco, Westmoreland County Community College; Lois Einhorn, State University of New York, University Center at Binghamton; Anne Holmquest, University of Louisville; Harold J. Kinzer, Utah State University; John Lyne, University of Iowa; Beth Waggenspack, Virginia Polytechnic Institute and State University; and David Walker, Middle Tennessee State University.

I want to give special thanks to the entire Wadsworth team involved in the production of this book, with special thanks to John Bergez, who helped me realize how I could come closer to achieving my goals for creating this textbook in the first place. Thanks are also due to the subjects of the three case studies in this edition of *Challenge*, all of whom gave generously of their time in order to share their experiences with students: Steve Burrill, Jill Fox, and Joe Marshall.

Finally, I express my gratitude to my wife Kathie who continues to provide both valuable insight and inspiration, and to my daughter Allison who is learning by example that writing well is a long, sometimes frustrating, but always exhilarating process.

PART I

ORIENTATION

The goal of this one-chapter unit is to introduce you to public speaking. In addition to discussing the importance of public speaking, public speaking as communication, and the responsibilities of public speaking, a preview of public speaking principles also is included that will lead you in the preparation of a first speech. Because your course may require an introductory speech even before you have had a chance to study the fundamental principles presented in Part II, the chapter concludes with a narrative speech assignment that enables you to use information with which you are already familiar.

Prior to each of the next four sections of this book, we will preview what is to come in that unit and explain both why the unit is organized as it is and how you can make the most of the material in that section.

Chapter 1 | Introduction to Public Speaking

Most people are aware of the importance of public speaking to success in nearly any walk of life. Those who doubt its importance misunderstand what it means to "give a speech." A speech is an oral presentation, usually given without interruption, and delivered to entertain, to help people to understand, to help people to form or alter beliefs, or to move people to action. Speeches occur on at least three levels, only one of which conforms to most people's idea of a speech.

First is the formal level of a noted speaker delivering a prepared speech to an audience that has assembled expressly to hear that speaker. We all recognize that when an organization such as the American Medical Association invites a famous person to give a "keynote address" to open a national convention, the keynoter will be giving a speech. Likewise, when you attend a town meeting to learn about the ideas of candidates for public office, you expect to hear speeches. Although on this level the number of speeches you give may be few, they are likely to be very important in bringing an important message to an audience or in getting you elected. A course in public speaking can be justified on this basis alone.

The second level is the kind of speech that most people give as part of their jobs. For instance, as a college professor, I give speeches in every one of my classes. Now some of my colleagues may prefer to call these presentations something other than speeches. But when they explain an assignment for the next class or when they clarify a difficult concept that was a part of the day's reading, they are giving a speech, whatever they may choose to call it. Similarly, lawyers give speeches to judges and juries, salespeople give speeches to prospective customers, and waiters give speeches to their customers as part of their jobs.

A third level is the impromptu, off-the-cuff speaking that nearly all of us do at some time each day. For instance, we give directions to a person on how to get to the hotel or to the French Chateau restaurant or how to use the Fax machine. We explain our views on a movie, a novel, a play, or a television program. We present our views on gun control, the minimum wage, taxes. Now you might be saying, "Those aren't speeches," but they are. When they are well done, they use all the principles that we will discuss as methods of preparing and presenting speeches.

In spite of the importance of our various levels of speechmaking, most people accept their communication strengths and weaknesses without paying attention to the development of skills that might make them more effective. Enrollment in this course is the first step toward a commitment to work on improved communication. Countless people have discovered that they can learn to improve their speaking, just as you will.

Although speeches are given to meet a variety of situations, in this book we will focus primarily on those principles of speechmaking that are directed at two important goals: communicating information and changing attitudes and behaviors. You will learn how to clarify people's understanding of information and increase their retention of that information. In addition, you will learn to give clear reasons, support your reasons with evidence, and present your reasons and evidence in a compelling manner to increase the likelihood of influencing others.

In this chapter we will consider public speaking as communication, examine legal and ethical responsibilities of public speaking, and preview material that will lead you toward the preparation and presentation of your first speech.

Public Speaking as Communication

Public speaking, like writing a letter to your folks or saying "I love you" to that special man or woman, is a communication event. But it is a special form of communication. What separates public speaking from other types

Many people think of speeches as formal affairs, but in fact we give speeches to meet the demands of a wide variety of situations. Effective communication skills are relevant to all kinds of speaking, from explaining the specialty of the house to inspiring supporters at a public rally.

of communication is that it is characterized by one person, a speaker, who prepares a speech with the intention of achieving a specific goal and delivers that speech to an audience of one or more people who listen to the speech and have the freedom to accept or reject the speaker's goal.

Although this sounds straightforward, a speech is a communication transaction that is affected by several variables: context, speaker (source), speech (message), channel, audience (receivers), feedback, and noise. Let us take a closer look at these variables and consider how they relate to one another to form a public-speaking communication transaction. To make this discussion concrete, imagine that your company's management has asked you to explain to your fellow workers why each person is being asked to donate an hour each week to the company's Right-to-Read program.

The Context

Every communication transaction takes place in a specific *context*, the interrelated conditions of communication. In the case of speech, one aspect of context is the *physical setting* in which the speech occurs. The components of the physical setting include location, time, light, temperature, and seating arrangements. Each component affects the speech. The meeting-room setting in which you give a speech to your fellow workers is likely to differ from the town hall setting in which you may explain the company's program.

A second aspect of context is *historical*. Previous communication episodes affect the communication transaction. For instance, if you said, "The company would like the same kind of support we gave to last year's Free Store program," a person who was not familiar with the company's involvement would have no idea what you were talking about.

A third aspect of context is *norms*, or the guidelines that we establish (or perceive as established) to conduct transactions. If the occasion for your speech is perceived to be a formal one, for example, then your behavior and that of the audience will differ from those when an occasion is perceived to be informal. If corporate executives are to attend a formally arranged "speech," then people are likely to behave differently than if you are asked to talk to a group that is eating lunch.

The Source of the Message: The Speaker

The *speaker* is the source or the originator of the speech or communication message.

How speakers perceive their material depends on the field of experience that affects their thoughts and feelings. When you speak, you are affected by your past and present experiences, feelings, ideas, moods, gender, occupation, and religion, as well as by aspects of your total environment. Thus, how you have lived your life determines to some extent what you will choose to say and how you will say it. For instance, as you think about how you will explain the company's support for the Right-to-Read program, you may develop feelings of concern about those who cannot read and the problems they face.

In addition, an audience will have or will develop a perception of the speaker's *credibility*, the *persona* or image that the speaker presents. The more credible the audience perceives the source to be, the more likely that its members will trust or have confidence in the accuracy of the information the speaker presents. For this reason, effective speakers will consider what they can do or say that will help the audience perceive them as qualified, caring, and engaging individuals.

The Message: A Speech

A public-communication transaction takes place through the sending and receiving of messages in the form of a speech. Speech messages comprise meanings communicated through symbols; these meanings are encoded and organized by the speaker and decoded by members of the audience.

MEANINGS   Meanings are the pure ideas and feelings that exist in the mind of a person. You may have ideas about how to study for your next exam, what your career goal is, and whether taxes should be raised or lowered; you also may have feelings such as jealousy, anger, and love. The meanings you have within you, however, cannot be transferred magically into another's mind. To share these ideas and feelings you must form messages comprising both verbal and nonverbal elements.

Symbols are words, sound, and actions that represent meaning. As you speak, you choose words to convey your meaning. At the same time, facial expressions, gestures, and tone of voice — all nonverbal cues — accompany your words and affect the meaning that your listener receives. The listener takes both the verbal symbols and nonverbal cues and assigns meanings to them.

ENCODING AND DECODING   The process of transforming ideas and feelings into symbols and organizing them is called *encoding a message*; the process of transforming messages back into ideas and feelings is called *decoding*. You have been communicating for so long that you probably do not consciously think about either encoding or decoding processes. When your eyes grow bleary and you say, "I'm tired," you are not thinking, "I wonder what symbols will best express the sensation I am now experiencing." Conversely, when you hear the words, "I'm tired" and see the bleary eyes of the other person, you are not likely to think, "*I* stands for the person doing the talking, *am* means that the *I* is linked to some idea, and *tired* means growing weary or feeling a need for sleep; therefore, the person is feeling a need for sleep and the bleary eyes confirm the accuracy of the statement." At the same time, you are not likely to consider whether you have the same mental picture of "tired" as the person using the word. Nevertheless, these encoding and decoding processes do occur. There are, of course, times when you *are* aware of the encoding process. If you are giving a speech and you get the idea that your audience is not understanding a point you are trying to make, you may go through a conscious encoding process to select expressions that are likely to be better understood. Likewise, you become aware of the decoding process when you must figure out the meaning of an unfamiliar word by the way it is used in a sentence.

When you speak, you may communicate meaning intentionally or unintentionally. *Intentional meaning* occurs when you make a conscious effort to select symbols to communicate. Under these circumstances you are acting purposefully. Yet at the same time, you may be giving *unintentional meaning* by sending a conflicting message through nonverbal cues. Suppose you are complimenting your audience for its contribution to the Right-to-Read program and notice that some audience members are frowning and shifting in their chairs. You may have intended to be very gracious with your compliments, but the edge in your voice has given away your belief that the group's effort actually has fallen short of your hopes for it. As a result of the negative thought, you sent an unintentional nonverbal message that some audience members perceived as sarcasm.

Although unintentional communication can be either verbal or nonverbal, it is more likely to be nonverbal. People do on occasion blurt out something that they did not intend to say, but most of us are far better able to control verbal reactions than we are such nonverbal cues as a higher pitch level, a scowl, or a reddening of the face. When unintentional messages compete with intentional ones, listeners are more likely to pay attention to the unintentional because they believe that spontaneous reaction is more likely to be honest. As we discuss in Chapter 6, when you deliver speeches, you should make sure that both the verbal and the nonverbal communication send the same message.

Because the processes of encoding and decoding messages are at the heart of public speaking, many of the skills that you will learn from this book relate directly to improving your message formation and the accuracy of interpretation so that your communication effectiveness is increased.

FORM OR ORGANIZATION   When meaning is complex, it may need to be communicated in sections or in a certain order for people to grasp it more easily. In short, the meaning must be organized. Your co-workers will expect that your explanation of company interest in the Right-to-Read program will be organized and not just a random expression of your thoughts. Furthermore, if your argument moves logically from reason to reason, your meaning is likely to be clearer than if you randomly present bits and pieces of argument and evidence.

At first, organizing statements will take time and may seem quite difficult. As you gain experience, however, you will find that you can organize even your spur-of-the-moment thoughts clearly.

The Channel

The *channel* is both the route traveled by the message and the means of transportation. Your words are carried to others by airwaves; your facial expressions, gestures, and movement are carried by light waves. Usually, the more channels that you can use to carry a message, the more likely that your communication will succeed. Although our everyday communication is carried intentionally and unintentionally by any sensory channel—a fragrant scent and a firm handshake both may communicate—public speaking is basically two-channeled—that is, carried by sound and sight.

In addition, public speaking may be in person or mediated (delivered over radio or television). Any mediated channel introduces different variables that the speaker must understand and adapt to.

The Receiver: The Audience

The *audience*—or, in communication terms, the receiver—is the end and object of your speech. Your entire reason for speaking is to gain a specific response—for example, to motivate your co-workers to donate one hour a month to tutor adults in reading.

Whether you are able to get the response you desire is likely to depend on your audience's interest in hearing you out and its understanding of what you are saying, and then its attitude toward what you have said. If your co-workers are not interested enough to pay attention to your plea to donate one hour a month, if they do not understand what you mean by tutoring adults, or if they are strongly opposed to the idea of donating time, then you have very little chance of achieving your goal. Chapter 2, "Selecting Your Topic and Refining Your Goal," discusses audience analysis in detail.

As a result of the complexity of audience attention, interest, understanding, and attitudes, the effect of your message may be different from the one you intended. If you say in your speech, for instance, "People who need help learning to read have a right to the help we can give them," some audience members may hold an entirely different view of what constitutes rights, or they may lack your empathy for illiterate adults. As a result, they may not accept your line of argument.

Feedback

Whether your audience decodes the meaning of your messages properly or not, they will have some mental or physical response to your messages, and that response often enables you to determine whether your audience really understands you. Audience response—called *feedback*—tells you whether your message has been heard, seen, or understood. If the verbal or nonverbal response tells you that your message was not received, was received incorrectly, or was misinterpreted, you can send the message again, perhaps in a different way, so that your intended meaning is the same as the meaning your audience gets.

Different kinds of public-speaking situations provide for different amounts of feedback. Giving a speech on television brings *zero feedback*, because the speaker is unaware of the audience's response.

In-person speeches enable the speaker to monitor nonverbal feedback. If you say, "It's the responsibility of citizens to help those who are unable to help themselves," you might be able to tell by facial expression whether the audience agrees with you. If many people knit their brows, frown, or shake their heads, then you will know that you need to discuss the idea more fully.

Some in-person speeches occur in a setting that is informal enough for people to ask questions. Direct interaction between speaker and audience represents the highest level of feedback, but such free flow does not occur in most speech settings.

In their research, Leavitt and Mueller concluded that communication effectiveness improved markedly as the situation moved from zero feedback to complete interaction.[1] In your speeches, you want to stimulate as much feedback as possible, and you want to learn to make the most of even a limited amount of feedback.

Noise

Noise often limits the audience's ability to interpret, understand, or respond to symbols. *Noise* is any stimulus that gets in the way of sharing meaning. Much of your success as a speaker depends on how you cope with external, internal, and semantic noises.

External noises are the sights, sounds, and other stimuli that draw people's attention away from intended meaning. For instance, during your presentation on literacy, the audience's attention may be drawn to the sound of an airplane overhead. The airplane sound is external noise. External noise does not have to be sound, however. Perhaps during your speech people's eyes are drawn to a chart on the wall behind you that shows your company's drop in sales during the last month. Such visual distraction also is external noise.

Internal noises are the thoughts and feelings that interfere with meaning. Have you ever found yourself daydreaming during a speech? Perhaps you let your thoughts wander to the good time you had at a party the night before or to the argument you had with a friend that morning. If you have tuned out the speaker's words and tuned in a daydream or a past conversation, then you have created internal noise. Of course, the same thing can happen to your audience when you are the speaker.

Semantic noises are alternate meanings aroused by a speaker's symbols. Suppose you told your co-workers that the company was liberal — meaning generous — in its attitude toward the Right-to-Read program. If your audience has associated a political philosophy, they will probably miss your meaning. Because meaning depends on personal experience, others may at times decode a word or phrase differently from the way that you have intended. When this happens, semantic noise is interfering with your attempt to communicate.

Model of Public Speaking as Communication

Let us summarize these variables of public speaking in model form. Figure 1.1 illustrates the communication process in terms of a one-to-one relationship between the speaker and one audience member. The left-hand circle represents you, the speaker. In the center of that circle is a speech, a message, or series of messages that you send. The nature of your thought or feeling is created, shaped, and affected by your total field of experience, represented in the outer circle by such specific factors as your values, culture, environment, experiences, occupation, gender, interests, knowledge, and attitudes. The bar between the circles represents the channel. By both words and actions you send your speech through the sending channel (upper half of the bar).

Figure 1.1

*A model of communication
between two individuals.*

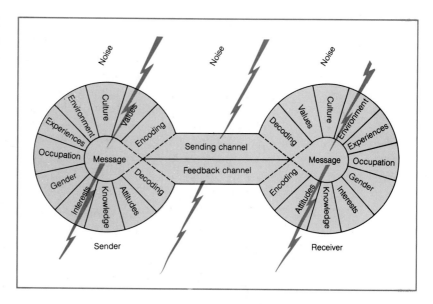

The right-hand circle represents one receiver—or one audience member. The message(s) in your speech moves to the center of the circle. The receiver decodes the message, thus giving it meaning. The receiver's total field of experience, especially his or her attitudes, beliefs, and values, affects the decoding process. Upon decoding and interpreting the messages of the speech, the receiver sends verbal and nonverbal reaction back to you through the receiving or feedback channel (lower half of the bar). You then receive and decode the feedback to interpret the receiver's response.

The area that surrounds you and the receiver represents the context—the setting or occasion in which the speech occurs. During the process, external, internal, and semantic noise may be occurring at various places in the model. These noises may affect how well you and the receiver share meanings. Note that this model will differ in its particulars for each person in the audience.

Public Speaking Carries Responsibilities

So far we have been considering public speaking as a process—a communication transaction. More than other forms of communication, however, public speaking also has an ethical dimension. Although the First

Amendment to the U.S. Constitution guarantees freedom of speech, it is interpreted by the courts as carrying certain legal and ethical responsibilities that you, as a student of public speaking, bear. In 1972, the Speech Communication Association, the national association of teachers of speech communication in the United States, endorsed the "Credo for Free and Responsible Communication in a Democratic Society." Two paragraphs of the document lay a foundation for your persuasive speaking responsibilities:

> We accept the responsibility of cultivating by precept and example, in our classrooms and in our communities, enlightened uses of communication; of developing in our students a respect for precision and accuracy in communication, and for reasoning based upon evidence and a judicious discrimination among values.
>
> We encourage our students to accept the role of well-informed and articulate citizens, to defend the communication rights of those with whom they may disagree, and to expose abuses of the communication process.

These two paragraphs provide the overall approach to speech responsibilities. Now let us take a look at specific legal and ethical responsibilities.

Legal Responsibilities

As a public speaker you have at least three major legal responsibilities.

First, you must refrain from any communication that may be defined as constituting a "clear and present danger." Speeches that present a clear and present danger are those that incite people to panic, to riot, or to overthrow the government. From the time you began studying civics, you learned that a person cannot yell "fire" in a public place just to see what might happen — that would be speech to incite panic. You also can be prosecuted for giving a speech that incites a mob of students to riot against the administration or a mob of citizens to riot against the government.

Second, you must refrain from using obscene language. Despite a relaxation of society's attitude toward the use of vulgar language, a person still can be prosecuted for obscene public speech. Because the U.S. Supreme Court has defined obscenity as behavior that is outside the boundary of "community standards," what is considered illegal varies from one place to another.

Third, you must refrain from using language that will defame the character of another person. *Defamation* is harming another person by making statements that convey an unjust unfavorable impression. Thus, if in a political campaign Carson calls Simpson a card-carrying Communist, then Simpson can sue Carson for defamation. If Carson made a statement on the basis of hearsay or solely to cast doubt on the political aims of Simpson, then Carson will be held guilty of defamation. If, however, Carson can *prove* to the satisfaction of the jury or judge that Simpson is a Communist, Carson will be acquitted. Truth is the best defense against any charge of defamation. Thus, if you are planning to say anything that could be interpreted as defamation, you will want to make sure that you have the evidence to uphold your opinion.

Ethical Responsibilities

Ethical issues according to Richard Johannesen, focus "on degrees of rightness and wrongness in human behavior."[2]

Although legal responsibilities are codified, what is ethical is far more likely to be a personal matter. Still, we expect the society in which we live to hold to certain standards that can help us with our personal value judgments. The family, schools, and church all share the responsibility of helping the individual develop ethical standards that can be applied to specific situations. Yet, as we are all aware, ethical judgments are seldom easy. In this initial look at ethical responsibilities for persuasive speaking, we will present two broad guidelines that were reflected in the Speech Communication Association's credo and that are endorsed by most, if not all, communication scholars.

1. *You as a public speaker are responsible for what you say.* Your audience has the right to hold you accountable for what you say. If, for instance, you say that Peters (your opponent in a hotly contested election) received campaign funds from illegal sources, your audience holds you responsible for the truth and accuracy of that statement.

    You uphold this ethical responsibility in at least two ways. First, you should have solid evidence, not personal opinion or hearsay, on which to build your arguments. Before you make any statement about Peters's campaign funds, you are responsible for finding the facts. If you have not found facts to support your claim, it is unethical to present such a claim as if you had such facts.

    Second, you should present the facts for your audience to examine. You have the right to advocate a position—however unpopular it may be—but the listener has the right to examine the bases for the conclusions you have drawn. If you state that Peters received funds from illegal sources, you should share with the audience the facts that led you to that conclusion. Although an audience may be willing to trust your judgment on such matters, you owe them — and Peters for that matter — the right to examine the facts for themselves.

2. *You as a public speaker have a responsibility to allow free choice on the part of your audience.* Often this means allowing the other side to be heard. Freedom of speech applies equally to both sides of an issue or controversy. You do not have the right to suppress the speech of those who hold different views from your own. If you have accused Peters of getting illegal campaign funds, you have the responsibility to allow Peters to reply to your accusations. Any effort to suppress that right or to deny Peters access to the same audience is unethical.

Everything we say or do in our speeches has a potential effect on our audience. If we know that we have a solid basis for what we say, are willing to share the facts on which our statements are based, and are willing to listen to opposing views, we are reasonably certain that our public speaking will meet our ethical responsibilities.

Ethical speaking helps you build respect for yourself and others.

Toward Your First Speech

Because you may be called upon to give a short speech before you have had a chance to read and master the fundamentals presented in Part II of this textbook, in this section we preview the eight steps of speech preparation that are fully developed over the next five chapters. In addition, we begin a discussion of coping with speech nervousness, a feeling that most speakers experience before they deliver their speeches.

Preparing Your First Speech
In many cases the first speech assignment in a public-speaking course is to narrate a personal experience in a speech lasting anywhere from two to five minutes. We will focus the discussion of the eight steps of speech preparation on such an assignment.

1. *Select a topic you know something about and that you are interested in.* Whether you are preparing a speech for a class or for some organization that has invited you to speak, you are likely to be asked to select the topic. Your criteria for selecting a topic are your expertise with and your interest in that topic.

   Thus, if you are asked to prepare a narrative speech, think about your own humorous, suspenseful, or dramatic experiences and select one that you think your audience would enjoy hearing about. For example, in the sample speech included at the end of this chapter, Andy Gilgoff thought of an embarrassing experience that he had at the local gym when he thought that his clothes had been stolen from his locker.

2. *Determine the response that you want from your audience.* Every effective speech has a specific goal that the speaker intends to achieve. For speeches that you give in this class, your goal is likely to be that your audience enjoy the material, understand information, believe something, or behave in a specific way. For instance, Andy wanted the audience to laugh at his realization that his clothes had not been taken.

3. *Analyze your audience and your occasion.* Although there are times when the audience or occasion or both will determine or inspire a specific speech goal, it is more likely that you will analyze your audience and occasion to determine the kind of information you will use in your speech and how you will discuss that information. The key to your audience analysis is to gather demographic information that will enable you to make predictions about audience interests, knowledge, and attitudes. By gathering information about the size of the audience, the members' average age, gender, educational levels, occupation, income level, race, religion, nationality, geographic uniqueness, and group affiliation, you can make assessments about the kinds of material they are likely to respond to. Although the quality of your audience analysis may well determine the eventual success or failure of your speech, for this opening assignment, you should consider whether your audience will respond to the material that you are planning to use.

   Because most students have had fears of forgetting their locker number, forgetting the lock combination, or losing valuables, Andy thought that the class would be able to relate to his experience.

4. *Gather and evaluate material that you can use in the speech.* For speeches you prepare this term you will draw material from your own experience, observations you have made, interviews you have conducted, and library sources you have read.

For this first speech you should be able to draw information primarily from your own experience. For instance, because Andy had had the experience, he needed only to reconstruct the details of the experience. As you recall details, keep the following ideas that relate specifically to narratives in mind.

Usually a narrative has a point to it, a climax that the details build up to. Think carefully about the point of your story.

A narrative is developed with supporting details that give background and build the story so that the point has maximum effect. Try to select and develop details that heighten the impact.

A narrative often includes dialogue. A story will be much more enjoyable to an audience if it can hear the story unfold through dialogue.

A narrative often is humorous. Although not all narratives are funny, most will have elements of humor. If what happened can be made funny, the humor will hold attention.

5. *Choose an organizational pattern that clearly communicates the material.* A speech comprises an introduction, a body, a conclusion. For most speeches you prepare the body of the speech first, then determine how you will introduce and then conclude the speech.

Although speeches can be organized in many ways, you are likely to find that a narrative speech can be presented chronologically. For instance, Andy Gilgoff arranged his personal experience by talking about what happened first, second, third, and so on.

Because there are never any guarantees that your audience is ready to pay full attention to the speech, you should find a way to start the speech that will focus audience attention on your topic. In a short first speech, this may well be done by asking a question or making a startling statement.

Finally, you should usually prepare a speech conclusion that wraps up the speech in a way that reminds the audience of what you have said and that hits home in such a way that the audience will remember your words. In a narrative speech the conclusion often is the climax of the experience.

Although a major speech has a clearly delineated introduction, body, and conclusion, a narrative is a single, unified story.

6. *Outline the speech on paper.* Although some speakers do not prepare outlines, most write one to test the logic of the structure of their speeches.

Figure 1.2

```
Narrative Speech

Specific Goal:  I want my audience to laugh at
my realization that my clothes had not been
taken.

Introduction

    I.  I had joined a local gym so that one day I
        could look like Arnold Schwarzenegger.

Body

    I.  I returned to my locker from my usual
        bone-crushing workout.
        A. The lock was ajar.
        B. My clothes, wallet, and keys were gone.
   II.  I raced to the clerk's cage to report the
        robbery.
        A. I described what had happened.
        B. I pleaded for the attendant to call the
        police.
  III.  I returned to my locker to wait for the
        police.
        A. To my amazement the lock was back on
        the locker.
        B. When I opened the door my clothes were
        there.
        C. I had looked in the wrong locker!

Conclusion

    I.  Totally embarrassed, I envisioned being man
        enough to admit my mistake.
   II.  Instead, I said to myself, "I think I'll
        just go out the back door."
```

A narrative outline will be much shorter than an outline for an informative or persuasive speech. You will likely limit the outline to the key points of the sequence of events (see Figure 1.2).

7. *Choose the wording of main points and supporting materials carefully.* Your ideas are communicated to your audience through verbal and nonverbal means. If you have not given thought to how you will

phrase your key ideas, you run a great risk of missing a major opportunity for communicating your ideas effectively. In practice sessions you should work on clarity, vividness, emphasis, and appropriateness of language.

For a narrative, make sure that you are being as specific as possible in relating the details.

8. *Practice delivering the speech orally.* Because delivery is likely to be the most important variable in determining how the audience reacts to your speech, you will want to make sure that you have practiced in a way that ensures that you can speak with enthusiasm, use good eye contact, and leave the impression that ideas are fresh. Regardless of your language, how your audience reacts to your wording will depend on your use of voice and bodily action.

You will want to practice the speech two or three times to make sure that you can tell the story within the time limits. Do not try to memorize the speech. Throughout this text we emphasize the extemporaneous speaking method. A speech that is delivered extemporaneously is one that is researched, outlined, and practiced until the ideas of the speech are firmly in mind, but the wording varies from practice to practice and in the speech itself. By keeping your mind on the main points of the sequence, you will find that you can lengthen or shorten the story by including or deleting details of the experience.

Coping with Nervousness

Nearly everyone who speaks in public, whether for the first or the fiftieth time, experiences some nervousness. Effective speakers, however, learn to channel their nervousness. In fact, you need to be a little nervous to do your best: If you are lackadaisical about giving a speech, you are not likely to do a good job.

As you prepare your first speech, keep the following points in mind:

Despite nervousness, you can make it through your speech. Very few people are so bothered that they are literally unable to function. You may not enjoy the experience, but you can do it.

Listeners are not nearly as likely to recognize your fear as you might think. The thought that audiences will notice an inexperienced speaker's fear often increases that fear. Thoughts that an audience will be quick to laugh at a speaker who is hesitant or that it is just waiting to see how shaky a person appears can have devastating effects. But the fact is that members of an audience, even speech instructors, greatly underrate the amount of stage fright they believe a person has.[3]

The more experience you get in speaking, the better you can cope with nervousness. Beginners experience some fear because they do not really understand speaking in public. As you give speeches, and see improvement in those speeches, you will gain confidence and worry less about any nervousness you might experience.

The better prepared you are, the better you will cope with nervousness. Many people show extreme nervousness because either they are not well prepared or they think they are not well prepared. This entire textbook is devoted to helping you learn the kind of material necessary to be well prepared for your speeches. As you learn to recognize when you are truly prepared, you will find yourself paying less attention to your nervousness.

Later, in the chapter on speech delivery, we will consider some of the specific behaviors that you can use to relieve nervousness as the time for speaking approaches.

Part II of this book offers an integrated development of the steps of speech preparation. The six-chapter unit includes a complete explanation of all eight steps. Chapter 2 includes the first three steps: selecting a topic, determining a speech goal, and analyzing audience and occasion. Chapter 3 discusses finding sources of information and recognizing the kinds of information you will use in your speeches, Chapter 4 explains speech organization, Chapter 5 gives insights into speech wording, Chapter 6 analyzes effective speech delivery, and Chapter 7 focuses on critical listening and speech evaluation.

In addition, the six-chapter unit includes a series of exercises that, when completed with care, lead to the development of a complete speech that will meet the requirements of your first major speech assignment.

Assignment *Preparing a Narrative* *Speech*	Prepare a two- to three-minute personal experience (narrative). Think about experiences that you have had that were humorous, suspenseful, or dramatic, and select one that you think your audience would enjoy hearing about. Figure 1.2 illustrates the kind of outline that is suitable for a short, narrative speech. Figure 1.3 is an example of a student speech that was given to meet this assignment.[4]

Figure 1.3

A while back, I joined a local gym with the express purpose of taking up weight lifting in hopes that someday people would have difficulty in telling me and Arnold Schwarzenegger apart. One day, when I had returned to my locker after my usual bone-crushing workout, I noticed that my lock was through the handle of my locker, not through the hole at the bottom that locks the locker. "Dumbhead," I said to myself, "That's a sure way of ending up in trouble." And sure enough, when I opened the locker my worst fears were confirmed--my wallet was gone, my keys were gone, and my pants were gone. I was outraged. I couldn't even drive myself home. I went running out of the locker room and up to the clerk who worked at the desk. I started yelling at him, "Call the police--I've been robbed."

"What happened?" he asked.

"I've been robbed!" I repeated.

"Are you sure?" he asked.

"Of course I'm sure," I said, "I looked in my locker and my clothes are gone!"

"Okay," he said, "I'll call the police."

Because I knew it would take a while for the police to come, I thought that maybe if I went back to the scene of the crime I could find some evidence--perhaps the thief had dropped part of my clothing, or maybe a credit card had fallen from my wallet. So I approached the locker the second time and did a doub le take when I noticed that now the lock was through the hole at the bottom of the handle as it should have been. "Great," I said, "Now that everything is gone I remembered to put the lock back on right." So I unlocked the locker, opened the door--and found my pants, my wallet, and my keys. A slow red burn of embarrassment began to form. I had looked in the wrong locker--one that was one row behind.

What could I do? "No problem," I said to myself. "I'm a man, right? I can take it, right? I can swallow my pride, look directly at the clerk, and announce, 'I've made an error. I'm sorry you had to call the police. In fact, I'll even make the call myself and apologize directly to the police.'"

I took several firm strides back toward the desk, full of resolve and feeling very proud of my manly behavior. Then I stopped and said to myself, "Nah, I'll just go out the back door."

Summary

Public speaking is important to success in nearly every walk of life. Speeches, oral presentations that are usually given without interruption, occur at formal occasions where an audience has assembled expressly to hear that speaker, in less formal employment contexts, and informally as a part of our everyday conversations.

Public speaking is a special kind of communication transaction that involves a speaker giving a prepared speech to an audience through both oral and visual symbols in a specific context. The audience, the speech's end and object, gives verbal or nonverbal feedback that tells the speaker whether the message of the speech was understood or whether some kind of noise interfered with understanding.

The public speaker has at least three major legal responsibilities: to refrain from any communication that may be defined as constituting a clear and present danger, to refrain from using obscene language, and to refrain from using language that will defame the character of another person.

In addition, a speaker has ethical responsibilities that are based on guidelines reflected in the Speech Communication Association's credo and endorsed by most communication scholars: You as a public speaker are responsible for what you say and have a responsibility to allow free choice on the part of your audience.

Preparing a speech involves the following eight steps: (1) Select a topic you know something about and in which you are interested. (2) Determine the response that you want from your audience. (3) Analyze your audience and your occasion. (4) Gather and evaluate material that you can use in the speech. (5) Choose an organizational pattern that clearly communicates the material. (6) Outline the speech on paper. (7) Choose the wording of main points and supporting materials carefully. (8) Practice the delivery of the speech to your audience.

Despite nervousness, you *can* make it through your speech. Listeners are not nearly as likely to recognize your fear as you might think. The more experience you get in speaking and the better prepared you are to speak, the better you will cope with your nervousness.

Notes

1. H. J. Leavitt and Ronald A. H. Mueller, "Some Effects of Feedback on Communication," *Human Relations* 4 (1951), 11.
2. Richard L. Johannesen, *Ethics in Human Communication*, 3d ed. (Prospect Heights, Ill.: Waveland Press, Inc., 1990), 1.
3. Theodore Clevenger, Jr., "A Synthesis of Experimental Research in Stage Fright," *Quarterly Journal of Speech* 45 (April 1959), 136.
4. Delivered in speech class, University of Cincinnati. Used with permission of Andy Gilgoff.

PART II

FUNDAMENTAL PRINCIPLES

This section systematically leads you through the five fundamental principles of effective speaking and the eight steps of effective speech preparation that come from them. Each chapter begins with a principle and then takes you through the steps necessary to achieve that principle in your speaking. To help you in preparing for your first major speech, twelve individual exercises have been included that correspond to specific stages of your preparation. If you work carefully to complete each assignment, by the time you have finished all twelve, you should be fully prepared to present your first major speech.

In addition, each chapter contains other learning-by-doing activities that give you a chance to express your understanding of key ideas and methods. The final chapter of this section, "Listening Critically to Speeches," prepares you to increase your listening efficiency and to evaluate others' speeches.

The case study "'The More I Do It, the More Comfortable I Am'" follows on pages 26 and 27.

Case Study
*"The More I Do It,
the More
Comfortable I Am"*

If they could peer into the future, many students in public-speaking courses would be surprised to discover that speech has come to play a far larger part in their lives than they ever dreamed it would.

To illustrate, consider the example of Jill Fox, a freelance book editor in her mid-thirties who readily agreed to share her experience with readers of this book.

As a college student, Jill took a public-speaking course with little notion of becoming a frequent or proficient speaker. Even when she embarked on her present career, Jill could not have foreseen how much she would need her speaking skills. "I didn't know editors had to talk!" she said with a laugh. "It wasn't something that came in any job description."

In fact, she discovered, the ability to speak convincingly to a group is essential to her business. Twice a year, Jill is called upon to make persuasive presentations to groups of marketing executives about books she has produced. Although part of her task is to articulate the editorial concept behind a particular book, in these talks her specific goal is to excite her listeners about her products.

"It's critically important to be very enthusiastic," Jill pointed out, "so that the marketing people will be enthusiastic, so that the bookstore people will be enthusiastic, so that the books will sell. Because if they don't, I don't have any more work!"

Needless to say, Jill devotes careful preparation to these talks. Part of her task is to find creative ways of making an impression so that her books stand out in her listener's memories. One technique she employs to give her presentations more impact is the use of slides or other visual aids. For example, in describing a cookbook, she may display photographs of food prepared according to the recipes in the book. On occasion, she has even prepared hors d'oeuvres from instructions in the book and served them as part of her talk. "I do like to 'razzmatazz' these things!" she remarked.

Public speaking has become an integral part of Jill's life in other ways as well—often unexpected ones.

It is interesting that her major formal speaking engagements of late resulted from her enrollment in a continuing-education course at a local university. When the instructor of her publishing class asked her to share her experience as a freelance editor, her ten-minute talk (done in lieu of a term paper) was so successful that it turned into a half-hour guest lecture that she now gives every year. In turn, that led to an invitation to speak on the same subject to a local professional association.

To prepare her speeches, Jill composes an outline of her talks on a personal computer, building them around some four or five points she wants to make. She then fills in the outline with personal anecdotes, notes she has made from conversations, and information acquired through her reading. She revises and edits, but her speeches are extemporaneous. "They're not verbatim talks—I use only an outline and notes."

Throughout her speeches, Jill skillfully uses external transitions and topic statements to mark the start of a new idea, often in a succinct and memorable way. For example, she introduced the theme of keeping one's personal and business life separate while working at home by saying, "I work at home. That also means I *live at work*." Personal experiences, vivid details, and humor illustrate her points and adapt her content to her audience. As she developed the hazards of working at home, for instance, she told a story that many in her audience could readily appreciate.

Food can be a real problem. It's very tempting to eat too much. Your kitchen is right there, and it's a great excuse to avoid work. A couple of years ago, when I was writing a book, I put on thirty pounds — most of it Pepperidge Farm Goldfish.

Jill's personal interests and activities have also led her into many kinds of public speaking, from giving reports as an officer in her alumni association to working as a volunteer docent for the California Historical Society. A history buff, twice a month she leads hour-long tours of a Victorian mansion to groups ranging from one or two visitors to twenty or more. There are no fixed scripts for these tours; the specific content Jill presents depends on the makeup of the group and its members' particular interests and questions.

This type of impromptu speaking requires on-the-spot adaptation of the wealth of information Jill has prepared on California history, decorative arts, and the mansion's architectural features. "I always start by asking people where they're from and what they want to know," Jill explained. "Basically, I adjust to the situation and to whoever shows up."

With all her current speaking activity, does Jill still become nervous before a speech engagement? "I'm less nervous as time goes on," she said, "but there are a few things I do. First, I make sure I'm *prepared*. Even on the docent tours I give so regularly, I try to plan at least a few minutes to go over my notes. Second, I try to get wherever I'm speaking *early* enough so that the whole ordeal of getting somewhere and getting parked and set up and knowing where I'm supposed to stand is over with. And I also take a few deep breaths just to make sure I'm relaxed."

Now that public speaking has become a significant part of her life, Jill keeps working at getting better by observing lecturers and speakers, critiquing her own performances, and revising her presentations to improve and keep them fresh. Like most good speakers, she knows that the real secret to a fluid, apparently spontaneous speech is the hard work and preparation the audience never sees.

Nor would most people suspect the personal triumph that effective speaking represents for Jill. Like many speakers who seem to radiate confidence when they stand in front of a group, Jill was very shy as a child. In fact, when she was asked whether she had had some special training that would account for the clarity of her speaking style, she gave a surprising answer.

"As a child, I was a stutterer," she said. "So I had a little speech therapy in early elementary school. That's really the only special training I can think of."

And does this once-shy person now enjoy public speaking?

"Yes! I enjoy it very much. That's something that has evolved — the more I do it, the more comfortable I am."

| Chapter 2 | Selecting Your Topic and Refining Your Goal |

Principle I

Effective speaking begins with a specific speech goal adapted to your audience and occasion.

Suppose you were the chief executive officer (CEO) of a major business in your community and you received the following invitation: "We invite you to speak about the characteristics of leadership at The Banker's Association meeting on Thursday, February 15, at 7 P.M."

Whether you accept an invitation to speak to a group such as the Banker's Association or whether you are required to speak to meet a classroom assignment, your challenge is much the same — to select a clear speech goal that is adapted to your audience and to your occasion. Although the principle is specific enough, giving guidance in accomplishing that principle poses the dilemma of "Which comes first, the chicken or the egg?" But with guidelines for speech preparation, the question of "which comes first" includes five choices: topic, audience, occasion, goal, and thesis. Although the steps are not always separate or always accomplished in this order, the following five steps are recommended: (1) Select your topic, (2) determine your speech goal, (3) write a thesis statement, (4) analyze your audience, and (5) analyze your occasion. As each is discussed, it will become apparent why this order may be the most helpful for you in your first few speeches. When you are comfortable with the procedures necessary to get started, you then can determine the order that seems best for you.

Selecting Your Topic

People are invited to give speeches because of their expertise on or insight in certain broad subject areas. Nevertheless, they usually are given the freedom to select their specific topic and their speech goal. What is the difference between subject area and topic? A *subject* is a broad area of knowledge, such as American history, cognitive psychology, baseball, or the Middle East. A *topic* is some specific aspect of a subject. For instance, under the subject of American history, a historian might be prepared to speak on such diverse topics as the Continental Congress, the Civil War, or the Roaring Twenties; likewise on the subject of baseball, a professional athlete might choose to speak on specific topics as the art of base stealing, learning the strike zone, or playing shortstop. For instance, groups ask me to speak because they want insight into some aspect of the subject of *speech communication*. Sometimes they leave the specific topic entirely to me; sometimes they give me broad guidelines, such as "We need advice on what leaders should do," and sometimes they are very specific, such as "We want you to talk about some of the most important elements of good lecturing." The point is that even professional speakers may have to select their specific speech topics. The goal of this section is to help you identify a suitable subject area and then select potential specific topics from those subject areas.

When you are asked (or required) to give a speech, you should use the same criteria for identifying subjects as those used by professional speakers: Start by identifying subject areas that (1) you know something about and (2) interest you, and select suitable topics from those subject areas. Just as Lee Iacocca draws many of his topics from the subject of automobiles, Gloria Steinem draws from the subject of feminism, and Jesse Jackson draws from the subject of social and political issues, you should draw your topics from subjects that you know something about and that interest you.

The subjects of your present expertise and interest probably include such things as your vocation (major, prospective profession, or current job), your hobbies or spare-time activities, and special interests (social, economic, educational, or political concerns). These are subject areas from which you can draw topics for your speech assignments. Thus, if retailing is your actual or prospective vocation, tennis is your favorite activity, and problems of illiteracy, substance abuse, and toxic and nontoxic waste are your special concerns, then these are subject areas from which you would draw topics.

At this point you might be thinking, "Why not just select a 'hot' topic that every one is talking about?" or even "Why not just talk on something I know an audience wants to hear?" There is one very good reason for avoiding either of these temptations: An audience listens to a speaker because of perceived expertise on or insight in a particular subject area. If you start believing that you can talk about anything, you will find it very easy to get in "over your head." You will notice that people such as Lee Iacocca, Jesse Jackson, and Gloria Steinem stay within their areas of expertise. For when even widely read individuals talk about topics outside of their areas of expertise, they are far more likely to get into trouble and lose the respect of their audiences. Of course, over time you can become an expert in a particular subject area, but to begin with you will want to speak about those subject areas in which you have already spent months or years developing expertise and insight.

This does not mean that you should not be sensitive to the needs of audience and occasion. As we will see, you use this information about the audience and occasion to shape your goal and determine the kinds of information you should use in your speeches.

Brainstorming for Topics

To generate a list of specific topics from the subject areas you have identified, you can use a form of brainstorming. *Brainstorming* is an uncritical, nonevaluative process of generating ideas, much like the old word-association process: To the words *rock music* you might associate "beat," "new wave," "punk," "electronic," or "amplifiers." When you start with a subject area of expertise and interest you often can list twenty, thirty, fifty, or even more related words.

Start by dividing a sheet of paper into three columns. Label column 1 "Major" or "Vocation," column 2 "Hobby" or "Activity," and column 3 "Personal Concerns (Issues)." Work on one column at a time. If you begin

Figure 2.1

Brainstorming.

Hobby: Computers

games	history	hardware	home units
software	CRTs	costs	chips
printers	technology	crime	memory
floppy disks	hard disks	terminals	languages
	FORTRAN	terminology	word processing
BASIC	capabilities	programming	graphics
list processing			

with column 2, "Hobby," you might write "pocket billiards." Then you would jot down every word that comes to mind, such as "cues," "English," "games," "tables," "equipment." Work for at least a few minutes on a column. Then begin a second column. Although you may not finish in one sitting, do not begin an evaluation until you have listed at least twenty items in each column.

When you believe your list under each column is complete, read the entries and check the three or four words or phrases that sound most compelling to you, that strike you as particularly important, or that you think would be of particular interest to your audience. Brainstorming allows you to take advantage of a basic commonsense principle: It is easier to select the correct answer to a multiple-choice question than it is to think of the answer to the same question without the choices. And it is easier to select a topic from a list than to come up with a fresh topic. Instead of asking yourself, "What should I talk about?" ask yourself, "What are the one, two, or three topics under each subject heading that are most compelling to me?" The computer buff whose brainstorming list is shown in Figure 2.1 will find it much easier to decide to talk about memory, computer crime, or chips from the twenty-four topics listed than to think of new choices.

If you select two or three topics from each of the three subject areas of your brainstorming list (Speech Preparation Exercise 1), you will have six to nine good topics to work with in preparing your speeches for this course.

Speech Preparation
Exercise 1
*Brainstorming for
Topics*

Divide a sheet of paper into three columns. Label column 1 with your major or vocation, such as "art history"; label column 2 with a hobby or activity such as "chess"; and label column 3 with a concern or issue, such as "water pollution." Working on one column at a time, brainstorm a list of at least twenty words for each column; then check three of the topics in each column that are most compelling—of special meaning to you or of potential interest to your audience.

Writing Your Speech Goal

Now that you have identified a subject area and tentative topics within the subject area, you are ready to set about writing a speech goal. You will begin by identifying a general goal and then write a specific goal.

General Goals

As you think about what you want to achieve with your audience in your speech, you will find that almost all of your general goals can be grouped under three major headings: entertaining or amusing the audience, helping the audience understand information, and changing an audience attitude or moving an audience to action. In short, speeches can be categorized in terms of their general goals as entertainment speeches, informative speeches, or persuasive speeches.

Because speech is a complex act that may actually affect an audience in different ways, these headings are useful only in showing that in any public speaking act one overriding general goal is likely to predominate. For example, Johnny Carson's opening monologue is a speech that may give some insight into information and may even contain some intended or unintended persuasive message, and yet his general goal is to entertain his audience. Your history professor's discussion of the events leading to World War I may use humor to gain and hold attention, and the discussion of the events may affect your class's attitudes about war, but the professor's primary goal is to explain those events in a way that will help the class understand them. Political candidates may amuse you with their anecdotes about life in politics and may give you some information that clarifies aspects of key political issues, but their goal is to persuade you to vote for them.

Because one common way of assigning speeches is by goal, and methods of organizing and developing speeches differ according to goal, the assignments discussed later in this book are made by goal. In Chapter 1 we talked about a narrative speech, a popular entertainment speech. In the remainder of this text, we focus attention on informative and persuasive speeches, which are the kinds of speeches you will give in most real-life situations. Part III deals with informative speeches that are intended to gain audience understanding, and Part IV concerns persuasive speeches that are intended to affect audience attitudes, move an audience to action, or both.

Specific Goal

Your specific goal, or specific purpose, is a single statement that specifies the exact response you want from your audience. For a speech on the topic of "evaluating diamonds" you might state your goal as, "I would like the audience to understand the four major criteria for evaluating a diamond." For a speech on "supporting the United Way," you might state your goal as, "I would like the audience to donate money to the United Way." In the first example, your goal is informative: You want the audience *to understand* the criteria. In the second example, your goal is persuasive: You want your audience *to donate* money. Let us look at several other examples:

Entertainment Goals

I would like my audience to be amused by my portrayal of an over-the-hill football player.
I would like my audience to laugh at my experience as a waiter.

Informative Goals

I would like my audience to understand the characteristics of the five common types of coastlines.
I would like my audience to understand the three basic forms of mystery stories.

Persuasive Goals

I would like my audience to believe that drug testing by business and industry should be prohibited.
I would like my audience to join Amnesty International.

Now let us consider a step-by-step procedure for writing the specific speech goal:

1. *Keep writing until your tentative speech goal is a complete sentence that states the specific response or behavior you want from your audience.* Suppose you want to talk about illiteracy in the workplace. The topic itself is just the start of a complete speech goal. "Effects of illiteracy in the workplace" indicates the aspect of the topic you want to consider. "Three effects of illiteracy" limits what you will say to a specific number. "I would like the audience to understand three effects of illiteracy in the workplace" is a complete-sentence statement of a speech goal.

2. *Write out three or more different wordings of the goal, reflecting your sensitivity to the needs of the audience and the occasion.* Even if you like your first sentence, write at least two more. You may find that the second, third, or fourth sentence turns out to be the clearest statement of your goal. For example, in addition to "I would like the audience to understand three effects of illiteracy in the workplace," you might write the following: "I would like the audience to know three ways that illiteracy hurts the workplace." "I would like the audience to understand the three major effects that illiteracy has on the workplace." Each of the three is similar. After writing all three, you might decide that the third one is the best statement of your goal because it stresses "major" effects "on" the workplace.

3. *Do not write the goal as a question or as a capsule statement.* "Is illiteracy a way of life in the workplace?" is a good question for discussion, but it is not a good speech goal because it does not show the specific response you want from your audience. Likewise, "Illiteracy — a detriment to success" is a capsule statement that may be a good title, but it also fails as a speech goal for much the same reason: It does not give clear direction.

4. *Write the goal so that it focuses on only one idea.* "I would like the audience to understand three effects of illiteracy in the workplace and to prove how illiteracy is detrimental to both industry and the individual" includes two distinct focuses; either can be used, but not both because the two goals suggest different approaches to the material. Make a decision. Do you want the audience to understand the effects? Then the goal "I would like the audience to understand three effects of illiteracy in the workplace" is the better statement. Do you believe that illiteracy is a problem that must be solved? Then

the goal "I want my audience to believe that illiteracy is detrimental to both the individual and to society" is the better goal. (You may find that you will have to talk about the effects of illiteracy to meet this goal, but the *focus* of the speech is on getting the audience to believe that illiteracy is detrimental to the individual and to society.)

5. *Revise the infinitive until it indicates the specific audience reaction that you desire.* Such wordings as "to understand" or "to believe" are infinitives. If you regard your ideas as noncontroversial, universally accepted, or an expression of observation, then your intent is basically informative, and the infinitive will be "to understand" or "to know." If, however, your idea is controversial, a statement of belief, or a call to action, then your intent is persuasive, and that intent will be shown with such infinitives as "to believe" or "to attend."

Writing a Thesis Statement

Before you actually begin constructing your speech, you will want to refine your goal by writing a thesis statement. Whereas the specific goal is a statement of how you want your audience to respond, the *thesis statement* is a sentence that outlines the specific elements that were forecast in the goal statement. Although the speech goal "I would like the audience to understand the four major criteria for evaluating a diamond" clearly states what you want the audience to do (understand the criteria), it does not tell what those criteria are. The thesis statement for such a speech would be, "Diamonds are evaluated on the basis of carat (weight), color, clarity, and cutting." Likewise for the speech goal "I would like my audience to donate money to the United Way," a thesis statement would be "You should donate to the United Way because it covers a wide variety of charities with one gift, it spends a very low percentage on overhead, and it allows you to designate your dollars to specific agencies if you so desire."

You may not be able to write a clear thesis until you complete your research for your speech. For instance, you may know that you want "to have the audience understand the criteria for evaluating a diamond," but you may not yet have enough material to fill in the specifics. That is, you may think that there are at least four major criteria, but you want to read more and perhaps talk to a jeweler before you settle on the specific coverage of the speech.

Relationship Among Elements

So far in this chapter we have shown that there are many potential speech topics under a single subject area. Likewise, a topic can be the basis for three general goals and many different specific goals. And, finally, a specific goal then can be explained in a thesis statement. Let us illustrate this relationship among subject (heading of brainstorming list), topic (word or phrase you have checked), general speech goal, specific goal, and thesis statement with different examples:

Subject Area: Career counseling
Topic: Networking
General Speech Goal: Informative
Specific Goal: I want the audience to understand the procedure for networking in career development.
Thesis Statement: You can use networking most effectively if you make networking a high priority, position yourself in places of opportunity, advertise yourself, and follow up on your contacts.

Subject Area: Finance
Topic: Debt
General Speech Goal: Informative
Specific Goal: I would like the audience to understand two major factors that are increasing the problem of personal debt in the United States.
Thesis Statement: Personal debt is facilitated by easy access to credit and need for instant gratification.

Subject Area: NCAA
Topic: Sanctions
General Speech Goal: Persuasive
Specific Goal: I would like the audience to believe that sanctions are an ineffective means of punishing colleges that violate NCAA rules.
Thesis Statement: NCAA sanctions do not deter colleges from violating rules, they do not make it difficult for schools to field winning teams, and they do not prevent sanctioned colleges from receiving financial support.

Having a clearly stated specific goal at this stage of preparation will pay big dividends for you later. How? First, a clearly written goal will help you to limit your research. If you want the audience to understand "the effects of illiteracy in the workplace," you can limit your reading to "effects" with focus on "the workplace," saving you many hours of preparation time. Second, a clearly written goal will assist you in organizing your ideas logically. The main points of a speech grow directly from the goal and will be forecast in the wording of the thesis statement. Thus, the main points for the specific goal "I want the audience to understand the major effects of illiteracy in the workplace" could be: (1) illiteracy in the workplace locks people out of career advancements, (2) illiteracy in the workplace prevents people from understanding even the simplest of written instructions, and (3) illiteracy in the workplace leads to frustration that is manifested in chemical abuse and criminal activity.

Speech Preparation Exercise 2
Writing Speech Goals

1. Write three well-worded speech goals for a topic for which you indicated a preference on your brainstorming sheet (Speech Preparation Exercise 1, p. 32). Which of the three best meets the first five tests of a specific goal?
2. Write a complete thesis statement for the specific goal that you selected above. (Note: If you do not yet have enough information to complete your thesis statement, wait until you have found sufficient information on your topic.)

Analyzing Your Audience

Because a speech is for an audience, regardless of how much of an expert you are on the topic and regardless of how meaningful or important that topic may be, you have the responsibility of adapting the speech to your listeners in such a way that it arouses their interest, complements and adds to their knowledge, and speaks to their particular attitudes. Moreover, you have the responsibility of adapting the speech to the occasion in such a way that it will not be perceived as inappropriate. We will consider the analysis of an audience in this section and the analysis of an occasion in the next section.

Audience analysis is the study of audience composition, knowledge, interests, and attitudes. You will use the results of this analysis to guide you in selecting supporting material, organizing your speech, and presenting your speech.

Audience analysis is a three-part process: (1) You gather essential audience data; (2) you make predictions about the level of audience interest in your topic, level of knowledge about your topic, and strength of attitude about your position on the topic; and (3) you consider strategies for adapting to interests, understanding level, and attitude of your audience.

Gathering Audience Data

You get data about your audience in one of three ways:

1. If you are a member of the group comprising the audience to which you are speaking, you can get information directly from experience you have had with the group. For instance, you are a member of the class who will be hearing your classroom speeches; in a non-classroom situation, you may be a member of a community action group to which the speech will be given.

2. If you are not a member of the group comprising the audience, you can interview the person who scheduled your speech. For example, if your speech is to be delivered to a community action group, you should find out about your audience from the person who contacted you.

3. If the contact person cannot answer all of your questions satisfactorily, you can make informed guesses based on an analysis of the situation and other indirect information. For instance, because a community action group is made up of people who live in a specific community, you can make predictions about the audience based on observation and inferences about people who are likely to belong to such a group.

Now let us consider the specifics for which it is most important to have accurate data: size; education; age; gender; occupation; income; race, religion, or nationality; geographic uniqueness; and group affiliation.

SIZE   You need to know how large your audience will be — whether it will be small (fewer than 50 people), medium (50 to 100), or large (more than 100). The size of the audience will help you decide how formal you will be in your presentation. If you are anticipating an audience of 25 to 35 people, you will gear yourself for a relatively informal setting in which you are close to all members of the audience. With a small audience you can talk in a normal voice and feel free to move about as you talk. In contrast, if you anticipate an audience of 200 or more people, in addition

Both of these speakers are giving informative presentations on scientific topics, but the goals, content, and delivery of their speeches are likely to be quite different. Adapting to the knowledge, interests, and attitudes of specific audiences is a key task in all types of public speaking.

to needing a loudspeaker, you will make your delivery, language, and even the nature of your development more formal.

EDUCATION You need to know the education levels of the members of your audience. You want data to confirm whether audience members have high school, college, or postcollege educations, or whether their educational levels are mixed. For either informative or persuasive speeches, information about audience education is a necessity. For informative speeches, the higher the education level of your listeners, the more likely they will be to understand literary, historical, and geographical references and allusions. Likewise, they are more likely to have the background necessary to understand complex explanations. For persuasive speeches, the higher the education level of the audience, the more likely its members will be able to process complex arguments.

AGE You need to know the age level of the majority of the audience members. You will want data to confirm both the average age and the age range. Age provides a primary key to determining an audience's life experiences. When you have an accurate picture of average age, you can select examples that will be most relevant. For example, suppose you are planning to use examples of popular music in your speech to help you relate to your audience. Obviously, you will want to pick different examples for an older audience than for a younger audience. In a speech to an audience dominated by teenagers, you will get only blank stares with allusions to the music of Glenn Miller and Tommy Dorsey; likewise in a speech to an audience composed of older people, you might be met with bewilderment and perhaps even hostility if your *only* references are to heavy metal and hard rock performers.

GENDER You will want data to confirm whether your audience will be primarily male, primarily female, or will be reasonably balanced. The gender makeup of an audience becomes especially important if the audience is predominantly of one gender. Although gender differences are less marked than they once were (for example, females no longer can be stereotyped as housewives and males no longer can be stereotyped as breadwinners), men and women still have different perspectives on many issues. If the audience comprises mostly people of the opposite gender, you will need to make sure that your language and illustrations relate to the differing orientation.

OCCUPATION You need to know whether the majority of your audience members are of the same occupation or occupational status. If the majority has a single occupation such as nursing, banking, drill-press operating, teaching, or sales, it will be easier to make accurate predictions about the kinds of information that will be of interest and of educational value to them. Similarly, your choice of information and examples probably will be different if you are speaking to an audience made up mostly of students, blue-collar workers, such professionals as doctors and lawyers, and so on.

INCOME You need to know whether the majority of your audience members are at about the same income level. If you have data to confirm that the average income level of the audience is high, low, or average, you can make predictions about how the audience might react to speeches that have an economic focus. There is no sense in trying to convince an audience of people with well below average incomes of the value of investments, purchases, or recreational opportunities that require huge resources. On the other hand, people of lower incomes are sometimes more sympathetic to appeals to support the needy, even if the level of support they can afford is marginal. Moreover, whether any audience considers money an obstacle may well depend on its financial circumstances.

RACE, RELIGION, OR NATIONALITY You need to know whether the majority of your listeners are of one race, religion, or nationality. Data of this kind may affect the kinds of material you will use to illustrate or support your arguments as well as provide a basis for making predictions about how they might stand on an issue. For instance, an all-Catholic audience is likely to hold a negative attitude toward abortion on demand.

GEOGRAPHIC UNIQUENESS You need to know whether the majority of your audience members are from the same state, city, neighborhood, or some other definable area. The knowledge that an audience has a geographic bond can help you select meaningful examples. For instance, it is much easier to paint a vivid picture of the harms of littering or pollution if you are able to personalize the issue by relating these harms to your audience's city or neighborhood. Most people will be more inclined to support a project to improve the environment if they see the problem as in "their own backyard."

GROUP AFFILIATION You need to know whether the majority of your listeners are members of the same group or organization. Group affiliation is a bonding element. If you have evidence to verify that the majority of audience members belong to the same group, then again you can predict with more certainty the kinds of information that they will perceive as relevant to them. Group affiliation can be especially important when determining the kinds of developmental material that will appeal to the audience. For example, a group of auto mechanics will respond more favorably to allusions to working with hands, mechanical analogies, and so forth than to historical allusions or literary parallels.

Making Predictions About Audience Reactions

The next step in your audience analysis is to use the data you have gathered to assess the audience's potential interest, level of knowledge, and strength of attitudes about your topic in general and your specific speech goal in particular.

AUDIENCE INTEREST You need to assess whether the audience is likely to have an immediate interest in your topic or whether you will need to elicit its interest. Moreover, you need to think of what you can do to build or maintain audience interest.

Occasionally a topic will create an immediate interest with all members of an audience. Suppose you are planning to give a speech on the topic of cholesterol. If your audience is composed mostly of males between the ages of forty and sixty, you may predict that they would have greater potential interest in the speech than an audience of males and females eighteen to twenty-two years of age. Why? Because the cholesterol and heart attack connection is more prevalent and of greater immediate concern to older men. Young people, as a group, tend to take warnings about cholesterol levels and other potential health risks far less seriously. But just because the audience is less likely to have an immediate interest, you still have the possibility of building interest by the way you develop your speech.

In most speeches, the amount of audience interest depends upon what the speaker does with the topic. Even if you are talking about recycling to a group of environmentalists, they can lose interest if your material is not new to them or is not explained creatively.

AUDIENCE UNDERSTANDING You need to make predictions about the level of audience understanding of the information that you plan to present. You need to assess whether this particular audience has enough background information to understand your speech; conversely, you need to assess whether the audience may already possess as much or more understanding of the topic than you plan to include in the speech. Then you need to determine what you might do to provide either the background information necessary for understanding or a greater depth of information to meet the needs of the audience.

For some speech topics special knowledge is unnecessary. Because most people are familiar with automobiles, for example, you may predict that an audience has enough background information to understand the content of a speech explaining the special features of new models. For other topics, some basic orientation information may be necessary before the speech will make sense. For instance, before most audiences will understand the importance of quality circles (plant committees of eight to ten workers who meet weekly to uncover problems and present their ideas to managers) in increasing morale and productivity in assembly plants, you will have to explain the meaning of quality circles and how they function in an industrial setting.

AUDIENCE ATTITUDE   You will need to know the direction and strength of audience attitudes about your topic in general and your specific goal in particular, especially when the response you are seeking is a change of belief or an action. On the basis of the data you have collected, you need to predict whether your listeners will be favorably disposed, neutral (perhaps apathetic), or unfavorably disposed (perhaps even hostile) toward your topic and goal.

Audience attitudes are expressed by opinions. These opinions may be distributed along a continuum from highly favorable to hostile. Even though any given audience may have one or a few individuals' opinions at nearly every point of the distribution, audience opinion will tend to cluster at a particular point on the continuum. That point represents the general audience attitude on that topic. Except for polling the audience, there is no way to be sure about your assessment, but you can make reasonably accurate estimates based on demographic knowledge.

Skilled workers, for example, are likely to look at minimum wage proposals differently than are business executives; men will look at women's rights proposals differently than will women; a meeting of the local "Right-to-Life" chapter will look at abortion differently than will a meeting of NOW (National Organization for Women) members. The more data you have about your audience and the more experience you have in analyzing audiences, the better are your chances of judging their attitudes with accuracy. A precise differentiation of opinion is seldom necessary. You are likely to be able to classify most of your audiences as predominantly one of the following: no opinion—either no information or no interest; in favor—already holding a particular belief; or opposed—holding an opposite point of view. These classifications may overlap. Because you will, however, have neither the time nor the opportunity to present a line of development that will adapt to all possible attitudes within the audience, you should assess the prevailing attitude and work from there.

If you believe your audience will be favorably disposed, what will you do to heighten its positive attitude? Because the audience already is with you, you can put most of your emphasis on what they can do about the topic. If you believe your audience will be neutral or apathetic, what can you do to get them to think more favorably? With a neutral or apathetic audience you need to present evidence that supports your goal, and you need to use materials and language that will arouse the audience members' interests. If you believe your audience will be negative or hostile, what can you do to lessen its negative attitude or at least not arouse its hostility? With a negative audience you must be careful to be objective with your material and hope to make your case clearly so that those who are only mildly negative may be persuaded and those who are very negative will at least understand your position.

Attitudes and attitude change will be discussed in more detail in Part IV, Persuasive Speaking.

Strategy for Adapting to Your Audience

The final phase of your audience analysis is to write an overall strategy for adapting to your audience. Let us consider two specific examples — one in which audience factors are known and in your favor and one in which audience factors are inferred (from the data available about your audience, you would make predictions about audience interest, understanding, and attitude, and then you would determine a strategy for adapting to that audience).

In the first case, suppose your goal is to inform the members of the secretarial pool about a new word-processing package that the company will be installing on all secretarial word processors. If you had found out that the audience would be comprised of about twenty-five Cincinnati women of mixed race, religion, and nationality ranging in age from nineteen to forty whose education ranged from graduates of high school to graduates of two-year college secretarial programs, you could predict many factors that would work to your advantage. First, their interest is likely to be high because they will have to use the new package. Second, since their background knowledge is high, their understanding of the information is likely to be great. Because the members of the audience work at the same company they have had common experiences and are likely to have the same minimum competencies. Moreover, since they have already been working with word processing, their knowledge of computer use in general and word processing in particular will be similar.

And third, their attitude about changing packages may vary, but they still are likely to be open to the information if they see the new package as an improvement. As a result of these predictions, you might write the following strategy:

> Because interest is likely to be high at the beginning of the speech, I will place my emphasis on maintaining that interest. Since they already have knowledge of and practice in word processing, I can move directly to specific elements of this new package. To adapt to their knowledge, I will compare key features of the new package to operations they are familiar with. Although their attitude is likely to be favorable, I will still attempt to feature improvements so they will understand why they need to spend their time and energy learning the new system.

In the second case, suppose your goal is to inform a local adult community organization about computer software packages. If the only information you have about the audience is that they will be adult members of a community organization, you could still infer data about them that would help you make the kind of predictions necessary to determine a speech strategy. Because it is an adult organization, you could begin by inferring that the audience would be comprised of both males and females of mixed race, religion, and nationality, with a mixed educational background, and ages ranging from about twenty-five upward. Moreover, you could infer that most of the audience will be married, many will have homes and families, and because they are members of a local community organization, they will have a geographic bond.

Even though your data is inferred, you could still make predictions about interests, understanding, and attitude. First, their interests are likely to vary, since they are likely to have no natural need for information about computer packages. Second, their background knowledge is likely to range from little to moderate. Because they are adults, you can assume they have some knowledge about computers in general, and though a few may own personal computers, you cannot predict that all of them will be knowledgeable about computer use. Third, their attitude is likely to range from favorable to neutral about software packages. Your prediction about attitude will come from the likelihood of their varied experiences: some will be very positive about what computers may be able to do for them; others will be fearful and will see the computer as an intrusion into their privacy.

As a result of these predictions, you might write the following strategy:

> Because interest levels will vary, I will have to begin the speech in a way that will capture their interest. I will also try to develop a need to gain

information about computer software packages. Since they are unlikely to share the same background information, I will include orientation information about the usefulness to all adults of computers and computer packages in general. Moreover, I will use examples and illustrations that relate to adult experiences. To increase their understanding, I will compare computer package information to information they are familiar with. Because their attitudes are also likely to vary, I will want to use examples and illustrations of "average Americans" who have found interest in computer packages.

Analyzing the Occasion

While you are analyzing your audience, you also will want to analyze the occasion and the effect it will have on determining your specific goal as well as its effects on speech development. Analyzing the occasion is especially important for determining the tone of your speech. Speeches often are given in conjunction with a particular occasion, and when they are, knowledge of the occasion will provide you with guidelines for both meeting audience expectations and determining the tone of the speech. For example, a high school or college commencement is a formal occasion; moreover, because it celebrates graduation, the audience will expect you to speak to the needs of graduating students. Chapter 18, "Adapting to Special Occasions," outlines some of the expectations that must be met in speeches that celebrate such occasions.

If the speech is not in commemoration of any special occasion, there are still several questions that you should answer:

When will the speech be given? The question of *when* includes at what time of day the speech will occur, and where on the program it will occur.

What hour of the day will the speech be given? The time of day the speech will be delivered can affect how it is received. If you are scheduled to speak after a meal, for instance, your audience might be lethargic, mellow, or even on the verge of sleep. As a result, you will want to insert more "attention-getters" to counter potential lapses of attention.

Where does your speech occur on the program? If you are the featured speaker, you have an obvious advantage: You are the

Analyze your audience by completing the audience analysis checklist.

Checklist

Audience Analysis

Complete the following questions about your audience:

Data

a. The size of the audience is _____ small, _____ medium, _____ large.

b. The audience education level is _____ high school, _____ college, _____ post college.

c. The age range is from _____ to _____ . The average age is about _____ .

d. The audience is approximately _____ percent males and _____ percent females.

e. My estimate of the income level of the audience is _____ below average, _____ average, _____ above average.

f. The audience is basically _____ the same race or _____ a mixture of races.

g. The audience is basically _____ the same religion or _____ a mixture of religions.

h. The audience is basically _____ the same nationality or _____ a mixture of nationalities.

i. The audience is basically of the same _____ state, _____ city, _____ neighborhood, or _____ other definable area.

Predictions

j. Audience interest in this topic is likely to be _____ high, _____ moderate, _____ low.

k. Audience understanding of the topic will be _____ great, _____ moderate, _____ little.

l. Audience attitude about the topic will be _____ in favor, _____ neutral, _____ opposed.

Strategy for Adapting to Your Audience

In light of your predictions, write a one-paragraph overall strategy for adapting to your audience.

focal point of audience attention. In the classroom, however, yours will be one of many speeches, and your place on the schedule may affect how you are received. In your classroom speech you will be guaranteed enough speaking time, but going first or last still will make a difference. If you go first, you may have to be prepared to meet the distraction of a few class members strolling in late; if you speak last, you must counter the tendency of the audience to be a bit weary from listening to several speeches in a row.

What are the time limits for the speech? The amount of time you have to speak greatly affects the scope of your speech and how you develop it. Keep in mind that the time limits for your classroom speeches are going to be quite short. Students often get overly ambitious about what they can accomplish in a short speech. "Three major causes of World War I" can be briefly discussed in five minutes, but "A history of World War I" cannot. Problems with time limits are not peculiar to classroom speeches. Any speech setting will include actual or implied time limits. For example, a Sunday sermon is usually limited to about twenty minutes; a keynote speech for a convention may be limited to thirty minutes; a political campaign speech may be limited to forty-five minutes or an hour. Whatever the time limit, speakers must consider realistically how much can be covered within that time limit. Although you want your topics to have depth, you will need to avoid covering too broad an area.

What are the expectations for the speech? Every occasion provides some special expectations. For your classroom speeches, one of the major expectations is meeting the assignment. Whether the assignment is made by purpose (to inform or to persuade), by type (expository or descriptive), or by subject (book analysis or current event), your goal should reflect the nature of that assignment.

Meeting expectations is equally if not more important for speeches outside of the classroom experience. For instance, if you attend an Episcopalian Sunday service, you will expect the minister to have a religious theme; if you attend a campaign rally, you will expect a speech revealing the candidate's issues or platform.

Where will the speech be given? The room in which you are scheduled to speak also will affect your presentation. If you are fortunate, your classroom will be large enough to seat the class comfortably. But classrooms vary in size, lighting, seating arrangements, and the like. Giving a speech in a room that is long and narrow creates different problems from one that is short and wide. In a long narrow room, for instance, you must talk louder to reach the back row, but your eye contact can be more limited to a narrow range. Likewise, if a room is dimly lit, you must try to get the lights turned up. You must be able to meet the demands of any situation.

Outside of the school setting you may encounter even greater variations. You need specific information about the room in which you are scheduled to speak, such as seating capacity, shape, number of rows, nature of lighting, existence of a speaking stage or platform, distance between speaker and first row, and so on, before you make final speech plans. If possible, visit the place and see it for yourself. In most instances you will have some kind of speaking stand, but you can never count on it. You must be prepared for the situation as it exists.

What facilities are necessary to give the speech? For some speeches you may need a microphone, a chalkboard, or an overhead or slide projector and screen. If the person who has contacted you to speak has any control over the setting, make sure you explain what you need. But always have alternative plans in case what you have asked for is unavailable.

Checklist | **Analyzing the Occasion or Setting**

1. Complete the following questions about the occasion or setting.

   a. When will the speech be given? _____

   b. Where will the speech be given? _____

   c. What facilities are necessary to give the speech? _____

   _____

   d. What are the time limits for the speech? _____

   e. What is the specific assignment? _____

2. What effect will the occasion or setting have on your speech? _____

   _____

3. What is the most important factor you must take into account to meet the demands of the setting? _____

Analyze your speech occasion or setting by answering the questions in the preceding checklist.

Summary

The first step of effective speech preparation is to determine a clear speech goal that is adapted to your audience and occasion.

Select a subject area that you are interested in and that you know something about, and then brainstorm a list of potential topics under each potential subject area. You will consider items on the list that seem most meaningful to you and that you believe you can make stimulating for your audience.

Determine a general speech goal. Are you giving your speech for purposes of entertaining? informing? or persuading? Write a specific goal. Keep writing until your tentative specific goal is a complete sentence. Write out at least three different wordings for the goal. Write it as a statement rather than as a question or as a capsule statement. Write the specific goal so that it contains only one idea. Use an infinitive or infinitive phrase that indicates the specific audience reaction that you desire.

Write a thesis statement that explains the specific goal in detail.

Analyze your audience to decide the direction of the speech goal. You can get data directly from experience you have had with the audience, from the member of the group who scheduled you to speak, or indirectly from inferences you make. The specific audience data you gather relates to its size, education, age, gender, occupation, income, race, religion, nationality, geographic uniqueness, and group affiliation. From the gathered data you can make predictions about audience interest, understanding, and attitude and you can develop a strategy for adapting to your specific audience.

You will also analyze the speech setting by determining where in the program, at what time of day, and in which location the speech will be given, and by determining what the time limits and audience expectations are for the speech.

Chapter 3 | # Finding, Recording, and Using Information

> **Principle II**
> *Effective speaking requires high quality information.*

I t is said that you cannot make a silk purse out of a sow's ear, and indeed, whether it is purses, buildings, or speeches, you can get a lot farther if you have high quality material to work with. In the case of speeches, your primary material is the information that gives your speech its substance. Effective speaking requires knowing where to look for information, what kinds of information to look for, and how to record information once you have found it.

Sources of Information

To be sure you have the best material, you need to start with your own knowledge and work outward to other sources.

Your Own Knowledge

If you look carefully at your own knowledge and experience, you will find that you already have a foundation of quality information for your speeches. For instance, athletes have special knowledge about their sports, coin collectors about coins, detective-fiction buffs about mystery novels, do-it-yourself advocates about the house and garden, musicians about music and instruments, farmers about animals or crops and equipment, and camp counselors about camping. Your first-hand knowledge will contribute to the unique, imaginative, and original development of your speeches. Even if your own knowledge is incomplete, it still will provide a good starting point for further research. Moreover, your knowledge and experience can guide you in the analysis and interpretation of other sources.

You will want to verify the facts that you plan to use. Our memories are not always accurate, and you may find that some fact that you remember is not really a fact at all. Still, verifying a fact is far easier than discovering new information.

Observation

For many of your topics you can get additional valuable information through direct observation. For example, if you plan to talk about how newspapers are printed, you can learn about printing procedures by taking a tour of your local newspaper's printing plant and observing the process in action. Or if you plan to talk about the effectiveness of your city council, you can observe the council in action by attending a couple of its meetings. Through observation you can get information that will add a personal touch to your speech and thus make it more interesting.

To get the most from your observation you must identify what you want to gain from your observation and concentrate on what is taking place. Suppose you wanted to learn more about the duties of individual football players. Instead of just watching the game, which for most people means trying to follow the ball, you should determine which player or players you will follow. For instance, select a given offensive or defensive player and follow his every move for six or seven plays in a row. Try to see not only *what* is taking place but also *how* it is taking place and why. If you are observing an offensive lineman, you can see how his blocking technique differs depending upon whether the play is a run or a pass. You also will see when he stays in one place blocking the player in front of him and when he moves from his position to set up a special blocking pattern. If you are observing a defensive back, you can see when and how he covers a pass receiver, and when and how he moves when he discovers that the play will be a run. You may want to take notes of what you see. By keeping your focus on specifics, you will discover detailed information that you can use in your speeches.

Interviewing

You often can get a great deal of valuable information from an interview. Ask yourself, "Who are the people most likely to have the kind of information I need?" For instance, for a speech on newspapers, you should consider interviewing a reporter or one of the editors; for a speech on the city council, you should consider interviewing a council member or the mayor. Will people take the time to talk with you? You will be surprised how cooperative people will be if you approach them correctly. When you have decided whom you want to interview, call well in advance to make an appointment.

A good interview is a product of good questions. If you have written down exactly what you hope to find out, you will maximize the available time and not waste the time of people who are willing to talk with you. (Interviewing will be discussed in detail in Chapter 13.)

Taking Surveys

One variation of the interview is the survey. A *survey* is a list of one or more questions that can be asked of many people. For example, if you want to know what people think of the chances of the local sports team, or how well the council is doing in governing the city, or what people's attitudes are toward a proposed program such as testing employees for drugs, banning automatic rifles, or increasing property taxes, you can take a survey.

Sometimes a survey can be taken on one question. For instance, you could write:

> The College of Arts and Sciences is considering requiring all Arts and Sciences students to take the three-hour course "Fundamentals of Effective Speaking" for graduation. Please indicate your reaction to this proposal:
>
>   ——— I agree.
>   ——— I disagree.
>   ——— I have no opinion.

Of course, a survey can be considerably longer, but the shorter the survey, the more likely you are to get a larger number of responses.

In addition to considering what you will ask, you will want to make sure that you have polled enough people and that you have sampled

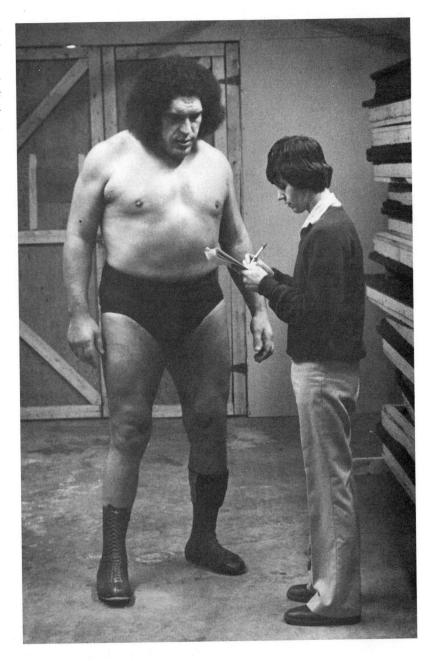

Information for speeches can be found in many places besides the library. For many speech topics, interviews can be an excellent source of firsthand information and expert opinion.

different segments of the population before you attempt to draw any significant conclusions from your poll. For instance, for a poll of college students you should sample freshmen, sophomores, juniors, and seniors, an equal number of males and females, Greeks and independents, and people of all races.

Reading

However much information you may have gained from other sources, some of your best information will come through reading. Effective speakers also are effective researchers. In this section we discuss sources of both primary and secondary information.

BOOKS Whether your library is large or small, it is likely to have books on nearly any subject you choose. The *card catalog* indexes all library books and holdings by title, author, and subject. Increasing numbers of libraries are putting their card catalogs on computer. If your school's catalog is computerized, you need to know whether all library holdings have been computerized and if not, what the exceptions are.

Whether your library uses cards or computers, you may need to be creative to uncover all the books your library holds on a particular topic. If, for example, you were researching the topic "illiteracy," you also would want to search such related headings as "literacy" and "reading problems."

PERIODICALS AND MAGAZINES *Periodicals* and publications that appear at fixed periods: weekly, biweekly, monthly, quarterly, or yearly. Generally, material that you obtain from periodicals and monthly magazines is more current than what you find in books. Of course, some magazines are more accurate, more complete, and more useful than others. Because you must know where and how to find articles before you can evaluate them, you should know and use several indexes, in particular the *Readers' Guide to Periodical Literature, Magazine Index, Education Index, Humanities Index*, and *Social Sciences Index*.

The *Readers' Guide to Periodical Literature* is a yearly index of articles in some 200 U.S. general circulation journals. Articles from such diverse magazines as *Atlantic, Ebony, Business Week, New Yorker, Newsweek, Reader's Digest, Time*, and *Vital Speeches* are all indexed by topic in the *Readers' Guide*.

Education Index, a cumulative subject index to a selected list of some 200 educational periodicals, proceedings, and yearbooks, will lead you to material that is either directly or indirectly related to the field of education.

The *Social Sciences Index* and *Humanities Index* are both guides to more than 250 periodicals. These indexes have been published separately since 1974, when the *Social Sciences and Humanities Index* was divided in two. In contrast to *Readers' Guide*, which indexes popular magazines, these indexes cover scholarly journals. The *Social Sciences Index* includes such journals as the *American Journal of Sociology, Economist*, and *Psychological Review*; the *Humanities Index* includes such journals as the

Modern Language Quarterly, Philosophical Review, and *Quarterly Journal of Speech.*

To be a good researcher, you must know when a periodical index is likely to be the best source. First, a magazine may be your best source when the focus of the topic you are considering is less than two years old. Second, a magazine is probably your best source when the topic is so limited in scope that it is unlikely to provide enough material for a book or when you are looking for a very specific aspect of that particular topic. Third, a magazine may be your best source when you are looking for contemporary reactions to events at the time they actually occurred.

If you decide to use magazine indexes, you should know how to proceed to find the material you need. Indexes are published yearly for years before the current edition and in monthly and quarterly supplements for the current year. To find appropriate articles about your topic, you need to determine when the event occurred or during what years the topic was actively discussed. For example, if you were researching the overthrow of communist leadership in Eastern Europe, you would begin with October 1989, and work forward and backward until the supply of articles dries up. If you are preparing a speech on our nation's dependency on oil and you wanted to document the effects of the first Arab oil embargo, you would use an encyclopedia or an atlas to locate the correct year, 1973, and then work through that year in various magazine indexes.

ENCYCLOPEDIAS   *Encyclopedias* are books or series of books that promise to cover all subjects from A to Z. For such subjects as animals, countries, art, and other broad headings, you are likely to find important basic information about the subject. Encyclopedias not only give you an excellent overview of many subjects, but also include bibliographies. As a result, an encyclopedia may be a good starting point for some broad subjects. But because the material covered includes only what is called "common knowledge," you should never limit your reading to an encyclopedia. Most libraries have a recent edition of *Encyclopaedia Britannica, Encyclopedia Americana,* or *World Book Encyclopedia.*

STATISTICAL SOURCES   *Statistical sources* are books devoted to presenting statistical information on a wide variety of subjects. When you need facts and details — such as statistics about population, records, continents, heads of state, weather, or similar subjects — you should refer to one of the many single-volume sources that report such data. Two of the most popular sources in this category are the *World Almanac and Book of Facts* and the *Statistical Abstract.*

BIOGRAPHICAL SOURCES *Biographical sources* provide accounts of people's lives. When you need biographical details, from thumbnail sketches to reasonably complete essays, you can turn to one of the many available biographical sources. In addition to full-length books and encyclopedia entries, you should use such books as *Who's Who* (British subjects) and *Who's Who in America* (short sketches of U.S. citizens) or the *Dictionary of National Biography* and *Dictionary of American Biography* (rather complete essays about prominent British subjects and U.S. citizens, respectively).

Biographical sources are excellent places to find information and personal details about people you plan to mention in your speech.

NEWSPAPERS Newspapers are especially good sources for information on local problems, and in some cases they may be the only information. You will have to consult your reference librarian for information about which newspapers your library indexes, although most libraries hold indexes of the nearest major daily and the *New York Times*.

UNITED STATES GOVERNMENT PUBLICATIONS The following are some of the government publications that are especially useful for locating primary sources:

United States Code. Published every six years since 1926, the *Code*, includes *federal* laws. The tenth edition includes fifty content areas.

Federal Register. The *Register* publishes daily regulations and legal notices issued by the executive branch and all federal agencies.

Monthly Catalog of United States Government Publications. The *Monthly Catalog* covers publications of all branches of the federal government. It has semiannual and annual cumulative indexes by title, author/agency, and subject.

MICROFILM INDEXES A new indexing format that is available in libraries is called Computer Output Microform (COM). These consist of rolls of microfilm prepared from a database and stored in a mechanized reader. These are updated frequently. Although they are quite comprehensive, they usually only cover the preceding three to five years. Two of the most widely used are the *Magazine Index*, which indexes more than 370 U.S. periodicals, and the *Business Index*. You will want to consult with your reference librarian to see which of these special indexes your library has.

Skimming Sources

For any topic you will uncover more sources than you can use. How can you make a quick evaluation of a source to determine whether or not it should be read in full? A method that can help you make this decision is *skimming*, or rapidly going through the work to determine what is covered and how. If you are evaluating a magazine article, spend a minute or two finding out what it covers. Does it really present information on the part of the topic you are exploring? Does it contain any documented statistics, examples, or quotable opinions? Is the author qualified to draw valid conclusions? If you are evaluating a book, read the table of contents carefully, look at the index, and skim pertinent chapters, asking the same questions as you would for a magazine article. During this skimming period you will decide which sources should be read in full, which should be read in part, and which should be abandoned. Minutes spent in such evaluation will save you hours of reading.

**Speech Preparation
Exercise 5**
Listing Sources

For one of the three speech goals you wrote for Speech Preparation Exercise 2 (p. 37), answer the following questions:

1. What is your personal knowledge base for this topic?
2. What, if anything, could you observe to broaden your personal knowledge base?
3. Who are the persons you could interview for additional information for this topic?
4. What are three specific articles or books that you have found that provide information for your topic?

What to Look for: Kinds of Research Material

Whether you are drawing information from your own background or from interviews, surveys, or books, the two major kinds of research material you are seeking are factual statements and expert opinions. Let us consider each of these separately.

Factual Statements

Factual statements are objective statements about things that exist or occurrences that can be documented. "Compact disks are 'read' with a laser beam," "The Macintosh II Computer comes with a hard disk drive," and "Chicken pox vaccines are now available to the public," are all statements of fact about things that exist. "Six persons died and more than 600 were injured in Santa Cruz County during the October earthquake," "Johannes Gutenberg invented printing from movable type in the 1400s," and "Romanian reform leaders executed ousted ruler, Nicolae Ceausescu and his wife Elena on December 26, 1989," are all statements of fact about occurrences that can be documented.

Objects and occurrences do not achieve "factual" status until they are verified in some way. For example, in 1989, chemists B. Stanley Pons and Martin Fleischmann reported achieving "desktop fusion," thus asserting that "desktop fusion" was a fact. In the months that followed, many other scientists attempted to replicate or validate the "fact" of desktop fusion. Because they could not, "desktop fusion" was not given "factual" status.

Reports of alleged past occurrences are not all factual. Obvious examples are the headlines of the tabloids at the checkout stands of supermarkets: "Man Talks with Martians," "Women Abducted by Extraterrestrials for Third Time," and so on are examples. But even more respectable sources can report "facts" that are not so. For instance, in the morning after the Bay Area earthquake of October 1989, early reports of "facts" about deaths and earthquake damage from various locations proved untrustworthy. Before you use "factual statements" in a speech, you should verify their accuracy.

One way to determine the accuracy of a factual statement is to check it against the original source, if one is given, or against material from another article or book on the same subject. Although checking accuracy may seem a waste of time, you will be surprised at the difference in "facts" reported in two or more sources. If at least two sources say essentially the same thing, you can be a little more confident. On the other hand, if two or more sources give different slants on the material, you will know that what is being discussed may be a matter of opinion. Only after you have examined many sources are you in a position to make an objective value judgment.

Expert Opinion

A second kind of research material that you will use in your speeches is expert opinion. *Expert opinions* are interpretations of facts made by authorities in a particular subject area. For example, when using facts that give the numbers of illiterate Americans and that show the kinds of problems these people face, we might find expert authorities giving the opinion that illiteracy leads to poverty.

Although you cannot rely entirely on opinions in speeches, expert opinion can be used to interpret and give weight to facts that you have discovered. Moreover, in situations where you cannot get facts, where they are inconclusive, or where they need to be supplemented, you will have to further support your claims with expert opinion.

The quality of opinion depends on whether its source is an expert. If a co-worker at a department store gives an opinion about the relationship between drug abuse and birth defects, the statement would not be evidence: The opinion is not expert; his expertise lies in other areas. On the other hand, if a neonatologist who has studied the relationship between drug use and birth defects says that such defects are observed in higher numbers when the mothers are drug users, her opinion is expert. Of course, opinions are most trustworthy when they are accompanied by factual data. If the physician can give data from tests she has conducted to support her opinion, then her opinion is worth even more.

How do you choose experts? How do you tell an expert from a "quack"? Experts are those who have earned a reputation for knowledge on the specific subject in question. Thus, in a court of law an attorney may call on a handwriting expert to give an opinion on whether the signature on a document was written by the person named. Yet even experts hold opinions that turn out to be incorrect. The best way to test the trustworthiness of an expert is by his or her record. The higher the percentage of true claims, the more trustworthy that person's opinion is likely to be.

Opinions often may be classified as being either inferences or judgments. An *inference* is a conclusion or generalization based on what has been observed. Let us clarify the distinction between an inference and a verifiable factual statement with an example. When, in her speech on the environment, Ellen says, "Rainfall for the last two years in Ohio has been below average," Ellen is relating factual information—it can be verified. If, however, Ellen adds, "According to Paul Jorgenson, a biologist, 'We're in a pattern of drought brought on by the Greenhouse effect,'" she would be citing an opinion that is an inference. The expert would be concluding—without actually knowing—that the two years of drought resulted from the Greenhouse effect. Other interpretations, or inferences, could be drawn from the fact of drought. Perhaps another expert would say that this is a normal statistical pattern that suggests that two years of below-average rainfall simply means that the next year has a higher probability of above-average rainfall.

A *judgment* is an expression of approval or disapproval. If Ellen's expert went on to say, "It is really a shame that our awareness of the Greenhouse effect has resulted in so little corrective action," the expert would be making a judgment.

If you plan to use expert opinions in your speech, instead of passing them off as facts, you should indicate to your audience the level of confidence that should be attached to the statement. For instance, an informative speaker may well say, "The temperatures throughout the last half of the 1980s were much higher than average. Many scientists believe that these higher-than-average temperatures represent the first stages of the Greenhouse effect, but the significance of these temperatures is still in doubt."

Recording Data

Whether the research materials you have found are classified as facts or opinions, you need to record the data accurately.

You record data so that you can provide the information and its source in a speech or report the documentation to anyone who might question the information's accuracy. Many times when question periods are provided at the end of a speech, members of an audience will ask for sources of information. Whether or not there is a question period, however, the listeners need the assurance that they can find the material you used in your speech if they should decide to look for it.

In your research (including not only printed sources, but also personal knowledge, observation, and interviews), you will find specific materials that you will want to save to use in your speech. How should you record these materials? Because you will use only some of the material and can never be sure of the order in which you will use it, you need to record the material so that you can easily select and move it around. The *notecard method* is probably the best.

You should record each factual statement or authoritative opinion along with bibliographical documentation on its own 4″ × 6″ or larger index card. Although it may seem easier to record all material from one source on a single sheet of paper (or to photocopy source material), sorting and arranging material is much easier when each item is recorded separately. On each card, indicate the source, the name of the author if one is given, and the page number from which it was taken. Bibliographical material should be in enough detail to ensure that you can find the information later if you need to. Figure 3.1 illustrates a useful notecard form. As your stack of information grows, you then can sort the material. Each item goes under a heading to which it is related. If the same item seems to belong to two headings, make another copy of that item and sort it accordingly.

The number of sources that you should use depends in part on the type of speech. For a narrative of a personal experience, you obviously will be the main if not only source. For reports and persuasive speeches,

Figure 3.1

Example of a notecard recording information.

```
Topic:  College tuition--slowing increases

"Data from the American Council on Education
indicates that, for both public and private
schools, 1990-91 tuition could rise as little
as 6 percent overall--the lowest rate in a
decade. . . . Public-school tuitions, after
yearly increases of up to 12 percent in the
mid-'80s, are now at about 6 percent."

                    "Slowing Tuitions,"
                    Newsweek, March 19, 1990, p. 8
```

however, you should use several sources, and certainly never fewer than three. One-source speeches often lead to plagiarism; furthermore, a one- or two-source speech simply does not give you sufficient breadth of material. By selecting, combining, adding, cutting, and revising, you will develop an original approach to your topic.

Citing Sources in Speeches

In your speeches, as in any communication in which you use ideas that are not your own, you should attempt to work the source of your material into the context of the speech. Such efforts to include sources will not only help the audience evaluate the content but also will add to your credibility as a speaker. In a written report, ideas taken from other sources are designated by footnotes; in a speech these notations must be included within the context of your statement of the material. In addition, citing sources will give concrete evidence of the depth of your research. Your citation need not be a complete representation of all the bibliographical information. Figure 3.2 gives examples of several appropriate source citations.

Although you do not want to clutter your speech with bibliographical citations, you do want to make sure that you have properly reflected the sources of your most important information. If you practice these and similar short citations, you will find that they soon will come naturally.

Figure 3.2
*Appropriate source
citations.*

"According to the feature article about the
rising costs of medicine in last week's <u>Time</u>
magazine . . ."

"In a speech on 'Computer Security,' before
the Annual Computer Security Conference last
November, Thomas Horton, CEO of the American
Management Association said . . ."

"An article on ethnic clashes in Russia in
the March 19, 1990, issue of <u>Newsweek</u> reported that, . . ."

"But in order to get a complete picture we
have to look at the statistics. According
to the most recent <u>Statistical Abstract</u>,
the balance of payments during the last
three years have been . . ."

**Speech Preparation
Exercise 6
*Using Notecards***

Using at least four different sources that you identified in the exercise on listing sources (p. 59), complete six notecards, four of factual statements and two of expert opinions. On your notecards be sure to cite the title, source, date, and page number of the source, whether an article or a book.

Verbal and Visual Speech Material

The factual statements and expert opinions you gather from your research may be presented in a variety of forms. Some of the material you find may be in a form you can use just as it is. For instance, if you found the fact that Joe Jones had graduated from high school without learning how to read, you might present that fact in your speech as you found it. Or you might present that fact as one in a series of examples, or as part of a comparison, or you might develop it into a narrative.

Depending on your topic and your speech goal, you may use facts and opinions verbally in any of the following ways: as examples, illustrations, anecdotes, narratives, statistics, quotable explanations and opinions, comparisons, definitions, descriptions, and also visually as charts, diagrams, and other visual aids.

Examples and Illustrations

Examples are specific instances that illustrate or explain a general statement. The generalization "American cars are beginning to rival the quality of foreign cars," for instance, may be illustrated or explained with the following specific example: "Ford Escorts' and Plymouth Horizons' frequency-of-repair records this year are much closer to those of cars made by Nissan and Toyota." The use of examples is a commonly used mode of idea development because examples are so readily available or easily constructed.

You can use examples individually or in series. In the following passage, notice how Mario Cuomo, the governor of New York, uses a series of examples to support his point about the importance of family education:

> I learned to do all the basic things from my family before I ever went to school. . . . The real tough teaching jobs were left up to my mom and pop: things like tying my shoes, not playing with fire, learning my way to the potty, picking up my own toys and socks, not hitting my brother or sister, standing up to the bully down the block. In short, I learned to be a worker, a citizen, a neighbor, a friend, a husband and — I hope — a civilized human being — all under the tutelage of this marvelous university called the family — and all before I set foot in a school.[1]

Although you will want to develop most of the general statements in your speech with real examples, at times you may want to develop generalizations with hypothetical examples. *Hypothetical examples* are those drawn from suppositions — they develop the idea, "What if . . . ?" In the following excerpt, John A. Ahladas presents hypothetical examples of what it will be like in the year A.D. 2039 *if* global warming continues:

> In New York, workers are building levees to hold back the rising tidal waters of the Hudson River, now lined with palm trees. In Louisiana, 100,000 acres of wetland are steadily being claimed by the sea. In Kansas, farmers learn to live with drought as a way of life and struggle to eke out an existence in the increasingly dry and dusty heartland. . . . And reports arrive from Siberia of bumper crops of corn and wheat from a longer and warmer growing season.[2]

If you are planning to use only one example in your speech and you want to make more of it, then you should cast your example in illustration form. An *illustration* is an example that has been developed with added detail. The following segment shows the difference between casting the same information in example form and in illustration form:

> *Generalization:* Most people want to accomplish an objective with the least amount of effort.
>
> *Example:* When entering a building people will wait for an open door rather than use the energy to open a closed door.
>
> *Illustration:* "I remember watching the entrance of a large office building. There were five doors. The one on the far left was open, the rest closed. Most everybody used the open door, even waiting for people to come out before they could enter just because the door was easier than the effort of pushing another door open. This is true of much of life."[3]

Now let us consider guidelines for the selection and use of examples.

First, the examples should be clear and specific enough to create a clear picture for the audience. If you were to exemplify the generalization "American car manufacturers give long warranties" with the statement "Many companies give warranties of several years," the example would not give a clear picture. But if you were to give the examples "Chrysler and General Motors are now giving five- to seven-year warranties on all models," the point would be more specific.

Second, the examples you use should not be the only examples available. For instance, if Chrysler was the *only* manufacturer to give a long warranty, then it would be unethical to start with the generalization "American car manufacturers give long warranties."

Third, you should use examples that actually relate to the generalization. If you say, "American car manufacturers are becoming more sensitive to environmental issues," and then give the statement, "Chrysler Corporation has run a series of commercials urging drivers not to throw litter on the highways on their trips," the example may have something to do with the environment, but it does not relate to the point that Chrysler Corporation is itself doing anything that shows sensitivity to environmental issues.

Because specifics both clarify and substantiate, a good rule of thumb to follow is: Never let a generalization stand without at least one example.

Statistics

Statistics are numerical facts. *Statistical* statements, such as "Seven out of every ten local citizens voted in the last election," or "The cost of living rose 4.5 percent in 1988," enable you to pack a great deal of information into a small package. When statistics are well used, they can be most impressive; when they are poorly used, they may be boring and, in some instances, downright deceiving. How can you use statistics effectively?

1. *Make sure the statistics are true.* Taking statistics from only the most reliable sources and double-checking any startling statistics with another source will help you avoid the use of faulty statistics.

2. *Use recent statistics so as not to mislead your audience.* For example, if you used the statistic that only 12 of 435, or 2.8 percent, members of Congress were women (true in 1971), you would be misleading your audience. If you wanted to make a point about the number of women in Congress, you would want the most recent figures.

3. *Use statistics comparatively whenever possible.* By themselves, statistics are hard to interpret, but when used comparatively, they have much greater impact. Notice how John Lawn, Administrator, Drug Enforcement Administration, uses comparisons of his statistics in the following passage: "Drug users are $3\frac{1}{2}$ times as likely to be involved in a plant accident. Drug users are 5 times as likely to file a workers' compensation claim. Drug users receive 3 times the average level of sick benefits. Drug users function at 67% of their work potential."[4]

    In your comparisons, be careful not to present a misleading picture. If you say that during the past six months Company A doubled its sales while its nearest competitor, Company B, improved by only 40 percent, the implication would be misleading if you did not indicate the size of the base; Company B, with a larger base of sales, could have more sales, even though its improvement was only 40 percent.

4. *Do not overuse statistics.* Although statistics may be an excellent way to present a great deal of material quickly, be careful not to overuse them. A few pertinent numbers are far more effective than a battery of statistics. When you believe you must use many statistics, try preparing a visual aid, perhaps a chart, to help your audience more easily visualize them.

    Donald Baeder points out that whereas in the past chemicals were measured in parts per million, today they are measured in parts per billion or even parts per trillion. In the following passage, he goes on to use comparisons to show the meaning of these statistics: "One part per billion is the equivalent of one drop — one drop! — of vermouth in two 36,000 gallon tanks of gin — and that would be a very dry martini even by San Francisco standards! One part per trillion is the equivalent of one drop in two thousand tank cars."[5]

Anecdotes and Narratives

Anecdotes are brief, often amusing stories; *narratives* are tales, accounts, personal experiences, or lengthier stories. Each presents material in story form. Do you remember the last time one of your professors said, "That reminds me of a story"? Probably more people listened to the story than to any other part of the lecture. Because holding audience interest is so important in a speech and because audience attention is likely to be captured by a story, anecdotes and narratives are worth looking for, creating, and using. For a two-minute speech, you have little time to tell a detailed story, so one or two anecdotes or a very short narrative would be preferable. In longer speeches, however, including at least one longer anecdote or narrative will pay dividends in holding audience attention as well as in fostering audience understanding.

The key to using stories is to make sure that the point of the story states or reinforces the point you make in your speech. In his speech about managers, Michael Durst, president of Training Systems, made a point about the impact of people who love their jobs. In the following excerpt, notice how he clearly states his point and then gives an anecdote that really supports the point:

> People who love their job make more positive impact than those who don't. I can think of an example. In Chicago, we have a singing bus driver. This guy is incredible. He sings from the time he gets on the bus in the morning until he finishes that evening. When he was interviewed on Channel 5, he said, "Actually, I'm not really a bus driver, I'm a professional singer. I only drive a bus to get a captive audience every single day." His job description does not include "singing to the people who ride the bus." The truth is, because he is in touch with that purpose, his job becomes aligned with it, and that alignment created a further alignment with the Chicago Transit Authority because people wait in line to get on his bus. Because they're happier, they ride more often.[6]

Neither the anecdote nor the narrative needs to be humorous to be effective. In her speech on the subjects of blacks and women in universities, Pattie Gillespie told the following story to show the inaccuracy of perceptions even among university faculty:

> I recently heard a male senior professor say with considerable pride that on his faculty there were now an equal number of men and women. His observation was quickly affirmed by one of the junior men in the department. Because I knew the department and could not get the figures to tally, I asked that we go through the faculty list together. Both men were surprised when we discovered that, by actual count, the current faculty consisted of nine men and five women, that is almost two men for each woman.[7]

Comparison and Contrast

One of the best ways to give meaning to new ideas is through comparison and contrast. *Comparisons* show similarities; *contrasts* show differences. Although you can create comparisons easily, you should still keep your eye open for comparisons in your research.

Your comparisons may be literal or figurative. Literal comparisons show similarities of real things: "The walk from the lighthouse back up the hill to the parking lot is equal to walking up the stairs of a thirty-story building." Figurative comparisons express one thing in terms normally denoting another: "I always envisioned myself as a four door sedan — I didn't know she was looking for a sports car!"

Comparisons not only make ideas clearer but also more vivid. Notice the way that Stephen Joel Trachtenberg used figurative comparison to demonstrate the importance of willingness to take risk, even in the face of danger, when he said in his speech to the Newington High School Scholars' Breakfast: "The eagle flying high always risks being shot at by some hare-brained human with a rifle. But eagles — and young eagles like you — still prefer the view from that risky height to what is available flying with the turkeys far, far below."[8]

Whereas *comparisons* show similarities, *contrasts* show differences. Notice how this humorous contrast dramatizes the difference between "participation" and "commitment": "If this morning you had bacon and eggs for breakfast, I think it illustrates the difference. The eggs represented 'participation' on the part of the chicken. The bacon represented 'total commitment' on the part of the pig!"[9]

Quotation

When you find an explanation or an opinion that seems to be exactly what you are looking for, you may quote it directly in your speech. Because we want to see *your* creative processes at work, we do not want to hear long quotations strung together to form your speech. Nevertheless, a well-selected quotation might be perfect in one or two key places. If you keep quotations relatively short and few in number, they can and should serve you well.

You will find that you can use quotations both to explain and to vivify.

Use contemporary quotations to explain. Often you will find that another person has made a point in a way that is far more clear or more vivid than you can make it. For example, in his speech "The Spur of Ignorance" James Olson, used the following quote from the British psychologist Edward DeBono to help him make a point about how needing to be right can be an impediment to progress: "the need to be right at every stage and all the time is probably the biggest bar there is to new ideas."[10]

Use historical or literary quotations to vivify. You also will want to be on the lookout for material that will add punch to your speech. Frequently you can find historical or literary quotations that are well enough related to your subject matter that quoting them will reinforce your point and in a vivid way.

In his introduction to a speech on "Integrity," Ronald W. Roskens quoted Sir Harold MacMillan, the former British prime minister, as saying, "If you want to know the meaning of life . . . don't ask a politician."[11] For another example, we can turn to C. Charles Bahr, chairman of Bahr International, who in his speech on telling the truth to sick companies, quoted Mark Twain on the importance of telling the truth: "Always do right. It will amaze some people and astonish the rest."[12]

To take advantage of such opportunities, you need access to one or more of the many available books of quotations. One of the newest is *The International Thesaurus of Quotations* compiled by Rhoda Thomas Tripp.[13] If you look in the reference section of your library, you will find several books of quotations, which are often organized by topic and from which you may find a particularly appropriate quote to use in your speech.

Keep in mind that if you use a direct quotation, you should credit its source. The use of any quotation or close paraphrase that is not documented is plagiarism.

Descriptions and Definitions

In your speeches you also will find that your information is clearer when you define words carefully and describe material completely.

A *definition* is a statement about what something is. Our entire language is built on the assumption that we, as members of a culture, share common meanings of words. And although that may be true, many of the words we use in our speeches may not be totally understood by our audiences. As a result, we must define words carefully when they are important to audience understanding.

A *description* is a verbal picture or an account in words. We can describe a room, a city, a park, a dog, or any other object, place, person, or thing with the goal of enabling the audience to hold a mental picture that corresponds to the actual thing.

Because definition and description may be the impetus for an entire speech, we discuss the two in separate chapters in Part III, Informative Speaking. Any speaker will want to build his or her facility with definition and descriptions, so you will want to study the material of those chapters carefully even if you are not asked to prepare descriptive or definition speeches.

Visual Aids

So far, all of our discussion of developmental material has focused on the verbal, but a speech may comprise both visual and verbal material.

A visual aid is a form of speech development that allows the audience to both see and hear about the material. Visual aids are likely to take two forms in a speech: (1) as a means of *showing* verbal information so that as a speech progresses, members of the audience will gain visual as well as auditory impressions; (2) as a means to create moods, emotions, and attitudes that supplement or take the place of verbal information.

The major rationale for the use of visual aids in any speech is that information is more likely to be understood and retained when oral expression is supplemented with visual aids. Whether a picture is worth a thousand words or not, research has shown that people learn considerably more when ideas appeal to both the eye and the ear than when they appeal to the ear alone.[14]

As you prepare your speeches, you should consider graphic visuals, including charts, diagrams, maps, drawings, flipcharts, photographs, films, slides, overheads, and the chalkboard. Because visual aids are a major contributor to increasing the clarity of informative speeches, an entire chapter in Part III, Informative Speaking, is devoted to the construction and use of visual aids.

Summary

Effective speaking requires high-quality information. You need to know where to look for information, what kind of information to look for, how to record it, and how you can use it in your speeches.

To find material, you must explore your own knowledge as well as observe, interview, survey, and read.

In your sources, you will look for factual statements and expert opinions. Factual statements are about things that have an actual, concrete existence or report actual, documentable occurrences. Expert opinions are interpretations of facts made by authorities in your particular subject area.

When you find material that you want to consider using in your speech, you should record each bit of data along with necessary bibliographical documentation on a separate notecard.

Although you will use some of your material as you find it, you may want to present the information in a different form. Depending on your topic and your speech goal, you may use facts and opinions orally as examples, illustrations, anecdotes, narratives, statistics, quotations, comparisons, definitions, and descriptions and also as visual aids.

Notes

1. Mario M. Cuomo, "The Family," *Vital Speeches*, February 15, 1980, 268.
2. John A. Ahladas, "Global Warming," *Vital Speeches*, April 1, 1989, 382.
3. Guernsey Jones, "How Deep Are Your Convictions?," *Vital Speeches*, June 1, 1987, 493.
4. John C. Lawn, "Drugs in America," *Vital Speeches*, March 15, 1986, 323.
5. Donald L. Baeder, "Chemical Wastes," *Vital Speeches*, June 1, 1980, 497.
6. G. Michael Durst, "The Manager as a Developer," *Vital Speeches*, March 1, 1989, 313.
7. Patti P. Gillespie, "Campus Stories, or the Cat Beyond the Canvas," *Vital Speeches*, February 1, 1988, 237.
8. Stephen Joel Trachtenberg, "Five Ways in Which Thinking Is Dangerous," *Vital Speeches*, August 15, 1986, 653.
9. G. Michael Durst, "The Manager as a Developer," *Vital Speeches*, March 1, 1989, 309–310.
10. James E. Olson, "The Spur of Ignorance," *Vital Speeches*, March 15, 1988, 340.
11. Ronald W. Roskens, "Integrity," *Vital Speeches*, June 1, 1989, 511.
12. C. Charles Bahr, "Sick Companies Don't Have to Die," *Vital Speeches*, September 1, 1988, 685.
13. *The International Thesaurus of Quotations*, compiled by Rhoda Thomas Tripp (New York: Harper & Row, 1987).
14. Bernardette M. Gadzella and Deborah A. Whitehead, "Effects of Auditory and Visual Modalities in Recall of Words," *Perceptual and Motor Skills*, 40 (February 1975), 260.

Chapter 4 | Organizing Speech Material

Principle III

Effective speaking occurs when material is organized and developed to heighten the speech's goal.

P lato, the famous classical Greek philosopher, was one of the first people to recognize the organic nature of a speech. He wrote, "Every discourse like a living creature, should be put together that it has its own body and lacks neither head nor feet, middle nor extremities, all composed in such a way that suit both each other and the whole."[1] Or to put it in a way that follows the old military guideline: First you tell them what you're going to tell them, then you tell them, then you tell them what you told them.

From the beginning of the organizational process, you should work in outline form. Your goal is to develop a complete speech outline, which is a short representation of the speech with key points expressed in complete sentences. Think of an outline not as a complete speech written in outline form, but as a blueprint you can follow as you make language choices and practice the delivery. The value of working with an outline is that you can test the logic, development, and overall strength of the structure of your speech before you prepare the wording or begin practicing its delivery.

Does a speaker really need to write such an outline? Most of us do. Of course, some speakers do not prepare outlines; they have learned, through trial and error, alternate means of planning speeches and testing structure that work for them. Some accomplish the entire process in their heads and never put a word on paper—but they are few indeed. As a beginner, you can save yourself a lot of trouble if you learn to outline ideas. Then you will *know* the speech has a solid, logical structure and that the speech really meets its goal. Over the years I have seen ample proof of the generalization that there is a direct relationship between quality of outline and quality of speech content.

In this chapter, we will begin with the basic rules of outlining and then discuss the development of each part of the outline: the body, the introduction, and the conclusion. The chapter concludes by examining a complete outline and discussing the tests you should make before practicing the speech.

Rules of Outlining

What rules should you use to guide your writing in developing the speech? The following six rules will help you test your thinking and produce a better speech.

1. *Use a standard set of symbols.* Main points usually are indicated by Roman numerals, major subdivisions by capital letters, minor subheadings by Arabic numerals, and further subdivisions by lowercase letters. Although further breakdown of ideas can be shown, a speech outline rarely will be subdivided beyond the level shown here. Thus, an outline for a speech with two main points might look like this:

   I.
      A.
         1.
         2.
      B.

```
II.
    A.
    B.
        1.
            a.
            b.
        2.
```

2. *Use complete sentences for major headings and major subdivisions.* By using complete sentences you are able to see (1) whether each main point actually develops the thesis of your speech goal and (2) whether the wording really makes the point you want to make. Although a phrase or key-word outline works best when the outline is to be used as a speaker's notes, for the planning stage — the blue-print of the speech — complete sentences are preferable. Unless you write key ideas out in full, you will have difficulty ensuring that the following two rules are obeyed.

3. *Each main point and major subdivision should contain a single idea.* By following this rule you will ensure that development will be relevant to the point. Let us examine an incorrect and a correct phrasing:

Incorrect	**Correct**
I. The park is beautiful and easy to get to.	I. The park is beautiful. II. The park is easy to get to.

Trying to develop the incorrect example will lead to confusion, because the development cannot relate to both ideas at once. If your outline follows the correct procedure, you will be able to line up your supporting material with confidence that the audience will see and understand the relationship.

4. *Minor points should relate to or support major points.* This principle is called *subordination*. Consider the following example:

I.   Proper equipment is necessary for successful play.
      A. Good gym shoes are needed for maneuverability.
      B. Padded gloves will help protect your hands.
      C. A lively ball provides sufficient bounce.
      D. And a good attitude doesn't hurt.

Notice that the main point deals with equipment. A, B, and C (shoes, gloves, and ball) relate to the main point. But D, attitude, is not equipment, and should appear somewhere else, if at all.

5. *Main points should be limited to a maximum of five.* A speech usually will contain from two to five main points. Regardless of the length of time available, audiences will have difficulty really assimilating a speech that has more than five points. If a speech does seem to have more than five points, you usually can group points under headings to limit them to five or fewer. Audiences will remember two main points with four divisions each more easily than they will remember eight main points.

6. *The total words in the outline should equal no more than one-third to one-half of the total number anticipated in the speech.* An outline is a skeleton of the speech and should be a representation of it — not a manuscript with letters and numbers. One way to test the length of an outline is by computing the total number of words you will be able to speak during the time limit and then limiting your outline to one-third of that total. Because approximate figures are all that are needed, you can assume that your speaking rate is about average — 160 words per minute. Thus, for a two- to three-minute speech, which would include roughly 320 to 480 words, the outline should be limited to 110 to 160 words. The outline for an eight- to ten-minute speech, which will contain roughly 1,200 to 1,500 words, should be limited to 400 to 500 words.

Preparing the Body of the Speech

Many students assume that because the introduction is the first part of the speech to be heard by the audience, they should begin outlining with the introduction. If you think about it, however, you will realize that it is difficult to work on an introduction until you have considered the material you will be introducing. Unless you know exactly what will be in the speech, you probably should outline the body first.

To do so, you select and state the main points, determine the best order, and then select and develop the examples, quotations, and other elements that explain or support the main points.

Selecting and Stating Main Points

Main points are the key building blocks of your speech. You expect your audience to remember the main points of the speech if nothing else. Because main points are so important, they should be carefully selected and worded.

If your speech goal is well written, the main points already will be stated or at least suggested. For instance, what would be the main points for a speech with the goal "I want my audience to know the four most important considerations for planting roses"? Each main point would be one of the four considerations. If the thesis statement is well written at this stage of preparation, the selection and statement of main points becomes even easier. If the thesis statement is "Roses should be planted in an area that receives morning sun, that is close to a supply of water, that contains well-drained soil, and that is away from trees and shrubs," writing out the main points will be no problem whatsoever. Written in outline form, the main points would be as follows:

I. Plant the roses in an area that receives four to six hours of morning sun.
II. Plant the roses close to a supply of water.
III. Plant the roses in an area with good, well-drained soil.
IV. Plant the roses away from other trees and shrubs.

Once you have selected the main points, you must state them in complete sentences that are specific, vivid, and parallel in structure.

Main points are *specific* when their wording is likely to call up the same images in the minds of all members of the audience. For the speech on roses, suppose that Dora first wrote two of the main points as follows:

I. Plant the roses in a pretty sunny place.
IV. Plant the roses out of the way.

This wording is so general that the audience is unlikely to understand what she means: The directions are not phrased in a way that is likely to create clear mental images. Thus, as Dora revises the main points for clarity, she seeks wording that will increase the likelihood of audience understanding:

I. Plant the roses in an area that receives four to six hours of morning sun.
IV. Plant the roses several feet away from trees and shrubs.

Main points are *vivid* when their wording produces strong sensory impressions on the audience. Often the more specific the sentence, the stronger the sensual impression will be. Thus, the revised wording of points I and IV above are more vivid as well as more clear than the first drafts. But vividness goes beyond clarity. Suppose that Dora had written her third main point as follows:

III. Plant the roses in an area with good, arable soil.

The wording of this point is reasonably clear. In reference to soil, "good" is likely to denote cultivatable, and "arable" is a specific word meaning tilled or tillable. Still, neither "good" nor "arable" is a vivid word. As Dora revised her main points for vividness, she seeks words that will strike sharper images. The end result is the following:

III.   Plant the roses in an area with rich, easily cultivated soil.

"Rich" is more striking than "good"; "easily cultivated" is likely to create a sharper visual image than "arable." In the next chapter, "Speech Language," we will discuss clarity, vividness, emphasis, and appropriateness of language more completely.

Main points are *parallel* when their wording follows the same structural pattern, often using the same introductory words for each main point. For example, in the speech about roses mentioned above, each main point begins with the words "Plant the roses." Sometimes parallelism is achieved by less obvious means. One method is to start each sentence with an active verb. For instance, suppose Kenneth wished to have his audience understand the steps involved in antiquing a table. He might write the following main points in the first draft of his outline:

I.   Clean the table thoroughly.
II.   The base coat can be painted over the old surface.
III.   A stiff brush, sponge, or piece of textured material can be used to apply the antique finish.
IV.   Then you will want to apply two coats of shellac to harden the finish.

Do you see how the wordings do not present a clear, parallel structure? If Ken then revised the wording to meet the test of parallel language, he would write the main points as follows (parallel active verbs are italicized):

I.   *Clean* the table thoroughly.
II.   *Paint* the base coat over the old surface.
III.   *Apply* the antique finish with a stiff brush.
IV.   *Harden* the surface with two coats of shellac.

To further illustrate the evolution of topic ideas into complete-sentence main points, let us examine three contrasting ways of stating the same main points:

Specific Goal: I want the audience to understand the insights our clothes give us into our society.

Thesis Statement: Our clothing gives insight into the casual approach, youthful look, similarity in men's and women's roles, and lack of visual distinction between rich and poor in our society.

Set 1	Set 2	Set 3
I. Casual	I. They are casual.	I. Our clothes indicate our casual look.
II. Youthful	II. They are youthful.	II. Our clothes indicate our emphasis on youthfulness.
III. Similarities	III. There is a similarity in men's and women's roles.	III. Our clothes indicate the similarity in men's and women's roles.
IV. Little distinction	IV. There is little distinction between rich and poor.	IV. Our clothes indicate the lack of visual distinction between the rich and the poor.

The labels in the first column indicate the subject areas only. Although the words *casual, youthful, similarities,* and *little distinction* relate to the purpose and indicate the subject areas of the thesis statement, how they are related is unknown. These labels might be useful as idea triggers on notecards, but they will not work at this stage of preparation. In the second set, the complete-sentence main points are clearer than the labels. Nevertheless, the use of *they* and *there is* along with forms of the verb *to be (are, is)* makes the statements vague.

Notice the significant improvement in the third set. The main points not only include each of the classifications but also explain the relationships of the categories to the goal sentence. In addition, starting each item with "Our clothes indicate" makes the main points parallel. If the listeners remember only the main points of set 3, they will know exactly what our clothes tell us about our society.

As you begin to phrase prospective main points, you may find your list growing to five, seven, or even ten points that seem to be main ideas. Because every main point must be developed in some detail, it usually is impractical to have more than two to five main points. If you have more than five, you should rework your speech goal to limit the number of points or group similar ideas under a single heading.

Preparing a complex meal calls for a good deal of advance preparation and organization—and so does explaining how to do it. Unless this cooking instructor organizes his material carefully, it's unlikely that his audience will be able to understand or remember the main points he wants to convey.

Determining the Best Order

A speech can be organized in many different ways. Your objective is to find or create the structure that makes the most sense of your material and best achieves your goal. An audience is likely to understand and remember main points better if they are organized in an order that emphasizes time, space, topic, causality, reasons, or problem solution. As we discuss each option, you will notice that order is determined by the nature of the information and the perception of the information you want to leave with your audience.

TIME OR CHRONOLOGICAL ORDER   *Time order* follows a chronological sequence of ideas or events. When you select a time-order arrangement of material, the audience understands that there is a particular importance to the sequence as well as to the content of those main points. Time order is most appropriate when you are explaining how to do something, how to make something, how something works, or how something happened. In the following example, notice how the order of main points is as important to the logic of the speech as the wording of its main points:

Specific Goal: I want the audience to understand the three steps involved in magazine production.

Thesis Statement: The steps of magazine production include imposition, composition, and printing.

    I.   Imposition is the first step of production.

    II.   Composition is the second step of production.

    III.   Printing is the final step of production.

SPACE ORDER   *Space order* follows a spatial relationship of main points. Space order is likely to be used in descriptive, informative speeches. When you use a space order, you are telling the audience that there is a special significance to the positioning of the information. In explanations of a scene, place, person, or object, a space order helps to create an orderly picture for your audience. To emphasize the logical pattern of your description, you should proceed from top to bottom, left to right, inside to outside, or in any constant direction that the audience can picture. In the following example, notice how the spatial order helps us see the three layers of the atmosphere:

Specific Goal: I want the audience to picture the three layers that make up the earth's atmosphere.

Thesis Statement: The earth's atmosphere comprises the troposphere, the stratosphere, and the ionosphere.

    I.   The troposphere is the inner layer of the atmosphere.

    II.   The stratosphere is the middle layer of the atmosphere.

    III.   The ionosphere is the succession of layers that constitute the outer regions of the atmosphere.

TOPIC ORDER   *Topic order* emphasizes categories or divisions of a subject. Because any subject may be subdivided or categorized in many different ways, a topic order allows you to select those divisions or categories that are most informative for an audience. The internal order of the topics may go from general to specific, least important to most important, or in some other logical order. If all the topics are of equal weight, their order is unimportant. For example, in a speech on extrasensory perception, the three topics of telepathy, clairvoyance, and precognition are of equal weight and thus can be placed in any order on the outline.

If topics vary in weight and in importance to the audience, how you order them may influence your audience's understanding or acceptance of them. For example, because the topics of the major roles of the presidency vary in weight, they can be presented in order of importance, with greatest importance last.

Specific Goal: I want the audience to understand the major roles of the presidency.

Thesis Statement: The president is chief of foreign relations, commander-in-chief of the armed forces, head of a political party, and head of the executive branch.

   I.   The president is the chief of foreign relations.
  II.   The president is commander-in-chief of the armed forces.
 III. The president is the head of a political party.
 IV. The president is the head of the executive branch.

CAUSAL ORDER *Causal order* emphasizes the causal relationship between main points and subject. That is, it shows that the subject results from specific conditions. When you use a causal order, you are telling the audience that each main point is one of the factors that is instrumental in bringing about the subject.

Specific Goal: I want the audience to understand the major causes of juvenile crime.

Thesis Statement: Juvenile crime is a result of poverty, lack of discipline, and broken homes.

   I.   One major cause is poverty.
  II.   A second major cause is lack of discipline in the home.
 III. A third major cause is broken homes.

REASONS ORDER *Reasons order* emphasizes why you believe an audience should believe in a statement or behave in a particular way. Unlike the first four arrangements of points, the reasons order is most appropriate for a persuasive speech. In Chapter 14, we consider additional ways of phrasing and ordering reasons for persuasive speeches.

Specific Goal: I want the audience to donate money to the United Way.

Thesis Statement: Donating to the United Way is appropriate because your one donation covers many charities, a high percentage of your donation goes to charities, and you can stipulate which specific charities you wish to support.

   I.   You should donate to the United Way because your donation will be used to meet the needs of your community.
  II.   You should donate to the United Way because your one donation will be apportioned to many charities.

III. You should donate to the United Way because a high percentage of your donation reaches the charities.

PROBLEM–SOLUTION ORDER *Problem–solution order* is a form of organization in which the main points are written to show (1) that there is a problem that requires a change in attitude or behavior (or both), (2) that the solution you are presenting will solve the problem, and (3) that the solution is the best way to solve that problem. Because the problem–solution order is used when you want to prove to the audience that a different solution is needed to remedy a major problem, this type of organization will work best for a persuasive speech. Notice how the three points of the problem–solution order are presented in the following example:

Specific Goal: I want the audience to believe that business and industry should be allowed to conduct random drug tests on all employees.

Thesis Statement: Businesses should be allowed to conduct random drug tests on employees because drug abuse creates major problems in the workplace, random drug testing lowers instances of drug abuse, and drug testing is the best solution to the problem.

I. Drug abuse is creating major problems in the workplace.
II. Random drug tests lower instances of drug abuse.
III. Random drug testing is the best solution to the problem.

In summary then, (1) state each main point as a complete sentence, (2) state each main point so that it develops the key words in the speech goal, (3) state each main point clearly, (4) state each main point vividly, (5) state each point in parallel language, (6) limit the number of main points to five, and (7) organize the main points to follow one of the six standard patterns.

Selecting and Outlining Supporting Material

Taken collectively, your main points outline the structure of your speech. Whether your audience understands, believes, or appreciates what you have to say usually will depend upon how well you have developed those main points.

In Chapter 3 you learned that factual statements and expert opinions were the types of research information you use in your speech. Now you must select the most relevant of those materials and decide how you will use them to develop each of the main points.

1. *List supporting material.* First, write down each main point and under it state the information that you believe develops that main

point. For example, for the first main point of a speech with the goal "I want the audience to understand the four C's that determine the value of a diamond," you might write the following:

I. Carat, the first C, is the weight of a diamond.
Recently standardized.
Used to be weighed against the carob seed.
Now the weight is a standard 200 milligrams.
Weight also is shown in points.
How much a diamond costs depends on its size.
But the price of high-quality diamonds may multiply as they get larger: A ½-carat diamond may cost $1,000; a 1-carat diamond, $3,000.
The price is determined by the amount of rock that has to be mined.

2. *Subordinate the material.* Once you have listed the items of information that make the point, you look for relationships between and among ideas. You are likely to find that several items can be grouped under a more general heading. In outline form, then, you are likely to see that a main point will have two or more subdivisions and that each subdivision may have two or more sub-subdivisions. The eight lines of information might be grouped and subordinated in the following way:

I. Carat, the first C, is the weight of the diamond.
A. Diamond weight has been standardized only recently.
1. Originally, merchants measured the weight of diamonds against the carob seed.
2. Now the carat has been standardized as 200 milligrams.
3. Partial weight of a carat is shown in points.
a. One point is one-tenth of a carat.
b. Five points is half of a carat.
B. As diamond weights increase, the costs multiply.
1. A high-quality ½-carat stone may cost $1,000.
2. A high-quality 1-carat stone may cost $3,000.

In your speech you then might develop each of the points with additional examples, illustrations, anecdotes, and other supporting material. In the outline you put enough factual statements and expert opinions down on paper to ensure that you can explain and clarify the point you are making.

Speech Preparation Exercise 7
Outlining the Speech Body

1. Outline the main points of your speech. Indicate whether the main points follow a time order, space order, topic order, causal order, reasons order, or problem–solution order. Check the wording of your main points to make sure that each is written in language that is clear, vivid, and parallel in structure.

2. Begin to outline factual statements and expert opinions that develop each of the main points. Subordinate material so that each subpoint contains only one idea.

Preparing the Introduction

At this stage of preparation, the body of the speech is sufficiently well developed and you can concentrate on ways of beginning your speech. Let us consider what you hope to accomplish in a speech introduction.

Goals of the Speech Introduction

Although your audience is captive (few of them will get up and leave), their physical presence does not guarantee that they will listen. A good introduction will (1) gain initial attention, (2) set the tone for the speech, (3) create a bond of goodwill between you and your audience, and (4) lead into the content of your speech. Let us examine each of these goals separately.

GETTING ATTENTION   Many audiences are like the one you face in class: a group of people who may not throw tomatoes but also may have little motivation to give you their undivided attention. They hope they will like your speech, but if they do not, they can always daydream their way through. Your first goal, therefore, is to create an opening that will win your listeners' undivided attention by involving them with the content.

Some speakers fail to realize that attention must be accompanied by involvement, or the attention may be short-lived. For instance, you may get momentary attention by pounding on the stand, by shouting "Listen!," or by telling a joke, but if an attention-getting device does not relate to the subject matter of the speech, you may lose audience attention as soon as the impact of the attention getter has passed. The attention getter comprises one or more sentences that *directs* audience attention to the body of the speech.

SETTING THE TONE How you approach your topic, your audience, and the occasion will vary from speech to speech. For example, in some speeches you may intend to take a serious look at a grave problem, while in some you may intend to take a more light-hearted look at the foibles of humankind. Each of these intentions will be carried out through the tone you set for your speech. Although the occasion (a funeral or an awards banquet) will suggest a tone, in many speeches you establish the tone by what you say, particularly in your introduction.

Therefore, if you want to set a light-hearted tone, then a humorous opening is appropriate; if you want to set a serious tone, then the opening of the speech should be serious. A speaker who starts with a rib-tickling ribald story is putting the audience in a light-hearted, devil-may-care mood; if that speaker then says, "Now let's turn to the subject of abortion (or nuclear war, or drug abuse)," the speech probably is doomed from the start.

CREATING A BOND OF GOODWILL If your listeners have heard you before, they may be looking forward to hearing you again. On the other hand, they may not know you at all. Or they may even view you as a potential threat, as a person who will tell them things they do not want to hear, who will make them feel uncomfortable, or who will make them think about things they do not necessarily want to think about. If they are going to invest time in listening to you, they must be assured that you are all right, that you are worth listening to. To create this bond of goodwill between speaker and audience, your opening must make the audience *want* to listen to you. You may create goodwill with a separate statement, but in most speeches it is conveyed through the sincerity of your voice and your apparent concern for the audience as people as shown by personal pronouns and direct forms of address. Active efforts at creating goodwill are especially important for persuasive speeches.

LEADING INTO THE CONTENT The introduction must focus the audience's attention on the goal of the speech. In most speech introductions you tell your listeners what you will be talking about. For instance, in an informative speech on campaigning, after your attention getter you may say directly, "In this speech I'll explain the four stages of a political campaign." In a persuasive speech you may proceed less directly and keep the audience in suspense until its attention is firmly established. We will discuss some indirect approaches to content when we consider alternate organizations in the section on persuasive speaking.

Because your thesis statement is a forecast of your main points, it can be used to lead into the speech. Position it as the last point of your outline of the speech introduction (as you will see in the model outline on pp. 94–96). If there is some strategic reason for *not* stating the thesis statement, you still will write it on the outline but put it in parentheses. This means that your speech has a thesis statement but that you have a reason for not stating it in the introduction.

How long should the introduction be? Although I have heard many a professional speech in which the introduction took up 25 to 30 percent of the speech, most introductions range from 5 to 10 percent of the speech. Thus, for a five-minute speech (approximately 750 words), an introduction of 35 to 75 words is appropriate; for a thirty-minute speech, an introduction of two to four minutes is appropriate. Yours should be long enough to put your listeners in the frame of mind that will encourage them to hear you out. Of course, the shorter the speech, the shorter the introduction.

Types of Introductions

Ways to begin your speech are limited only by your imagination. You will want to try three to five different introductions in practice and pick the one that seems best suited to your purpose and that meets the needs that you identified in your analyses of audience and occasion. Let us look at representative approaches that will work for short and long speeches, including startling statements, questions, stories, personal references, quotations, suspense, and compliments. Most of the examples represent introductions that could be used for speeches as short as five minutes.

STARTLING STATEMENT   Especially in a short speech, the kind you are likely to be giving in your first assignment, you must grab your listeners' attention and focus on the topic quickly. One excellent way to do this is by opening with a startling statement that will override the various competing thoughts in your listeners' minds. The following example illustrates the attention-getting effect of a startling statement: "If I pointed a pistol at you, you would be justifiably scared. But at least you would know the danger to your life. Yet every day we let people fire away at us with messages that are dangerous to our pocketbooks and our minds, and we seldom say a word. I'm talking about television advertisers."

QUESTION   Asking a question is another way to get your listeners thinking about your ideas. Like the startling statement, this opening also is adaptable to the short speech. Whether the question method works will depend on how the audience perceives it. The question has to have enough importance to be meaningful to the audience. Notice how a student began her speech on counterfeiting with a series of short questions: "What would you do with this ten-dollar bill if I gave it to you? Take your friend to a movie? Treat yourself to a pizza and drinks? Well, if you did either of these things, you could get in big trouble—this bill is counterfeit!"

STORY   Nearly everyone enjoys a good story, so an introduction that includes story material will get an audience's attention. Keep in mind that a good opening also must lead into the speech as well as get attention. If your story does both, you probably have an unbeatable opening. If your story is not related to the subject, save it for another occasion. Because most good stories take time to tell, they are usually more appropriate for longer speeches; however, you will occasionally come across a short one that is just right for your speech. How do you like this opening to a speech on making money from antiques?

> At a recent auction bidding was particularly brisk on an old hand-blown whiskey bottle, and finally a collector on my left was the successful taker at $50. When the purchase was handed over to him, an aged but sharp-eyed farmer standing nearby leaned over and took a good look at the bottle. "My God," he gasped to his friend. "It's empty!"
>
> To that farmer an empty bottle wasn't worth much. But in today's world anything that's empty might be worth a fortune, if it's old enough. Today I want to talk with you about what might be lying around your basement or attic that's worth real money—a branch of antiques called "collectables."

PERSONAL REFERENCE   Although any good opening should engage the audience, the personal reference is directed solely to that end. In addition to getting attention, a personal reference can be especially good for building goodwill between you and your audience. A personal reference opening such as this one on exercise may be suitable for a speech of any length:

> Say, were you panting when you got to the top of those four flights of stairs this morning? I'll bet there were a few of you who vowed you're never going to take a class on the top floor of this building again. But did you ever stop to think that maybe the problem isn't that this class is on the top floor? It just might be that you are not getting enough exercise.

QUOTATION   A particularly vivid or thought-provoking quotation makes an excellent introduction to a speech of any length. You will need to use your imagination to develop the quotation so that it yields maximum benefits, however, as in the following:

> George Bernard Shaw once wrote, "The road to hell is paved with good intentions." Probably no statement better describes the state of our tort system in this country. With the best of intentions, the scales of a system

designed to render justice have been tipped. The balance has moved so far toward the desire to compensate all injuries and all losses that the overall cost to society has become too high. We have reached a point where exposure to liability is becoming almost limitless and incalculable, making everyone — governments, businesses and individuals — a victim.[2]

SUSPENSE   An extremely effective way to gain attention is through suspense. If you can start your speech in a way that gets the audience to ask, "What is she leading up to?" you may well get them hooked for the entire speech. The suspense opening is especially valuable when the topic is one that the audience might not ordinarily be willing to listen to if started in a less dramatic way.

Consider the attention-getting value of the following: "It costs the United States more than $116 billion per year, it has cost the loss of more jobs than a recession. It accounts for nearly 100,000 deaths a year. I'm not talking about cocaine abuse — the problem is alcoholism."

COMPLIMENT   It feels good to be complimented. We like to believe we are important. Although politicians often overdo the compliment, it still is a powerful opening when well used. Consider the following opening on the free economic system:

> Thank you, Ladies and Gentlemen. I am honored to be speaking to such a fine group of concerned Americans. Your membership in the United States Industrial Council, and your presence at today's National Issues Seminar, affirm your belief in the central role played by millions of individual businesses in creating jobs, wealth and managerial skills for a world that desperately needs all three.[3]

Selecting Your Introduction

How do you know whether the introduction you have prepared is the best for your speech? You cannot tell unless you have something to compare it with. Try working on three or four different introductions; then pick the one you believe will work best for your specific audience.

For example, if you were giving a speech on juggling, you might prepare the following three introductions:

> It takes physical skill, agility, and dexterity. It promotes an overall mind and body balance. It is meditation and it is relaxation. What am I talking about? The art of juggling. Today, I'd like to teach you how to juggle.

> They called him the Lord of the Rings. Cool, confident, and graceful, Anthony Gados recently won the overall title in the thirty-ninth annual International Jugglers' Association competition with a score of 94.83 out of 100, which is five full points above the highest score ever achieved. He can

juggle eight rings, nine balls, and almost anything else, and he makes an average of $1000 per show. Also, Anthony was scolded at the IJA for spitting milk at his brother. You see, Anthony is only thirteen years old, and he's the world's juggling genius. Today, I'd like to teach you what Anthony could do at the age of five, the three-ball cascade.

One night on the David Letterman show, I saw a man juggle a chili dog, a mug of beer, and a slinky. As I watched him, I said to myself, "Nancy, if this man can juggle a chili dog, a mug of beer, and a slinky, you can juggle three stupid beanbags." So, I started off with a mission — to teach myself how to juggle. And I did. Today, I'd like to teach you the basic steps in juggling.

Which introduction would you prefer if you were giving this speech to your classmates?

Although each type of introduction has been discussed individually, they may be used either alone or in combination, depending upon the time you have available and the attitude of your audience. The introduction will not make your speech an instant success, but it can get an audience to look at and listen to you. That is about as much as you have a right to ask of an audience during the first minute or two of your speech.

Speech Preparation Exercise 8
Writing Speech Introductions

For the speech (your) that you outlined in Speech Preparation Exercise 7 (p. 85), prepare three separate introductions that would be appropriate for your classroom audience. Which is the best for your audience and your specific goal? Why?

Preparing the Conclusion

Shakespeare said, "All's well that ends well," and nothing could be truer of a good speech. The conclusion offers you one last chance to hit home with your point. Too many speakers either end their speeches so abruptly that the audience is startled or ramble on aimlessly until they exhaust both the topic and the audience. A poor conclusion — or no conclusion at all — can destroy much of the impact of an otherwise highly effective speech. Even the best conclusion cannot do much for a poor speech, but it can heighten the effect of a good speech.

Goals of the Conclusion

What is a conclusion supposed to do, and how can you make your conclusion do it? A conclusion has two major goals: (1) wrapping the speech up in a way that reminds the audience of what you have said, and (2) hitting home in such a way that the audience will remember your words or consider your appeal. Look at it this way: You may have talked for five minutes or fifty-five minutes, but when you get near the end you have only one last chance to put the focus where you want it. So even though the conclusion will be a relatively short part of the speech — seldom more than 5 percent (thirty-five to forty words of a five-minute speech) — it is worth the time and effort to make it an effective one.

Types of Conclusions

Now let us look at several of the most common types of conclusions.

SUMMARY By far the easiest way to end a speech is by summarizing the main points. Thus, the shortest appropriate ending for a speech on the warning signs of cancer would be, "So remember, if you experience a sudden weight loss, lack of energy, or blood in your urine or bowels, then you should see a doctor immediately." Such an ending restates the main points, which are, after all, the key ideas of the speech.

Because the conclusion may be important for heightening the emotional impact of the speech, even when you are using a summary you may want to add something that will provide greater impact. The following represent several ways of supplementing or replacing the summary.

STORY Storylike material works just as well for the speech conclusion as for the speech introduction. In his speech, "Profitable Banking in the 1980s," Edward Crutchfield ends with a personal experience showing that bankers must be ready to meet competition coming from any direction:

> I played a little football once for Davidson — a small men's college about 20 miles north of Charlotte. One particularly memorable game for me was one in which I was blindsided on an off-tackle trap. Even though that was 17 years ago, I can still recall the sound of cracking bones ringing in my ears. Well, 17 years and 3 operations later my back is fine. But, I learned something important about competition that day. Don't always assume that your competition is straight in front of you. It's easy enough to be blindsided by a competitor who comes at you from a very different direction.[4]

APPEAL TO ACTION The appeal to action is a common way to end a persuasive speech. The appeal describes the behavior that you want your listeners to follow after they have heard the arguments. Notice how Marion Ross, professor of economics at Mills College, ends her speech on living a full and creative life with a figurative appeal to her students:

> We, the faculty, want you to grow wings that won't melt in the sun as did those of Icarus. We want to give you the materials to make your *own* wings,

and we are bold enough to say the thoughts of great thinkers, works of great art and, in some cases, musings of tinkerers of the past are wrought of gold. They won't melt. Use them. It is you who must take these materials, forge them with your own energy and burnish them with your own imagination to make your own wings.[5]

EMOTIONAL IMPACT   No conclusion is more impressive than one that drives home the most important point(s) with real emotional impact. Consider the powerful way in which General Douglas MacArthur finished his speech when he ended his military career:

> But I still remember the refrain of one of the most popular barrack ballads of that day, which proclaimed most proudly that "Old soldiers never die; they just fade away."
> And like the old soldier of that ballad, I now close my military career and just fade away — an old soldier who tried to do his duty as God gave him the light to see that duty.
> Goodbye.[6]

Selecting Your Conclusion

As with introductions, it is difficult to tell whether a conclusion you have prepared is effective unless you have something to compare it with. Try out several conclusions for your speech; then choose the one that you believe will work best with your audience.

If you were speaking on juggling, you might create the following conclusions:

> So, the four steps of learning to juggle are to choose your weapons, get into position, practice your tosses, and begin the cascade.

> And you can learn to juggle, too. Just follow my directions. Choose your weapons (start with something like a beanbag). Get into position. Practice your tosses. And finally, begin the cascade. Come on, you can all learn to do it — juggle!

> So, if you will just learn to choose your weapons, get into position, practice your tosses, and begin the cascade, you can learn to juggle. And who knows? Maybe one night you'll be on the David Letterman show.

Which conclusion would you prefer if you were giving this speech to your classmates?

Speech Preparation Exercise 9
Writing Speech Conclusions

For the speech that you outlined in Speech Preparation Exercise 7 (p. 85), prepare three separate conclusions that would be appropriate for your classroom audience. Which is the best for your audience and your specific goal? Why?

Writing a Title

For most of your classroom speeches you will not need titles unless your professor requires them. You will be called upon to speak, you will walk to the front of the class, and you will begin. But in most situations outside of the classroom, you will want a title. A title is probably necessary when you will be formally introduced, when the speech is publicized, or when the speech will be published. When the group that has invited you is trying to motivate people to attend the speech, a good title may play an especially important part in attracting an audience. A title should be brief, descriptive of the content, and, if possible, creative.

Three kinds of titles are: (1) the simple statement of subject, (2) the question, and (3) the creative title. For many speeches, the title may be a shortened version of your speech goal. For instance, if your goal is "to help the audience understand three major causes of juvenile crime," the title may be "The Causes of Juvenile Crime" or, even more simply, "Juvenile Crime." Sometimes you can put the title in question form. Depending on what you planned to do in the speech on juvenile crime, you might title the speech "Can the Causes of Juvenile Crime Be Eliminated?" In some cases, however, you may want to create some catchy title to help build an audience for the group that has engaged you. Under these circumstances, you may want to use a brainstorming process to find a title.

The following three lists of titles illustrate the types we have mentioned:

Simple Statement of Subject

The Peace Movement
Women and Work
A Good Business Climate
Selling Safety
Office Automation
Domestic Manufacturing
The Housing Crisis

Question

Too Much of a Good Thing?
Do We Need a Department of Play?
Are Farmers on the Way Out?
What Is the Impact of Computers on Our Behavior?
Is Industrial Policy the Answer?

Creative

Teaching Old Dogs New Tricks: The Need for Adult Computer Literacy

Promises to Keep: Broadcasting and the Public Interest

The Tangled Web: How Environmental Climate has Changed

Freeze or Freedom: On the Limits of Morals and Worth of Politics

Sense and Sensitivity: The Engineer and the Public Conscience

The descriptive statement and the question give a clear idea of the topic, but they are not especially eye- or ear-catching. Creative titles capture interest but do not give a clear idea of content unless they include subtitles.

Once you have your goal written, you can write a title. When you are trying to be creative, you may find a title right away or not until the last minute.

<table>
<tr><td>

**Speech Preparation
Exercise 10**
Writing Speech Titles

</td><td>

Write three titles — simple statement of subject, question, and creative — for the speech you have been working on. Which do you like best?

</td></tr>
</table>

The Complete Outline

Now that we have considered the various parts of an outline, let us put them together for a final look. The following outline illustrates the principles in practice. Note that the analysis in the left-hand margin focuses on each of the rules we have considered.

Analysis

Writing the specific purpose at the top of the page before the outline of the speech reminds the speaker of the goal. The speaker should refer to the specific purpose to test whether everything in the outline is relevant.

The heading Introduction *sets this section apart as a separate unit. The introduction (1) gets attention, (2) gains goodwill, and (3) leads into the body.*

OUTLINE FOR A 4–6 MINUTE SPEECH

Specific Goal: I want my audience to understand why Roquefort cheese is unique.

Introduction

I.   For millions of Americans, the answer to the question, "What kind of dressing would you like on your salad?" is "Roquefort, please."

II.   Yet very few of us realize how truly unique this delectable product is.

Thesis Statement: The three distinct elements of Roquefort cheese are that it's trademarked, it's made from ewe's milk, and its distinct flavor comes from a mold grown only one place in the world.

Body

I. Roquefort cheese is trademarked.
   A. Cheesemakers still follow legislation of the Parliament of Toulouse that dates from 1666.
   B. All salad dressings claiming to be Roquefort must contain at least 15 percent legislated Roquefort.

II. Roquefort cheese is made exclusively from ewe's milk, instead of from cow's or goat's milk.
   A. This particular type of sheep dates back to Neolithic times.
   B. Ewe's milk is quite precious.
      1. It takes thirty ewes to produce the amount of milk that could be gotten from one cow.
      2. It takes 800,000 ewes to keep the cheesemakers in business.

III. Roquefort cheese is made from molds grown only in caves located in Roquefort-sur-Soulzon.
   A. The mold is grown in caves that were discovered four to six thousand years ago.
      1. The caves are 1-¼-miles long and 300 yards deep.
      2. The caves are made up of blocks that resemble sugar cubes.
   B. The specific mold, *Penicillium roquefortii*, grows in cracks and fissures of these caves.
   C. The mold is cultivated in bread, ground, and injected into the cheese to give the distinctive color and flavor.

Conclusion

I. We see then that Roquefort cheese is truly unique because it is trademarked, made from ewe's milk, and flavored with a mold grown in only one place in the world.

II. The next time you ask for Roquefort on your salad, you'll have a better appreciation of what you are getting.

Bibliography

"Cheese," *Encyclopedia Americana* 6 (1983): 354–358.

Lecler, René. "Hommage á Fromage," *Saturday Review* (June 24, 1972): 77.

Marquis, Vivienne, and Patricia Haskell. *The Cheese Book*. New York: Simon & Schuster, 1985.

Wernick, Robert. "From Ewe's Milk and a Bit of Mold: A Fromage Fit for a Charlemagne," *Smithsonian* (February 1983): 57–63.

Speech Preparation Exercise 11 *Completing Your Outline*

Complete the outline for your first speech assignment and then test it to make sure that it conforms to the rules discussed previously. If you wish, include a title for your speech.

Summary

After determining content, the next step in effective speech preparation is to outline the speech material. To prepare your outline, use a standard set of symbols, use complete sentences for major headings and major subdivisions, limit each point to a single idea, relate minor points to major points, limit main points to a maximum of five, and make sure your outline is no more than one-third of the speech.

First, outline the body of the speech. The main points will reflect the points made in the thesis of the speech: (1) State each main point as a complete sentence, (2) state each main point so that it develops the key words in the speech goal, (3) state each main point clearly, (4) state each main point vividly, (5) state all points in parallel language, (6) limit the number of main points to five, and (7) organize the main points to follow one of the six standard patterns.

Second, outline the introduction to gain attention, set the tone for the speech, create good will, and lead into the body of the speech. Typical speech introductions include startling statements, questions, stories, personal references, quotations, suspense, and compliments.

Third, outline the conclusion. A well-designed speech conclusion ties the speech together and ends it on a high note. Typical conclusions include summaries, stories, appeals to action, and emotional appeals.

Most speeches have a title. Three kinds are the simple statement of subject, the question, and the creative title.

You then can test the logic and development of the speech by analyzing the speech outline.

Notes

1. Plato, *Phaedrus* (Indianapolis, Ind.: Bobbs-Merrill, 1956), 53.
2. William M. McCormick, "The American Tort System," *Vital Speeches*, February 15, 1986, 267.
3. Based on Rafael D. Pagan, Jr., "A System That Works," *Vital Speeches*, July 15, 1980, 594.
4. Edward E. Crutchfield, Jr., "Profitable Banking in the 1980's," *Vital Speeches*, June 15, 1980, 537.
5. Marion Ross, "Go, Oh Thoughts, On Wings of Gold," *Vital Speeches*, February 15, 1989, 284.
6. Douglas MacArthur, "Address to Congress," in William Linsley, *Speech Criticism: Methods and Materials* (Dubuque, Iowa: Brown, 1968), 344.

Chapter 5 | Speech Language

Principle IV

Effective speaking is a product of clear, vivid, emphatic, and appropriate wording.

When you are ready to begin thinking about presenting your speech, the emphasis switches from *what* you plan to say to *how* you plan to say it. The next two chapters consider the question of how you get from the outline stage of preparation to presenting the speech.

In this chapter we consider what criteria you can use to measure whether your words contribute to an effective oral style, one that is clear, vivid, emphatic, and appropriate. Before we examine these criteria and show how you can meet them in your speeches, let us take a brief look at certain aspects of language that affect your speech or writing.

Your Overall Language Goal

As a unique, individual person, your overall goal is to develop a personal oral style that captures your uniqueness. Still, you must be aware of the awesome power of your language. Richard Weaver, a major figure in contemporary rhetorical theory, has stated that all language is "sermonic."[1] That is, whether or not you are aware of it, you can strike special and sometimes unique chords in each member of your audience by *how* you word your ideas. Thus, wording is not to be taken lightly. Again, paraphrasing Weaver, each of us has an ethical responsibility to use our language with care, for as a result of mindless, sloppy, or unknowingly provocative language, we will create images over which we have no control.[2]

By coping with issues of clarity, vividness, emphasis, and appropriateness, you can preserve your uniqueness, while ensuring that you have approached your goal responsibly. Because language is the device that controls the perceptions that the audience gets from your speech, it is too important to leave to chance. If you are not in control of your wording, you lose the opportunity to communicate effectively.

Words and Meaning

First, we must remind ourselves that language is symbolic. The words we use in our speeches *represent* ideas, objects, and feelings—but they are not of themselves those ideas, object, and feelings. The word "chair" is only a symbol for an object you sit in. Meanings for words are passed on from generation to generation, but in passing on meanings, people learn neither exactly the same meanings for words nor exactly the same words. We must never assume, therefore, that another person will know what we are talking about just because we have used the "right" word.

What makes the challenge of wording so exciting is that words can call up so many different kinds of audience reactions.

Most of us make the mistake of thinking that wording is based on what often is called denotation. *Denotation* is the direct, explicit meaning or reference of a word; in short, denotation is the dictionary meaning. Unfortunately, even on the denotative level you still face certain challenges, which we will briefly consider. First, many of the most common words in our language have many definitions—some similar, but some quite different. For example, *The Random House Dictionary of the English Language* offers fifty-one meanings for *low*. Number one is "situated, placed, occurring not far above the ground"; the seventeenth is "soft, subdued, not loud"; the twenty-second is "depressed or dejected"; and the twenty-sixth is "mean, base, or disreputable."[3] No matter how we look at these three definitions, we have to admit that they are quite different. How does a listener know which definition you are using? Often the "correct" meaning comes from context. For example, when you say, "He really plays a mean drum," your audience probably will recognize the different meaning for *mean* than if you had said, "He's a mean professor." Still, these problems with denotation contribute to our difficulties in expressing ideas clearly.

Far more important to your consideration of wording is the reality that *words evoke thoughts and feelings in listeners*. When we speak of the feelings that a word evokes, we are referring to word *connotation*. For example, when you use the word *home* in a speech, individual listeners' connotations of that word will affect their perceptions of what you are saying. If *home* to one person is a place filled with fun, love, understanding, warmth, and good feelings, it will carry a different meaning than if the person thinks of home as a place filled with fighting, bickering, punishment, confinement, and harsh rules. Some words may evoke stronger thoughts and feelings than others.

In sum, as a speaker you must keep in mind the pitfalls of making assumptions about meanings. In choosing your wording, you must ask both whether the audience is likely to hold the correct dictionary meaning for a word and whether that word is likely to arouse feelings that enhance or interfere with the message you want to convey.

Speaking Clearly

The first goal you want to achieve in your speeches is clarity; that is, you want your audience to have an instant understanding of the words you use. You are more likely to achieve clarity if you select words that are precise, simple, specific, and concrete and if you work to eliminate unnecessary clutter.

Use Precise Words

Precision of language is the goal of using the word that most accurately depicts your meaning. Precision begins with being careful with the words you use to communicate factual details. Suppose you were reporting the graduation rate of college athletes. You might say, "At our school some athletes are graduating more or less on time, but a whole lot of them aren't." In this context "some athletes" and "a whole lot" are not precise.

The range of what people might see as "some" and "a whole lot" is too wide. How could you phrase that sentence so that it would be more precise? See how much more clear the sentence would be if you said, "Here at State University, roughly 60 percent of athletes on scholarship graduate within five years of the time they started. The problem is that in such 'revenue' sports as football and men's basketball the number drops to less than 30 percent." Being precise can involve doing research to nail down specific facts and figures.

Too often, especially in extemporaneous, or off-the-cuff impromptu comments, speakers tend to get sloppy. They use a word that is not quite right, hoping that the audience will understand the point anyway. Suppose a speaker talking about budgetary problems to the board of directors says, "The problem lies in marketing." Marketing is a precise word, but it is the wrong one if the problem actually is in advertising and not marketing.

Precision is especially important when you are trying to communicate a specific shade of meaning. Suppose you wanted to make a point about a politician defending her principal advisor, who has been charged with mishandling campaign funds. Notice the changes in the meaning of the sentence "What she's trying to get is a complete acquittal" if, instead of *acquittal*, you used *vindication, justification,* or *whitewashing*.

How can you increase your precision? A good learning exercise is to play "synonyms." Think of a word, then list as many words as you can that mean about the same thing. When you have completed your list, refer to a book of synonyms such as *Roget's Thesaurus* to see which words you have omitted. Then write what you think is the meaning of each word, focusing on the shades of difference among the words. When you are done, look up each word, even those of which you are sure of the meaning. You will be surprised to find how many times the subtle meaning of even a familiar word escapes you. The goal of this exercise is not to get you to select the rarest word, but to select the best word, the most precise word, to get your idea across to an audience.

As you practice the wording of your speeches, you must constantly ask yourself, "What meaning do I want my audience to get?" Then check to see whether the words you are planning to use are the precise words for carrying those meanings.

Skill Development Exercise
Practicing with Synonyms

For each of the following, indicate five different words that you could use for the italicized words to express the meaning of the sentence:

Scientists have discovered tools that give a clearer picture of what it was like to live in the *past*.

The investigators discovered that the dealings were definitely *phony*.

The position she held gave her a great deal of *authority*.

The committee concluded that he had *imagined* the entire plan.

His lack of interest in group activities suggested that he was a real *hermit*.

To communicate more precisely, you may need to enlarge your vocabulary. The smaller your vocabulary, the less chance you have of communicating effectively. As a speaker you will have fewer choices from which to select the word that you want; as a listener you will be limited in your ability to understand the words that speakers use.

One way to enlarge your vocabulary is to work through a basic vocabulary book such as Ehrlich's *Super Word Power*.[4] Another way is to take a more active role in working with the words you hear and read every day. Begin by noting words that people use in their conversations with you that you cannot define precisely. For instance, suppose Jackie says, "I was *inundated* with phone calls today!" If you cannot give a precise definition for *inundated*, you could ask Jackie what she meant by that word. But if for some reason you do not wish to ask, you can still make a note of the word, look up its meaning at the first opportunity, and then review what Jackie said to see whether the dictionary meaning seems to be what Jackie meant. Most dictionaries define *inundated* as synonymous with *overwhelmed* and *flooded*. If you then say to yourself, "Jackie was inundated — overwhelmed or flooded — with phone calls today," you will tend to remember that meaning and apply it the next time you hear the word. You can follow the same procedure in your reading. As you read a book or magazine, circle any words about which you have a question. After you have finished the section, return to those words and look them up.

Specific and Concrete Words

Specific and *concrete* words help to clarify ideas. Such words call up a single image. People who do not discipline themselves to think sharply fill their speeches with words that are too general or abstract, and which allow the listener the choice of many possible images rather than a single intended image. The more that listeners are called upon to provide their own images, the more they will see meanings different from what you have intended.

Compare the word selection shown in italics in the following sentences:

The senator brought *several things* with him to the meeting.
The senator brought *recent letters from his constituency* with him to the meeting.
She lives in a *really big house*.
She lives in a *fourteen-room Tudor mansion*.

The backyard has *several different kinds of trees.*
The backyard has *two large maples, an oak, and four small evergreens.*

Students say that Morgan is a *fair grader.*
Students say that Morgan uses *the same standards for grading all students.*

I just get really angry with people who *aren't honest* in class.
I just get really angry with people who *cheat on tests* in class.

What are the differences? In the first sentence of each pair, the italicized words and phrases are general and abstract; in the second sentence, the italicized words and phrases are specific and concrete. Words such as *things, trees,* and *car* are general: They communicate no definite visual image. In contrast, *recent letters from his constituency, fourteen-room Tudor mansion, two large maples, an oak, and four small evergreens* are specific phrases that limit what the listener can picture. *Fair* and *aren't honest* are abstract — they cover a variety of possible behaviors; *the same standards for all students* and *cheat on tests* are concrete — they reduce choice to single specific behaviors.

When you select a general or abstract word to carry your meaning, you are inviting confusion. Listeners may take the time to ask you questions to help sharpen the meaning of your message, but it is more likely that they will be satisfied with their own meaning, whether or not it coincides with yours. On the other hand, if you select specific or concrete words to carry your meaning, people will more likely share your meaning without having to question you.

You can find out how precise, specific, and concrete your word selections are by recording portions of your practice speech. As you listen to the playback, write down words that you believe are imprecise and general or abstract. Then try to think of words that would create a clearer mental picture. If your speech is not clear, it may be that your thinking is not clear. For practice, look around the room you are in and label various objects. Do you see a lamp? How could you describe it more specifically? Perhaps it is a fluorescent table lamp or a Tiffany floor lamp. The more success you have in thinking clearly and using precise, specific language in practice sessions, the more success you will have in your speeches.

Use Simple Words

Some speakers get the idea that to be effective they must impress their audience with their extensive vocabularies. As a result, instead of looking for precise, specific, and concrete words, they go overboard and use words that appear pompous, affected, or stilted to the listener. Speaking precisely and specifically does not mean speaking obscurely. So when you have a choice, select the simplest, most familiar words that convey your specific meaning. The following story illustrates the problem with pretentious, unfamiliar words:

> A plumber wrote to a government agency, saying that he found that hydrochloric acid quickly opened drain pipes but that he wasn't sure whether it was a good thing to use. A scientist at the agency replied, "The efficacy of hydrochloric acid is indisputable, but the corrosive residue is incompatible with metallic permanence."
>
> The plumber wrote back thanking him for the assurance that hydrochloric acid was all right. Disturbed by this turn of affairs, the scientist showed the letter to his boss, another scientist, who then wrote to the plumber: "We cannot assume responsibility for the production of toxic and noxious residue with hydrochloric acid and suggest you use an alternative procedure."
>
> The plumber wrote back that he agreed, hydrochloric acid worked fine. Greatly disturbed by this misunderstanding, the scientists took their problem to the top boss. He wrote to the plumber: "Don't use hydrochloric acid. It eats hell out of pipes."

The decision rule is to use a more difficult word when you believe that it is the very best word for a specific context. Suppose you wanted to use a more precise or specific word for *building*. Using the guideline of simplicity, you might select *house, apartment, high-rise,* or *skyscraper,* but you would avoid *edifice.* Each of the other choices is more precise or more specific, but *edifice* is neither more precise nor more specific, and in addition to being less well understood, it will be perceived as affected or stilted.

Similarly, unless you have reason to do otherwise, you should say *clothing* instead of *apparel, bury* instead of *inter, engagement* instead of *betrothal, begin* instead of *commence, avoid* instead of *eschew, wedding* instead of *nuptials, predict* instead of *presage, beauty* instead of *pulchritude, home* instead of *residence, view* instead of *vista,* and so on.

Eliminate Clutter

One of the greatest enemies of clarity in speech is verbal clutter, which includes extraneous words, unnecessary repetition of words, repetitious modifiers, and empty adjectives. Clutter not only crowds out meaning, but also drives listeners up the wall. Although we tolerate such clutter in conversation, we are far less likely to accept it in public speeches.

Clutter is particularly noticeable in early stages of rehearsal when people still are unsure of what they will say. Suppose a person wanted to begin a speech on earthquakes with a reference to the 1989 quake that rocked San Francisco. Her first practice of a speech might be worded like this:

> It was a night to be remembered, but not for the reasons that most people might be likely to remember the night. You know what I'm talking about. It

was a night in the middle of October, the night of October 17 to be exact, the night scheduled for the third game of the World Series in San Francisco when San Francisco was hit with an earthquake that took many lives and caused billions in property damage.

Although such wordiness is accepted more readily in oral than in written language, clutter or wordiness interferes with clarity. The example above not only suffers from wordiness, but also wastes precious time, time needed to develop more important points in the speech. Let her try it again:

October 17, 1989, was a night to be remembered, but not for the reasons that most people expected to remember the night — not for the third game of the World Series, but for a fifteen-second earthquake that took at least fifty-five Bay Area lives and caused more than seven billion dollars in property damage.

Note also how vague and general expressions have been replaced with specific ones.

The following examples illustrate four of the ways that you can use to eliminate clutter.

1. Eliminate repetitions that do not add emphasis.
   Wordy: He found that *the bill that he supported* is not one *that he should have supported*.
   Better: He found that he should not have supported that bill.
2. Eliminate empty words and phrases — especially meaningless modifiers — that add nothing to the meaning.
   Wordy: Sarah became the leader she is through *very, very* hard work and *a lot of* attention to detail.
   Better: Sarah became an accomplished leader through hard work and attention to detail.
3. Boil down long sentences into shorter, harder-hitting sentences.
   Wordy: A few *of the* people *who had become very angry* rose *to take the opportunity of* refuting the arguments set forth by Councilman Roddy.
   Better: A few angry people rose to refute Councilman Roddy's arguments.
4. Combine sentences or simplify phrases and clauses that include the same ideas.
   Wordy: *The speeches prepared by* Martin Luther King, Jr., are different from *those speeches prepared by* other Civil Rights speakers of the period.
   Better: Martin Luther King, Jr.'s speeches are different from those by other Civil Rights speakers of the period.

How do you practice eliminating clutter? Tape a one- or two-minute segment in which you narrate an event that you have witnessed. Perhaps you could talk about a portion of a professor's lecture, a segment of a game that you witnessed, or the plot of a situation comedy you saw. Then transcribe the one- or two-minute section. Edit the segment following the guidelines of eliminating repetitions and empty phrases — those that add nothing to the meaning — boiling down long sentences into shorter, harder-hitting sentences, and combining sentences or simplifying phrases and clauses. Then record another segment describing the same event, but concentrating on eliminating the kinds of problems that you found in the first session.

During your first practice sessions, your speaking may not appear to be natural. You may concentrate so heavily on speaking without clutter that meaning may suffer. But the more you practice, the more easily you will find yourself reducing clutter.

Improvement in speeches should come naturally as a result of improvement in practice. Just as an athlete works on skills in practice but concentrates on the game in competition, so you can stress work in practice but concentrate on your ideas and on the audience when you are giving a speech. Nevertheless, if practice is successful, you will find yourself able to monitor even public speaking *without* conscious effort.

Speaking Vividly

While clear language helps the audience grasp the meaning, vivid language paints meaning in living color. *Vivid* means full of life, vigorous, bright, and intense. Vivid speech begins with vivid thought. You must have a striking mental picture before you can communicate one to your audience. If you cannot feel the bite of the wind and the sting of the nearly freezing rain, if you cannot hear the thick, juicy sirloin-strip steaks sizzling on the grill, if you cannot feel the exhilaration as the jet climbs from takeoff, then you will not be able to describe these sensations vividly. The more imaginatively you can think about your ideas, the more likely you can state them vividly.

To illustrate the major means of increasing vividness, contrast the differences in the following two sentences:

> A great deal of potential was seen in Helen Keller by Anne Sullivan. She worked hard on Helen until the potential that enabled Helen to help people such as herself all over the world was realized.

Anne Sullivan saw great potential in Helen Keller. "She loved her, disciplined her, played, prayed, pushed, and worked with her until the flickering candle that was her life became a beacon that helped light the pathway and lighten the burdens of people all over the world."[5]

The first passage describes what Sullivan did with and for Helen Keller. The second passage from Beverly Chiodo's speech on "Choosing Wisely" vivifies the passage through active rather than passive voice, specific active verbs that create mental pictures, and figurative language. Let us consider each of these methods for increasing vividness.

Use active rather than passive voice. Voice is the form of a transitive verb that tells whether the grammatical subject performs the action stated in the verb or is acted upon. Casting all your sentences in active voice will lay a foundation for vivid speech. "A great deal of potential *was seen*" is passive voice — "potential," the grammatical subject, is acted upon; "Anne Sullivan *saw* great potential" is active voice — "Anne Sullivan," the grammatical subject performs the action stated in the verb.

Use specific, verbs that form sharp mental pictures. For instance in the first example, "Anne worked hard on Helen," *worked hard* does not create a sharp mental picture of what Anne did. In contrast, Beverly Chiodo's phrasing, "Anne *disciplined her, played, prayed, pushed*," uses specific verbs that each call up a different image.

Use figurative language. Figurative language involves using a word or words in an imaginative rather than literal sense. In the first Anne Sullivan example, we saw that Anne's work "enabled Helen to help people such as herself." This passage states Helen's contribution literally. The second passage, "the flickering candle that was her life became a beacon that helped light the pathway and lighten the burdens of people all over the world," contains figurative language that uses words in an imaginative rather than literal sense. "The flickering candle" is a figurative expression of a life that was lacking in potential; "her life became a beacon" is a figurative expression of a life that served as a role model.

Although there are many types of figurative language,[6] you should practice using two of the most common, similes and metaphors, in your speeches.

Similes

Perhaps the easiest comparative figure to create is the simile. A *simile* is a direct comparison of dissimilar things. Similes usually contain the word *like* or *as*. Many common clichés are similes. To make a point

Throughout history, skilled orators like Jesse Jackson have capitalized on the power of vivid and evocative language to strike chords in the hearts of their listeners.

about lack of speech, we may hear a person say, "He runs like a turtle" or "She's slow as molasses." Likewise, to dramatize a negative description, we may hear a person say, "He swims like a rock" or "She's built like a pencil." The problem with using clichés in your speeches is that their familiarity destroys the vividness they once possessed. Similes are vivid when the basis for the direct comparison is imaginative or different. Thus, "Trucks are like monstrous boxcars that eat highways for breakfast"[7] is a vivid simile. Likewise, talking about public school teachers who send their children to private schools by saying, "That's like sitting in a restaurant and watching the chef go next door to eat"[8] is a fresh, imaginative simile.

Metaphors

A second common comparative figure of speech is the metaphor. *Metaphors* are much like similes, but instead of a direct comparison using *like* or *as*, metaphors build a direct identification between the objects being compared. Metaphors are such a common part of our language that we seldom think of them as special. We call problem cars "lemons"; we describe a baseball team's infield as a "sieve."

As you create metaphors for your speeches, try to avoid the trite or hackneyed. Try to match the creativity shown in the following examples:

Human progress is a chain, and every generation forges a little piece of it.[9]

It is imperative that we weave our fabric of the future with durable thread.[10]

And my personal favorite, describing New Orleans:

I can attest to the fact that this fair city must surely be the one place on earth where sound travels faster than light. Here is a circus of curved mirrors and distorted images of lights and shadows, of leads and red herrings — where it daily becomes more difficult to separate fact from fiction.[11]

Skill Development Exercise
Practicing Vividness

1. Revise each of the following five sentences by substituting more vivid words or phrases for the underlined words or phrases.

It was a *very, very dreary day.*

Don surprised everyone by *making a great catch.*

A lot of damage to Charleston was caused by Hurricane Hugo.

We've got to *generate income* to enable us *to improve education.*

Writers have found that working at a word processor really helps them *a lot.*

2. For each of the following clichés, create a fresher image.

as cold as ice

as happy as a lark

selling like hot cakes

he's playing with fire

we have to nip that in the bud

Speaking Emphatically

In a 500-word speech, not every word is of equal importance. You neither expect nor necessarily want an audience to remember every word spoken. Still, if you leave it up to listeners to decide which words and ideas are most important, they may select the wrong ones. You are the speaker; you should know what you want to emphasize. How can you do it? Although you can emphasize with your voice and body, in this section we want to consider how you can emphasize your wording by means of proportion, repetition, and transition.

Emphasizing Through Proportion

Proportion means spending more time on one point than on another. If a speaker devotes five minutes to the president's role as head of the executive branch and only two minutes each to the president's roles as head of the party and commander-in-chief of the armed forces, the audience will assume that the role as head of the executive branch is the most important.

To improve the audience's perception of the importance of a point, you can add examples or an illustration to build its strength. If the point really is important, you should have enough material to use to build it.

Although proportioning is effective by itself, it may be too subtle for some audiences. Consequently, you also should consider emphasizing crucial ideas through repetition and transition.

Emphasizing Through Repetition

Deliberate—as opposed to wordy—*repetition* is another way to emphasize an idea. If you say, "There are 500 steps—that's 500," a listener will probably perceive the repetition as an indication that the point should be remembered. Repetition is widely used because it is relatively easy to practice and quite effective.

If you want the audience to remember your exact word, then you can repeat it once or twice: "The number is 572638—that's 5, 7, 2, 6, 3, 8" or "A ring-shaped coral island almost or completely surrounding a lagoon is called an atoll—the word is *atoll*."

If you want the audience to remember an idea but not necessarily the specific language, you probably will restate it rather than repeat it. Whereas repetition is the exact use of the same words, *restatement* means echoing the same idea but in different words; for instance, "The population is 975,439—that's roughly one million people" or, "The test will be composed of about four essay questions; that is, all the questions on the test will be the kind that require you to discuss material in some detail."

Emphasizing Through Transition

Transition is a third way to emphasize ideas. Transitions are the words, phrases, and sentences that show relationships between and among ideas. Transitions summarize, clarify, forecast, and, in almost every instance, emphasize. Of the three methods of emphasis discussed here, transition is perhaps the most effective and yet the least used.

INTERNAL TRANSITION *Internal transition* are words and phrases that link parts of a sentence in ways that help people to see the relationships of the parts. In the following sentences, notice how the relationships between ideas are clarified and emphasized through the use of internal transition words.

> Miami gets a lot of rain. Phoenix does not.
> Miami gets a lot of rain, *but* Phoenix does not; (or) Although Miami gets a lot of rain, Phoenix does not.
> You should donate money to United Way. It will make you feel better.
> You should donate money to United Way *because* it will make you feel better.
> Buckeye Savings is in good financial shape. Buckeye pays high interest.
> Buckeye Savings is in good financial shape; *moreover*, it pays high interest.

Our language contains many words that show idea relationships. Although the following list is not complete, it indicates many of the common transition words and phrases that are appropriate in a speech.[12]

Transitions	**Uses**
also and likewise again in addition moreover	You will use these words to add material.
therefore and so so finally all in all on the whole in short	You will use these expressions to add up consequences, to summarize, or to show results.

but	
however	
yet	
on the other hand	You will use these expressions to indicate
still	changes in direction, concessions, or a re-
although	turn to a previous position.
while	
no doubt	

| because | You will use these words to indicate reasons |
| for | for a statement. |

then	
since	You will use these words to show causal or
as	time relationships.

in other words	
in fact	
for example	You will use these expressions to explain,
that is to say	exemplify, or limit.
more specifically	

EXTERNAL TRANSITION *External transitions* are complete sentences that are placed between major sections of a speech to call attention to shifts in meaning, degree of emphasis, and movement from one idea to another. External transitions tell the audience exactly how it should respond.

First, external transitions act like a tour guide leading the audience through the speech. You use them because you do not want to take a chance that the audience might miss something. Speakers make use of the following kinds of statements:

(At the start of the body of the speech) This speech will have three major parts.
(After a main heading in a speech in which you are showing how to antique furniture) Now that we see what the ingredients are, let's move on to the second step: stripping the surface.

Second, external transitions can announce the importance of a particular word or idea. You know which ideas are most important, most difficult to understand, or most significant. If you level with the audience and state that information, the audience will know how to react. For example, you might say any of the following:

Now I come to the most important idea in the speech.

If you don't remember anything else from this presentation, make sure you remember this.

But maybe I should say this again, because it is so important.

Pay particular attention to this idea.

These examples represent only a few of the possible expressions that interrupt the flow of ideas and interject keys, clues, and directions to stimulate audience memory or understanding.

Speaking Appropriately

Speaking appropriately is the final way to improve your speech language. *Appropriateness* means using language that adapts to the needs, interests, knowledge, and attitudes of the audience. Appropriate language cements the bond of trust between speaker and audience.

Speaking appropriately begins when you examine the materials you are planning to use in light of the analysis you have made of your audience. It continues with choosing phrasing that the listeners will perceive as relating to their experience. Let us see how you can adapt your language to your audience and avoid language that alienates it.

Use Personal Pronouns

In most situations the more personal you can make your language, the more appropriate it will be. Merely by speaking in terms of "you," "us," "we," and "our," you often will give listeners a verbal clue to your interest in them. In a speech on football defenses, instead of saying, "When *people* go to a football game, *they* often wonder why defensive players change their position just before the ball is snapped," why not try, "When *you* go to a football game, *you* may often wonder why players change their position just before the ball is snapped." Although this pronoun change may seem to be a very small point, it can mean the difference between attention and indifference in your audience.

Ask Rhetorical Questions

Although public speaking is not direct conversation with your audience, you can create the impression of direct conversation by asking rhetorical questions. *Rhetorical questions* are those phrased to stimulate a mental response on the part of the audience rather than an actual spoken response. For instance, one more change in the football example we used previously would increase audience participation. Instead of saying, "When you go to a football game, you may often wonder why players change their position just before the ball is snapped," you might ask, "When you go to a football game, have you ever said to yourself, 'I wonder why Kessel moved to the other side of the line before the snap' or 'I wonder why Jones started to rush the passer and then all of a sudden stepped back'?" Notice how we also have improved the question by substituting specifics for a general phrasing.

Rhetorical questions generate audience participation; once the audience starts participating, it becomes more involved in the content. To be effective, however, rhetorical questions must sound sincere. Practice until you can ask such questions naturally and sincerely.

Share Common Experience

If you think your audience has had experiences like yours, share them in the speech. Talking about common experiences will allow your audience to identify with you. If you were talking to a group of Girl or Boy Scouts, you might drive home the point that important tasks require hours of hard work by saying, "Remember the hours you put in working on your first merit badge? Remember wondering whether you'd ever get the darned thing finished? And do you remember how good it felt to know that the time you put in really paid off?" (Notice how this example incorporates common experience along with personal pronouns and rhetorical questions to heighten the sense of shared experience.) When members of an audience identify with you as a speaker, they will pay more attention to what you have to say.

You want your listeners to identify with the common experience so that they will think about it. In the following example, businessperson Edward Reavey is talking with other businesspeople about a common experience:

> The deterioration of costly service is partly our fault. We experience the consumer's service problems every day. As business people we know that the same kind of treatment is being given to our customers. Still, we don't do much about it. We tolerate the terrible, when it comes to service.[13]

Build Hypothetical Situations

Although you cannot involve every audience directly with every topic, you can relate to them by speaking hypothetically. Suppose you wanted to show an audience with interests in home improvement how it could turn a cast-off table or chair into a fine piece of refinished furniture. You could start the speech by placing audience members in the following hypothetical situation:

> Many times we relegate our cast-off end tables, a desk, a record cabinet to the land of the lost — the storage room of our basement. We know the piece of furniture is worth saving, but we don't know why. That cast-off is probably a lot heavier and a lot more solid than most furniture being made today. So what are we going to do with it? Why not refinish it? Let's assume for this evening that you have just such a piece of furniture in your basement. Let's take it out of that storage room and go to work on it. Where do we start? Well, first of all, we have to gather the right materials to do the job.

Whether members of the audience actually have such pieces of furniture is unimportant. Because of the hypothetical situation, they still can involve themselves in the procedure. The hypothetical situation is another excellent way of involving an audience in your speech.

Personalize Examples

Suppose you are planning to give a speech on Japanese management techniques to the Society for Advancement of Management and you want to begin the speech with geographic data. In reading the 1987 *World Almanac*, you draw the following conclusion: Japan is small and densely populated. The nation's 120 million people are crowded into a land area of 145,000 square miles. The population density is 827 persons per square mile.

Although you have the essential statistics about population and area, you will not want to present them in your speech in this form because the passage does not bring the information down to a personal level.

Notice how the following revision would be more likely to get members of an audience on the west coast of the United States to feel that the material is related to them:

> Japan is a small, densely populated nation. Her population is 120 million — only about half that of the United States. Yet the Japanese are crowded into a land area of only 145,000 square miles — roughly the same size as the state of California. Just think of the implications of having one-half the population of the United States living in California, where 23 million now live. In addition, Japan packs 827 persons into every square mile of land, whereas in the United States we average about 64 persons per square mile. Japan, then, is about 13 times as crowded as the United States.

This revision includes an invented comparison of the unknown. Japan, with the familiar, the United States and California. Even though most Americans do not have the total land area of the United States on the tip of the tongue, they know that the United States covers a great deal of territory. Likewise, a west-coast audience would have a mental picture of the size of California compared to the rest of the nation. If you were speaking to an audience from another part of the country you could make your comparison to a different state, such as Texas, New York, or Florida. It is through such detailed comparisons that the audience is able to visualize just how small and crowded Japan is.

To adapt material to your audience, use these guidelines: (1) If you have choices of which material you will use, choose the material that best relates to the audience; (2) if the material lacks audience adaptation, use your imagination to adapt it to the audience.

Avoid Inappropriate Language

Appropriate language has the positive value of cementing the bond of trust between speaker and audience. If audience members like and trust you, they are likely to believe you. The more hostile the audience is to your ideas, the more care you need in using language that will be accepted by that audience. Yet, under strain, or in your eagerness to make a point, you sometimes can say things you do not really mean or express feelings in language that is unlikely to be accepted by strangers. If you do that, you may lose all that you have gained.

EFFECT OF INAPPROPRIATE LANGUAGE You have heard children shout, "Sticks and stones may break my bones, but words will never hurt me." I think this rhyme is so popular among children because they know it is a lie, but they do not know what else to do. Whether we are willing to admit it or not, words do hurt—sometimes permanently. Think of the great personal damage done to individuals throughout history as a result of being called "hillbilly," "nigger," "wop," "yid." Think of the fights started by one person calling another's sister or girlfriend a "whore." Of course, we all know that it is not the words alone that are so powerful; it is the context of the words—the situation, the feelings about the participants, the time, the place, or the tone of voice. You may recall circumstances in which a friend called you a name or used a four-letter word to describe you and you did not even flinch; you also may recall other circumstances in which someone else called you something far less offensive and you became enraged.

The message to remember is that we always must be aware that our language may have accidental repercussions. When we do not understand the frame of reference of the audience, we may state our ideas in language that distorts the intended communication. Many times a single inappropriate sentence may be enough to ruin an entire speech. For instance, if you say, "And we all know the problem originates downtown," you may be referring to the city government. But if the audience is composed of people who see downtown not as the seat of government but as the residential area of an ethnic or social group, the sentence will have an entirely different meaning to them. Being specific will help you avoid such problems; recognizing that some words communicate far more than their dictionary meanings will help even more.

I also must caution against using words such as "genocide" for their shock value. Such language often backfires on the user. Arousing anger and hostility toward an issue often results in anger and hostility toward the speaker.

Avoiding inappropriate language requires sensitivity to an audience's feelings. Some of our mistakes result from using expressions that are perceived as sexist or racist. Although the speaker may be totally unaware of being offensive, the audience may take legitimate offense.

SEXIST, RACIST, AND OTHER UNFAIR LANGUAGE   Sexist, racist, and other unfair language is any language that is perceived as belittling any person or group of people by virtue of their gender, race, age, handicap, or other characteristic. Two of the most prevalent linguistic uses that result in unfair perceptions are nonequal language and nonparallel language.

Nonequal language is exclusionary; that is, it involves eliminating a sex or race, grammatically or connotatively. Let us consider some examples:

1.   *Generic "he."* Traditional English grammar calls for the use of the masculine pronoun *he* to stand for the entire class of humans regardless of sex. Thus, standard English calls for such usage as, "When a person shops, he should have a clear idea of what he wants to buy." Even though such statements are *grammatically* correct, because they contain an inherent bias, they are by definition sexist.

     Guideline: Do not construct sentences that use male pronouns when no sexual reference is intended. You often can avoid the dilemma by using plurals. For instance, instead of saying, "Because a doctor has high status, his views may be believed regardless of topic," you could say, "Because doctors have high status, their views may be believed regardless of topic." The change may seem small, but it may be the difference between persuading or failing to persuade an audience.

2. *Generic "man."* A second example of exclusion results from the reliance on the use of the generic *man*. Many words have become a common part of our language that are inherently sexist. Look at the term *man-made*. What this means is that a product was produced by human beings rather than by machines; but what it *says* to many people is that a *masculine* human being was involved. Using such terms when speaking about human beings in general is bad enough; using them to describe actions done by women (as in the sentence, "Sally is particularly proud of her pies because they are totally man-made") becomes ludicrous.

   Guideline: Avoid using words that have built-in sexism, such as *policeman, postman, chairman, man-made,* and *mankind*. For most expressions of this kind you can use or create suitable alternatives. For the first three examples, you can use *police officer, mail carrier,* and *chairperson*. For *man-made* and *mankind,* you can change the constructions. For "All of mankind benefits," you might say "All the people in the world benefit." For "The products are man-made," you might say "The products are made entirely by hand" (or by people or by human beings).

Nonparallel language also is belittling. Three common forms of nonparallelism are marking, destructive word pairings, and stereotyping.

1. *Marking. Marking* means adding gender, race, age, or other designations unnecessarily to a general word. For instance, *doctors* is a word representing *all* people with medical degrees. To describe Jones as a doctor is to treat Jones linguistically as a member of the class of doctors. For example, you might say, "Jones, a doctor, contributed a great deal to the campaign." If, however, you said, "Jones, a female doctor" (or "a black doctor," or "an aging doctor," or "a handicapped doctor") you would be marking. By marking, you are trivializing a person's role by emphasizing an irrelevant characteristic of the person. For instance, if you say "Jones is a really good female doctor" (or "black doctor," or "old doctor," or "handicapped doctor"), you may be intending to praise Jones. In reality, your audience can interpret the sentence as saying that Jones is a good doctor *for a female* (or *for a black, for an old person,* or *for a handicapped person*), but not necessarily good compared to a white, young unhandicapped male.

   Guideline: Avoid markers by treating all groups equally. If it is appropriate to identify the person by gender, race, age, and so on, do so but leave such markers out of your labeling when they are irrelevant. One test of whether a characteristic is relevant and appropriate is whether you would mention the person's gender, race, age, and so on regardless of what that happened to be. It is relevant to specify "female doctor," for example, only if it would be equally relevant in that context to specify "male doctor."

2. *Unnecessary Association.* Another form of nonparallelism is emphasis of a person's association with another when you are not talking about the other person. Often you will hear a speaker say, "Gladys Thompson, whose husband is CEO of Procter and Gamble, is the chairperson for this year's United Way campaign." In response to this sentence, you might say that the association of Gladys Thompson with her husband gives further credentials to Gladys Thompson. But using the association seems to imply that Gladys Thompson is important not in herself but because of her relationship with her husband. The following illustrates a more flagrant example of unnecessary association: "Dorothy Jones, the award-winning principal at Central High School, and wife of Bill Jones, a local contractor, is chairperson for this year's United Way campaign." Here Bill Jones's occupation and relationship to Dorothy Jones is clearly irrelevant.

In either case the pairing takes away from the person who is supposed to be the focus. For instance, I recall reading such statements as, "Robin Smith, wife of dancer Fred Astaire, was one of the leading jockeys at Belmont Park this year." Now Fred Astaire was certainly a famous person, but what did he have to do with Robin Smith's riding success? Again, the test of parallel treatment is whether you would do the same thing for all people. How often do you see statements such as "Fred Astaire, husband of Robin Smith, a leading jockey, is starring in a new made-for-television movie"?

Guideline: Avoid associating a person irrelevantly with his or her partner. If the person has done or said something noteworthy, it should stand alone.

3. *Stereotyping. Stereotyping* consists of assigning characteristics to people solely on the basis of their class or category. Stereotyping represents a shortcut in thinking. By developing an attitude or belief about an entire group and then applying that attitude to every member of the group, a person no longer has to consider the potential for individual differences — the stereotype applies to all persons in the group. It provides some people with a certain comfort to talk about social issues in such a way that states or implies that blacks are lazy, that Italians are naturally hotheaded, that old people are cantankerous, and that white Americans are racist.

Guideline: Avoid making statements that treat groups of people as if they can be identified by the same characteristics. Thus, in a speech, if you must make value judgments about people, make them about specific individuals, and make such a statement without reference to any group of people to which the person may be associated.

Few people escape all unfair language. By monitoring your usage, however, you can guard against frustrating your communication by assuming that others will react to your language the same way you do, and you can guard against saying or doing things that offend others and perpetuate outdated sex roles, racial stereotypes, and other unfair language.

Summary

Your overall language goal is to develop a "personal" oral style that captures your uniqueness. Your language usage should be guided by the knowledge that words are only representations of ideas, objects, and feelings. Meaning is often a product of word denotation, or dictionary meaning, and connotation, or the thoughts and feelings that words evoke.

Specific goals of language use are to state your ideas clearly, vividly, emphatically, and appropriately.

Ideas are clarified through precise, specific, simple language that is devoid of clutter. Precise words are those that accurately depict your meaning. Specific words are those that call up a single image. Simple words are the least pretentious but most precise words you can find. You can eliminate clutter by eliminating repetitions that do not add emphasis; eliminating empty phrases; boiling down long sentences into shorter, harder-hitting sentences; and combining sentences and phrases with like ideas.

Vividness means full of life, vigorous, bright, and intense. You can increase the vividness of your language by using active rather than passive voice; using specific, active verbs that form sharp mental pictures; and using figurative language, especially similes and metaphors.

Emphasis means giving certain words and ideas more importance than others. One way to emphasize is through proportion, or spending more time on one point than another. A second way is through repetition. A third way is through transitions, or words and phrases that show relationships between ideas.

Appropriateness means using language that adapts to the needs, interests, knowledge, and attitudes of the audience and avoids language that alienates. Appropriateness is achieved through using personal pronouns and rhetorical questions, sharing common experience building hypothetical situations, and personalizing examples. Inappropriate language can be minimized by avoiding such exclusionary usages as the generic *he* and *man* and by eliminating such nonparallel usages as marking, unnecessary association, and stereotyping.

Notes

1. Richard L. Johannesen, Rennard Strickland, and Ralph T. Eubanks, *Language Is Sermonic: Richard M. Weaver on the Nature of Rhetoric* (Baton Rouge: Louisiana State University, 1970).
2. Ibid.
3. *The Random House Dictionary of the English Language*, 2d college ed. (New York: Random House, 1987), 1140.
4. Eugene Ehrlich, *Super Word Power* (New York: Harper & Row, 1989).
5. Beverly Chiodo, "Choose Wisely," *Vital Speeches*, November 1, 1987, 42.
6. For instance, in his analysis of language, Walter Nash discusses more than 20 figures of syntax and semantics in Walter Nash, *Rhetoric: The Wit of Persuasion* (Cambridge, Mass.: Basil Blackwell, Inc., 1989), 112–129.
7. Robert H. Schertz, "Deregulation: After the Airlines, Is Trucking Next?" *Vital Speeches*, November 1, 1977, 40.
8. David T. Kearns, "Economics and the Student," *Vital Speeches*, July 1, 1986, 566.
9. Gerry Sikorski, "Will and Vision," *Vital Speeches*, August 1, 1986, 615.
10. Ronald W. Roskens, "Webs of Sand," *Vital Speeches*, February 1, 1986, 233.
11. James N. Sites, "Chemophobia," *Vital Speeches*, December 15, 1980, 154.
12. After Sheriden Baker, *The Complete Stylist* (New York: Thomas Y. Crowell, 1966), 73–74.
13. Edward Reavey, Jr., "The Critical Consumer Need," *Vital Speeches*, October 15, 1971, 25–26.

Chapter 6 | Practicing the Delivery

Principle V

Effective speaking requires enthusiastic, direct, and spontaneous delivery.

Meaningful, well-organized words do not become a speech until they are delivered to an audience. When people think of great orators such as Jesse Jackson or such effective communicators as former president Ronald Reagan, they often think first of the way the speaker delivered the message. Why do people place such emphasis on the importance of delivery? Primarily because delivery is the source of the audience's contact with the speaker's mind.

Delivery refers to the use of voice and body to communicate the message of the speech; it is what the audience sees and hears. Think of delivery as a window through which we see a speech: When it is cracked, clouded over, or dirty, it obscures the content, organization, and language of the speech; when it is clean, it allows us to appreciate every aspect of the speech more fully. Although delivery cannot improve the ideas of a speech, it can help to make the most of those ideas.

Many people believe in the myth that only those who were born with good voices or some other innate talent have any chance to develop a powerful delivery. The fact is that most of the characteristics of good delivery are more a matter of practice than the luck of genetics. In this chapter we focus on those elements of delivery that you can improve or perfect if you are willing to take the time to practice. Then we consider how to practice your speech and how to cope with nervousness. Let us begin with the essentials of good delivery.

What to Practice: Characteristics of Good Delivery

In your speech practice, as well as in the speech itself, you should be using your voice, articulation, and bodily action to develop a *conversational quality*, a speech delivery that *sounds* like conversation to your audience. Although speeches and conversation are different, using certain techniques characteristic of conversation in your speeches will give listeners the feeling that you are conversing with them.

Essentials of Conversational Quality

The three essentials of conversational quality are enthusiasm, eye contact (directness), and spontaneity.

ENTHUSIASM   A review of research shows that one of the most important elements of effective speaking is speaker *enthusiasm*. A speaker who looks and sounds enthusiastic will be listened to, and that speaker's ideas will be remembered.[1]

The source of enthusiasm is a real, sincere *desire to communicate*. If you genuinely want to communicate, if you care about your topic and your audience, your voice will convey your enthusiasm, and your audience will listen.

If you are an outgoing person who displays feelings openly, you may find it easy to sound enthusiastic in your speech. If you are rather reserved, your audience may not pick up as readily on the more subtle signs of your enthusiasm. In this case you may have to work to intensify your feelings about what you are doing so that your emotions can be communicated. How can you do this?

First, select a topic that excites you. The outgoing person might be able to show enthusiasm about an uninspiring topic; the reserved person probably cannot. Second, get involved in the material. Focus on why you care about the topic. Mental activity will lead to physical activity. That is, if you can rekindle your initial excitement for wanting to accomplish your goal, your voice is more likely to show your enthusiasm. Third, remind yourself how the content of your speech will benefit the audience. If you are convinced that it is in the audience's best interests to listen, that thought may raise your level of enthusiasm.

EYE CONTACT *Eye contact* involves looking at various groups of people in all parts of your audience throughout your speech. So long as you are looking at people (at times at those in front of you, or in the left-hand rear of the room, or in the right center of the room, and so on) and not at your notes or at the ceiling, the floor, or out the window, *everyone* in the audience will perceive you as having good eye contact. Do not let your eyes linger too long on those immediately in front of you. The people at the ends of the aisles and those in the back of the room are every bit as important as those right in front of you.

Maintaining eye contact is important for several reasons. First, eye contact helps audiences concentrate. If speakers do not look at us while they talk, we are unlikely to continue to maintain eye contact with them. This break in mutual eye contact is likely to decrease concentration on the speaker's message.

Second, eye contact increases the audience's confidence in the speaker. Just as you are likely to be skeptical of people who do not look you in the eye when they converse with you, so too audiences will be skeptical of speakers who do not look at them. Eye contact is perceived as a sign of sincerity.

As you gain skill in speaking, you will learn the third reason for the importance of maintaining eye contact: gaining insight into the audience's reaction to what you are saying. Because communication is two-way, your audience is speaking to you at the same time you are speaking to it. In conversation the audience's response is likely to be both verbal and nonverbal; in public speaking, the response is more likely to be shown by nonverbal cues alone. Audiences that pay attention are likely to look at you with varying amounts of intensity. Listeners who do not pay attention are likely to yawn, look out the window, and slouch in their chairs. By monitoring your audience's behavior, you can determine what adjustments, additions, and deletions you should make in your plans. As you gain greater skill, you will be able to make more and better use of the information you get about your listeners through eye contact with them.

SPONTANEITY Spontaneity means being responsive to your ideas and their meaning while you are speaking. A *spontaneous* speech is fresh; it sounds as if the speaker is really thinking about both the speech and the audience as he or she speaks. In contrast, a speech that sounds like a rote recitation decreases the audience's attention to you and your speech. Yet many speakers deliver their speeches sounding like students reciting memory work in a literature class. Remember how painful it was to listen to class members reciting bits of prose or poetry that they had memorized? Because they were struggling so hard to remember the words, they did not communicate any sense of meaning. The words sounded memorized, not spontaneous. Although good actors can make lines that they have spoken literally thousands of times sound spontaneous, most public speakers cannot.

How can you make your outlined and practiced speech sound spontaneous? The answer lies in the difference between knowing ideas and memorizing words. Because you know where you live and how to get there, if someone asked you for directions to your house, you would be able to give them spontaneously. But if you were asked for directions to another person's house, even if you had memorized written directions prepared for you, your delivery of those directions would not be as good. Your delivery probably would sound labored because the word-for-word language you tried to memorize would not be a part of you—you would struggle as you tried hard to remember individual words instead of communicating ideas.

You develop spontaneity in public speaking by getting to know the ideas for your speech as well as you know how to get home. You study your outline and *learn* the material you are going to present, but you do not try to memorize *how* you are going to present it. We will consider spontaneity more when we get to methods of speech rehearsal.

Physical Elements of Delivery

The physical elements of your delivery include your voice, articulation, and bodily action.

VOICE Your voice is the vehicle you use to communicate the words of your speech to your audience. Not only does your voice carry your words, but also the sound of your voice, your *paralanguage*, helps shape

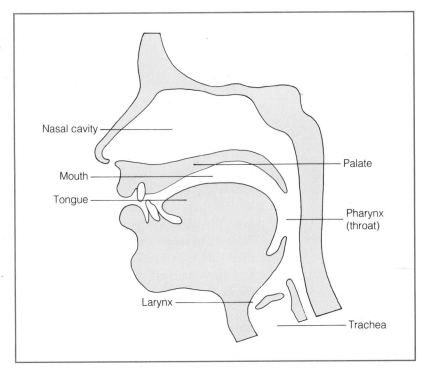

the meanings that your audience receives. *How* you sound may emphasize the meaning, supplement the meaning, and at times even contradict the meaning of the words you speak.

How you use your voice may make the difference between the success or failure of your speech, so you will find it useful to understand how your voice works.

Your voice is produced in your larynx. As you exhale, you bring your vocal folds together closely enough to vibrate the air as it passes through them (Figures 6.1 and 6.2). This vibration (called *phonation*) produces a weak sound that is then built up or *resonated* as it travels through the pharynx (throat), mouth, and, in some cases, the nasal cavity. The resonated sound is then shaped by the *articulators* (tongue, lips, palate, and teeth) to form the separate sounds of our language system. These individual sounds then are put together into words or distinguishable oral symbols.[2]

To improve your delivery, you must learn to coordinate the four major characteristics of voice (pitch, volume, rate, and quality) in a way that creates enough vocal variety and emphasis to help you communicate your meaning effectively.

Figure 6.2

Section of the breathing apparatus, showing a lung, bronchial tubes, and trachea that lead to the cartilage area housing the larynx.

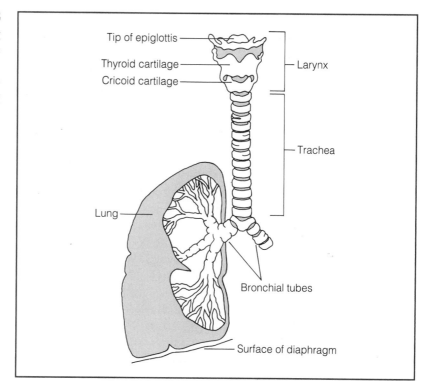

Pitch refers to the highness or lowness of your voice. As we said, your voice is produced in the larynx by the vibration of your vocal folds. To feel this vibration, put your hand on your throat at the top of the Adam's apple and say "ah." Now, just as the pitch of a violin string is changed by making it tighter or looser, so the pitch of your voice is changed by the tightening and loosening of the vocal folds. Most people have a working pitch range of more than an octave.

Most people speak at a pitch level that is about right for them. A few, however, have pitch problems — that is, they talk using tones that are too high or too low for their best voice. If you have questions about your pitch level, ask your professor about it. If you are one of the few people with a pitch problem, your professor can refer you to a speech therapist for corrective work. Because for most of us our normal pitch is satisfactory, the question is whether we are making the best use of our pitch range.

Volume is the loudness of the tone you make. When you exhale normally, the diaphragm relaxes, and air is expelled through the trachea. When you speak, you supplement the force of the expelled air on the vibrating vocal folds by contracting your abdominal muscles. This greater force behind the air you expel increases the volume of your tone.

To feel how these muscles work, place your hands on your sides with your fingers extended over the stomach. Say "ah" in a normal voice. Now say "ah" as loud as you can. If you are making proper use of your muscles, you should feel an increase in stomach contractions as you increase volume. If you feel little or no muscle contraction, you probably are trying to gain volume from the wrong source; such a practice can result in tiredness, harshness, and lack of sufficient volume to be heard in a large room.

Each person, regardless of size, can make his or her voice louder. If you have trouble talking loudly enough to be heard in a large classroom, work on increasing pressure from the abdominal area while exhaling.

Rate is the speed at which you talk. Although most of us utter between 130 and 180 words per minute in normal conversation, the rate that is best for anyone is a highly individual matter. Whether you speak at an acceptable rate is determined by whether listeners can understand what you are saying. Usually, even very fast talking is acceptable if words are well articulated and if there is sufficient vocal variety and emphasis.

If your instructor believes you talk too rapidly or too slowly, he or she will tell you and may suggest ways in which you can improve. If you want to change your speaking rate, start by working with written passages — it makes it easier to compute your speaking rate. First, read aloud for exactly three minutes. When you have finished, count the number of words you have read and divide by three to compute the number of words you read per minute. If you perceive your reading as too fast or too slow, re-read the same passage for another three-minute period, making a conscious effort to decrease or increase the number of words you read. Again, count the number of words and divide by three.

At first, you may not be able to significantly change speed. With practice you will see that you can read much faster or much slower when you want to. You may find that a different rate, whether faster or slower, will sound strange to you. To show improvement in your normal speaking, you have to learn to adjust your ear to a more appropriate rate of speed. But if you practice daily, within a few weeks you should be able to accustom your ear to changes so that you can vary your rate with the type of material that you read. As you gain confidence in your ability to alter your rate, you can practice with portions of your speeches. You will talk faster when material is easy or when you are trying to create a mood of excitement; you will talk slower when the material is difficult or when you are trying to create a somber mood.

Quality is the tone, timbre, or sound of your voice. The best vocal quality is a clear and pleasant tone. Problems of quality include nasality (too much resonance in the nose on vowel sounds), breathiness (too much escaping air during phonation), harshness (too much tension in throat and chest), and hoarseness (a raspy sound). If your voice tends to one of these undesirable qualities, consult your professor. Although you can make some improvement on your own, significant improvement can require a great deal of work and rather extensive knowledge of vocal anatomy and physiology. Severe problems of vocal quality should be referred to a speech therapist.

Variety and Emphasis

In addition to the positive or negative effect of these individual vocal characteristics, the interaction of these characteristics also can affect your delivery. Effective speakers strive for vocal variety and emphasis. By *variety*, we mean contrasts in pitch, volume, rate, and quality. Even if each of the characteristics is satisfactory individually, the net effect on the audience can be positive or negative depending on the presence or absence of variety.

To illustrate, consider the sentence "I am not going to the office." The meaning of the sentence depends entirely on how you say it. If you emphasize *not*, the sentence means you are answering the question of *whether* you are going; if you emphasize *office*, the sentence means you are answering the question of *where* you are not going. Effective vocal variety and emphasis give the voice the dimension that makes it easier for an audience to pay attention and to understand.

If you want to check your variety and emphasis, have someone listen as you read short passages aloud. Ask the person to tell you which words were higher in pitch, or louder, or slower. If you recognize that you tend to speak in a monotone or in a constant pattern, you should take time to practice. As you prepare to read or speak, determine which words you are trying to emphasize. When you find that you can read or speak in such a way that the person working with you recognizes which words you were trying to emphasize, you will be showing improvement in using vocal variety to clarify meaning.

Problems of Voice

Two problems of voice that have the greatest effect on your delivery are monotone and vocal interferences.

A *monotonous* voice is one in which the pitch, volume, and rate remain constant, and with no word, idea, or sentence differing significantly from any other. Although few people speak in a true monotone, many severely limit themselves by using only two or three pitch levels and relatively unchanging volume and rate. An actual or near monotone lulls an audience to sleep. If you were to speak the sentence "Congress should pass laws limiting the sale of pornography" in a monotone with all words at the same pitch, volume, and rate, the listener could not be sure whether your emphasis is on who should pass laws, what laws should be passed, or what such laws should emphasize.

A variation of the true monotone is the use of a monotonous pattern, a melody pattern in which vocal variation is the same for every sentence regardless of meaning. This pattern is nearly as detrimental as a true monotone. For example, you might end every sentence with an upward pitch or go up in pitch in the middle and down at the end of every phrase. Changes in pitch, volume, and rate will not help communicate meaning unless they are appropriate to that intended meaning. To cure a monotonous pattern, you must learn to correlate changes in voice with meaning.

VOCAL INTERFERENCES   A second problem of voice is the peppering of speech with such vocal interferences as "uh," "er," "well," and "O.K.," as well as those nearly universal interrupters of thought, "you know" and "like."

The "you know" habit may begin as a way people seek to find out whether what they are saying already is known by others. For some, "you know" may be a source of identification; some people seek to show that they and those to whom they are talking have common knowledge as a binding element. For most people, however, the flooding of sentences with "you know" is simply a bad habit resulting in such abominations as "you know, Maxwell is, you know, a good, you know, lecturer."

Similarly, the use of "like" may start from making comparisons such as "He's hot, he looks like Tom Cruise." Soon the comparisons become shortcut as in "He's, like, really hot!" Finally, the use of "like" becomes pure filler: "Like, he's really cool, like, I can't really explain it, but I'll tell you he's, like, wow!"

Curiously, no matter how irritating the use of "you know" or "like" may be, listeners are unlikely to acknowledge their irritation. Seldom, if ever, do people say openly to others, "Your use of 'you know' or 'like' at every break in thought is really very annoying to me." If it seems appropriate, you might start pointing out this irritant in others' speech; most important, you should request others to tell you whether you are an offender.

In the normal give and take of conversation, even the most fluent speakers may throw in an occasional "uh" or "you know"; few people can completely avoid their use. Interferences become a problem when they are perceived by others as excessive and call attention to themselves and thus prevent a person from concentrating on meaning. These interferences become especially detrimental to public-speaking effectiveness. With some practice, you can limit their occurrence in your speech. Remember, although people may not be willing to tell you, they are likely to be distracted or irritated by your interferences. So what do you do? Try the following suggestions.

1. Train yourself to hear your interferences. Even people with a major problem seem unaware of the interferences they use. You can train your ears in at least two ways: by tape recording and through friendly feedback.

    Tape record yourself talking for several minutes about any subject—the game you saw yesterday, the course you plan to take next term, or anything else that comes to mind. Before you play it back, estimate the number of times you used interferences. Then compare the actual number with your estimate. As your ears become trained, your estimates will be closer to the actual number.

    Have a close friend listen to you and raise a hand every time you say "like" or "you know." You may find the experience traumatic or nerve-racking, but your ear soon will start to pick up the interferences as fast as the listener.

2. Practice to see how long you can go without using a vocal interference. If you can learn to practice without vocal clutter, you will do better in your speeches. Set up practice periods two or three times a week. Start out by trying to talk for fifteen seconds. Continue to increase the time until you talk for two minutes without using an interference. Meaning may suffer; you may spend a disproportionate amount of time avoiding interferences. Still, it is good practice.

    During practice sessions, your speaking may not appear to be natural. You will concentrate so heavily on speaking without interferences that meaning may suffer. Eventually, however, you will speak more naturally and listen for and eliminate interferences. As your speaking becomes less cluttered, create practice situations that may ordinarily lead to increases in clutter. If you lapse into vocal interferences when you are under pressure, mentally re-create situations in which you are required to speak under pressure. Likewise, if interferences occur when you are speaking to people in authority, create practice situations in which you are speaking to your parents, college professors, city officials, and so forth.

3. Mentally note your usage of vocal interferences in your speeches. You will be making real headway when you can reduce clutter in actual speaking situations, but do not worry about trying too hard in speeches. Improvement in speeches should come naturally as a

result of improvement in practice. If practice is successful, you will find yourself able to monitor even public speaking *without* conscious effort.

ARTICULATION *Articulation* is the shaping of speech sounds into recognizable oral symbols that combine to produce a word. Many speakers suffer from minor articulation problems of adding a sound where none appears (ath*a*lete for athlete), leaving out a sound where one occurs (li*b*ary for li*b*rary), transposing sounds (re*v*alent for re*lev*ant), and distorting sounds (tru*f* for tru*th*). Although some people have consistent articulation problems that require speech therapy (such as substituting *th* for *s* consistently in speech), most of us are guilty of carelessness that is easily corrected.

Articulation often is confused with *pronunciation*, the form and accent of various syllables of a word. In the word *statistics*, articulation refers to the shaping of the ten sounds (*s-t-a-t-i-s-t-i-k-s*); pronunciation refers to the grouping and accenting of the sounds (*sta-tis'-tiks*). If you are unsure of how to pronounce a word that you will use in your speech, consult a dictionary for the proper pronunciation.

Although true articulatory problems (distortion, omission, substitution, or addition of sounds) need to be corrected by a speech therapist, the kinds of articulatory problems shown by most college students can be improved during a single term. The two most common faults for most students are slurring sounds (running sounds and words together) and leaving off word endings. Spoken English always will contain some running together of sounds. For instance, everyone says "tha-table" for "that table." It is simply too difficult to make two "t" sounds in a row. But many of us slur sounds and drop word endings to excess. "Who ya goin ta see?" for "Who are you going to see?" illustrates both these errors. If you have a mild case of "sluritis" caused by not taking the time to form sounds clearly, you can make considerable improvement by taking ten to fifteen minutes three days a week to read passages aloud and trying to *overaccentuate* each sound. Some teachers advocate "chewing" your words—that is, making sure that you move your lips, jaw, and tongue carefully for each sound you make. As with most other problems of delivery, you must work conscientiously several days a week for months to bring about significant improvement.

Because constant mispronunciation and misarticulation suggest that a person is ignorant or careless (or both), you will want to try to correct mistakes you make. Figure 6.3 lists many common problem words that student speakers are likely to mispronounce or misarticulate.

Figure 6.3

Problem words.

Word	Correct	Incorrect
arctic	arc'-tic	ar'-tic
athlete	ath'-lete	ath'a-lete
family	fam'-a-ly	fam'-ly
February	Feb'-ru-ary	Feb'-yu-ary
get	get	git
larynx	ler'-inks	lar'-nix
library	ly'-brer-y	ly'-ber-y
particular	par-tik'-yu-ler	par-tik'-ler
picture	pic'-ture	pitch'-er
recognize	rek'-ig-nize	rek'-a-nize
relevant	rel'-e-vant	rev'-e-lant
theater	thee'-a-ter	thee-a'-ter
truth	truth	truf
with	with	wit or wid

BODILY ACTION   Your nonverbal bodily actions either help or hinder your efforts to convey meaning and emphasize ideas. If you get a stern look on your face when you say "City Council is not listening to the people," for example, your nonverbal expression adds power to your words. Let us consider the principal nonverbal variables that affect meaning: facial expression, gestures, posture, and movement.

Facial expression refers to eye and mouth movement. The eyes and mouth communicate far more than you might realize. You need only recall the icy stare, the warm smile, or the hostile scowl that you received from someone to understand that the eyes (and the mouth as well) mirror the mind. Your facial expression should be appropriate to what you are saying. Audiences will respond negatively to deadpan expressions and perpetual grins or scowls; they will respond positively to honest and sincere expressions that reflect your thoughts and feelings. Think actively about what you are saying, and your face probably will respond accordingly.

Gestures are movements of hands, arms, and fingers. We use gestures consciously to describe or to emphasize. When a person says "about this high" or "nearly this round," we expect to see a gesture accompanying the verbal description. Likewise, when a person says, "Put that down" or

"Listen to me," we look for a pointing finger, a pounding fist, or some other gesture that reinforces the point. If you gesture in conversation, you usually will gesture in speech. If you do not gesture in conversation, it is probably best not to force yourself to gesture in a speech. You probably should leave your hands free at all times to help you "do what comes naturally." If you clasp them behind you, grip the sides of the speaker's stand, or put your hands into your pockets, you will not be able to gesture naturally even if you want to.

If you wonder what to do with your hands at the start of the speech so that they do not seem conspicuous, you may either rest them on the speaker's stand partially clenched or hold them relaxed at your sides — perhaps with one arm slightly bent at the elbow. Once you begin the speech, forget about your hands: They will be free for appropriate gestures. If, however, you discover that you have folded your arms in front of you or clasped them behind you, put them back in one of the two original positions. After you have spoken a few times, your professor will suggest whether you need to be more responsive or somewhat restrained with your hands and arms.

Posture refers to the position or bearing of the body. Good posture — upright stance and squared shoulders — communicates a sense of poise to an audience. Speakers who slouch may give an unfavorable impression of themselves, including the impression of limited self-confidence and an uncaring attitude.

Movement refers to motion of the entire body. Some speakers stand perfectly still throughout an entire speech. Others are constantly on the move. In general, it probably is better to remain in one place unless you have some reason for moving. A little movement, however, adds action to the speech, so it may help hold attention. Ideally, movement should help to focus on transition, emphasize an idea, or call attention to a particular aspect of the speech. Avoid such unmotivated movement as bobbing and weaving, shifting from foot to foot, or pacing from one side of the room to the other. At the beginning of your speech, stand up straight and on both feet. If you find yourself in some peculiar posture during the course of the speech, return to the upright position with your weight equally distributed on both feet.

With any bodily action, avoid mannerisms that distract the audience such as taking off or putting on glasses, smacking the tongue, licking the lips, or scratching the nose, hand, or arm. As a general rule, anything that calls attention to itself is bad, and anything that helps reinforce the idea is good.

Bodily action says the same kinds of things in a speech as it does in normal interpersonal or group communication. It is true that when you stand up in front of an audience, you may tend to freeze up — that is, to limit your normal nonverbal action — and occasionally, the speaking situation may bring out nervous mannerisms that are less noticeable in your daily speaking. But if you are thinking actively about what you are saying, your bodily action probably will be appropriate. If you use either too much or too little bodily action, your instructor can give you pointers for limiting or accenting your normal behavior. Although you may find minor errors, you should not be concerned unless your bodily action calls attention to itself; then you should find ways of controlling or changing the behavior.

During practice sessions you may try various methods to monitor or alter your bodily action. Videotape provides an excellent means of monitoring your bodily action. You may want to practice in front of a mirror to see how you look to others when you speak. (Although some speakers swear by this method, others find it a traumatic experience.) Perhaps the best method is to get a willing listener to critique your bodily action and help you improve. Once you have identified the behavior you want to change, you can tell your helper what to look for. For instance, you might say, "Raise your hand every time I begin to rock back and forth." By getting specific feedback when the behavior occurs, you can make immediate adjustments.

Practicing Your Speech

Now that you understand what constitutes good delivery, you can begin to practice your speech. How you proceed with your practice sessions depends on your method of delivery.

Methods of Delivery

In this book I recommend cultivating the extemporaneous method. Although you may deliver speeches impromptu, from manuscript, or from memory, the extemporaneous method gives you by far the greatest flexibility.

IMPROMPTU   An *impromptu* speech is done on the spur of the moment, without previous specific preparation. Although nearly all of our conversation is impromptu, most speakers prefer to prepare their thoughts well ahead of the time they face an audience. Regardless of how good you are at daily communication, you would be foolhardy to leave your preparation and analysis for formal speeches to chance. Audiences expect to hear a speech that has been well thought out ahead of time.

MANUSCRIPT   A common and often misused mode of delivery is the *manuscript* speech, which is written out in full and then read aloud. The advantage is that the wording can be carefully planned with nothing left to chance. Although presidents and other heads of state have good reason to resort to the manuscript (even the slightest mistake in sentence construction can provoke national outcry), most speakers have little need to prepare a manuscript. Often their only reason for doing so is in the false sense of security that the written speech provides. The major disadvantages of manuscript speeches, as you can attest from your listening experience, are that they tend to be less spontaneous, stimulating, or interesting. Manuscript speeches tend not to allow the speaker to adapt to his or her audience. Because of these difficulties, you usually should avoid manuscript speaking, except as a special assignment. If sensitivity in wording warrants preparation of a manuscript, then you must practice reading the manuscript often so that you can both maintain some eye contact and deliver the speech enthusiastically.

MEMORIZATION   A *memorized* speech is merely a manuscript committed to memory. In addition to offering an opportunity to polish wording, memorization allows the speaker to look at the audience instead of a manuscript while speaking. Unfortunately for beginning speakers, memorization has the same disadvantages as the speech written out in manuscript. Few individuals are able to memorize so well that their speech sounds spontaneous. Because a speech that sounds memorized affects an audience adversely, you should avoid memorization, especially for your first speech assignment.

EXTEMPORANEOUS   Most speeches you give in class and elsewhere will be delivered extemporaneously. In ordinary conversation we often equate extemporaneous speaking with impromptu speaking. In a public-speaking context, however, an *extemporaneous* speech is prepared and practiced, but the exact wording is determined at the time of utterance. Why should most of your speeches be given extemporaneously? Extemporaneous speaking permits you to control the speech far more than does impromptu speaking, while at the same time allowing for far greater spontaneity and adaptation to the audience than does the manuscript or memorized speech. Most experienced speakers prefer the extemporaneous method for most of their speeches. Now let us consider how a speech can be carefully prepared without being memorized.

Practice sessions are just as much a part of "writing" a speech as preparing an outline or researching information are. Rehearsal enables a speaker to hone the wording as well as the delivery of the speech.

Practicing Effectively

Inexperienced speakers often believe that their preparation for a speech is complete once they have finished the outline. Nothing could be further from the truth. If you are scheduled to speak at 9 A.M. Monday and you have not finished the outline for the speech until 8:45 A.M. Monday, the speech will not be nearly as good as if you had allowed yourself sufficient practice time. Practice gives you a chance to revise, evaluate, mull over, and consider all aspects of the speech, including both its wording and delivery. Accordingly, you should try to complete your outline at least two days before the speech is due so that you will have time to practice your speech. As we will see, that means starting work at least a week ahead of time.

An effective practice session involves giving the speech, analyzing it, and then giving it again with changes based on the analysis. Although some speakers are not comfortable with their speech until they have practiced the entire speech several times, you will eventually reach a point of diminishing returns where additional practices do not help and actually may hurt. You have to learn how many times you must practice to cement the key ideas in your mind and to get the oral, conversational, and spontaneous quality that is so important to good speaking without becoming stale or beginning to memorize.

Suppose you are planning to practice at least twice. The following guidelines may help you to conduct more valuable practice sessions.

First Practice

1. *Read through your outline once or twice to get ideas in mind. Then put the outline out of sight.*

2. *Stand up and face your imaginary audience.* You want to make the practice as similar to the speech situation as possible. If you are practicing in your room, pretend that the chairs, lamps, books, and other objects in your view are people.

   You may want to record your practice session. If you do not own a tape recorder, then perhaps you can borrow one. If not, you may want to ask a friend or relative to listen to one or more of your practices. If you are self-conscious about practicing in front of an audience of friends or relatives, train your ear to really listen to what you say while you are practicing.

3. *Time the speech.* Write down the time that you begin.

4. *Give the speech.* Keep going until you have finished the ideas.

5. *Write down the time you finish.* Compute the length of the speech for this first practice.

Analysis

Look at your outline again. Then begin the analysis. If you have practiced in front of a friend or relative, you can ask that person to share in the criticism. But do not ask simply, "Well, what do you think?" Be specific. Did you leave out any key ideas? Did you talk too long on any one point and not long enough on another? Did you clarify each of your points? Did you try to adapt to your anticipated audience? For your first speech, you may want to use the universal critique sheet checklist (p. 166), as a basis for your analysis. For later speeches, you should use the critique sheet that correlates with the speech assignment you have been given.

Second Practice

Run through the entire process again, including the analysis.

After you have completed a session consisting of two practices and two analyses, put the speech away for awhile. Although you may need to go through the rehearsal process several times, there is no value in doing all your rehearsal at one time. You may find that a practice session right before you go to bed will be helpful; while you sleep, your subconscious will continue to work on the speech. As a result, you are likely to find a tremendous improvement in your mastery of the speech at the first practice session the next day.

How many times you practice depends on many things, including your experience, your familiarity with the subject, and length of your speech. When practicing, you should try to learn the speech, not memorize it. Learning the speech involves giving it differently during each practice.

What you do *not* want to do is to practice the speech the same way each time until you have it memorized. When people memorize, their attention is on mastering word order. During the practice, then, any mistake is likely to require backtracking or some other means of getting back to the proper word order. Unfortunately, this kind of practice does not make for mastery of content, it does not give additional insight into the topic, and it does not allow for audience adaptation during presentation. Sometimes speakers give the speech extemporaneously one time and then repeat the same wording over and over again. The result is about the same in both instances.

Let us illustrate the method of learning a speech by using a short portion of the speech outline on pages 94–96 of Chapter 4 as the basis for the practice. That portion of the outline reads as follows:

I.   Roquefort cheese is trademarked.
    A. Cheesemakers still follow legislation of the Parliament of Toulouse that dates from 1666.
    B. All salad dressings claiming to be Roquefort must contain at least 15 percent legislated Roquefort.

Now let us consider three practices that focus on point B of the outline, the amount of pure Roquefort that must be included before a salad dressing can be called "Roquefort."

First practice: "So, the point is that all salad dressings claiming to be Roquefort must contain at least 15 percent of legislated Roquefort — that's 15 percent of pure Roquefort."

Second practice: "So, let's say that you order Roquefort for your salad. How do you know what you're getting? According to law, that dressing you order must contain at least 15 percent of legislated Roquefort."

Third practice: "When you order Roquefort dressing for your salad you may find that the taste varies a little from restaurant to restaurant. Still, according to law, you can be sure that what you are getting has at least 15 percent of the real thing — legislated Roquefort."

Notice that point B of the outline is in all three versions. As this illustrates, the essence of the outline will be a part of all of your practices. Because you have made slight variations each time, when you finally give the speech, there will be that sense of spontaneity. In your speech you probably will use a wording that is most meaningful to you, and yet you will be assured that you are likely to get the key point across.

Using Notes in the Speech

Should you use notes in practice or during the speech itself? The answer depends on what you mean by notes and how you plan to use them. It may be best to avoid using notes at all for your first short speech assignment. Then, as assignments get longer, you will be more likely to use notes properly and not as a crutch. Of course, there is no harm in experimenting with notes to see what effect they have on your delivery.

Appropriate notes are composed of key words or phrases that help trigger your memory. Notes will be most useful to you when they consist of the fewest words possible written in lettering large enough to be seen instantly at a distance. Many speakers condense their written preparatory outline into a brief word or phrase outline. A typical set of notes made from the preparatory outline illustrated in Chapter 4 is shown in Figure 6.4.

For a speech in the five- to ten-minute category, one or two 3 × 5 notecards should be enough. When your speech contains a particularly good quotation or a complicated set of statistics, you may want to write them out in detail on separate 3 × 5 cards.

During practice sessions you should use the notes as you plan to use them in the speech. Either set them on the speaker's stand or hold them in one hand and refer to them only when needed. Speakers often find that the act of making a notecard is so effective in helping cement ideas in the

Figure 6.4

Notes.

```
ELEMENTS OF ROQUEFORT

Trademarked
    Toulouse 1666
    15% required

Ewe's milk
    Neolithic
    30 ewes to 1 cow
    800,000 ewes

Mold from caves
    Penicillium roquefortii
    in fissures
    injected
```

mind that during practice, or later during the speech itself, they do not need to use the notes at all.

Speech Preparation Exercise 12
Recording Your Speech Practice

Make a diary of your rehearsal program for your first speech. How many times did you practice? At what point did you feel you had a mastery of substance? How long was each of your practice periods?

Coping with Nervousness

In Chapter 1, we noted that nearly everyone who speaks in public experiences nervousness. Research has shown that up to 20 percent of the population may experience anxiety with real or anticipated communication.[3] Specific speech nervousness, or stage fright, however, is a normal reaction to speaking in public. The difference? If you have no major problems in interacting with people in other communication situations, your nervousness at the thought of giving a speech is likely to be less of a problem than you might think.

Let us start with the assumption that you are indeed nervous about delivering your speech — you may, in fact, be scared to death. Now what? To start with, realize that you are in good company. Even experienced speakers confess to nervousness when they speak. Now, you may say, "Don't give me that line — you can't tell me that [fill in the blank with the name of some person you know] is nervous when he [or she] speaks in public!" Ask that person. He or she will tell you. Even famous speakers such as Abraham Lincoln and Franklin D. Roosevelt were nervous before speaking. The difference in nervousness among people is a matter of degree. Some people tremble, perspire, and experience shortness of breath and increased heartbeat. As they go through their speech, they are so preoccupied with themselves that they lose all contact with the audience, jump back and forth from point to point, and on occasion forget what they had planned to say. Some people's anxiety is so great that they cannot eat or sleep before a speech, and some people avoid speaking at any cost.

Experience has proven that people can learn to cope with these fears. Recall from Chapter 1 that despite nervousness you can make it through your speech, your listeners are unlikely to recognize your fear, and the more experience you get in speaking, the more you will be able to cope with nervousness.

In addition, experienced speakers learn to channel their nervousness. The nervousness you feel is, in controlled amounts, good for you. It takes a certain amount of nervousness to do your best. What you want is for your nervousness to dissipate once you begin your speech. Just as a football player is likely to report that the nervousness disappears once he engages in body contact, so too a speaker should find nervousness disappearing once he or she gets a reaction to the first few sentences of an introduction.

Specific Behaviors

Now let us consider some of those specific behaviors that you can use to help you. Coping with nervousness begins during the preparation process and extends to the time you actually begin the speech.

1. *Pick a topic you are comfortable with.* The best way to control nervousness is to pick a topic you know something about and are interested in and, as a result of your audience analysis, one that you know your audience is likely to respond to. Public speakers cannot allow themselves to be saddled with a topic they do not care about. An unsatisfactory topic lays the groundwork for a psychological mind-set that almost guarantees nervousness at the time of the

Figure 6.4

Timetable for preparing a speech.

Days Before Speech	Task
7	Select topic; begin research
6	Continue research
5	Outline body of the speech
4	Work on introduction and conclusion
3	Finish outline; find additional material if needed
2	First rehearsal session
1	Second rehearsal session
Due date	Give speech

speech. By the same token, having a topic you know about and are truly interested in lays the groundwork for a satisfying speech experience. In Chapter 2 we emphasized how to ensure that you had the best topic possible. Heed that advice and you will be well on the way to reducing your nervousness.

2. *Give yourself enough time to prepare fully.* If you back yourself into a corner and must find material, organize it, write an outline, and practice the speech all in an hour or two, you almost guarantee failure and destroy your confidence. On the other hand, if you do a little work each day for a week before the assignment, you will experience considerably less pressure and increased confidence.

The timetable in Figure 6.4 will work for most of the short speeches that you prepare for class.

Experience in preparing and the length and difficulty of the speech will affect your preparation schedule. For instance, for a major speech I usually begin research a month before the date I am to give the speech; I then reserve an entire week for rehearsal and revision.

Giving yourself enough time to prepare fully includes sufficient time for rehearsal. Follow the steps outlined in the section on practice periods. Your goal is to build habits that will take over and control your behavior during the speech itself. If our national love affair with big-time athletics has taught us anything, it is that careful preparation enables an athlete (or a speaker) to meet and overcome adversity. Among relatively equal opponents, the team that wins is the one that is mentally and physically prepared for the contest.

When an athlete says, "I'm going into this competition as well pre-pared as I can possibly be," he or she is more likely to do well. In this regard, speech making is like athletics. If you assure yourself that you have carefully prepared and practiced your speech, you will do the kind of job of which you can be proud.

During the preparation period you also can "psych yourself up" for the speech. If you have a good topic, and if you are well prepared, your audience is going to profit from listening to you. That's right: Even though this is only a class and not a professional speaking experience, your listeners will be glad they have heard you. Now, before you say, "Come on, who are you trying to kid!" think of speeches you have heard. When a speaker had ideas that related to your needs and interests, were you *not* impressed? Of course you were. The fact is that some of the speeches you hear in class are some of the best and most valuable speeches you will ever hear. Students learn to put time and effort into their speeches, and many of their speeches turn out to be quite good. If you work at it, your class will look forward to listening to you.

3. *Try to schedule your speech at a time that is psychologically best for you.* When speeches are being scheduled, you may be able to control when you speak. Are you better off "getting it over with" — that is, being the first person to speak that day? If so, you can usually volunteer to go first. But regardless of when you speak, do not spend your time thinking about yourself or your speech. At the moment the class begins, you have done all you can do to be prepared. This is the time to focus your mind on something else. Listen to each of the speeches that comes before yours and become involved with what each speaker is saying. Then when your turn comes, you will be as relaxed as possible.

4. *When your turn comes, walk to the speaker's stand confidently.* Re-search indicates that it is during the period right before you walk up to give your speech and the time when you have your initial contact with the audience that your fear is most likely to be at its greatest.[4]

As you walk to the speaker's stand, remind yourself that you have good ideas, that you are well prepared, and that your audience wants to hear what you have to say. Even if you make mistakes, the audience will profit from your speech.

5. *Pause for a few seconds before you begin.* When you reach the stand, pause a few seconds before you start. Take a deep breath while you make eye contact with the audience; this may help get your breath-ing in order. Try to move about a little during the first few sentences; sometimes a few gestures or a step one way or another is enough to break some of the tension.

Figure 6.5

Speech Principles and Action Steps of Preparation.

The five fundamental principles of effective speaking are fulfilled through eight action steps of speech preparation.

Principle I: Effective speaking begins with a specific speech goal adapted to your audience and occasion.

1. Select a topic you know something about and that you are interested in.
2. Determine the response that you want from your audience.
3. Analyze your audience and your occasion.

Principle II: Effective speaking requires high quality information.

4. Gather and evaluate material that you can use in the speech.

Principle III: Effective speaking occurs when material is organized and developed to heighten the speech's goal.

5. Choose an organizational pattern that clearly communicates the material.
6. Outline the speech on paper.

Principle IV: Effective speaking is a product of clear, vivid, emphatic, and appropriate wording.

7. Choose wordings of main points and supporting materials carefully.

Principle V: Effective speaking requires enthusiastic, direct, and spontaneous delivery.

8. Practice delivering the speech orally.

Assignment

Presenting a Diagnostic Speech

Now that you have all the fundamentals in hand, you are ready for a first major speech. The purpose of this speech is to diagnose which of the fundamentals you are comfortable with and which may be giving you difficulty. (See the summary of speech principles and preparation steps in Figure 6.5.) When you have completed this assignment, you should be ready to move into specific informative-speaking assignments in the next part.

Prepare a three- to five-minute speech. The speech may be informative or persuasive. An outline is required. (Pp. 147–149 contain a sample three- to five-minute student speech. The preparatory outline the speaker submitted is on pp. 146–147.)

Criteria for evaluation will include the essentials of topic and purpose, content, organization, language, and delivery. The universal speech critique checklist in Chapter 7 (p. 166) is appropriate for evaluating this diagnostic speech. As you practice your speech, you may want to use the critique sheet as a checklist to assure yourself that you are meeting the basic criteria in your speech.

Speech — Classifications of Nursery Rhymes

Specific Goal: I want my audience to understand four major classifications of nursery rhymes.

Introduction
I.   "Hey diddle diddle, the cat and the fiddle, the cow jumped over the moon. The little dog laughed to see such sport, and the dish ran away with the spoon."
II.   Did you know that there are four major classifications of nursery rhymes?

Thesis Statement: The four classifications of nursery rhymes are ditties, teaching aids, historically based rhymes, and modern use rhymes.

Body
I.   Ditties are nursery rhymes with a prophetic purpose.
   A. A fortune-telling rhyme is told while counting the white spots on the fingernails.
   B. Just as in *Poor Richard's Almanack* by Benjamin Franklin, Mother Goose had her merry wise sayings.
   C. Traditionally, a rhyme on the topic of love fidelity is said while plucking the petals of a daisy.
II.   Some nursery rhymes were used as teaching aids.
   A. "Hickory Dickory Dock" is an example of onomatopoeia, an attempt to capture in words a specific sound.
   B. Song rhymes help children with their coordination.
      1. Historical background.
      2. Children's usage.
   C. Numbers in nursery rhymes obviously retain traces of the stages by which prehistoric people first learned to count.
III.   Many nursery rhymes have historical significance.
   A. Religious problems entered into nursery rhymes with "Jack Sprat."
   B. In England it is believed that some of these country rhymes may be relics of formulas the Druids used in choosing a human sacrifice for their pagan gods.
   C. Cannibalism is quite prevalent in nursery rhymes.
IV.   A modern classification of nursery rhymes is the parody.
   A. The famous prayer "Now I lay me down . . ." was first published in 1737, but has now been parodied.
   B. A joke has been created out of "Mary and Her Lamb."

Conclusion

I. Every song, ballad, hymn, carol, tale, singing game, dance tune, or dramatic dialogue that comes from an unwritten, unpublished word-of-mouth source contributes to the future culture of our nation.

II. Remember that with your next cute saying, teaching aid in the form of a rhyme, reference to history, or modern use of nursery rhymes, you may become the next Mother Goose.

Bibliography

Baring-Gould, William S., and Cecil Baring-Gould. *The Annotated Mother Goose.* New York: Clarkson A. Potter, 1962.

Bett, Henry. *Nursery Rhymes and Tales–Their Origins and History.* New York: Henry Holt, 1924.

Ker, John Bellenden. *An Essay on the Archaeology of Popular Phrases and Nursery Rhymes.* London: Longman, Rees, Orme, Brown, Green, 1837.

Mother Goose. *Mother Goose and the Nursery Rhymes.* London: Frederick Warne, 1895.

Read the following speech aloud at least once.[5] Examine it to see whether the specific goal is clear; whether the material really develops the points; whether the speech has a good opening, clearly stated main points, and a good conclusion; and whether the language is clear, vivid, emphatic, and appropriate.

Analysis

The speaker uses a common rhyme to capture our attention. From the beginning, the novelty of the topic and the development get and hold our attention. Notice the clever wording "There's more to nursery rhymes than meets the ear."

Throughout the speech, the speaker leads us through the organization. She begins the body of the speech by identifying the first classification. The next sentence gives us the three subdivisions of the major classification. The commendable part of this and all sections of the speech is the use of specific examples to illustrate the various types and subtypes.

SPEECH

"Hey diddle diddle, the cat and the fiddle, the cow jumped over the moon, the little dog laughed to see such sport and the dish ran away with the spoon." You recognize this as a nursery rhyme, and perhaps you always considered these nursery rhymes as types of nonsense poetry with little if any meaning. As we look at the four classifications of nursery rhymes, I think that you'll see as I did that there's more to nursery rhymes than meets the ear.

One of the major classifications of nursery rhymes is ditties. Ditties are fortune-tellings, little wise sayings, or little poems on love fidelity, and they are the most popular form of nursery rhyme. There are various ways of telling your fortune through ditties. One is saying, "A gift, a ghost, a friend, a foe; letter to come and a journey to go." And while you say this little ditty, this fortune-telling, you count the little white spots on your fingernails. Or you can say, "Rich man, poor man, beggarman, thief, doctor, lawyer, merchant, chief," and count your buttons. Whichever button you end on is the type of guy you are going to marry. Another kind of ditty is the wise saying. Just as in *Poor Richard's Almanack* by Benjamin Franklin, Mother Goose had her own little sayings. She said, "A pullet in the pen is worth a hundred in the fen," which today we say as "A bird in the hand is worth two in the bush." Love fidelity, the third kind of ditty, can be proven while plucking the petals off a daisy. "Love her, hate her, this year, next year, sometime, never." But today's usage has brought it up to "Love me, love me not, love me, love me not."

Another classification of nursery rhymes is those used as teaching aids, such as the saying "Hickory dickory dock." This is the use of onomatopoeia, which is trying to develop a sound from the use of words. In this case, he's trying to show the ticking of a clock. "London Bridge," although it has some historical background, is used for teaching children coordination, such as running around the circle raising their hands up and jumping back down. Similarly, in the ancient times, man made up rhymes in order to make things easier for him to remember, such as in the saying, "One, two, buckle my shoe; three, four, close the door." And as time went on, he eventually found out that he could use the fingers and toes to count. This is where "This little piggy went to market and this little piggy stayed home" originated.

Also, did you know that nursery rhymes have historical background? The third classification of nursery rhymes are those of historical significance. In the Middle Ages, which is when most nursery rhymes were formed, the saying, "Jack Sprat could eat no fat, his wife could eat no lean; and so betwixt the two of them, they licked the platter clean," refers to the Catholic Church and the government of the old Roman Empire. This is when the Catholic Church was blessing tithes, and wiping the country clean. The government came in and collected the taxes; and between the two of them, the country had no wealth and no money. The Druids, in their relics of old formulas for selecting human sacrifices, used the "eeny, meeny, miny, moe." And cannibalism is quite prevalent in almost all the nursery rhymes. Such as in "Jack and the Beanstalk," the big giant eater, and "Fee, Fi, Foe, Fum, I smell the blood of an Englishman. Be he alive or be he dead, I'm going to use him to make my bread." This also came up again in Shakespeare with *King Lear* and *A Midsummer Night's Dream*. "Little Jack Horner" is about a man named Jack Horner, who was steward of the abbot of Glastonberry. And in 1542, he was sent by this abbot to King Henry VII of England with a pie. And in this pie were documents which were the documents of the ownership of land around the Abbey of Glastonberry, in Somersetshire. And on his

Again the main point is clearly stated. She begins this section with an interesting look at a common rhyme. Once more, there is an excellent use of specifics to illustrate the point she is making. Although speech language should be informal, it should not be imprecise. Notice that the antecedent for "he" in "he's trying to show the ticking" is unclear. You should be careful to avoid these common grammatical errors. This section of the speech illustrates how information can sometimes be communicated in such an interesting way we are not even aware that we have learned anything.

Again the speaker moves smoothly into the statement of the main point. As far as the quality of information is concerned, this is probably the best section of the speech. Notice that she continues to use her examples and illustrations very well.

Of all the single examples in the speech, "Little Jack Horner" is probably the best.

way to the king, he stuck in his thumb and pulled out a document to the ownership of Meld, which he kept to himself. And until this day, over in Somersetshire, the Manor of Meld belongs to the Horner family.

The fourth classification of the nursery rhyme is the modern use — parodies and jokes — such as in "Mary had a little lamb, its fleece was white as snow." Today the kids go around saying, "Mary had a little lamb and was the doctor ever surprised." Or else they tend to make parodies of these nursery rhymes. Such as the famous little prayer, "Now I lay me down to sleep. I pray the Lord my soul to keep. If I should die before I wake, I pray the Lord my soul to take." It was first published in 1737, so you can see the age of this prayer. But, nowadays, the children say in joke, "Now I lay me down to sleep with a bag of peanuts at my feet. If I should die before I wake, you'll know I died of a stomach ache."

So every song, ballad, hymn, carol, tale, dance rhythm, or any cute little saying that you might come up with may contribute to the future culture of our nation. So remember, the next time you start spouting wise sayings, using rhymes as a teaching aid, referring to our history, or when you start making jokes of the traditional nursery rhymes, who knows, you might be the next Mother Goose.

Summary

Effective speeches are well delivered. Good delivery requires enthusiasm, good eye contact, and spontaneity and is achieved through voice and bodily action.

The physical elements of delivery include pitch, volume, rate, and quality. In addition to the effects of these individual characteristics, how they interact also can affect delivery. Effective speakers strive for vocal variety and emphasis that is free from monotonous patterns and such vocal interferences as "uh," "um," "well uh," "you know," and "like."

Effective speakers also are careful with their articulation, the shaping of speech sounds, and their pronunciation, the form and accent of various syllables.

Your nonverbal bodily actions affect your meaning. Facial expression, gestures, posture, and movement all work together in effective speaking.

Methods of delivery are impromptu, manuscript, memorization, and, the goal of this course, extemporaneous speaking. Extemporaneous speeches are prepared and practiced, but the exact wording is determined at the time of speaking.

Between the time the outline has been completed and the time the speech is to be given, you should practice the speech several times, weighing what you did and how you did it after each practice. During these practice periods you will work on presenting ideas spontaneously and using notes effectively.

Speech nervousness is a common experience and may be eased, if not entirely overcome, through careful speech preparation.

Notes

1. Reed G. Williams and John E. Ware, Jr., "Validity of Student Ratings of Instruction Under Different Incentive Conditions: A Further Study of the Dr. Fox Effect," *Journal of Educational Psychology*, 68 (February 1976), 50.

2. If you are interested in a more detailed analysis of the anatomy and physiology of the process, ask your instructor to recommend one of the many excellent voice and articulation books on the market (also see the Suggested Readings for Part II).

3. James C. McCroskey, "Oral Communication Apprehension: A Summary of Recent Theory and Research," *Human Communication Research*, 4 (1977), 78.

4. Larry W. Carlile, Ralph R. Behnke, and James T. Kitchens, "A Psychological Pattern of Anxiety in Public Speaking," *Communication Quarterly* 25 (Fall 1977), 45.

5. Delivered in speech class, University of Cincinnati. Used with permission of Susan Woistmann.

Chapter 7 | Listening Critically to Speeches

A s you begin this chapter you may be asking, "Why end a unit on fundamentals of effective speaking with a chapter on listening?" There are three main reasons.

First, effective listening is a critical part of the public speaking process. Recall from the model of speech communication presented in Chapter 1 that public speaking is a transactional process between a speaker and a group of listeners. Public speaking involves the listener directly. In this course, as well as in your role as a responsible citizen, you will be a listener much more often than you will be a speaker. Without effective listening, you can neither learn from the speaker's message nor weigh and evaluate the speaker's ideas.

Second, you can use effective listening to help you become a better speaker. By learning to listen effectively to speeches, you can validate how and why various speech methods and techniques work. As a result, your listening will help you determine which methods and techniques you should try in your own speeches. You also can see in action the kinds of mistakes you will want to avoid. As a bonus, the better you listen, the more you will learn about a great number of subjects. By listening carefully to the many speeches you will hear, you will supplement your liberal education, for the speeches are likely to be on subjects that cover nearly every discipline in your college or university.

Third, effective listening will help you to become a better speech critic. As you learn to listen critically for the way that speakers use or abuse the fundamental principles of public speaking, you will be able to provide much better constructive criticism for your fellow speakers.

In this chapter we will first define listening and show how negative listening behaviors may affect you. Next we will examine the skills that you can learn to use to improve your listening in general and your critical listening to speeches in particular. Finally, we will look at methods of critical analysis that you can use to evaluate speeches.

Listening: The Forgotten Communication Skill

If you were to examine your own communication behavior over the next few days, you probably would find that you spend more time listening than you do speaking, reading, or writing. For instance, studies have shown that college students spend approximately 16 percent of their time speaking, 17 percent reading, 14 percent writing, and as much as 53 percent listening![1] Yet most of us are likely to be least effective as *listeners*, even if we *hear* satisfactorily. Moreover, as Lyman Steil has pointed out, "After a ten-minute oral presentation, the average listener hears, receives, comprehends, and retains only about 50% of the message. After 48 hours, most listeners only remember about 25% of what they heard."[2]

Why is this the case? Mostly because few of us have had much instruction in listening. Of the four communication skills of reading, writing, speaking, and listening, far more hours of study have focused on reading and writing than on speaking and listening.

Let us examine the difficulties that many of us face as we listen to speeches. Suppose you were a real estate agent and you were attending the Monday morning briefing in which the regional manager brought all agents up to date on matters of mutual concern. Let us see what might interfere with your listening.

1. *You may not hear what the speaker is saying.* Many times we miss key ideas in and even large sections of spoken communication because of a momentary physical or psychological problem. If we have had emotional trauma such as a death in the family, the loss of a friendship, or a low grade on an assignment, we can be completely distracted while someone is trying to explain something to us. Even a simple head cold can distract us. You will recall from Chapter 1 that factors interfering with meaning are called *noise*.

2. *You may hear what is said but be unable to understand it.* For example, you might hear every word the regional manager is saying, but if the explanation includes words that you do not know or that are used in a way that you do not recognize, then the result is the same: You do not understand. Suppose, for instance, you are told that "your implementation is obfuscatory"; you may not understand that you are being told that what you are doing gets in the way.

3. *You may understand what is said, but you may assign it a meaning different from that intended by the originator.* For example, you are told that a delivery point is "within walking distance" of the branch office. Two miles later, when you stumble exhausted into the building lugging an armful of brochures, you realize that your interpretation of "walking distance" differs from that of the person who provided directions.

4. *You may hear and understand the message but behave inappropriately because you did not evaluate it properly.* For instance, you may act on a recommendation that you buy stock in the parent company on the basis of an appeal made by your regional manager at the meeting. When you discover that the stock drops by 15 percent within a month, you may realize that you did not properly evaluate the recommendation in terms of your own short-term needs.

5. *You may interpret information accurately but forget it.* The manager may say that your monthly written report is due on the fifth, but you may fail to submit it on time because you do not remember what the manager said—until her secretary calls to ask where the report is.

How do you overcome these common difficulties? *Listening* effectively to speeches is a four-step process that begins with attending (hearing) and then progresses through understanding, evaluating, and remembering.

Because each of the phases of listening requires distinct, specific skills, we will discuss each in detail. Before we begin our study, take a minute to complete the listening checklist.

Listening

To find out what kind of listener you are, complete the following. For each item score 5 for *almost always*, 4 for *usually*, 3 for *occasionally*, 2 for *seldom*, and 1 for *almost never*.

_____ 1. I listen *differently* for enjoyment, understanding, and evaluation.

_____ 2. I stop listening when what a person is saying is not interesting to me.

_____ 3. I consciously recognize the speaker's goal.

_____ 4. I pretend to listen to people when I am really thinking about other things.

_____ 5. When people talk, I differentiate between their main points and supporting details.

_____ 6. When a person's manner of speaking annoys me (such as muttering, stammering, or talking in a monotone), I stop listening carefully.

_____ 7. At various places in a speech I paraphrase what the speaker has said to check my understanding.

_____ 8. When I perceive the subject matter as very difficult, I stop listening carefully.

_____ 9. When I am listening for information or to evaluate, I take good notes of major points and supporting details.

_____ 10. When people use words that I find offensive, I stop listening and start preparing responses.

Add together your scores on all *even*-numbered items, which focus on negative listening behaviors. Then add together your scores on all *odd*-numbered items, which concern positive listening behaviors. If your total score for the odd-numbered items is much higher than your total score for the even-numbered items (20 or more points to 10 or fewer points), you are relatively skilled at listening. If your two scores are about the same, you need to work on limiting negative behaviors and perfecting skills that will raise your level of positive behaviors. If your score for the even-numbered items is much higher than for the odd-numbered items (20 or more points to 10 or fewer points), you probably need to work a great deal on developing skills that will improve your listening.

Attending (Hearing)

The first step in improving listening is to use skills that focus your attention. *Attending* (hearing) is the physical process of receiving sound waves and the perceptual process of attending to them. Why is it that we "hear" some sounds but not others?

Although the physical mechanisms in our ears respond to any sound waves emitted within our hearing range, our brain does not attend to them all, because we filter out those sounds that we choose not to hear. Sounds range from those that almost always get our attention to those that we can block out or control. Unexpected and loud noises such as alarms and other warning signals almost always take precedence over other sounds. When a fire alarm goes off in our building, we hear it and immediately focus our attention on its meaning. Likewise, the ringing of telephones and doorbells, the howling of ambulance sirens, and shouting of "Look out!" and "Fire!" usually get our attention.

With most sounds, however, there are times when we receive and attend to them as well as times we receive them but do not attend to them. For example, as you and a friend are chatting while you walk to class, you both receive and attend to each other's words. At the same time you may physically "hear" the chiming of school bells, but you may block them out, treating them as background noise. In fact, you may be so unconscious of background noise that you would deny that certain sounds had occurred. The phenomenon of receiving one sound while attending to others is called *dichotic listening.*[3]

Listening to speeches places a special listening burden on us for several reasons. Speeches are relatively uninterrupted one-way communication. Because we do not have the option of interjecting comments, it is easier for us to let our attention drift. Moreover, because our motivation to listen to every word may not be high, we are given even more encouragement to drift. If we are relatively poor listeners to begin with, we are likely to attend to any competing sound or image.

Improving your listening skills in general and your listening to speeches in particular begins with learning how to select some sounds to bring to the foreground while keeping others in the background. Let us consider what you can do to consciously focus your attention.

1. *Adopt a positive listening attitude.* There is no reason why you cannot be more attentive in any communication setting. But whether you are listening to a religious sermon, a political campaign speech, or a classroom lecture, it is up to you to stress to yourself the

possible benefits of listening. For instance, reminding yourself that a classroom lecturer is likely to explain and emphasize material that will be on a test might increase your motivation for listening.

2. *Analyze and, if possible, eliminate physical impediments to attending.* Nearly 15 million Americans suffer from some hearing impairment that can potentially affect their ability to listen.[4] If you are among this number, you may wear a hearing aid or you may have learned to adapt to the problem. If you often miss spoken words and have to ask that they be repeated, however, you may have a hearing impairment that you are unaware of. If you suspect that you have a hearing problem, have a complete hearing test. Most colleges have facilities for testing hearing acuity. The test is painless and usually is provided at minimal, if any, cost to the student.

3. *Get ready to listen.* You can start to increase your listening effectiveness by being physically and mentally ready to listen. Because physical alertness often encourages mental alertness, you need to sit in a way that will help you listen. Also, you should look directly at the speaker throughout the speech. The visual bond established between you and the speaker helps form a mental bond that improves listening effectiveness.

   Mentally, you need to direct your attention to what a person is saying; you must make a conscious decision to block out the thousands of miscellaneous thoughts that constantly pass through your mind. A speaker's message competes with whatever is on your mind at the moment—a basketball game, a calculus test, a date you are excited about, a movie you recently saw. And what you are thinking about may be more pleasant to attend to than the speaker's message. Attending to these competing thoughts and feelings is one of the leading causes of poor listening.

4. *Do not let your emotional reaction to content affect your listening.* All of us react emotionally to language. The problem comes when the mere utterance of certain words causes you to lose any desire to listen attentively. For example, you might ordinarily react strongly to one or more of the following words: *racist, gun control, male chauvinist, rape, AIDS, busing, gay, communist, feminist, Jew, welfare, yuppie,* or *abortion.* Often, poor listeners (and occasionally even good listeners) receive an emotional jolt from a speaker who touches a nerve with one of these words. When the speaker trips the switch to your emotional reaction, let a warning light go on before you cease to attend. Instead of tuning out or getting ready to fight, overcome this "noise" by working that much harder to be objective. If you can do it, you will improve your listening.

Listening is half of the communication transaction, but most of us pay too little attention to the way we listen. Like speaking, listening is a complex skill that requires a conscious effort to adapt to the demands of the occasion.

5.   *Adjust your hearing to the listening goals of the situation.* Listening is similar to reading in that you need to adjust how you listen to the particular goal you wish to achieve and to the degree of difficulty of the material you are hearing. For instance, when a speaker is narrating an experience to illustrate a point, you listen to get the point of the narrative. When, on the other hand, the speaker is attempting to prove a point with a series of examples, you not only have to "get the point," but also have to evaluate the quality of the examples and their relevance to the point being made. This second goal requires a different method of listening. Although many people approach all situations as if they were listening to stories, good listeners change

qualitatively when they are listening to understand and listening to evaluate, which are the subjects of the next two sections of this chapter.

Understanding

The second step in improving listening to speeches is to use specific skills that increase your understanding. *Understanding* may be defined as assigning the intended meaning to the messages you receive. One way to distinguish between hearing and understanding is to recall a time that someone spoke to you in a foreign language. For instance, if someone asks "Quelle heure est'il?" and you do not know French, you will hear and recognize all the *sounds*, but you will be unable to assign the intended meaning to them. You will not understand that the person is asking "What time is it?" A person does not have to be speaking a foreign language, however, for you to have difficulty understanding. In addition to using words outside of your vocabulary, speakers in any language sometimes talk quickly, shortcut sounds, and mispronounce words, so that you may have trouble decoding the message.

Vocabulary

Because word symbols are the primary vehicle of spoken messages, the size of your vocabulary will affect how well you understand what is being said and how hard you have to work to achieve the intended meaning. Listening effectiveness and vocabulary are definitely related. Chapter 5 emphasized the importance of building vocabulary to increase the precision of messages you send. Similarly, if you know the meaning of all the words that a person uses, you will understand messages more easily and thus can devote more energy to retaining those meanings. Some students who have average or above-average intelligence but who do not perform well in school are handicapped by a limited vocabulary. If your vocabulary is weak, you probably are spending so much time trying to figure out the meaning of an unfamiliar word in a sentence that you miss other parts of the message.

What do you do when a person uses a word that you do not understand? For too many people the answer is, "Nothing." If your professor tells you that the economy of a certain country has reached its "nadir," and you do not know what he or she is talking about, not taking the time to find out that *nadir* means the low point—the "pits"—seriously limits your understanding. Even people who have extensive vocabularies will encounter words with which they are unfamiliar. Serious listeners make notes of words they do not understand. If they cannot interrupt the speaker at the moment to find out the meaning, then they make note of the word and look it up as soon as possible.

As was pointed out in Chapter 5, two ways to improve your vocabulary are to work through a vocabulary book and to take a more active role in finding out meanings for words that you hear in speeches and conversation or encounter in your reading but do not understand.

Active Listening

One key to increasing your understanding is to practice active listening. *Active listening* includes mentally questioning to anticipate meanings, paraphrasing the meanings you have understood, and distinguishing among governing ideas, main points, and details in order to understand the relative importance of complex ideas. Active listening requires you to consciously think about the meaning of messages. Let us consider in detail these three procedures of active listening.

1. *Ask yourself questions to help you anticipate material.* Suppose your boss says, "There are four steps to coding data." You might ask yourself, "What are the four steps?" As your boss proceeds to tell you the steps, having posed the question can help you to attend to and recognize the steps as they are described. If the boss does not discuss the steps, your anticipatory questions will remind you to ask her. For instance, if a person says, "Swimming is an activity that provides exercise for almost every muscle," active listeners might inwardly question "How?" and then pay attention to the supporting material offered or request this information if the speaker does not supply it.

2. *Silently paraphrase to help you understand.* A *paraphrase* is a statement in your own words of the meaning you have assigned to a message. When you have listened to a message, you should be able to summarize your understanding. For example, after a person has spent a few minutes explaining the relationship between ingredients and amounts in recipes and the way a mixture is achieved, you can

say to yourself, "In other words, how the mixture is put together may be more important than the ingredients used." If you cannot paraphrase a message, either the message was not well encoded or you were not listening carefully enough.

3. *Separate the governing idea (or goal), key points, and details to help you understand a complex message.* Some people mistakenly think they have understood a message when they can feed back most of the words that made up the message. Understanding goes beyond that, however. In any extended message the speaker will have an overall purpose and will include both key ideas (or main points) and details. For example, as Gloria, a social worker, speaks on teenage crime, she mentions three apparent causes: poverty, permissiveness, and broken homes. She includes information she has read or observed that relates to each of these points. If you were listening carefully, when Gloria finishes speaking, you would identify *her goal* as explaining the causes of teenage crime, her *main ideas* as the three specific factors she sees as causes, and the *details* she has provided to support each cause.

Sometimes, people organize their messages in such a way that it is relatively easy to understand their goal, key points, and details. At other times, however, you must supply the structure for yourself if you are to understand.

Evaluating

The third step in improving your listening to speeches is to use skills that will increase your capacity to evaluate speech messages. *Evaluating* consists of the process of critically analyzing what you have understood and interpreted in order to determine how truthful, authentic, or believable you judge the meaning to be. This aspect of listening also is called *critical listening*. For instance, when a person explains the causes for a downturn in the economy or tries to convince you to vote for a particular candidate for office, you will want to listen critically to these messages to determine how much you agree with the speaker and how you wish to respond to the message. If you fail to listen critically to the messages you receive, you risk inadvertently agreeing with ideas or plans that may violate your own values, with ideas that may be counterproductive to achieving your goals, or with ideas that may be misleading to others (including the speakers) who value your judgment. Critical listening requires you to separate facts from inferences and to judge the accuracy of the inferences that have been made.

Separating Factual Statements from Inferences and Judgments

As mentioned in Chapter 3, a *factual statement* is one whose accuracy can be verified or proven; by contrast, an *inference* is a conclusion or generalization based on what has been observed, and a *judgment* is an expression of approval or disapproval. Just as it is important for you to make distinctions between factual statements, inferences, and judgments when you gather information for your speeches, it also is important for you to make these distinctions when you listen to speeches. If you identify a speaker's statement as either a judgment or an inference, you will want to look for the data upon which the judgment or inference is based.

Evaluating Inferences

Critical listeners not only can recognize inferences, but also evaluate them to determine their validity. As we already have said, *inferences* are conclusions or assertions drawn from or based upon factual information. Inferences usually are presented as arguments — that is, the speaker makes a claim and then presents other statements in support of the claim. Let us look at an example of a simple argument that you might hear someone make. Joyce says, "Next year is going to be a lot easier for my husband and me than the past year [*inference* — a statement that requires some kind of support to validate it]. I got a $200-a-month raise [*fact*] and my husband has been relieved of some of the extra work he's had to do while they were looking for a replacement for Ed [*fact*]." Notice that Joyce's argument suggests that she sees a relationship between her conclusion and the facts she presents. Her argument is based on the assumption that more money per month will make the year easier financially and that less work for her husband will make the year easier because it will relieve stress.

The critical listener asks at least three questions when evaluating any inference: (1) Is there factual information to support the inference? (2) Is the factual support relevant to the inference? (3) Is there known information that would prevent the inference from logically following the factual statements? In the example, Joyce does have factual statements for support: She received a raise, and her husband has less work to do. Moreover, increased income is one kind of information that is relevant to "having an easier time." At this stage it would appear that Joyce does have the makings of a sound argument; however, if we learn that to get the $200-a-month raise Joyce had to take on extra duties, then we still might question whether the year is likely to be "easier" than the last one.

Let us consider one more example. Dan says, "This is a great time to buy a house — interest rates are at the lowest point they've been in three years." The inference is that this is a great time to buy a house. First, does Dan give any support for the inference? Yes. Second, is the support relevant to the inference? Yes — interest rates are a factor in determining whether the time is right for home buying. Third, is there known information that would prevent the conclusion following from the data? If other indicators showed that we were entering a period of recession, the information might be more important to the decision than the stability of interest rates.

In Chapter 17 we will discuss the formation and testing of arguments in greater detail. For now however, asking these three questions will help you to evaluate the arguments you hear.

Remembering

The final step in improving your listening to speeches is to use skills that will help you retain the information you hear. Too often, people forget almost immediately what they have heard. Haven't you often been unable to recall the name of a person to whom you were introduced just moments earlier? On the other hand, there are times when ideas and feelings imprint themselves so deeply on your memory that a lifetime of trying to forget them will not erase the images. For instance, a song's lyrics may rattle around in your mind for days, or a cutting remark made by a loved one may haunt you for years. Deliberate remembering requires consciously applying techniques that imprint ideas on your memory. Let us consider four techniques that are likely to work for you.

Repetition

Repetition, of course, is the act of saying something more than once. Repeating information two, three, or even four times makes it far more likely that you will remember it at a later date. Thus, during a lecture when you hear that Aristotle wrote the first complete work on rhetoric, one of the easiest ways of ensuring that you will remember that fact is to say to yourself, "Aristotle, the first complete work on rhetoric," three or four times.

Recognition of Patterns

You are far more likely to remember material if you can find or create some organizational pattern for it. Good speakers will help you considerably in identifying a pattern, but when you are listening to a somewhat disorganized speech, you will have to work harder to discover a relevant pattern.

In Chapter 4 we discussed six common patterns of speech organization: time order, space order, topic order, causal order, reasons order, and problem–solution order. If you can identify which pattern the speaker is using, you can mentally follow the order and better remember the ideas of the speech. If the speech seems disorganized, you will have to create an organization for the speech. Thus, if the speaker is clarifying a process or procedure, if you can fit ideas into a time order, you are more likely to remember the necessary information.

Regrouping Material

You are far more likely to remember long lists of items if you can regroup them under two or three headings. Many times, people express their thoughts as a series of items of equal weight. A person who is trying to show you how to complete a woodworking project, for example, might tell you to gather the materials, draw a pattern, trace the pattern on wood, cut out the pattern so that the tracing line still can be seen, file to the pattern line, sandpaper edges and surfaces, paint the object, sand lightly, apply a second coat of paint, and varnish. This list includes ten steps of apparently equal weight, and the chances of remembering all ten steps in order are not very good. But if you analyze the ten steps, you will see that you can regroup them under three headings: (1) Plan the job (gather materials, draw a pattern, trace the pattern on wood), (2) cut out the pattern (saw so the tracing line can be seen, file to the pattern line, sand edges and surface), and (3) finish the object (paint, sand lightly, apply a second coat of paint, and varnish). The regrouping appears to add three more steps, but in reality, by turning ten separate steps of apparently equal weight into three steps with three, three, and four subdivisions, respectively, you are much more likely to remember the entire process.

This technique is effective because it takes into consideration the limitations of most people's abilities to process information. Psychologists who study human memory processes have discovered that most of us can hold a maximum of four to seven bits of information in our active consciousness at one time.[5] Thus, the list of ten steps is too long for us to remember. Instead, we "store" three main points and three to four subpoints, an amount of information that can more easily be retained.

Create Mnemonics

Another way of remembering the content of a speech is to create a mnemonic for the key ideas. *A mnemonic device* is any artificial technique used as a memory aid. Some of the most common rules for forming mnemonics are taking the first letters of a list of items you are trying to remember and forming a word. For example, an easy mnemonic for remembering the five great lakes is HOMES (Huron, Ontario, Michigan, Erie, Superior). Thus, if you are trying to remember the three goals of speaking that are discussed in this book (entertainment, information, persuasion), you could take the first letters of each word and rearrange them so that they spell *pie*. Then when you think of *pie* you will think of the three goals.

When you are trying to remember items in a sequence, you can form a sentence with the words themselves, or you can assign words using the first letters of the words in sequence and form an easy-to-remember statement. For example, when you studied music the first time, you may have learned the notes of the scale (EGBDF) with the saying "every good boy does fine." (And for the notes on the treble clef spaces (FACE) you may have remembered the word *face*.) A second way to organize information in a sequence is to see whether a chronological, spatial, or topical relationship exists among the ideas and then group them accordingly. Directions are best remembered chronologically, descriptions may be remembered spatially, and other kinds of material can be grouped topically.

Note-Taking

Although note-taking would be inappropriate in most casual encounters, it is perhaps the most important skill in improving retention of ideas presented in speeches. Writing notes reinforces points through a kind of repetition as well as preserves a record of key ideas.

What constitutes good notes will vary by situation. Good notes may consist of a brief list of main points, key ideas, or governing points plus a few of the most significant details. Or good notes may be a short summary of the entire concept (a type of paraphrase) after the message is complete.

For lengthy and rather detailed information, however, good notes probably will consist of a brief outline of what the speaker has said, including the overall idea, the main points of the message, and key developmental material. Using the principles of outlining, which were presented in Chapter 4, you create a structure for the information you want to retain and distinguish among main points, subpoints, and illustrative material. Good notes are not necessarily very long. In fact, many excellent lectures can be reduced to a short outline of notes.

Critical Analysis of Speeches

In addition to learning to prepare and present speeches in this course, you also are learning to critically analyze the speeches you hear. From a pedagogical standpoint, the critical analysis of speeches not only provides the speaker with both an analysis of where the speech went right and where it went wrong, but also gives you, the critic, insight into the methods that you want to incorporate as well as avoid in presenting your own speeches.

Critical listening is *context specific*; that is, the effectiveness of communication is determined by criteria that are specific to each communication context. Thus, for instance, analyzing the effectiveness of a public speech differs from analyzing the effectiveness of an interpersonal interaction or a group discussion. But just as there are different types of communication, so too there are different types of speeches. Thus, analyzing the effectiveness of an informative demonstration speech differs from analyzing the effectiveness of a persuasive action speech. In this section we will look specifically at criteria for evaluating public speaking in general. Later, when we consider specific speech contexts, we will consider specific criteria for evaluating those speeches.

A speech may be evaluated on at least two bases: (1) on its overall effectiveness and (2) on how well the speaker has met specific criteria of effective speaking.

Trying to determine a speech's overall effectiveness turns out to be a very difficult task. On the surface, a speech is effective when it is successful—that is, when it (1) achieves its specific goal or (2) brings the audience significantly closer to that goal. By this criterion, if as a result of the speech an audience now understands the steps of imposition, composition, and printing that are fundamental to the process of magazine

Checklist | **Universal Speech Critique**

Content

_____ 1. Was the goal of the speech clear? (pp. 32–35)

_____ 2. Did the speaker have high quality information? (pp. 59–62)

_____ 3. Did the speaker use a variety of kinds of developmental material? (pp. 64–71)

_____ 4. Did the speaker adapt the content to the audience's interests, knowledge, and attitudes? (pp. 38–46)

Organization

_____ 5. Did the introduction gain attention, gain goodwill for the speaker, and lead into the speech? (pp. 85–87)

_____ 6. Were the main points clear statements? (pp. 76–79)

_____ 7. Did the conclusion tie the speech together? (pp. 90–92)

Language

_____ 8. Was the language clear? (pp. 100–106)

_____ 9. Was the language vivid? (pp. 106–109)

_____ 10. Was the language emphatic? (pp. 110–113)

_____ 11. Was the language appropriate to the audience? (pp. 113–120)

Delivery

_____ 12. Did the speaker sound enthusiastic? (pp. 123–124)

_____ 13. Did the speaker look at the audience? (pp. 124–125)

_____ 14. Was the delivery spontaneous? (p. 125)

_____ 15. Did the speaker show sufficient vocal variety and emphasis? (pp. 129–130)

_____ 16. Were the pronunciation and articulation acceptable? (pp. 132–133)

_____ 17. Did the speaker have good posture? (p. 134)

_____ 18. Did the nonverbal elements of the speech complement the speech content? (pp. 133–135)

_____ 19. Did the speaker show sufficient poise? (pp. 141–144)

Based on these criteria, evaluate the speech as (check one) _____ excellent, _____ good, _____ satisfactory, _____ fair, _____ poor.

production or if the audience is convinced that Congress should pass stricter handgun control laws, then the speech is considered to be a success.

Of course, the problem that any critic faces is that in most situations there is no objective way to measure the audience's degree of understanding or conviction. Moreover, even if such a test could be made, the critic could not be sure that either the understanding or the conviction of the audience resulted directly from the speech or from other factors.

Because overall effectiveness is such a complex criterion, most critics base their evaluation on how well the speaker has met specific criteria of effective speaking. In the last five chapters you have been learning not only steps of speech preparation but also the criteria by which speeches are measured. The critical assumption is that if a speech has good content, is well organized, is well worded, and is well delivered, then it is more likely to achieve its goal. Thus, the critical apparatus for evaluating any speech comprises questions that relate to the basics of content, organization, style, and delivery.

The universal speech critique checklist shows a series of questions that can be adapted in the evaluation of any speech. Notice that for each question on the critique the pages where that issue has been discussed are specified. This universal critique would be appropriate for at least two speech situations. The first is when your goal is to provide feedback on all aspects of a speech. When people give their first speeches, it often is useful to provide a general diagnostic evaluation. That is, regardless of the specific speech goal, you want the speakers to understand the strengths they can build on in later speeches and the weaknesses that they will have to correct before more specific analysis is relevant.

I perform this diagnostic step whenever I am hired to help a speaker improve. I begin by asking the person to prepare a speech on any topic with either an informative or persuasive goal so that I can find out what aspects of the person's speechmaking at this stage are strengths and which seem to be the biggest weaknesses. One speaker I was working with showed a natural tendency toward a powerful speech delivery. The person had a good voice, showed tremendous enthusiasm, and gave me a sense of real communication. But the structure and development of the speech was dreadful. I knew then that I would not need to focus much on speech delivery, but that I would have to work closely with the person on building a coherent speech.

The second situation in which a universal critique sheet is useful is when you are not sure what kind of speech the person intends to give. Even knowing the speech title or subject may not tell you the general or specific goal of the speech.

For a truly comprehensive analysis, however, the speech analysis must relate to the specific type of speech and to its specific goal. Within each of the general categories of content, organization, language, and delivery, different questions may apply to different types of speeches. For instance, the evaluation of an informative demonstration speech must consider the visual aids that have been used in the demonstration; the evaluation of the persuasion speech of conviction must consider the reasons and evidence in support of those reasons that were used to support the proposition. Accordingly, in each of the following chapters where we focus on different types of speech skills, you will find specific critique checklists that focus on the features emphasized in that particular assignment as well as on the questions that apply to all kinds of speeches.

<table>
<tr>
<td>

Skill Development Exercise

Listening Actively

</td>
<td>

1. For one of the speeches you hear during the first round, take notes on the content in outline form as you listen. When the speech is finished, answer "yes" or "no" to the questions on the critique checklist. Evaluate the speech as excellent, good, satisfactory, fair, or poor. Then, using the answers to the questions in the checklist, support your evaluation in two to five paragraphs.

2. Break into groups of six. Members of the group should each talk in turn for one to two minutes on a topic with which they are familiar and on which they have an opinion. The other members should listen actively. When the speaker is finished, the listeners should quickly outline what they have understood to be the speaker's purpose and main points. These outlines should be shared, compared, and discussed to determine similarities as well as differences between the intended meaning and the received meaning. Because the speaker has (presumably) prepared both a specific goal and an outline, these written documents can be shared with the group and similarities and differences specifically noted.

3. Read the following story and evaluate each witness's statement as either F (fact) or I (inference).

   Two people came hurrying out of a bank with several large bundles, hopped into a long black car, and sped away. Seconds later, a man rushed out of the bank, waving his arms and looking quite upset. You listen to two people discuss what they saw and heard.

   _____ a. "The bank's been robbed!"

   _____ b. "Yes, indeed — I saw the robbers hurry out of the bank, hop into a car, and speed away."

   _____ c. "It was a long black car."

   _____ d. "The men were carrying several large bundles."

</td>
</tr>
</table>

_____ e. "Seconds after they left, a man came out of the bank after them — but he was too late, they'd already escaped."

Answers: a. I; b. I; c. F; d. I (men?); e. I.

4. For the following, underline the inference (conclusion) once; underline the supporting material (evidence) twice. Then answer the following questions: (1) Is the inference valid? (2) Is the evidence relevant?

    a. I see that, according to the published report, the chess club made $275 from its raffle. I think our ski club should hold a raffle, too.

    b. When I looked at my gradebooks I saw that three of my students last year got A's on this test, five the year before, and three the year before that. There certainly will be some A's this year.

    c. Maybe that's the way you see it, but to me when high city officials are caught with their hands in the till and when police close their eyes to the actions of people with money, that's corruption.

5. Have a friend assume the role of a fellow worker on your first day in an office job and read the following information to you once at a normal rate of speech. As the friend reads the instructions, take notes. Then give yourself the test that follows, answering true or false, but *without* referring to your notes. Then repeat the quiz using your notes. How much does your score improve? Although the temptation is great to read this item yourself, do not do so. You will miss both the enjoyment and the value of the exercise if you do.

Because you are new to the job, I'd like to fill you in on a few details. The boss probably told you that typing and distribution of mail were your most important duties. Well, they may be, but let me tell you, answering the phone is going to take most of your time. Now about the typing. Goodwin will give the most, but much of what he gives you may have nothing to do with the department — I'd be careful about spending all my time doing his private work. Mason doesn't give much, but you'd better get it right — she's really a stickler. I've always asked to have tests at least two days in advance. Paulson is always dropping stuff on the desk at the last minute.

The mail situation sounds tricky, but you'll get used to it. Mail comes twice a day — at 10 A.M. and at 2 P.M. You've got to take the mail that's been left on the desk to Charles Hall for pickup. If you really have some rush stuff, take it right to the campus post office in Harper Hall. It's a little longer walk, but for really rush stuff, it's better. When you pick up at McDaniel Hall, sort it. You'll have to make sure that only mail for the people up here gets delivered here. If there is any that doesn't belong here, bundle it back up and mark it for return to the campus post office.

Now, about your breaks. You get ten minutes in the morning, forty minutes at noon, and fifteen minutes in the afternoon. If you're smart, you'll leave before the 10:30 classes let out. That's usually a pretty crush time.

Three of the teachers are supposed to have office hours then, and if they don't keep them, the students will be on your back. If you take your lunch at 11:45, you'll be back before the main crew goes.

Oh, one more thing. You are supposed to call Jeno at 8:15 every morning to wake him. If you forget, he gets very upset. Well, good luck.

With Notes	Without Notes	
_____	_____	1. Mail that does not belong in this office should be taken to Harper Hall.
_____	_____	2. Mail comes twice a day.
_____	_____	3. You should be back from lunch by 12:30.
_____	_____	4. Paulson is good about dropping work off early.
_____	_____	5. Mason gives the most work.
_____	_____	6. Goodwin gives work that has little to do with the department.
_____	_____	7. Your main jobs, according to the boss, are typing and answering the telephone.
_____	_____	8. Mail should be taken to McDaniel Hall.
_____	_____	9. The post office is in Harper Hall.
_____	_____	10. You get a fifteen-minute morning break.
_____	_____	11. Call Jeno every morning at 8:45.
_____	_____	12. You don't have to type tests.

Answers: 1. F; 2. T; 3. T; 4. F; 5. F; 6. T; 7. T; 8. F; 9. T; 10. F; 11. F; 12. F.

Summary

Increasing your listening skill is important to you for three reasons: Effective listening is a critical part of the public speaking process because you can use effective listening to help you become a better speaker, and effective listening will help you to become a better speech critic.

Listening problems include completely missing the message, hearing the message but not understanding it, hearing the message but creating meaning not intended by the sender, listening accurately but changing the meaning over time, and listening accurately but forgetting the meaning. Effective listening to speeches involves hearing, understanding, evaluating, and remembering. Attending (hearing) effectiveness can be increased by (1) adopting a positive listening attitude, (2) preparing to listen, (3) adjusting your hearing to the types of situations, (4) making the shift from speaker to listener a complete one, (5) hearing a person out before you react, and (6) eliminating physical impediments to listening.

Understanding can be improved by enlarging your vocabulary and by practicing active listening: silently questioning, paraphrasing, and separating governing ideas, key points, and details.

Evaluating is the process of separating fact from inference and judging the validity of main points and their support. Once the logic of the inference is identified, critical listeners evaluate the truthfulness of the inference conclusions.

Remembering is increased by repeating information, looking for and storing information by an organization pattern, reorganizing information when there is too much to be remembered, and taking notes when feasible.

In addition to learning to prepare and present speeches, you also are learning to critically analyze the speeches you hear. The criteria for evaluating a speech correlate with the elements of speech content, organization, language, and delivery. Although a speech may be evaluated on the basis of its overall effectiveness, determining overall effectiveness is difficult to do. Consequently, the critic focuses criticism on the criteria of effective speaking that we developed in the last five chapters.

Notes

1. L. Barker, R. Edwards, C. Gains, K. Gladnes, and F. Holley. "An Investigation of Proportional Time Spent in Various Communication Activities by College Students." *Journal of Applied Communication Research* 8 (1980), 101–109.

2. Lyman K. Steil, Larry L. Barker, and Kittie W. Watson, *Effective Listening* (Reading, Mass.: Addison-Wesley, 1983). See also C. Day, "How

Do You Rate as a Listener?" *Industry Week* 205 (28 April 1980), 30–35; and R. W. Rasberry, "Are Your Students Listening? A Method for Putting Listening Instruction into the Business Communication Course." *Proceedings.* Southwest American Business Communication Association Spring Conference (1980), 215.

3. Florence I. Wolff, Nadine C. Marsnik, William S. Tacey, and Ralph G. Nichols, *Perceptive Listening* (New York: Holt, Rinehart & Winston, 1983), 113–115.

4. Arthur S. Freese, *You and Your Hearing* (New York: Charles Scribner's Sons, 1979), 67.

5. This limitation was discovered first by George A. Miller and presented in "The Magical Number Seven, Plus or Minus Two: Some Limits on Our Capacity for Processing Information," *Psychological Review* 63 (1956), 81–97.

Suggested Readings

Amato, Phillip, and Donald Ecroyd. *Organizational Patterns and Strategies in Speech Communication.* (Skokie, Ill.: National Textbook Company, 1975.) This book focuses on speech organization.

Brownell, Judi. *Building Active Listening Skills.* (Englewood Cliffs, N.J.: Prentice-Hall, 1986.) This book not only covers the major components of listening, but also contains an excellent section on communication contexts such as "Listening to Superiors," "Listening in the Family," and so forth.

Clevenger, Theodore, Jr. "A Synthesis of Experimental Research in Stage Fright." *Quarterly Journal of Speech* 45 (April 1959), 134–145. This article draws eleven conclusions about stage fright that are still consistent with recent data.

Haynes, Judy L. *Organizing a Speech: A Programmed Guide.* 2d ed. (Falls Church, Va.: Speech Communication Association, 1981.) The programmed approach enables you to check your understanding of organization systematically.

McCroskey, James C. "Oral Communication Apprehension: A Summary of Recent Theory and Research." *Human Communication Research* 4 (1977), 78. A companion article to the Clevenger article cited earlier.

Mayer, Lyle V. *Fundamentals of Voice and Diction.* 8th ed. (Dubuque, Iowa: Brown, 1988.) A short (228 pages) and very popular analysis of voice and articulation.

Nash, Walter. *Rhetoric: The Wit of Persuasion.* (Cambridge, Mass.: Basil Blackwell, Inc., 1989.) A unique look at the use of language.

Rubin, Rebecca B., Alan M. Rubin, and Linda J. Piele. *Communication Research: Strategies and Sources.* 2d ed. (Belmont, Calif.: Wadsworth, 1990.) This book gives a comprehensive analysis of research sources.

Wolvin, Andrew D., and Carolyn Gwynn Coakley. *Listening*, 2d ed. (Dubuque, Iowa: Brown, 1988.) This book has chapters on appreciative listening, discriminative listening, comprehensive listening, therapeutic listening, and critical listening. It also gives a list of skills involved in each of the types.

PART III

INFORMATIVE SPEAKING

Now that you have an understanding of the fundamentals of preparing any kind of speech, this part focuses on those issues that are particularly relevant to informative-speech contexts.

The effectiveness of informative speaking is measured by how well the audience attends to, understands, and retains the information you present. Accordingly, the first chapter of the unit focuses on principles of informative speaking that are designed to get and maintain your listeners attention, facilitate their understanding, and increase their retention of the information you present.

The remainder of the unit focuses on informative-skill development. Chapter 9 stresses visual aids and their use. Although visual aids are not unique to informative speaking, they are discussed in this unit because imparting understanding and stimulating retention often involve presenting information visually as well as orally. Chapters 10 through 13 stress the skills of demonstration (process explanation), description, definition, and reporting. To give you specific practice in applying these skills, each chapter includes both a speech assignment and an example of a speech modeling the application of that skill.

The case study "Making Complex Information 'More Interesting and Relevant'" follows on pages 176 and 177.

Case Study
Making Complex Information "More Interesting and Relevant"

Y ou might not think that an accountant who "came up the audit trail" after graduating from college with a Bachelor's degree in business administration would be in high demand as a public speaker. But for G. Steven Burrill, the dynamic national director of Manufacturing/High Technology Industry Services for the accounting and consulting firm of Ernst & Young, informative speaking is nearly an everyday task.

Steve gives between 100 and 150 speeches per year — approximately three per week — to audiences all over the globe, from venture capitalists and chief executive officers to college groups and industry associations.

Why is Steve in such demand as a speaker? Part of the answer is the unique content he is able to present. Early on, he confessed with a chuckle, "Most people were amazed that an accountant could know anything about anything." In fact, Steve's consulting and accounting practice, together with proprietary information developed through his company's own research, has made him an internationally recognized expert on high-technology industries such as aerospace, electronics, and biotechnology — a "hot" subject in today's economy. To Steve, being able to offer his audiences new and valuable information makes for both successful speaking and good business: "I always try to present some content, perspective, or knowledge that sets our company apart."

A second reason for Steve's popularity as a speaker is that he has learned to adjust his choice of topic — or the slant he takes on the topic he is asked to address — to the needs and interests of each specific audience.

"Very early in my speaking career, I changed the topics I selected from topics people would normally expect an accountant to talk about — which were mostly on technical, accounting-related developments — and moved to where most of my speaking is about what's happening in the business world or the financial world or high tech, what's hot and what's not. These were topics that were not my original area of expertise, but they were things I knew about from being around certain industries. I found out relatively quickly that the world said, 'Hey, here's someone who's pretty interesting,' and that people were interested in the perspective I had to offer."

Even given a good choice of topic, Steve emphasized, it's equally important to communicate information in ways that will be meaningful to diverse audiences. As he put it, "I think people feel I can take a lot of complexity and make it more interesting and more relevant."

How does he accomplish this goal? To begin with, Steve knows that he must be thoroughly prepared. "Good speaking," he asserted, "is largely a matter of your comfort level with your subject." To stay current and informed, he not only draws upon extensive survey data compiled by his firm but also "spends an incredible amount of time" reading widely to develop a broad awareness of events around the world that can have an impact on technology companies. When the time comes to speak, his immersion in his subject allows him to talk directly with his audience — "from the heart and mind" — using only an outline and notes.

Merely being knowledgeable, however, is no guarantee that audiences will understand and remember the content of a speech. For this reason Steve looks for creative ways of packaging the information he wants to convey.

In business settings, one of Steve's favorite techniques is to build a presentation around carefully prepared visual aids so that his audiences can isolate key points and absorb them visually as well as by ear. For instance, in one recent speech Steve wanted to report survey data showing how the heads of electronics companies view their competitive situation in the coming decade. Instead of merely reciting percentages, Steve converted the raw numbers to pie charts and graphs that enabled the audience to see trends and comparisons at a glance. Other slides presented bulleted lists that briefly recapped the conclusions he most wanted to emphasize.

While this approach works well for his business speeches, Steve knows he must adapt his presentation style to each specific situation. For example, talking about technical subjects with nonexpert audiences poses a different challenge. In these settings Steve is careful to bring his listeners "up to speed" by relating new concepts to the knowledge they already have. For instance, in speaking to a general audience about "what's happening in biotechnology," Steve uses familiar examples to impart an idea of what constitutes biotechnology.

"I point out that we've been doing biotechnology since the beginning of mankind, when we created cheese by using microorganisms, or when we fermented alcohol, or when we rather crudely changed plants through hybridization. Now what's changed is the tools. That gives people a context for understanding what biotechnology is all about."

As this example suggests, Steve is very conscious of the need to adapt the level and content of his speeches to his audiences.

"I will spend a lot of time before every speech trying to figure out who the audience is — what their level of sophistication is. Even then, before I go into the room, I'll look at the attendee list so that — no matter what I was told in advance — I can see who is really there. That way I can adjust quickly to what I perceive their level of knowledge to be."

Is good informative speaking, then, a matter of presenting solid content in an understandable way? To Steve, there is a third crucial element: the speaker's own person and point of view.

"My speeches aren't just data dumps," he emphasized. "My goal is not only to have some unique content that I can add to someone else's knowledge base, but also to make that information *relevant* by sharing my perspective. I always try to answer the question, 'So what?'"

For a business audience, answering the "So what?" question can mean identifying a trend in a set of data and venturing predictions about what it means for executives or investors. For a general audience, it might involve explaining how technological research and development will affect the lives of ordinary people. Whatever the specific topic, Steve believes that it is the personal perspective that he provides that makes factual information meaningful to his listeners.

In this sense, informative speaking — no less than persuasive speaking — involves having the courage of one's convictions. As Steve pointed out, sharing a personal viewpoint means having confidence in his grasp of his subject and his judgment of what an audience wants and needs to know. For this reason, he cited becoming more comfortable with himself — "being able to say, I am who I am" — as a key part of his development as a speaker. For Steve knows that whether he is speaking to researchers in biotechnology or a high-powered group of venture capitalists, "Speaking is very much putting yourself on the line."

Chapter 8 | Principles of Informative Speaking

R alph Waldo Emerson wrote, "Any piece of knowledge I acquire to-day has a value at this moment exactly proportioned to my skill to deal with it. Tomorrow, when I know more, I recall that piece of knowledge and use it better."[1] Especially now when literally millions of data items are at our fingertips, we look for people who can make sense out of data and in turn explain things to us in ways that are useful to us.

Whether you are invited to report on the status of urban renewal for a key downtown area to a community action group, to describe the nature of the problem of chemical abuse among students in public secondary schools to the local Parent–Teacher Association, or to demonstrate the use of computers in creating graphics for a marketing firm, your ultimate goal is to create understanding. In this chapter we will define the nature of informative speaking, discuss the factors involved in achieving your informative-speaking goal, and stress several principles that are useful to the preparation of *any* informative speech; in the next chapter, we will discuss in detail one of the most prevalent means of helping audiences to understand information — using visual aids. In Chapters 10 through 13, we will consider different forms in which information can be presented.

The Nature of Informative Speeches

An *informative speech* is one in which an audience gains understanding. The three dimensions that differentiate an informative speech from a persuasive one are speaker intent, function of information, and audience perception.

Speaking Intent

Whether a speech is classified as "informative" depends in part on the intention of the speaker in sharing information for the purpose of arriving at understanding. This intention contrasts with one of changing a belief or bringing an audience to action.

For instance, most people would agree that a speaker whose intention is "to have the audience understand the components of impressionistic painting" is more likely to produce an informative speech than a speaker whose intention is "to have the audience believe that Renoir is the best in the school of French impressionistic painters." An intention that is phrased "understand the components" suggests the presentation of objective information; the intention that is phrased "to believe that Renoir is the best" suggests affecting an audience's attitude — an intention that seems to go beyond just gaining an understanding.

Function of Information

Whether a speech is classified as "informative" also depends on how the substance or material of the speech functions. Because all speeches are likely to contain substance or material that can be labeled "information," it is not the inclusion of information alone that produces an informative speech. If the information *functions* to clarify and explain, then the speech may be primarily informative; if the information functions to substantiate or to prove, then the speech may be considered primarily persuasive.

For instance, if a speaker presents examples of how computers can be used to create graphic displays, then the examples would serve an informative function; if, however, a speaker uses examples to form arguments supporting the need of this company to upgrade its computer technology, then the examples function persuasively.

Audience Perception

Finally, whether a speech is classified as "informative" depends on how the audience perceives you and your speech. First, your audience is likely to define your speech as informative when it perceives the context as informative. For instance, the majority of college students who attend a history class in which the professor is lecturing on the primary causes of World War I will accept the professor's list of causes as information. Likewise, when a staff of salespersons attend the regional managers talk on "Recent decisions affecting realtor and client relationships," the sales staff will view that talk as informative.

But even when the audience does not define the situation as informative, it will still perceive the speaker's subject matter as information if the speaker meets two criteria: (1) The audience accepts the speaker as an authoritative source of information on this topic and (2) the audience perceives the speaker as being without ulterior motives. Many speakers enter a situation with the necessary reputation that the audience will empower them to speak as an authority. Thus, when Michael Jordan talks with a group of teenagers about elements of team defense in basketball or when Anne Klein talks with a group of designers about fashion trends, both audiences will respect those speakers as authoritative sources of information on their topics. There are times when the audience does not empower you as an authority until it hears your speech. If, for instance, you give a speech to your classroom audience on illiteracy, the audience members may reserve their judgment about your authoritativeness to give an informative speech on that topic. Thus, in various places in this book we will talk about the need for you to build your credibility with your audience.

Likewise, you may lose your empowerment if the audience comes to believe that you have ulterior motives. For instance, if in either Michael Jordan or Anne Klein's speeches the audience begins to believe that the speakers are more interested in selling Nike basketball shoes or Anne Klein dresses than they are in helping the audience understand team defense or fashion trends, that audience may cease thinking of the situation as information exchange.

In summary, then, your speech will more than likely be classified as "informative" if your intent is to create understanding, if you use the material in your speech so that it functions informatively, and if you behave in ways that will allow your audience to perceive you as an authoritative information source without ulterior motives.

Factors in Achieving Your Informative Speaking Goal

Because you expect that your audience will learn from your informative speeches, your rhetorical challenge is what you can do in your speech to achieve that goal. *Learning* usually is considered to be a result of three factors: attending to or showing interest in the information being presented, understanding that information, and retaining the information in a form that results in the ability to recall it on demand.

1. *You must generate enough interest in the information to arouse audience attention.* Whether or not they should, people are quick to make value judgments about whether they will listen to information you present. Thus, arousing attention in the information is especially important. For example, in a speech in which you intend to teach your audience how to antique a piece of used furniture, you must show audience members why this information is useful for them. If your listeners are not listening—if they show no interest in your speech—they cannot learn.

2. *You must explain the information in ways that will enable the audience to understand.* If audience members do not truly understand the information, they will not learn it. For example, in your speech on how to antique a piece of used furniture, if your instructions for mixing ingredients of the antiquing compound are not clearly understandable, the audience will not learn them.

3. *You must discuss information in ways that will enable the audience to remember it.* The minute we hear information, we begin to forget some of it. Within a relatively short time we may lose anywhere from one-third to all of what we heard. You must present the information in a way that audience members will retain it in a form that will allow them to recall it on demand. In your speech on how to antique a piece of used furniture, for example, you must consider means of explaining the steps so that at a later date audience members will be able to remember them.

These are the factors. Now let us turn to specific principles that you can follow to incorporate these factors in your speech. At the start of each discussion, each principle is stated in a way that suggests which factors are incorporated. We approach this discussion of principles with the assumption that you already have a tentative specific goal, that you have completed your research, and that you have a tentative time, space, topic, causal, or problem–solution order for your speech (patterns of organization that are relevant to informative speeches). The challenge you now are trying to meet is finding what you can do in the speech to create enough interest to get an audience to listen, to explain in a way that will help the audience understand, and to discuss the information in a way that will help the audience remember. To accomplish these goals you must consider principles related to creativity, credibility, newness, relevance, and emphasis.

Creativity

Principle 1

Audiences are more likely to show interest in, understand, and remember information that is presented creatively.

Creativity underlies all of the other principles discussed in this chapter because it affects every part of the learning process.

The Nature of Creativity

John Haefele defines creativity as "the ability of make *new* combinations."[2] *Creativity* in informative speaking involves using your material in an imaginative way. Right now you may be thinking, "I'm just not a creative person." In reality, some people may be *more* creative than others, but *everyone* can generate creativity in their speeches if they are willing to work at it. Creativity in speaking begins with the three guidelines that were discussed in the section on practicing your speech: (1) Assure yourself that you have enough information so that you can make choices, (2) give yourself enough time to let the creative process work, and (3) force yourself to practice different sections of the speech in different ways. Creativity and choice are inseparable. If you simply do not have enough information to choose from, then it is far more difficult to be creative in presenting the information. If you do not give yourself enough time between gathering information and giving the speech, then you are not allowing your mind the necessary freedom for thinking creatively. And

As this French instructor knows, finding creative ways to make information memorable is a key element of informative speaking.

if you do not force yourself to practice in different ways, then you allow yourself to be content with the *first* way of presenting material that comes to mind rather than considering the *best* way.

Developing Creativity

At the heart of the creative process is the development of alternative methods of presenting factual material. Start with the premise that from any body of factual material an infinite number of lines of development are possible. By using a creative process you can discover the available lines of development and select the one that will work best for you in the speech. To illustrate the creative process, suppose you are planning to give a speech on climatic variation in the United States and in your research you uncovered the data shown in Table 8.1.

In the following section, we want to show that (1) one set of data can suggest *several* lines of development on one topic and (2) the same point can be made in many different ways.

1. *One set of data can suggest several lines of development.* Before you read the following material, study Table 8.1. What conclusions can you draw from it? If you are thinking creatively, you can draw the following conclusions:

    a. Yearly high temperatures in U.S. cities vary far less than yearly low temperatures.

	Temperature					Precipitation	
	January		Yearly				
City	Max.	Min.	High	Low	Extremes	July	Annual
Cincinnati	41	26	96	2	109 −17	3.3	39
Chicago	32	12	93	−6	103 −39	3.4	33
Denver	42	15	100	−5	105 −30	1.5	14
Los Angeles	65	47	88	39	110 28	T	14
Miami	76	58	96	44	100 28	6.8	59
Minneapolis	22	2	96	−21	108 −34	3.5	24
New Orleans	64	45	98	23	102 7	6.7	59
New York	40	17	97	11	106 −15	3.7	42
Phoenix	64	35	114	27	118 16	T	7
Portland, Me.	32	12	93	−6	103 −39	3.9	42
St. Louis	40	24	97	2	115 −23	3.3	35
San Francisco	55	42	86	33	106 20	T	18
Seattle	44	33	91	15	99 0	.6	38

Table 8.1

Climatic data.

b. It hardly ever rains on the West Coast in the summer.

c. In most of the major cities cited, July, a month thought to be hot and dry, produces more than the average one-twelfth of the precipitation that you might expect for the year.

   Thus, this one table will produce at least three conclusions that suggest three different lines of development for a single speech on climate.

2. *The same point can be made in different ways.* Let us consider the statement, "Yearly high temperatures in U.S. cities vary far less than yearly low temperatures."

   a. Statistical development: Of the thirteen cities selected, ten (77%) had yearly highs between 90° and 100°; three (23%) had yearly lows above freezing; six (46%) had yearly lows between zero and 32°; and four (31%) had low temperatures below zero.

   b. Comparative development: Cincinnati, Miami, Minneapolis, New York, and St. Louis, cities at different latitudes, all had yearly high temperatures of 96° or 97°; in contrast, the lowest temperature for Miami was 44°, and the lowest temperatures for Cincinnati, Minneapolis, New York, and St. Louis were 2°, −21°, 11°, and 2°, respectively.

   c. Can you find another way of making the same point?

Credibility

Principle 2

Audiences are more likely to attend to your speech if they like, trust, and have confidence in you.

You probably have noticed that you tend to have more confidence in some people's explanations of information than in others'. In fact, people are more inclined to listen and pay attention to speakers they like and trust. The Greeks had a word for this concept — *ethos*; today, students of communication theory use the term *credibility*. Thus, if you wish to increase the likelihood that your audience will listen to you, you will want to make sure that you are perceived as being credible.

Characteristics of Credibility

Although speech experts differ in listing the characteristics of credibility, most include competence, intention, character, and personality.

COMPETENCE   Your qualifications or capability are a major aspect of your competence, what we might call your "track record." What is your level of competence for your speech? Are you (or can you be) recognized as having necessary expertise? Do you have good material from reliable sources? Are you sure of your facts and figures? If you have a history of giving good advice, being a clear thinker, and so forth, your audience probably will see you as competent.

Think of how you are affected by the competence of your professors. Although all professors are supposed to know the information and topics they discuss, some are more convincing than others. Professors demonstrate their competence by having information that proves accurate and by presenting additional detail — an example, a story, or a list of reading material — when students ask questions. But not all professors maintain high credibility with their students. When a professor constantly corrects what he or she said earlier or gives "facts" that differ greatly from what other sources say, a student's faith in that professor drops considerably.

INTENTION   This second characteristic refers to a person's apparent motives. Remember that we discussed motive as an integral part of determining whether a speech really will be perceived as "informative." For instance, when an employee of your gas and electric company talks about testing your house for air leaks, you are likely to see his or her motives as "pure," because if you have such leaks repaired and lower your gas and electric use, the company stands to lose money. On the other hand, if representatives of a local home-repair business offer to give you a "free inspection for air leaks," you may suspect their motives, because if their inspection shows "major air leakage" they probably will want to sell you on having them do "necessary" repairs. The more positively your audience views your intentions, the more credible your words will seem.

What are your intentions in your speech? Are you presenting material that your listeners will perceive as informative so that they will not suspect you of having ulterior motives?

CHARACTER A speaker's character is made up of his or her mental and ethical traits. We are more likely to trust and believe a person whom we perceive to be honest, industrious, trustworthy, dependable, strong, and steadfast. We often will overlook what are otherwise regarded as shortcomings if a person shows character.

Will your audience perceive you as honest, industrious, and trustworthy?

PERSONALITY The final characteristic that we will discuss, personality, represents the sum total of a person's behavioral and emotional tendencies. In short, it is the impression a person makes on us. Sometimes, we have a strong gut reaction about a person based solely on a first impression. Based on such traits as enthusiasm, friendliness, warmth, a ready smile, and caring or its absence, we take a natural liking or disliking to a person.

Are you enthusiastic about your subject? Will your audience perceive you as friendly, warm, and caring?

Demonstrating Credibility

Credibility is not something you can gain overnight or turn on or off at will. Nevertheless, you can avoid damaging your credibility and perhaps even strengthen it somewhat during a speech or a series of speeches.

1. *Be well prepared.* Always approach your speech situation with the confidence that you have more knowledge and expertise than your audience. If the audience already perceives your knowledge and expertise before you begin, that is a plus. For instance, when well-known professional athletes appear at clinics to talk about how to hit a baseball, make a football block, or rebound a basketball, they are assured an attentive audience — their expertise precedes them. But even if you do not come into the speech with a reputation, if you talk knowledgeably and fluently with command of your information and without stumbling and making a variety of misstatements, you will build credibility during your speech.

2. *Emphasize your interest in the audience.* You can show your good intentions by emphasizing the benefits to be gained from your ideas. You want your listeners to understand that you really care about them and what happens to them. For example, suppose you were speaking to an audience of young adults about the need to monitor cholesterol levels. To show that your information is directed to them, you might say, "Learning about methods of lowering your cholesterol may be more important to you than you realize, because recent studies have revealed that high cholesterol levels are being discovered in large numbers of people in their teens and early twenties."

3. *Look and sound enthusiastic.* If you have a positive attitude about your topic, your audience is likely to become enthusiastic as well. If listeners suspect that you do not really care, however, they certainly are not going to.

   You probably will see the cumulative effect of credibility during this term. As your class proceeds from speech to speech, some speakers will grow in stature in your mind and others will diminish. Let us look at two more things you can do that relate primarily to classroom behavior.

4. *Be ready to speak on time.* Your credibility is enhanced by a positive attitude toward the schedule. Being ready to speak on time shows the class that you are willing to assume responsibility.

5. *Evaluate others' speeches thoughtfully.* If you can explain why a speech was good and apply that understanding of speech principles to your own speeches, classmates will develop a respect for your public-speaking capabilities. Then they will be more likely to respect your ideas when you present your speech.

Newness of Speech Information

> **Principle 3**
>
> *Audiences are more likely to listen to information they perceive to be new.*

When audience members think they already know the information you are presenting, they are less likely to pay attention. It is up to you as speaker not only to find information that will be new to your audience but also to feature its newness.

But how do you know what is new to your audience? Beginning speakers often overestimate an audience's familiarity with specific information. For example, your classroom audience probably will comprise many people, including some extremely intelligent and able students. Nevertheless, even intelligent people do not necessarily know a great deal about those subjects they are familiar with. Recently, a young woman speaking in her class mentioned the name of Adolf Hitler and proceeded to say that Hitler was a twentieth-century example of tremendous oppression. She was quite surprised when many of the people in her audience had vaguely unknowing expressions.

In most of your speeches, then, you will want to make sure you take time to give details about information that you regard as key to audience understanding of your topic. Your ability to do this depends on how well you have analyzed your audience. Recall that a good audience analysis includes predicting the audience's knowledge level for your topic.

Even when you are talking about a topic that most of the people in your audience are familiar with, you can uncover new angles, new applications, or new perspectives on the material. For example, if you plan to talk about football, it is likely that most people will know what the game of football is and how points are scored. But a speech on zone defenses may provide new information even to listeners who think they have a pretty good grasp of football. The idea is not to change the topic but to keep thinking about the topic in different ways until you have uncovered an aspect that will be new to most of the audience.

New information is even better received when it is novel. *Novelty* is newness with a twist, something unexpected that commands our attention. In a speech on the perils of cliff diving, for example, an audience is likely to listen because of the novelty of the topic itself. But if a topic is not novel, the next best thing is to identify specific features of the topic that will be perceived as novel. For instance, for a segment of your speech on computers, you may be able to focus on advancements in voice-activated word processing that are leading to the development of computers that will turn speech directly into printed messages on the monitor.

Relevance of Information

Principle 4
Audiences are more likely to listen to and understand information they perceive to be relevant.

Rather than acting like a sponge to absorb every bit of information that comes our way, most of us act more like filters: We listen only to that information we perceive to be relevant. *Relevance* is the personal value that people see in information and refers to how much information relates to audience needs and interests. Relevance might be called the "need to know."

Vital information, information that is seen as truly a matter of life or death, is the ultimate in relevance. Police cadets, for instance, will see information explaining what they should do when attacked as vital. Similarly, students may perceive information that is necessary to their passing a test as vital. If you can show your listeners that your speech information is critical to their well-being, they will be more likely to listen.

For your speeches you must ask yourself whether the material you plan to present is truly important to the audience. If so, you will want to emphasize that point in your speech. Some topics and some information are highly relevant on their own. People look for information that affects them personally. For example, in Cincinnati the Labor Day fireworks have attracted national attention. On that day some 300,000 to 500,000 people attempt to see the fireworks in person—at least that many more watch them on television. Thus, several weeks before the event a speech on strategies for seeing the fireworks would be highly relevant.

Developing relevance is more of a challenge when your information seems far removed from audience experience. Still, you usually can build relevance if you think creatively and take the time to work at it. For example, a speech on Japan can focus on the importance of Japanese manufacturing to our economy; a speech on the Egyptian pyramids can be related to our interest in building techniques. Audience relevance can be shown for *any* topic. It is up to you to determine what your audience needs to know and how your information meets those needs.

Although relevance is important throughout the speech, you should be sure to emphasize it in your introduction. Suppose you were giving a speech to show the class the steps used to compute readability levels. As class members listen to such a speech, they are sure to ask themselves, "Why should I listen to a speech on readability?" The following opening shows the relevance of readability levels to college students:

> Have any of your textbooks just given you fits? Have you found yourself saying, "I just can't seem to understand this stuff"? Most of us have. Although we may have a gut reaction that the book's at fault, we are equally likely to blame our own lack of concentration. Yet, many times your gut reaction is correct. How can you tell whether the book is at fault? Perhaps the best way is by taking a few minutes to determine the readability level of the text. Today, I'm going to show you how you can quickly and easily test the readability level of any of your textbooks.

Emphasis of Information

Principle 5

Audiences are more likely to understand and to remember information that is emphasized.

To help audiences retain information, a speaker must use devices that give the listener oral and verbal cues.

To make the best use of emphasis, you must determine what it is that you want the audience to retain. Because it is unrealistic to expect an audience to remember every word or every idea of your speech, you must help by prioritizing information. Think of your speech as comprising not only the highest priority information—that is, the information that you want everyone in the audience to remember—but also information that is likely to be lost over time.

The highest priority information should include your specific goal, the main points of the speech, and key facts that give meaning to the main points. If you were giving a speech on evaluating diamonds, you would want to make sure that the audience remembered: (1) That it heard a speech on the four criteria for evaluating a diamond (the goal); and (2) that the four criteria are carat (the weight of the diamond), clarity (the purity of the diamond), color (the tint of the diamond), and cutting (the shaping of the diamond). These are the main points. In addition you would hope that the audience would remember the following facts: (1) That a carat weighs 200 milligrams; (2) that clarity is marred by internal blemishes, such as bubbles, feathers, clouds, and inclusions, all of which detract from diamond purity; (3) that the most expensive diamonds are without color; and (4) that diamonds can be cut into six common shapes—emerald, oval, marquise, brilliant, heart, and pear.

Once you have identified your highest priority information, you can plan a strategy for increasing the retention of that information. The following specific devices can be used in this strategy: repeating information, using external transitions, suggesting memory aids, using humor, and using visual aids.

Repeat Information

Repetition is the easiest, but often the most abused, device for increasing emphasis. Repeating a key item of information increases its likelihood of later recall. Thus, during a speech on diamonds, one of the easiest ways to emphasize the fact that a carat equals 200 milligrams is to repeat it. "Today the weight of a carat has been standardized at 200 milligrams—that's 200 milligrams." Because repetition is so easy, speakers sometimes abuse it by repeating ten or fifteen different items in a speech. But when overdone, repetition loses its power. Use repetition for emphasis only a few times in a speech.

Lead the Audience Through the Speech with External Transitions

Recall from the discussion of emphasis in the chapter on language that another emphasis method is announcing to the audience how it is supposed to regard the coming material. If, for instance, you want the audience to remember that clarity is the second criteria for evaluating a diamond, you might say, "I now come to the second criteria that you will want to remember. The second criteria for evaluating a diamond is clarity, the purity of the diamond."

The value of transitions as signposts and emphasizers cannot be overemphasized. From the speaker's standpoint, everything you say is a gem. But from the listener's standpoint, each sentence you utter is just another group of words. And because listener's minds may wander, you must exercise control in how you want the audience to perceive what you say. I have heard listeners swear that a speaker never stated the second main point of the speech when in reality the point was stated, but in a way that had no effect on the audience. External transitions help your audience recognize where you are in the speech and why your point is significant.

Suggest Memory Aids

Good listeners create memory aids for themselves when they really want to remember. Good speakers help good listeners by suggesting memory aids for use during a speech. In describing the criteria for evaluating diamonds, suppose the speaker said, "There are four criteria: weight, clarity, tint, and shape." Although these four criteria may be remembered, notice how the speaker can help the audience by labeling the four with words that all start with "C": "There are four C's of evaluation: carat, clarity, color, and cutting."

Another kind of a memory aid is association. *Association* is the tendency of one thought to stimulate recall of another similar thought. That means that when one word, idea, or event reminds you of another, you are associating. Suppose that you are trying to help the audience remember the value of color in a diamond. Because blue is the most highly prized tint and yellow or brown tints lower diamond value, you might try to get the audience to associate blue tint with "the blue ribbon prize" and yellow (or brown) tint with "a lemon." Thus, the best diamond gets the "blue ribbon" and the worst diamond is a "lemon." It is quite likely that these two associations will help your audience's retention immensely.

Associations naturally fall into categories of similes and metaphors. Recall that a simile is a comparison using "like" — "The blue tint is like a blue ribbon." A metaphor is a direct comparison, "Yellow tinted diamonds are lemons." I still remember vividly a metaphor I heard a student use in a speech nearly twenty years ago. The student explained the functioning of a television tube by saying, "A television picture tube is a gun shooting beams of light." If you make your associations striking enough, your audience will remember your point as well as I remember that point about how a television tube works.

Use Humor to Cement a Point

Another way to emphasize a point is through *humor*. Audiences are likely to remember the point of a humorous story. For instance, suppose you were giving a speech on the importance of perspective. Your highest priority point might be that because a problem that seems enormous at the moment might turn out to be minor in a few days, being able to put events into perspective saves a great deal of psychological wear and tear. Then to cement the point you might tell the following story:

> A first-time visitor to the races bet two dollars on the first race on a horse that had the same name as his elementary school. The horse won and the man was ten dollars ahead. In each of the next several races he bet on horses such as "Apple Pie," his favorite, and "Kathie's Prize," his wife's name, and he kept winning. By the end of the sixth race he was 700 dollars ahead. He was about to go home when he noticed that in the seventh race, Seventh Veil was scheduled in the number seven position, and was currently going off at odds of seven to one. The man couldn't resist — he bet his entire 700 dollars. And sure enough, the horse came in seventh. When he got home his wife asked, "How did you do?" Very calmly he looked at his wife and said, "Not bad — I lost two dollars."

That's perspective.

Use Visual Aids

A final way to create interest and increase understanding as well as to emphasize is to present your ideas visually. You are more likely to emphasize your point if you can show it as well as talk about it. Visual aids

Checklist	Informative Speech Critique

Check all items that were accomplished effectively.

Specific Goal

_____ 1. Was the specific goal clear?

_____ 2. Was the specific goal designed to increase audience information?

Content

_____ 3. Was the speaker effective in establishing his or her credibility on this topic?

_____ 4. Did the speaker get and maintain audience interest in the information throughout the speech?

_____ 5. Was the speaker able to show the relevance of the information?

_____ 6. Did the speaker have information that was new to the audience?

_____ 7. Did the speaker explain information in a way that helped the audience understand the information?

_____ 8. Did the speaker use _____ repetition? _____ transition? _____ association? _____ humor? _____ visual aids? to help the audience understand and/or retain the information?

_____ 9. Did the speaker show creativity in idea development?

Organization

_____ 10. Did the introduction _____ gain attention? _____ gain goodwill for the speaker? _____ lead into the speech?

_____ 11. Did the speech follow a _____ time order? _____ space order? _____ topic order? _____ causal order? _____ problem–solution order?

_____ 12. Was the order appropriate for the intent and content of this speech?

_____ 13. Did the conclusion _____ tie the speech together? _____ leave the speech on a high note?

Language

_____ 14. Was the language _____ clear? _____ vivid? _____ emphatic? _____ appropriate?

Delivery

_____ 15. Was the speech delivered _____ enthusiastically? _____ with good eye contact? _____ spontaneously? _____ with appropriate vocal variety and emphasis? _____ with good pronunciation? _____ with effective bodily action?

Evaluate the speech as (check one) _____ excellent, _____ good, _____ average, _____ fair, _____ poor.

Use the information from your check sheet to support your evaluation.

are so important to the informative-speaking process that the entire next chapter is devoted to their discussion.

Assignment
Evaluating Informative Speeches

1. Prepare a four- to six-minute informative speech. An outline is required. Criteria for evaluation will include means of ensuring interest, understanding, and retaining information.
2. Write a critique for at least one of the informative speeches you hear in class. Outline the speech. As you outline, answer the questions on the informative speech critique checklist.

Speech — Dyslexia

OUTLINE: INFORMATIVE SPEECH (4–7 Minutes)

Specific Goal: I want my audience to understand the nature, causes, symptoms, and treatments of dyslexia.

Introduction
I.   Try to read the following sentence (visual aid).
II. Dyslexia can be a frustrating disorder.

Thesis Statement: Dyslexia is a disorder that affects large numbers of people, has at least three potential causes, is characterized by any combination of six major symptoms, and is treated through drugs and education.

Body
I.   Dyslexia is a disorder that affects large numbers of children.
  A. Dyslexia is "a serious difficulty with reading that cannot be attributed to other causes."
  B. Dyslexia affects more than 10 percent of the population.
    1. More than 25 million people suffer from it.
    2. It affects four times as many boys as girls.
II. Dyslexia has several potential causes.
  A. Dyslexia may be caused by abnormalities in areas of the left hemisphere of the brain.
  B. Dyslexia may begin during fetal development because of abnormal levels of a male hormone.

C. Dyslexia may be caused by malfunctions in the inner ear.
III. Dyslexia is characterized by six symptoms that can occur in different combinations.
    A. Reading skills of dyslexics are far behind those of peers and without any apparent explanation.
    B. Letters, words, and numbers frequently are reversed.
    C. There is confusion between left and right with lack of preference.
    D. Speech reversals occur well past infancy.
    E. There is difficulty in learning and remembering printed words or symbols.
    F. There are problems with organizing and managing simple tasks.
IV. Dyslexia is treated with drugs and education.
    A. Drugs have shown both long-term and short-term effects.
    B. The greatest amount of emphasis has been on education.
      1. Dyslexics improve by tracing letters in the air and on paper.
      2. Dyslexics improve by repeating familiar sounds.
      3. Dyslexics improve by repeating words.
      4. Dyslexics learn through phonic analysis.

Conclusion

I. We have seen the nature of, the causes of, the symptoms of, and the treatment for dyslexics.
II. If Albert Einstein was able to contribute, others can.

Bibliography

Daugherty, Jimi. "Dyslexics: Learning to Cope with a Different View," *News Record* (February 24, 1984).

"Dealing with Dyslexia," *Newsweek* (March 22, 1982): 55–56.

"Details on Dyslexia," *Consumer Research Magazine* (August 1985): 38.

"Facts about Dyslexia," *Child Today* (November/December 1985): 23–27.

Kaercher, D. "Diagnosing and Treating Dyslexia," *Better Homes and Gardens* (August 1984): 119–120.

Levinson, Harold. *Smart but Feeling Dumb.* New York: Warner Books, 1985.

Read the following speech aloud at least once.[3] Examine it to see how well the topic has been limited, how substantial the research is, how well bibliographical citations have been introduced, and how creatively the information has been developed.

SPEECH

I'd like to ask you all to read this for a moment [speaker shows a visual aid].

Imagine for a moment just how frustrating it would be to have everything you read look as jumbled as this sentence.

As a result of this very good opening, the audience experiences first-hand the frustration of the dyslexic.

The speaker clarifies the four areas that she will cover in the speech.

Here the speaker begins the first main point. Although we get a good idea of where we are in the speech, the speaker needs to state the first point more specifically.

Notice that throughout the speech the speaker uses a great deal of specific material. Some of her material came from interviews (specifically, the material about the size of the problem) and some from written sources.

Good use of a quotation. I like the way she personalizes the material in this section.

Notice that the speaker gives short, but satisfactory, citations of the sources of supporting material.

Good transition to the causes, the second main point of the speech.

You probably found this effort a frustrating experience. What it said was, "Imagine for a moment just how frustrating it would be to have everything you read look as jumbled as this sentence." Yet, this is how people with dyslexia are likely to perceive what they read [refers again to visual aid]. Today, I'd like to help you understand the nature of dyslexia, its probable causes, its major symptoms, and its treatments.

Dyslexia is defined as "a serious difficulty with reading that cannot be attributed to other causes." According to Dr. Kaiser of the Office of Veterans Affairs and Handicapped Services here on the University of Cincinnati campus, about one in every ten Americans is affected by this problem. Roughly, that's more than 25 million Americans. Moreover, the disability occurs in four times as many boys as girls, and it affects adults as well as children. Many dyslexics are frustrated people living in a topsy-turvy world where nothing seems to go right. According to Earl Chambers, a Cincinnati graduate of a couple of years ago who is a dyslexic, "It's the not knowing that frustrates you," he says. "When facing a time-testing situation, for example, a dyslexic might panic at the thought of having to read and answer fifty questions and not ever have time to finish the test." Mary Lou Danefield, coordinator of disability programs in the Minnesota schools, says, "Dyslexia can be combated—but first it must be understood." Dyslexia is the most challenging of the learning disabilities that have been discovered in recent years. The point is that many children who in the past have been diagnosed as retarded and who are treated as untrainable may well be dyslexics who can be helped to lead a relatively normal life.

Although researchers have been studying dyslexia seriously for the past thirty years, the primary causes are still a mystery. Nevertheless, researchers have focused their studies on several potential causes. According to an article in the March 22, 1982, issue of *Newsweek*, researchers at the Beth Israel Hospital in Boston are in search of clues to the biological roots of dyslexia. Some researchers have found abnormalities in the left hemisphere of the brain associated with language development. Other researchers hypothesize that the disorders may result from damage to the left side of the brain during fetal development, perhaps due to abnormal levels of a male hormone. These researchers point to the fact that there is an increased rate of left-handedness among dyslexics. Some recent research has suggested that dyslexia is linked to a defect on the fifteenth chromosome. From a different angle, Dr. Harold Levinson, in his book *Smart but Feeling Dumb*, chronicles his efforts to validate the hypothesis that brain dysfunction comes from inner ear problems. Researchers are hoping that by eventually pinpointing causes, they will discover means of prevention.

Whatever the causes of dyslexia, researchers are in agreement about the major symptoms. While a trained psychologist is the best judge of when dyslexia occurs, he is likely to look especially for these six symptoms or combination thereof.

One symptom is exhibition of reading skills that are far behind those of peers *without any apparent explanation*. We're aware that many retarded children have reading difficulties — but we're talking about otherwise normal people.

A second is the frequent reversal of letters or numbers in both reading and writing — *God* for *dog* or *was* for *saw*, for example.

A third is confusion between left and right and the lack of preference for using one hand over the other. By the age of six, most children develop a hand preference — dyslexics may not.

A fourth symptom is reversal in speech well past infancy. For example saying *aminal* instead of *animal*.

A fifth is serious difficulty in learning or remembering any kind of printed words or symbols. When confronted with the number 537, for instance, the dyslexic may not recognize it and, if he or she can recognize it, may quickly forget it.

A sixth problem is organizing simple patterns — a difficulty in following simple instructions. A dyslexic might not be able to respond correctly to "Walk to the first stop light, turn right, and go to the third house."

Now that we have looked at the nature, suspected causes, and symptoms, let's move on to the treatment of dyslexia. According to Dr. C. Keith Conners of the Children's Hospital National Medical Center, and reported in *Newsweek*, dyslexia is like alcoholism: "It is never really cured." But, nearly every dyslexic can achieve a sixth-grade reading level, and dyslexics have finished college and gone on to graduate school.

Dyslexia is being treated by drugs and by education. Some researchers who are trying to deal with root causes are experimenting with drug therapy. For instance, Dr. Levinson is working with antihistamines to deal with what he believes are inner ear problems. Another treatment of dyslexia is with a drug called piracetam, which resembles a brain chemical. It has proved somewhat effective in treatment by aiding transmission between two hemispheres of the brain. But to date the best treatment for dyslexia is education. Dyslexics can be helped to improve their condition by professionals who work on a one-to-one basis to help them do activities like tracing letters in the air or on paper until they become familiar with the letters. Another educational method is the use of spelling. By learning and repeating a letter time and time again, dyslexics become familiar with the way that letter is pronounced. The third form of treatment is through the use of phonics. They are taught to sound out letters rather than to memorize whole words.

By learning more about dyslexia — by understanding the causes, symptoms, and treatment — we can better understand this disorder that affects so many people. If Albert Einstein, Woodrow Wilson, and Nelson Rockefeller, who were dyslexics, were able to deal with their problems, we should certainly be able to hope for the best.

A clear statement of the specifics of treatment, drugs, and education.

A good job of comparing the value of treatments. She shows that although there has been some success with drugs, the greater success has been with education.

Good short summary.

Excellent final point. It leaves the speech on an upbeat note.

Summary

A speech is considered informative when your intention as a speaker is to share information for purposes of getting understanding, when the information functions to clarify and explain, and when the audience respects you as an objective source of information without ulterior motives.

Your rhetorical challenge then is determining what you can do in your speech to help your audience learn the information that you present. Learning is usually considered to be a result of three factors: attending to or showing interest in the information being presented, understanding that information, and retaining the information in a form that results in the ability to recall the information on demand. To get audience attention, facilitate understanding, and increase retention, you must consider principles related to creativity, credibility, newness, relevance, and emphasis.

First, audiences are more likely to show interest in, understand, and remember information that is presented creatively, that is by using your material in an imaginative way. You can increase your chances of speaking creatively by having enough information so that you can make choices, giving yourself enough time to let the creative process work, and forcing yourself to practice sections of the speech in different ways.

Second, audiences are more likely to attend to your speech if they like, trust, and have confidence in you and your information. Most definitions of credibility include competence, intention, character, and personality. In order to develop your credibility in your speeches you need to be well prepared, emphasize your interest in the audience, and look and sound enthusiastic. In addition, in your classroom speeches you need to be ready to speak on time and you need to evaluate others' speeches thoughtfully.

Third, audiences are more likely to listen to information they perceive to be new. When members of your audience think they already know the information you are presenting, they are less likely to pay attention. It is up to you as a speaker not only to find information that will be new to your audience but also to feature the newness.

Fourth, audiences are more likely to listen to and understand information they perceive to be relevant. Relevance is the personal value people see in information. For your speeches you must ask yourself whether the material you are planning to present is really important to the audience. If so, you will want to emphasize that in the speech.

Fifth, audiences are more likely to understand and to remember information that is emphasized. To help audiences retain information a speaker must use devices that give the listener oral and verbal cues. You can emphasize information through repetition, by leading the audience through the speech with external transitions, and by using such memory aids as association, humor, and visual aids.

Notes

1. Ralph Waldo Emerson, *Natural History of Intellect and Other Papers* Vol. 12 (New York: AMS Press, 1979), 91.
2. John W. Haefele, *Creativity and Innovation* (New York: Reinhold, 1962), 6.
3. Delivered in speech class, University of Cincinnati. Used with permission of Kelley Kane.

Chapter 9   Using Visual Aids

Although visual aids may be a part of any speech, they play a primary role in many informative-speaking contexts. For instance, at business meetings, visual aids are major means of illustrating a company's profit and loss; at city council meetings visual aids are used to illustrate the progress of city projects; and in the classroom, visual aids emphasize and illustrate a professor's lectures.

A visual aid is a form of speech development that allows the audience to see as well as hear about the material. Visual aids are likely to take two forms in a speech: (1) as a means of showing verbal information so that audience members will gain visual as well as auditory impressions; (2) as a means of creating moods, emotions, and attitudes that supplement or take the place of verbal information.

The major rationale for the use of visual aids in any speech is that information is more likely to be understood and retained when oral expression is supplemented visually. Allan Pavio states the general theory that images manage to facilitate the development of verbal associations. Studies by Pavio and others have shown that memory for pictures often is remarkable, even over long periods.[1] Details may not be well retained, but more general features are remembered. Mandler and Ritchey studied retention and found that some pictorial information was retained without loss of accuracy for more than four months.[2] Whether a picture is worth a thousand words or not, research has shown that people learn considerably more when ideas appeal to both eye and ear than when they appeal to the ear alone.[3]

Kinds of Visual Aids

As you find material for your speeches, you should consider whether and how you might use visual aids to complement or supplement your verbal information. You will want to consider the following types of visual materials: yourself; objects; models; films, slides, and overhead projections; and various other kinds of visual aids.

You the Speaker

For many speeches, *you* may be your best visual aid. For instance, through descriptive gestures you can show the size of a soccer ball, the height of a tennis net, and the shape of a lake; through your posture and movement, you can show the correct stance for skiing, a butterfly swimming stroke, and methods of artificial respiration; and through your own attire, you can illustrate the native dress of a foreign country, the proper outfit for a mountain climber, cave explorer, or scuba diver, or the uniform of a firefighter, police officer, or soldier.

Objects

When your speech involves objects, the objects themselves may make good visual aids, provided that they are large enough to be seen and small enough to be carried with you. A vase, soccer ball, braided rug, and sword are the kinds of object that can be seen easily by an audience of ten to thirty-five people; these might not be appropriate for audiences of fifty or more. Thus, before you decide whether to use an object, you must consider whether it is appropriate for the size of your audience.

A common example of visual aids: the maps used by television weather reporters to graphically display the main features of the day's weather patterns. Notice that only selected information is presented — a complete picture would be overkill and would defeat the purpose of the graphic display.

Models

When an object is too large to bring to the speech site or too small to be seen, a model may prove a worthwhile substitute. A *model* is a representation used to show the construction of an object or to serve as a copy. If you were to talk about a turbine engine, a suspension bridge, an Egyptian pyramid, or the structure of an atom, a model might well be the best visual aid. Working models are especially eye-catching.

Graphic Visuals

Graphic visuals include pictures, photographs, drawings, charts, maps, and graphs.

Pictures and photographs are popular because they are readily available. Although both often give an accurate representation, they often are too small to be seen from more than a few rows away. Moreover, they usually include more detail than you need to make your point.

Figure 9.1

A sample drawing.

When you select a picture or photograph, make sure that the central features you wish to emphasize stand out. Colored items usually are better than those in black and white. Above all, you must be sure that they are large enough to be seen. The all-too-common apology "I know you can't see this picture but . . ." is of little help to an audience.

Drawings are popular visual aids because they are easy to prepare. If you can use a compass, a straightedge, and a measure, you can draw well enough for most speech purposes. For instance, if you are making the point that water skiers must hold their arms straight, with the back straight and knees bent slightly, a stick figure (see Figure 9.1) will illustrate the point every bit as well as an elaborate, lifelike drawing. Stick figures may not be as aesthetically pleasing as professional drawings, but they work just as well. In fact, elaborate, detailed drawings are not worth your time and effort and actually may obscure the point you wish to make. If your prospective drawing is too complicated for you to handle personally, then you may need professional help.

The major problems that people encounter with drawing visual aids involve size, color, and neatness. For some reason, people tend to make drawings and letterings far too small for everyone in the audience to see easily. What looks like large printing to you the drawer when you are only a foot away may be too small to be seen even twenty-five feet away. To test the size of lettering, move as far away from the visual aid as the farthest person in your audience will be sitting. If you can read the lettering and see the details from that distance, then both are large enough; if not, you

Figure 9.2

A sample word chart.

```
Computer Essentials

1. Central Processing Unit
2. Memory
3. Input/Output
```

should draw another sample and check it for size. Color selection also may cause problems. Black or red on white always are good contrasts, but some color combinations simply cannot be seen well. So again, before you go very far in preparation, draw sample color contrasts and judge them from at least twenty-five feet away. Finally, make sure that the visual aid is neat. There is no excuse for offering a tattered piece of smudged paper as a visual aid.

Charts are graphic representations of material that compress a great deal of information into usable, easily interpreted form. The most common charts are word charts, maps, and graphs.

Word charts are used frequently to preview material that will be covered in the speech, to summarize material, and to remind the audience of where you are in the speech. For a speech on the parts of a computer, the speaker might make a word chart listing the items shown in Figure 9.2. To make the points more eye-catching, the speaker may use a picture or a sketch to portray each word visually. Dover Publications has published a series of ready-to-use black-and-white illustrations of silhouette spot illustrations, sale announcements, and art nouveau borders that can be purchased for a few dollars each.[4]

A chart also is used to show organization, chains of command, or steps of a process. The chart in Figure 9.3 illustrates the organization of a student union board. Charts of this kind lend themselves well to what is called the "striptease" method of showing. The speaker prints the words on a large piece of cardboard, covers each word or phrase with pieces of cardboard or paper mounted with small pieces of cellophane tape, and then removes the cover to expose that portion of the chart as he or she reaches each point.

Maps are charts indicating key locations of a geographical territory. Maps allow you to focus on physical details such as mountains, rivers, and

Figure 9.3

A sample organizational chart.

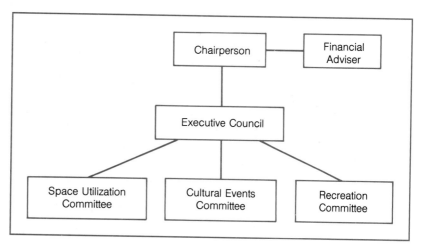

Figure 9.4

A sample map.

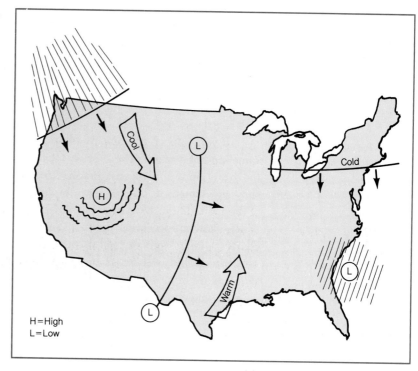

valleys; on the location of cities, states, nations, parks, and monuments; on automobile, train, boat, and airplane routes; or on statistical patterns; and so on. You can make a map that includes only the details you wish to show. For instance, the weather map in Figure 9.4 is a good example of a map that focuses on selected details.

Figure 9.5

A sample line graph show-
ing population increase
from 1800–1980
(in millions).

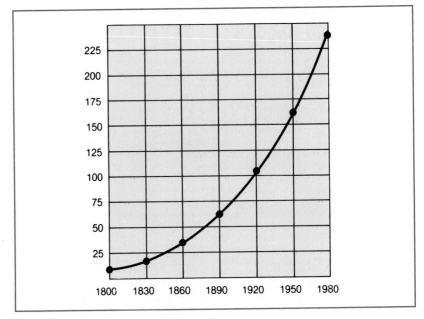

If your speech contains numbers, you may want to show them with some kind of a graph. The three most common types are the line graph, the bar graph, and the pie graph. Line charts are especially good for showing changes in time. If you were giving a speech on the population of the United States, for example, you could use the *line graph* in Figure 9.5 to show a population increase, in millions, from 1800 to 1990. Bar charts — graphs with vertical or horizontal bars — may be used to show relationships between two or more variables at the same time or at various times on one or more dimensions. For instance, if you were giving a speech on gold, you could use the *bar graph* in Figure 9.6 to show comparative holdings of the International Monetary Fund (IMF) and of world governments in gold (1985). Pie charts may be used to show the relationship among parts of a single unit. Although many chartmakers suggest putting the most important material to the right or to the left of 12 o'clock on the pie chart, try to finish the chart in a way that is appealing to the eye. For instance, in any speech where you want to show distribution of a whole, such as employment in Greater Cincinnati by industry category in 1986, a *pie graph* such as the one in Figure 9.7 could be used.

Figure 9.6

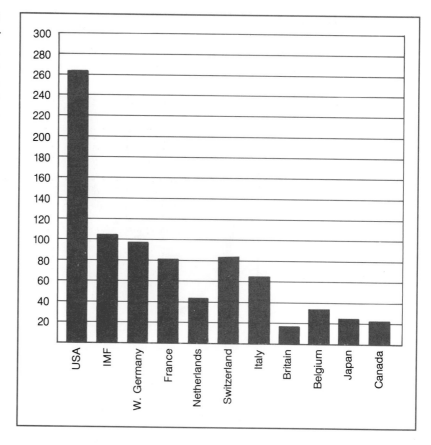

Comparative holdings of gold in 1985 by world governments that are IMF members (in millions of fine troy ounces). (Source: 1987 World Almanac.)

A flipchart is an excellent method of displaying a series of charts. A flipchart basically is a large pad of paper mounted on an easel. Today you can get flipcharts (and easels) in any of several sizes. For a presentation to four or five executives, a small table-top version may be used; for any larger audience you would be wise to use a larger size — one of the most widely used is the 30- × 40-inch chart.

When designing your flipcharts, leave several blank sheets between each chart. If you make a mistake in writing, you can tear out that sheet without disturbing the order. After you have finished all of the charts, you can tear out all but one sheet between each chart. The one sheet serves both as a transition page and as a cover sheet. Because you want your audience to focus on your words and not on unused visual material, when you finish a chart, you can flip to the empty page while you talk about

Figure 9.7

Breakdown of Greater Cincinnati employment, by industry category, in percent. (Source: Ohio Bureau of Employment Services, September 1986.)

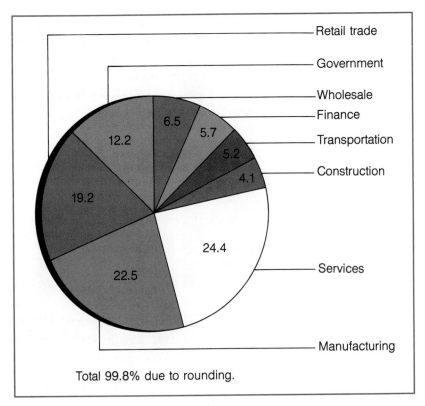

Total 99.8% due to rounding.

material not covered by your charts. The empty page between charts also ensures that heavy lines or colors from the next chart will not show through.

Films, Slides, and Overhead Projections

FILMS Although films may be beautifully done, they seldom are appropriate for speeches, mostly because they are so dominant that the speaker loses control. Occasionally it is possible that you may want to use short clips of no more than a minute or two each during a longer speech. Still, because using a film requires darkening a room, its use in a speech often is counterproductive.

SLIDES Slides are mounted transparencies that can be projected individually. The advantage of slides over film is that you can control when they will be shown. For instance, for a speech on scenic attractions in

London, a speaker might have one or more slides of the Tower of London, the British Museum, Buckingham Palace, and the Houses of Parliament, talking about each as long as necessary. But like films, their use requires a darkened room and so it is easy for less accomplished speakers to lose control of their audience. If you decide to use slides, make sure that the images are clear and sharp.

OVERHEAD PROJECTIONS An overhead projector is a machine that projects the image on a transparency onto a screen. Overheads often are the first choice in professional presentations because they can be made easily and inexpensively. They work well in nearly any setting, and unlike other kinds of projections, they do not require dimming room lights. Moreover, overheads are useful especially for showing how formulas work, for illustrating various computations, or for analyzing data — you can write, trace, or draw on the transparency while you talk.

Perhaps the major reason why overhead transparencies are the choice of many professional speakers is because they are relatively easy to make and, depending on the way they are made, can achieve truly professional quality. Transparencies can be handmade (either traced or hand-lettered) or machine-made (photocopied, thermographed, color lifted, or computer-drawn).

If you make overhead transparencies yourself, you probably will want to mount them in a way that avoids light leakage, makes them easier to store, and provides space for notes to yourself.

For a truly professional appearance, you may want to examine a book that is devoted specifically to the making and use of overhead transparencies, such as Lee Green's *501 Ways to Use the Overhead Projector.*[5]

Other Kinds of Visual Aids

CHALKBOARD As a means of visually portraying simple information, the chalkboard, a staple in every college classroom, is unbeatable. Unfortunately, the chalkboard also is easy to misuse and overuse. For instance, students and teachers often err by writing too much material while they talk, which often results in material that is either illegible or at least partly obscured by their body while they write. In addition, speakers tend to spend too much time talking to the board instead of to the audience.

Moreover, it is unlikely that the chalkboard would be your first choice for any major analysis of process or procedure. Yet effective use of the chalkboard should be a part of a speaker's repertoire, so let us analyze its strengths and weaknesses.

People are likely to use the chalkboard in an impromptu fashion because it happens to be available. Good visual aids, however, require considerable preplanning to achieve their greatest value. Keep in mind that anything that can be done with a chalkboard can be done better with the various pre-prepared visual aids that we have discussed.

If you still want to use the chalkboard, either put the material on the board before you begin or use the board for only a few seconds at a time. The chalkboard is best for short items of information that can be written in a few seconds. If you plan to draw your visual aid on the board before you begin, get to the speech site well before time so that you can complete your drawing beforehand. You may want to cover what you have done in some way. If you use the board for a classroom speech, it is not fair to your classmates to spend class time completing your visual aid. If you plan to draw or to write while you talk, practice doing so. If you are right-handed, stand to the right of what you are drawing. Try to face at least part of the audience while you work. Although it may seem awkward at first, your effort will allow your audience to see what you are doing while you are doing it.

COMPUTER GRAPHICS   With the ever-increasing advancements in computer graphics, computers have become a primary vehicle for producing visuals beforehand and then developing visuals during a presentation. Today's computers are so easily accessible and so advanced in capabilities that any professional speaker should experiment with computer graphics to prepare visual material for speeches. If you have not tried a presentation graphics package or if you are unsure of which to try and what its capabilities might be, you should investigate various reviews of graphics in computer magazines, such as *PC Magazine*'s 1989 review of seven of the best programs.[6]

When you learn to use one of the many computer graphics packages you will find that with a few computer key strokes or with the click of a "mouse" you can change lines of facts and figures into a variety of graphic displays. One caution comes with the construction of visual aids, however, especially with computer graphics: Speakers can become so excited about visuals that they forget that visuals are not the primary focus of a speech. Visuals are only aids. That is, they are but another form of developmental material that supports, elaborates, or emphasizes verbal material. Even when visuals are computer-developed and the product of the highest level of technology, they are still only aids. Thus, in preparing your analysis of a process, your primary questions are, "What kinds of visuals would make the best aids for this speech and audience?" and "What are the best uses that I can make of these aids in my speech?"

Using Visual Aids

As with any other speech skill, you must practice using visual aids to get the most from them. The following are useful guidelines for you to consider in your practice:

1. *Plan carefully when you are going to use your visual aids.* As you practice your speech, you may want to make notes on your outline indicating when and how you will use each visual aid.

2. *Carefully consider the needs of your audience.* Your use of visual aids is determined not only by the nature of your material, but also by the needs of your audience. If your audience would find it easier to understand and remember a portion of your speech, then using a visual aid at that point is appropriate. On the other hand, regardless of how exciting a visual may be, if it does not contribute directly to the audience's attention to, understanding of, or retention of information on your topic, then you may want to reconsider its use.

3. *Show visual aids only when you are talking about them.* You are competing with visual aids for attention. When you use a visual aid to make a point, you expect the audience's attention to be directed to it. But if your visual aids are still in view when you talk about something else, the audience will be inclined to continue to look at them. Thus, when the visual aid is not contributing to the point you are making, keep it out of sight. For instance, if you are using a chart, either have it face down on a table or covered if it is on a tripod. As soon as you are done, either return it to its face-down position or recover it. If you are using a projection, turn off the machine when you are not talking about the visual aid.

4. *Talk about the visual aid while you are showing it.* Although a picture may be worth a thousand words, you know what you want your audience to see in the picture. You should tell your audience what to look for, explain the various parts, and interpret figures, symbols, and percentages.

5. *Display visual aids so that everyone in the audience can see them.* If you hold the visual aid, do it away from your body and point it toward the various parts of the audience. If you place your visual aid on a chalkboard or easel or mount it in some other way, stand to one side and point with the arm nearest the visual aid. If it is necessary to roll or fold the visual aid, mount it to the chalkboard or wall with transparent tape so that it does not roll or wrinkle.

6. *Talk with your audience, not to your visual aid.* You may need to look at the visual aid occasionally, but you want to maintain eye contact with your audience as much as possible to see its reaction to

your visual material. When speakers become too engrossed in their visual aids, they tend to lose audience contact entirely.

7. *Do not overdo the use of visual aids.* You can reach a point of diminishing returns with visual aids. If one is good, two may be better; if two are good, three may be better. But somewhere along the line, you will reach a point where one more visual aid is one too many. Because they are a form of emphasis, showing too many visual aids will result in no emphasis at all. First, decide which visual aids would be of the most informative value. If you have no real purpose for the visual aid, then omit it. Second, determine exactly what you want to achieve with the aid. If you are not sure, then do not use it. Keep in mind that a visual aid is an *aid* and not a substitute for good speechmaking. There is no specific number that is best, but as you practice your speech you will get a sense of which visual aids are central to your goal and which are extraneous.

8. *Pass objects around the audience at your own risk.* People look at, read, handle, and think about whatever they hold in their hands; and while they are so occupied, they may not be listening to you. If you decide that passing out objects will be helpful, keep control of your listeners' attention by telling them what they should be looking at and when they should be listening to you. Anytime you actually put something in your listeners' hands, you are taking a gamble; make a conscious decision whether it is worth the risk.

Assignment
Using Visual Aids

1. Prepare a three- to six-minute informative speech in which visual aids are the major kind of supporting material. An outline is required. Criteria for evaluation will include selection and use of visual aids. For an example of a speech using visual aids, refer to the sample speech on juggling on pages 224–227 of Chapter 10.

2. Write a critique of one or more of the speeches you hear in class. As you outline the speech, answer *yes* or *no* to the following questions about visual aids. (To assist you in a complete analysis of the speech, you may also want to answer the list of questions on page 193 in Chapter 8 that deal specifically with informative speeches.)

Visual Aids

_____ Did the speaker select and construct useful visual aids?
_____ Were the visual aids and any printing or drawing large enough to be seen clearly by everyone in the audience?
_____ Did the speaker explain the visual aids?

_____ Did the speaker show the visual aids so that everyone could see them?

_____ Did the speaker talk to the audience and not to the visual aid?

_____ Did the speaker overdo the number of visual aids?

_____ As objects were passed around to the audience, was the speaker still able to keep audience attention on the speech?

Summary

Although visual aids are useful for any kind of speech, they are especially appropriate for informative speeches.

The most common kinds of visual aids are the speaker; objects; models; pictures, drawings, and sketches; charts; films, slides, and projections; and the chalkboard. Advancements in computer graphics give the speaker a wide range of flexibility in creating professional-looking visual materials.

Major guidelines for using visual aids are: (1) show visual aids only when you are talking about them, (2) talk about a visual aid while you are showing it, (3) display visual aids so that everyone in the audience can see them, (4) communicate with the audience, and not the visual aid, (5) strive for an optimal number of visual aids, and (6) pass objects around the audience at your own risk.

Notes

1. Allan Pavio, _Imagery and Verbal Processes_ (New York: Holt, Rinehart & Winston, 1971, 1979).

2. J. M. Mandler and G. H. Ritchey, "Long-Term Memory for Pictures," _Journal of Experimental Psychology: Human Learning and Memory_, 3 (1977), 386–396.

3. Bernadette M. Gadzella and Deborah A. Whitehead, "Effects of Auditory and Visual Modalities in Recall of Words," _Perceptual and Motor Skills_, 40 (February 1975), 260.

4. Write Dover Publications, Inc., 31 East 2nd Street, Mineola, NY 11501, for a free *Complete Dover Pictorial Archive Catalog*. You also may be able to find copies of these Dover publications at art supply or bookstores.

5. Lee Green, *501 Ways to Use the Overhead Projector* (Littleton, Colo.: Libraries Unlimited, Inc., 1982).

6. Robin Raskin, "The Packages Behind the Presentation," *PC Magazine*, (October 17, 1989), 95–145. This article reviews "Xerox Presents," "Lotus Freelance Plus," "Graph Plus," "Harvard Graphics," "The Graphics Gallery Collection," "Kinetic Graphics System," and "SlideWrite Plus."

Chapter 10 | Demonstrating Processes

Perhaps one of the most common informative speeches is the demonstration of a process. In businesses, trainers give numerous demonstrations to new employees on such topics as using computer packages and operating and caring for office equipment; in manufacturing plants, engineers demonstrate how their designs for new machinery will save time and money.

Although a *demonstration* usually involves a hands-on explanation of a process, for our purposes we will define a *demonstration* as any speech in which the speaker attempts to show the audience how to do something, how to make something, or how something works. Sometimes it is a complete hands-on, step-by-step demonstration, and sometimes it is a partial demonstration using various visual aids instead of actual demonstration. Thus, you demonstrate a process when you *show* an audience how to get more power on a forehand table-tennis shot, how to make fettucine noodles at home, or how to purify water.

To make effective demonstrations, a speaker needs the audience to accept his or her personal expertise, a clear time-order organization, and facility with the materials of the demonstration.

Speaker Expertise

In Chapter 8, "Principles of Informative Speaking," we indicated that audiences are more likely to attend to your speech if they like, trust, and have confidence in you and your information.

In this section we want to consider the specifics you must concern yourself with to ensure that your audience will accept your credibility to demonstrate a particular process.

You have a special advantage when the audience recognizes your expertise before the speech. For instance, with the recent popularity of Cajun cooking, sponsors of a speech would know that they could fill the hall if they could advertise Paul Prudhomme, the man who may be most singularly responsible for the national fascination with this Louisiana cuisine. Nearly every city has a person who is recognized as the top chef in town; again, people will make a special effort to attend a meeting when that person is advertised as the key speaker.

If you have gained such personal reputation, you have a tremendous advantage. Why? Because experts become their own authorities. For instance, when Joe Montana talks about running the "two-minute-drill" in professional football, or when Anne Klein talks about creating stylish clothes, *they* become the most important sources. One of the purposes of research is to give yourself additional credibility for your speech. Thus, a relatively unknown person talking about football will quote from Joe Montana—just as a relatively unknown person talking about fashion will quote from Anne Klein.

If you do not have the kind of reputation that allows you to be your own best source, then you have to rely on other means to build your credibility.

First, as we have discussed throughout this text, your credibility will rise as people respect your choice of source material. In other words, the more qualified your sources of information, the greater your credibility will become. If you cannot build your credibility in any other way, then you can earn it by using the best information available.

Second, you can show that you have special facility with the process even though you do not enter your speech with that reputation. The speech that is used as a model at the end of this chapter uses this method very well. Nancy Grant was *showing* her audience how to juggle. At the start of the speech and at various other times she *demonstrated* her facility as a juggler. She was not simply talking about juggling, she was cultivating the perception of herself as an experienced juggler. Once the audience recognized her facility, they were even more willing to *learn* from her demonstration.

Many informative speaking situations call for skill in combining words and example to demonstrate how something is done.

Another value of experience is that you can discuss the process in a way that shows that you know the possible variations and can tell the audience which aspects must be done a certain way and which may be done another way. People who are expert cooks, for example, know the kinds of variations that need to be made to even a "kitchen-tested" recipe to help the inexperienced cook avoid the risk of at least partial failure. They can talk about when Egg Beaters or another egg substitute will work in a recipe and when it will not, or why letting a sauce sit for even a minute too long can mean disaster. As a result of expertise, you can guide your listeners in a way that would be impossible for someone with only "book learning."

Organizing Steps

Chapter 4, "Organizing Speech Material," pointed out that a time order usually is the best organization for a process speech. Moreover, it was noted that a speech is best when it has only three to five main points. But as any experienced person learns, all but the simplest processes require many explanatory steps. The question then becomes, "What do I do when the process seems to have nine, eleven, or even fifteen steps?" Of course, you cannot leave any of them out. As a knowledgeable speechmaker you must redefine the steps in a way that seems to result in five or fewer steps. To do this, you will need to organize by grouping steps into common units that can be understood and recalled easily.

One way to do this is by chunking material. *Chunking* is the process of grouping like ideas under common headings. Although you should not sacrifice accuracy for listening ease, you should use this principle whenever possible. For example, if you have more than five steps, group them so that the end product is fewer than five. Audiences will remember three points, each with three or four subdivisions, better than they will remember ten points. Do you doubt this? If so, hand your book to someone else and have them read the ten steps below in column A. When done, see if the person can repeat the steps. Now have the person read the three steps in column B. Even though column B has thirteen items (three steps and a total of ten subdivisions) most people have much less difficulty in repeating them.

A

1. Gather the materials.
2. Draw the pattern.
3. Trace the pattern on wood.
4. Cut out the pattern so the tracing line can still be seen.
5. File to the pattern line.
6. Sandpaper edge and surface.
7. Paint the object.
8. Sand lightly.
9. Apply a second coat of paint.
10. Varnish.

B

1. Plan the job.
   A. Gather materials.
   B. Draw a pattern.
   C. Trace the pattern on wood.
2. Cut out the pattern.
   A. Saw so the tracing line can be seen.
   B. File to the pattern line.
   C. Sandpaper edge and surface.
3. Finish the object.
   A. Paint.
   B. Sand lightly.
   C. Apply a second coat of paint.
   D. Varnish.

Although both sets of directions are essentially the same, the redefinition of steps in column B enables an audience to visualize the process as having just three steps instead of ten. If the process you plan to explain seems to have more than five steps, you probably will be able to work out similar groupings. The "plan–do–finish" organization shown in column B is a common type of grouping for explaining how to make something. A little thought on the best way to group similar steps will pay dividends in audience understanding the recall. And during the speech, using strong transitions between steps will help reinforce the points to aid retention.

Although demonstrations usually are organized in a time order (like the one above), occasionally you will find that your material is best explained in a topical order. In such cases, the subdivisions of each topic usually will be discussed in a time order. For instance, you might want to demonstrate the three ways of making spares in bowling. Your main points would be the three topics: spot bowling, line bowling, and sight bowling. Each of the methods then could be demonstrated in terms of the steps involved.

Specific Goal: I want the audience to understand the three major ways of bowling for spares.

Thesis Statement: Spot bowling, line bowling, and sight bowling are the three major ways of bowling for spares.

   I.   One way to adjust your aim for spares is the spot-bowling method.

  II.   A second way to adjust your aim for spares is the line-bowling method.

 III.   A third way to adjust your aim for spares is the sight-bowling method.

If you used this topical organization for your speech on bowling, each main point then would be explained in a time, or chronological, order.

Visualizing Through Demonstration

Most of your process explanations will be complete or modified demonstrations.

The Complete Demonstration

When the task is relatively simple, you may want to use a complete demonstration in which you actually show the entire process while you talk about it. As mentioned, the model speech at the end of this chapter is a complete demonstration. If you decide to demonstrate the process, you should practice many times until you can do it smoothly and easily. A demonstration calls for having all the necessary materials or ingredients on hand, having enough time to complete the entire process, and having a means of demonstrating so that everyone in the audience can see what you are doing easily enough to follow along. As a result, complete demonstrations are best with relatively small audiences. When a person demonstrates a product in a department store, for example, usually only fifteen to thirty people can really see what is being done.

A complete demonstration has several potential problems. One is completing it professionally. Under the pressure of speaking before an audience, demonstrating even an apparently easy process can become quite difficult. Control of the material will be much more difficult in front of an audience than at home. Have you ever tried to thread a needle with twenty-five people watching you? Laudibly, Nancy Grant accomplished her juggling demonstration without a hitch, but it takes practice and strong nerves to juggle in front of an audience unless you are truly accomplished.

A second problem involves time. Demonstrations often take longer than planned. In practice you may be able to complete the demonstration in three minutes. But that same demonstration in front of an audience might take five to six minutes. Why? Because you will be conscious of the audience's attention. You will sense when the audience does not understand, and you will tend to slow down or develop the explanation more fully than you did during practice. Although this kind of adaptation is a sign of good speechmaking, it plays havoc with a tight time schedule.

As a result of these potential problems, you may want to select an alternative method to demonstrate your process.

Modified Demonstration

For a relatively complicated process, you may want to consider the modified demonstration, completing various stages of the demonstration at home and then doing only part of the actual work in front of the audience.

Suppose you were going to demonstrate the construction of a floral display. You would have a complete set of materials to begin the demonstration, a mock-up of the basic floral triangle, and a completed display. During the speech you would first talk about all the needed materials and then would begin demonstrating how to make the basic floral triangle. Rather than attempt to get everything together perfectly in a few seconds, you could remove the partially completed floral triangle from a bag or some other concealed place. You then would use this in your demonstration, adding flowers as if you were planning to complete it. From another bag you then might remove a completed arrangement that illustrated one of the effects you were discussing. Conducting a modified demonstration of this type often is easier than trying to complete an entire demonstration in a limited period of time.

Presentation in Demonstrations

Presentation in your demonstration will be improved by making sure that you speak slowly and work for audience participation.

Speak Slowly
Throughout your demonstration, speak slowly and repeat key ideas. When you demonstrate a process, it is important that an audience has time to absorb the details. Do not rush. Especially during the visualization steps, you want the audience to have a chance to think about the steps. Give the audience sufficient time to absorb your words and your visual aids. In addition to using strong transitions, you will want to repeat key ideas to increase audience retention.

Work for Audience Participation
We learn best by doing, so if you can include audience participation, you may be even more successful. In a speech on origami, or Japanese paper folding, you could explain the principles and then pass out paper and have audience members each make a figure. Actual participation will increase interest and ensure recall. Finally, through other visual aids you might show how these principles are used in more elaborate projects.

Assignment	1.	Prepare a three- to six-minute speech in which you show how something is made, how something is done, or how something works. An outline like that on pages 223–224 is required. Evaluation will focus on quality of the topic; selection, construction, and use of visual aids; and skill in organization and presentation. The following are the kinds of topics that would be appropriate for this assignment.

Assignment
Demonstrating
a Process

| **Checklist** | **Demonstration** |

Demonstration

Check all items that were accomplished effectively.

Specific Goal

_____ 1. Was the specific goal clear?

_____ 2. Was the specific goal appropriate for this assignment?

Content

_____ 3. Did the speaker have the necessary materials to demonstrate the process?

_____ 4. Did the speaker select or construct useful visual aids?

_____ 5. Were the materials used in the demonstration large enough to be seen clearly by everyone in the audience?

_____ 6. Did the speaker show expertise with the process?

_____ 7. Did the speaker use any special strategies to help the audience remember main points and other key information necessary to replicating the process?

Organization

_____ 8. Did the introduction _____gain attention? _____gain goodwill? _____lead into the speech?

_____ 9. Did the speech follow a time order?

_____ 10. If not, was the order appropriate for a process demonstration?

_____ 11. Were the steps grouped so that main points did not exceed five in number?

_____ 12. Did the conclusion _____tie the speech together? _____leave the speech on a high note?

Language

_____ 13. Was the language _____clear? _____vivid? _____emphatic? _____appropriate?

Delivery

_____ 14. Was the speech delivered _____enthusiastically? _____with good eye contact? _____spontaneously? _____with appropriate vocal variety and emphasis? _____with good pronunciation? _____with effective bodily action?

Evaluate the speech as (check one) _____excellent, _____good, _____average, _____fair, _____poor.

Use the information from your check sheet to support your evaluation.

How to Do It	How to Make It	How It Works
racing start	spinach soufflé	zone defense
racquetball killshot	fishing flies	helicopter
hanging wallboard	paper figures	compact disc
grading meat	wood carvings	photocopier

2. Write a critique of at least one demonstration you hear in class. As you listen to the speech, (1) take notes of the organization of the speech in outline form, and (2) use the demonstration checklist on page 222.

Speech — Juggling

OUTLINE: DEMONSTRATING A PROCESS

Specific Goal: I want my audience to understand the process of juggling.

Introduction
I. Watching a juggler on the David Letterman show motivated me to learn how to juggle.
II. Today, I want to show you the basics for learning the cascade, the basis for all advanced forms of juggling.

Thesis Statement: Learning to juggle involves choosing your weapon, getting into position, practicing basic tossing, and going for the cascade.

Body
I. Choose your weapon.
   A. The three types of objects for juggling are the ball, the club, and the ring.
   B. The ball is the easiest.
      1. You will not have to fight the rotation of a club.
      2. You will not have to fight the spin of a ring.
II. Get into position.
   A. Plant your feet.
   B. Position your arms.
      1. Keep your elbows at 90 degrees.
      2. Keep your forearms straight.

C. Keep your eye contact in front of you.
1. Focus high.
2. Don't follow the ball.
III. Practice basic tossing.
A. Start tossing with one ball.
1. Get a consistent height.
2. Keep a consistent distance from your body.
3. Practice with each hand.
4. Toss the ball back and forth.
B. Add a second ball.
1. Toss up and down with both hands.
2. Toss with one hand to the other.
C. Add the third ball.
1. Hold it in the hand you favor.
2. Hold it while you toss the other two.
IV. Go for the cascade.
A. Prepare physically.
1. Relax your muscles.
2. Breathe deeply.
B. Prepare mentally.
1. Concentrate.
2. Think in slow motion.
C. Toss the balls in the cascade.

Conclusion
I. I learned to juggle in about three weeks.
II. You can, too, if you will choose your weapon, get into position, practice your tosses, and begin the cascade.

Study this speech in terms of the topic's informative value, apparent knowledge and experience of the speaker, clarity of steps, and visualization of the process.[1] Read the speech through aloud at least once. After you have read and analyzed the speech, turn to the analysis in the other column.

Analysis

Notice how the opening captures audience interest and develops the speaker's expertise. I like the use of dialogue to help make the point.

SPEECH

One night on the David Letterman show, I saw a man juggle a chili dog, a mug of beer, and a slinky. As I watched him, I said to myself, "Nancy, if this man can juggle a chili dog, a mug of beer, and a slinky, you can certainly juggle three stupid beanbags. So I set off with a mission — to teach myself how to juggle. And I did. Today, I would like to teach you the four basic steps in juggling.

The first step is to choose your weapon. I call it a weapon because it can be just that when you're learning. You will see that it can fly out of control and break something or injure your dog. The three kinds of weapons a juggler will use are a ball-type, like these beanbags; a ring-type, like a Frisbee with a whole cut out; and a club-type, like an umbrella or a bowling pin. I suggest you begin with a ball-type. You have enough to worry about with three bags moving in front of your face to not have to worry about the spin of a ring or the rotation of a club [she juggled three beanbags as she completed this sentence]. When choosing your ball-type, make sure it is small enough to fit easily in the palm of your hand so you can catch it. It should be heavy enough so it will go in the air where you want it to and land firmly, unlike a Ping-Pong ball that goes where it wants to. Finally, get something that won't bounce. [She dropped a beanbag.] When you're starting to juggle you'll find that 90 percent of your time will be spent picking up. It's easier to pick up something that's landed at your feet than to chase a tennis ball across the room. For these three reasons, beanbags are ideal for learning.

The second step is to get into the proper position. Just as a batter needs to be in a certain stance to hit effectively, a juggler has to get into position to juggle. Start by planting your feet. This will give you balance and instill in your mind not to walk. Beginning jugglers have this nasty tendency to chase after the balls like this [she moved forward as she juggled]. Plant your feet. You cannot get control if you're running all over the room. Next, position your arms. You want your arms at your side with a 90-degree bend to your elbow and with your forearms straight, like this. Finally, you want your eyes focused high. You want your eyes focused where the *path* of the ball will go. If you let yourself follow the ball with your eyes, by the time you have three balls going, you're going to look like one of those little dogs in the back of people's cars with their heads bobbing back and forth as they go down the street.

The third step is to practice your tosses individually with each hand. Now this part can be a little monotonous, as you'll see. But practicing tosses is important to develop skill with each hand. Start with ball number one. Just toss it up and down like this until you get a consistent

The speech has four main points, and each is clearly stated.

I like the reference to "weapon" and her clever explanation of why she used such a designation.

A good explanation of the types of "weapons" and a good justification for beginning with the ball-type.

In this section we see why this speech is an excellent example of demonstration. Here and throughout the speech, the speaker uses herself and her beanbags as the primary visual aids.

"Unlike a Ping-Pong ball" is a good use of specific contrast.

Good explanation of why to use a nonbouncing ball-type object. In this section the speaker continues to show creativity of development.

Like the first main point, the second main point is clearly stated.

As a result of the speaker's method throughout this section, the audience was led to concentrate on her demonstration of the directions.

Here and in several other places the speaker uses humor to add to the effectiveness of her explanation. Through vivid description and precise word choice she is able to maintain a light touch — we enjoy listening to her explanations.

The third point is clearly stated.

height and consistent distance from your body. Then do it with your other hand. Okay, now begin to toss the bag from hand to hand. Now look at this diagram.

This is the only place in the speech where she uses a visual aid other than herself and her beanbags.

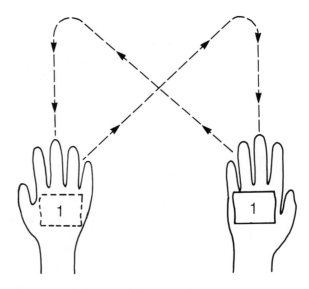

When you throw ball one, you want to aim at the point of the bow tie. You want to throw to that point and not to the middle. You want to throw it so that it reaches a high point here and then drops into your other hand. Now take ball two. Go back to tossing up and down until you get to the point where you can do it evenly, and then begin tossing from hand to hand again. Again, aim for that point. Now you're ready to add ball three. But don't juggle it. Hold it in your hand. Get the feel for it. And again just toss it from hand to hand like this. [She tossed the beanbag from hand to hand as she held the other bags, one in each hand.]

The way she goes through the demonstration, the audience gets a real sense of involvement.

This section is another example of the addition of personal touches that add to the informative value of the speech.

When you can feel it moving smoothly, you are ready to juggle. But there's something about releasing this third ball that will strike terror into the hearts of the bravest of us. I don't know why; it just does. Take a deep breath, relax your muscles, and concentrate: Think of these beanbags moving in front of your eyes as I do it. Think in slow motion. I know that while I'm doing this [she juggled the beanbags as she talked], to you guys it looks like these balls are going pretty fast, but they're not—in my mind they're moving slowly because I know I have enough time when I release the third ball to catch the first one.

Now, you're ready for the fourth step—to begin the cascade. Don't panic. Go for one turn. A turn is when all three balls change positions in your hands. When you've done it once, then do it again. Eventually you will be able to continue — that's juggling.

Now you may be asking yourself, Is it as easy as it looks? Yes, if you practice. It took me about three weeks till I could get to the point where I could keep the cascade going. And you can learn to do it too. Just follow my directions. Choose your weapons (start with something like these beanbags). Get into position. Practice your tosses. And finally, begin the cascade. Come on, you can all learn to do it — just juggle.

Summary

Demonstrating involves showing how to do something, how to make something, or how something works. The effectiveness of a demonstration depends on speaker expertise, organization of steps, and visualization through demonstration.

The greater your expertise, the more likely the audience will accept your credibility or authority with the demonstration. The greater the audience's acceptance of you, the more attention it will pay to your demonstration. In addition, the greater your expertise, the more likely you will be able to discuss the process comprehensively and show what variations in the process might improve the outcome.

Most demonstrations are accomplished by following a series of steps. When a process has more than five steps, you have to organize and group steps in a way that reduces them to a maximum of five.

You visualize a process through either a complete or a modified demonstration. A complete demonstration involves accomplishing all of the steps in front of the audience. In a partial demonstration, portions of the demonstration are completed before the speech so that you do not have to actually finish every detail in front of the audience.

Note

1. Delivered in speech class, University of Cincinnati. Used with permission of Nancy Grant.

Good conclusion. It lets the audience know what to expect and it summarizes the main points.

This is an excellent example of a demonstration speech.

Chapter 11	Describing

"Where is it located?" "How does it feel?" "What does it look like?" Questions such as these are answered by describing. Through description we are able to provide sensory impressions of sight, sound, touch, taste, and odor — in short, description answers to the question, "What is it like?"

Describing is an important skill for an informative speaker to cultivate, because showing what something is like may be used to get attention, increase understanding, and aid in retention. But in addition its use as a means of development in a speech, describing may be the speech's primary goal. For instance, travelogues are extremely popular types of descriptive informative speeches. Although visual aids are common speaker's aids in travelogues, in this chapter we focus on verbal description — creating mental images that are as sharp and meaningful as pictures.

Essentials of Description

Suppose a person begins her speech about the most impressive home on the Calvalcade of Homes tour with the following statement:

I was led into a family room so large that people standing at the far end seemed constructed on a smaller scale than I. The dominant feature of the room was a huge flagstone fireplace that was ten feet wide and extended upward more than twenty feet to the peak of a cathedral ceiling. On the inside of the fireplace was a grate that was large enough and strong enough to hold three logs that were at least ten inches in diameter and four to five feet long. The raging fire warmed the entire room. As I stood before it, I got a sense of what a fireplace must have been like in a medieval castle.

Can you *see* the fireplace? Can you picture its immensity? Speech is descriptive when it provides word pictures that allow the audience to mentally picture what you are talking about.

Effective Description

How do you describe accurately and vividly? Effective description requires at least two skills: (1) observing and (2) communicating the observation. The point cannot be overemphasized that description is a product of alert observation. Because effective description reflects firsthand observation, you must know first what to look for and then create accurate and vivid ways of reporting the essentials. You must be conscious of size, shape, weight, color, composition, age and condition, and the relationship among various parts.

SIZE How large is the object? Size is described subjectively by "large" and "small" and objectively by dimensions. But a description is more likely to be meaningful if it is comparative. For example, "The book, nine by six inches and three inches thick, is the same length and width as your textbook but more than twice as thick" is more descriptive than either "The book is a large one" or "The book is nine inches by six inches by three inches."

SHAPE What is the object's spatial form? Shape is described in terms of common geometric forms. *Round, triangular, oblong, spherical, conical, cylindrical,* and *rectangular* all are descriptive. A complex object is best described as a series of simple shapes. Because most objects do not conform to perfect shapes, you usually can get by with approximations and with comparisons to familiar objects. "The lake is round," "The lot is wedge-shaped," and "The car looks like a rectangular box" all give reasonably accurate impressions. Shape is clarified further by adjectives such as "jagged," "smooth," and "indented."

WEIGHT   How heavy is it? Weight is described subjectively as "heavy" or "light" and objectively by pounds and ounces. As with size, descriptions of weight are clarified by comparisons. Thus, "The suitcase weighed about 70 pounds; that's about twice the weight of a normally packed suitcase" is descriptive.

COLOR   What color is it? Although an obvious component of description, color is difficult to describe accurately. Although most people can visualize black and white, the primary colors (red, yellow, and blue), and their complements (green, purple, and orange), few objects are precisely these colors. Perhaps the best way to describe a color is to couple it with a common referent. For instance, "lemon yellow," "brick red," "green as a grape," or "sky blue" give rather accurate approximations.

COMPOSITION   What is it made of? The composition of an object helps us visualize it. A ball of aluminum does not look the same as a ball of yarn. A pile of rocks gives a different impression than does a pile of straw. A brick building looks different from a steel, wood, or glass building. Sometimes, you refer to what the object *seems like* rather than what it is. An object can appear metallic even if it is not made of metal. Spun glass can have a woolly texture. Nylon can be soft and smooth, as in stockings, or firm and sharp, as in toothbrush bristles.

AGE AND CONDITION   How old is it? What condition is it in? Whether an object is new or old can make a difference in its appearance. Because age by itself may not be descriptive, an object often is discussed in terms of condition. Although it is difficult to describe objectively, condition can be very important to an accurate description. The value of coins, for instance, varies tremendously depending on whether they are uncirculated or whether their condition is good or only fair. A 1917 Lincoln penny in fair condition may be worth two cents, while an uncirculated 1960 penny may be worth ten cents. Books become ragged and tattered, buildings become run-down and dilapidated, and land is subject to erosion. Age and condition together often prove valuable in developing informative descriptions.

RELATIONSHIP AMONG PARTS   First you may have to answer the question of number; "How many?" is an important element of description. Then you can ask, "How do the parts all fit together?" If the object you want to describe is complex, its parts must be fitted into their proper relationship before a mental picture emerges. Remember the story of the blind men who described an elephant in terms of what each felt? The one who felt the trunk said the elephant was like a snake; the one who felt a leg said the elephant was like a tree; and the one who felt the body said the elephant was like a wall. We must not only visualize size, shape, weight, color, composition, age, and condition, but also understand how the parts fit together.

Because the ultimate test of description is whether it enables the audience to visualize, you should include too much detail rather than not enough. Moreover, if some particular aspect is discussed in two or three different ways, everyone might get the mental image; a single description might make the image vivid only to a few listeners.

Descriptive Language

Description is aided by careful use of language. Instead of relying on visual aids to create a picture, words are used to develop mental pictures. Describing allows an excellent opportunity to use simile and metaphor to help the audience *see* what you are talking about.

In your description, try to avoid using florid description and excessive adjectives and adverbs, such as in "The Golden Gate Bridge silhouetted against the azure blue sky gives an awesome impression of majestic glory." Description should not sound like a page from a poor literary magazine. Your emphasis should be on clear, vivid sensory impressions.

For most people, description does not come easily—we are just not used to describing things vividly and accurately in ordinary conversation. To improve your descriptive skill, you must take the time to practice carefully. In your practices you will want to place special emphasis on revising language from general and bland to specific and vivid. Let us work with a single idea to illustrate the practice process. Consider the following sentence:

Several pencils were on Tom's desk.

This statement of fact tells us that pencils (plural) were on a desk, but it gives us no real description.

To begin revising this description, you should ask questions that relate to the essentials that we discussed. We might ask, "How many pencils? What color were they?" The following revision answers those questions:

Five yellow pencils adorned Tom's desk.

"Five" is more descriptive than "several" because it is more specific; "yellow" begins a description of how they looked; "adorned" is more descriptive than "on" because it carries a mental picture, although the word itself is a bit pretentious. Now let us ask the questions, "Specifically, what did the pencils look like? How were they arranged?" In the following two sentences we get completely different descriptions of the pencils:

Five finely sharpened yellow pencils lined the side of Tom's desk, side by side in perfect order from longest to shortest.

Five stubby, well-chewed pencils of different colors, all badly in need of sharpening, were scattered about Tom's desk.

These examples begin to show the different pictures that can be created depending on how you use the details you have observed.

Earlier you were cautioned about not memorizing a speech. Because you can describe any part of your topic in unlimited ways, keep the essentials in mind during each practice and use slightly different wordings each time to express your descriptions. By making minor changes each time, you will avoid memorization.

Assignment
Describing

1. Prepare a two- to four-minute description. Write an outline. Evaluation of your description will focus on clarity and vividness of the description.

   Topic: Any structure, place, object, or being can be described. For a descriptive exercise you will want a topic that provides new information for the audience. The following are suitable examples:

Structures	Places	Objects
Cape Hatteras Lighthouse	Grand Tetons	racing ice skate
Washington Monument	Natural Bridge	fisherman's seine
Golden Gate Bridge	The Alamo	pinking shears

   Organization: Because clear description often follows a space order, consider describing from foreground to background, back-

Checklist	**Descriptive**

Check all items that were accomplished effectively.

Specific Goal

_____ 1. Was the specific goal clear?

_____ 2. Was the goal appropriate for description?

Content

_____ 3. Did the speaker show good observation of the described structure, place, or objects?

_____ 4. Did the speaker give us clear description of _____ size? _____ shape? _____ weight? _____ color? _____ composition? _____ age and condition? _____ relationship among parts?

_____ 5. Did the speaker use any special strategies to help the audience remember the main ideas in the description?

Language

_____ 6. Was the description clear?

_____ 7. Was the description vivid?

Delivery

_____ 8. Was the speech delivered _____ enthusiastically? _____ with good eye contact? _____ spontaneously? _____ with appropriate vocal variety and emphasis? _____ with good pronunciation? _____ with effective bodily action?

Evaluate the speech as (check one) _____ excellent, _____ good, _____ average, _____ fair, _____ poor.

Use the information from your check sheet to support your evaluation.

ground to foreground, left to right, or top to bottom. Although space-order organization will be used most often, a topic order with space-order subdivisions is appropriate for longer descriptions. In a description of Yellowstone Park, for example, you might talk about Old Faithful and Fountain Paint Pot as two main topics, each of which then is described following a space-order arrangement of details.

2. Write a critique of one or more of the descriptions you heard in class based on the preceding descriptive checklist.
   a. Take notes outlining the speech.
   b. As you outline the speech, answer the checklist questions (p. 233) *yes* or *no* and fill in explanatory comments to clarify your response.

Speech — The Cape Hatteras Lighthouse

OUTLINE: DESCRIBING CAPE HATTERAS LIGHTHOUSE

Specific Goal: I want the audience to picture the exterior of the Cape Hatteras Lighthouse.

Introduction
I.   How many of you have been to America's tallest lighthouse?
II.   I recently visited the Cape Hatteras Lighthouse, the tallest in the United States.

Thesis Statement: The Cape Hatteras Lighthouse, located along the Outer Banks of North Carolina, has a 193-foot body and a 15-foot top that I will describe.

Body
I.   The lighthouse is located along the Outer Banks of North Carolina.
      A. It stands on the beach.
      B. It stands in stark contrast to its surroundings.
II.   The major portion of the lighthouse consists of its body.
      A. It is 193 feet tall.
         1. This would be the same as twenty stories.
         2. The interior has approximately 400 steps.
      B. The body is shaped like a cylinder, with the base wider in the diameter than the top.
      C. The walls are made of brick.
      D. Black and white stripes spiral the sides of the body.
      E. There are three windows on both the north and south sides.
      F. It was built in 1870.
III. The top of the lighthouse sits on a fenced platform in which the actual light is enclosed.

The Cape Hatteras Lighthouse. How vividly does the speaker's verbal description create a picture of this structure?

A. The height from the top of the body to the tip of the lighthouse is 15 feet.

B. The platform's base is shaped like a half cone, with the base of the cone fitting on top of the main portion.

C. The platform and the tip of the lighthouse are made of black steel.

D. The section containing the light is made of clear glass.

Conclusion

I. Although the Cape Hatteras Lighthouse is only 208 feet tall, it really looks taller against its background.

II. America's tallest lighthouse is a major scenic attraction of Cape Hatteras.

As you read this speech analyze the descriptions of size, shape, weight, color, composition, age, condition, and relationship among parts.[1] Which descriptions are clear? Which are vivid? Which need more or better development? After you have read the speech aloud at least once, read the analysis in the other column.

SPEECH

The speaker begins by trying to develop common ground with the audience. The question is used to heighten audience attention.

This sentence locates the lighthouse.

In this section the speaker does a good job of giving meaning to "200 feet."

I'm sure that some of you may have been atop the tallest building in this city or that country. But have any of you been up the tallest lighthouse? I've had a chance to visit the Cape Hatteras Lighthouse, the tallest lighthouse in America, and tonight I'd like to describe it to you.

The lighthouse is located along the Outer Banks of North Carolina. It stands on the beach in stark contrast to its surroundings. The lighthouse stands over 200 feet tall. Now, many of you may not think 200 feet is very much, but it is for a lighthouse, especially when it doesn't contain an elevator, and you try to climb the 400 steps that comprise the twenty flights of stairs. When you stop to think of it, that's the equivalent of a twenty-story building!

Now, 193 feet of this structure is the body. The body is a somewhat cylindrical figure with the base wider than the top; the base is about 50 feet wide and the top is about 15 feet wide. The outside walls are made of brick, which seems to last pretty well since the lighthouse was built in 1870 right after the Civil War, some 110 years ago. Still this is relatively young for a lighthouse; most famous lighthouses date from the sixteenth or seventeenth centuries. The body of the lighthouse is painted black and white stripes all the way up; the stripes are about 10 feet wide, and they spiral their way up the entire body.

On top of this main structure is a 24-foot-wide steel platform, which contains the glass structure that has the light inside it. This platform has a half-cone shaped body with the bottom of the cone fitting exactly on the top of the base of the main structure. Inside a fenced area is the solid glass-paned structure that contains the light. On top of the glass structure is a top with a pointed roof that's like an upside-down cone. Now, the tip of this roof and the steel platform are all black. And the glass is clear so the light can be seen from all directions.

I particularly like the phrasing "an upside-down cone."

The conclusion emphasizes the overall picture. Although the speech is not especially creative, it does present a clear, descriptive picture. I believe an audience can see the lighthouse as the speaker finishes.

Although the Cape Hatteras Lighthouse is only 208 feet tall, it really looks taller against its background. The black and white stripes make it stand out against the blue background of the ocean and sky whether it's day or night. America's tallest lighthouse is a major scenic attraction of Cape Hatteras.

Summary

Describing is an important skill for an informative speaker to cultivate, because showing "what is it like" may be used to get attention, increase understanding, and aid in retention.

Describing means creating a verbal picture. Describing requires skill in recognizing and portraying size, shape, weight, color, composition, age and condition, and the relationship among parts.

In your practices you will want to place special emphasis on revising language from general and bland to specific and vivid. To revise, answer questions related to the essentials of description.

Note

1. Delivered in speech class, University of Cincinnati. Used with permission of Karen Zimmer.

Chapter 12 | Defining

Because we cannot solve problems, learn, or even think without meaningful definitions, the ability to define clearly and vividly is essential for the effective communicator. In fact, Richard Weaver, a major twentieth-century figure in the development of rhetorical theory, labeled definition as the most valuable of all lines of development.[1]

The definitions you use in your informative speeches are likely to be of three types: short, stipulated, or extended.

Short Definitions

Short definitions are used to clarify concepts in as few words as possible. Effective speakers learn to define by synonym and antonym, classification and differentiation, use or function, and etymological reference.

Synonyms and Antonyms

Using a synonym or an antonym is the quickest way to define a word. Either one will enable you to indicate approximate, if not exact, meaning in a single sentence; moreover, because they are analogous to comparison and contrast, they often are vivid as well as clear.

Synonyms are words that have the same or nearly the same meanings; antonyms are words that have opposite meanings. Defining by synonym is defining by comparison. For instance, synonyms for *sure* are *certain, confident,* and *positive.* One antonym is *doubtful.* Synonyms for *prolix* include *long, wordy,* and *of tedious length.* Its antonyms are *short* and *concise.* Synonyms are not duplicates for the word being defined, but they do give a good idea of what the word means. Synonyms and antonyms are often the shortest, quickest, and easiest ways to clarify the meaning of a new word. Thus, we might define *compute* as *to calculate; ebullient* as *bubbling* or *boiling; pacific* as *appeasing* or *conciliatory;* and *sagacious* as *keenly perceptive, shrewd,* or *wise.* Of course, the synonym or antonym must be familiar to the audience or its use defeats its purpose.

Classification and Differentiation

The use of classification and differentiation, although slightly longer, is one of the most common ways to define. When you define by classification you give the class or group in which the object fits; then you focus on the feature or features that differentiate the object from other objects in that class. For instance, a definition of a clarinet may begin, "A clarinet is a woodwind instrument." This first statement places the clarinet in a class of instruments called *woodwinds.* The definition is completed by saying, "The clarinet is a single-reed instrument, consisting of a long tube made of wood, metal, or plastic that flares out at the end, with the tube containing holes and keys for playing." Saying that it is a single-reed instrument differentiates it from other woodwinds such as the oboe. Saying that its tube contains holes differentiates it from the saxophone; moreover, the additional description helps give a mental picture that enables us to recognize it when we see it.

Let us look at another example of classification and differentiation. A *mansard* is a *roof* (classification). The mansard has two slopes on each of the four sides; the lower slopes are steeper than the upper (description and differentiation). Many standard dictionary definitions are by classification.

Use or Function

Another short way to define is by explaining the use or function of the object represented by a particular word. Thus, when you say, "A plane is a handpowered tool that is used to smooth the edges of boards," or "A scythe is a piece of steel shaped in a half circle with a handle attached that is used to cut weeds or high grass," you are defining tools by indicating their use. Because the use or function of an object may be more important than its classification, this often is an excellent method of definition.

Etymology

Finally, another way to define is through *etymology*, the derivation or historical account of a particular word. Although historical accounts can be built into long definitions, a short historical account can be interesting and thus help an audience remember.

Consider the word *tantalize*, for instance, which means *to tease* (definition by synonym). Although "to tease" gives an approximation, definition by an etymological or historical example may give a more complete meaning that will help a person remember the meaning and use it appropriately. In the case of *tantalize*, the following explanation adds considerable insight. Tantalus, the mythical king of Phrygia, was the son of Zeus. Tantalus committed the crime of revealing the gods' secrets to mere mortals. For his punishment he was condemned to stand up to his chin in water that constantly receded as he stooped to drink and to be surrounded by branches of assorted fruit that eluded his grasp whenever he reached for them. Thus, for eternity Tantalus was tantalized by food and drink that were shown to him but were forever withheld.

In this and similar circumstances, etymology and historical example can give excellent assistance in defining a word. Like any illustration, anecdote, or story, etymology and historical example increase the vividness of the explanation. The best source of word derivation is the *Oxford English Dictionary*.

Regardless of which of the short definition forms you use, you are likely to have to supplement your statements with examples, comparisons, or both to make them truly understandable. This is especially true when you define abstract words. Consider the word *just* in the following sentence: "You are being just in your dealings with another when you deal honorably and fairly." Although you have defined by synonym, listeners still may be unsure of the meaning. If you add, "If Paul and Mary do the same amount of work and we reward them by giving them an equal amount of money, our dealings will be just; if, on the other hand, we give Paul more money because he's a man, our dealings will be unjust." In this case, you are clarifying the definition with both an example and a comparison.

For some words a single example or comparison will be enough. For other words or in communicating with certain audiences, you may need several examples and comparisons.

Stipulated Definitions

A stipulative definition is one in which a single definition from among many possible is selected for use in a particular instance. Because words may be used in many ways, a stipulative definition helps to direct the audience's thinking toward the one particular slant of definition that you wish to use. Although the following two definitions use contrasting methods, for example, they are equally clear in showing how the speakers will use the words they define:

> Let's talk for a moment about humanity. By humanity, I really mean "people skills" — our ability to work with each other.[2]

> A scenario is a kind of imaginary history of things that haven't happened — but might happen.[3]

You can stipulate a definition that is one of the standards of your word or create your own stipulated definition. Suppose you wished to define the concept of "responsible citizenry" in your speech. A dictionary will indicate that *responsible* means "accountable" and *citizen* means a "legal inhabitant who enjoys certain freedoms and privileges," but putting these two together does not really tell what a "responsible citizen" is. As you read about civic responsibilities, you may see such topics as "social," "civic," and "financial." This information would enable you to stipulate a responsible citizen as "one who meets his or her social, civic, and financial obligations."

Extended Definitions

Often a word is so important to your speech that an extended definition is warranted. An extended definition is one that serves as an entire main point in a speech or, at times, an entire speech.

How might you elaborate on the definition to explain what jazz is?

An extended definition begins with a single-sentence dictionary definition or stipulated definition. For example, *Webster's Third New International Dictionary* defines *jazz* as "American music characterized by improvisation, syncopated rhythms, contrapuntal ensemble playing, and special melodic features peculiar to the individual interpretation of the player." This definition suggests four topics ("improvisation," "syncopation," "ensemble," and "special melodies") that could be used as a basis for a topical order for the speech. Assuming you were familiar enough with jazz to talk about it, you might organize your speech as follows:

Specific Goal: I want my audience to understand the four major characteristics of jazz.

I. Jazz is characterized by improvisation.
II. Jazz is characterized by syncopated rhythms.
III. Jazz is characterized by contrapuntal ensemble playing.
IV. Jazz is characterized by special melodic features peculiar to the individual interpretation of the player.

The key to the effectiveness of the speech would be how well you explain each of the topics. Your selection and use of examples, illustrations, comparisons, personal experiences, and observations will give the speech its original and distinctive flavor.

<table>
<tr><td>**Checklist**</td><td>**Definition**</td></tr>
</table>

Check all items that were accomplished effectively.

Specific Goal

_____ 1. Was the specific goal clear?

_____ 2. Was the subject matter appropriate for definition?

Content

_____ 3. Did the speaker use _____classification? _____differentiation? _____synonym? _____use or function? _____etymology?

_____ 4. Did the speaker use examples to develop the definition?

_____ 5. Did the speaker show expertise with the subject matter?

_____ 6. Did the speaker use any special strategies to help the audience remember key aspects of the definition?

Organization

_____ 7. Did the speech follow a topical order?

_____ 8. If not, was the order appropriate for a definition?

_____ 9. Did each main point clarify an aspect of the definition?

Language

_____ 10. Was the language _____clear? _____vivid? _____emphatic? _____appropriate?

Delivery

_____ 11. Was the speech delivered _____enthusiastically? _____with good eye contact? _____spontaneously? _____with appropriate vocal variety and emphasis? _____with good pronunciation? _____with effective bodily action?

Evaluate the speech as (check one) _____excellent, _____good, _____average, _____fair, _____poor.

Use the information from your checklist to support your evaluation.

The model speech at the end of this chapter illustrates an extended definition of "impressionistic painting."

Assignment
Definitions

1. Prepare a two- to four-minute definition. An outline is required. Evaluation will focus on the definition's clarity, and the organization and quality of the developmental material.

Topics: Some of the best topics for extended definition are general or abstract words, words that give you leeway in definition and allow for creative development. The following are examples of the kinds of words for which extended definitions are appropriate:

expressionism	rhetoric	logic
existentialism	epicurean	acculturation
myth	fossil	extrasensory perception
epistemology	humanities	status

2. Write a critique of at least one of the definition speeches you hear in class. Outline the speech. As you outline, answer *yes* or *no* to the questions in the definition checklist on p. 243.

Speech — Impressionistic Painting[4]

OUTLINE: DEFINING IMPRESSIONISM

Specific Goal: I want the audience to understand the definition of impressionistic painting.

Introduction
  I. "I paint as the bird sings"; this quote from Monet describes the light, vibrant nature of impressionistic painting.
 II. Through the years, impressionism has become a highly appreciated art form.
III. *Impressionism* is defined as a practice in painting among French painters of the late 1800s in which subject matter was depicted in its natural setting, and painted in vibrant hues of unmixed color and with broad, fragmented brush strokes.

Thesis Statement: Impressionistic painting involves unique subject matter, use of color, and technique.

Body
  I. Impressionism involves the unique use of natural subject matter.
     A. Impressionistic painters painted visual impressions.
        1. The painters did not use conventional arrangements.
        2. They painted entirely out of doors.
     B. The painters used nature as their predominant source of subject matter.

1. They painted the effects of light on water.
2. They enjoyed painting landscapes.

II. Impressionistic painting also involves a unique use of color.

    A. The painters tried to record colors as they appeared in natural light.

        1. They used vibrant colors.

        2. The use of colors was nontraditional.

    B. Impressionistic painters were first to use color in shadows.

        1. Colors tended to cast complimentary tones on neutral backgrounds.

        2. Effects of shadow can be achieved by contrasts in color.

III. Most notably, impressionistic painting involves a unique technique.

    A. The painters developed the technique of using fragmented brush strokes.

        1. They blended colors by placing them side by side on canvas.

        2. The effect is similar to the dots of light in a television picture.

    B. They left their paintings "unfinished" by conventional standards.

        1. There were no clear outlines.

        2. This translated the immediacy and strength of the impression.

Conclusion

I. In its unique use of subject matter, color, and technique, impressionism has made quite an impression on the art world.

Bibliography

Hayes, Colin. *The Colour Library of Art.* London: Paul Hamlyn Limited, 1961.

Janson, David. *The History of Art.* New York: Harcourt Brace, 1985.

Martini, Alberto. *Monet.* New York: Avenel Books, 1978.

Rouart, Kenis. *Degas.* New York: Rizzoli International, 1988.

Analysis

After using an attention-getting quotation from Monet, the speaker gives a complete definition of "impressionism," focusing on the three key aspects that differentiate it from other styles of painting.

Notice the good transition leading into the body of the speech.

SPEECH

"I paint as the bird sings." This quotation from Claude Monet describes the light, vibrant nature of impressionistic painting. When impressionism first emerged in the late 1800s it was frowned upon by critics; however, as time has moved on it has become a highly appreciated art form. *Impressionism* is defined as a practice in painting among French painters of the late 1800s depicting subject matter in its natural setting, painted in vibrant hues of unmixed color, with broad, fragmented brush strokes. Let's consider each of these three aspects of impressionism.

The first aspect that makes impressionism unique is that it involves natural subject matter. Contrary to the practice of the time of arranging a basket of fruit or a basket of flowers or posing a model, impressionists painted natural objects primarily outdoors. In fact impressionists were the first artists to both start and finish a painting outdoors. Because they didn't bring the painting inside the studio at all, nature was the predominate source of their subjects. Many of their paintings featured landscape shots. And since impressionists were particularly fascinated with the effect of light on water — they often painted water scenes.

A second aspect of impressionism that defines it is the unique use of color. Again, in contrast to the typical practice of the time, instead of using muted tones impressionists captured the natural colors of nature by using more vibrant hues. More distinctive than just their selection of color was their use of color in shadows. Claude Monet who was one of the originators of impressionistic painting found that a color when cast on a neutral background would tend to cast in complementaries. For example, a red when cast on a gray background will tend to cast a bluish-green hue, because red is opposite blue-green on the color wheel. Yellow, on the other hand, would tend to cast a violet hue since yellow is opposite violet on the color wheel. Monet found that this same effect occurred in nature. Thus there was no longer a need to render shadows as dark harsh tones when you could render shadows by using complementary colors. This unique aspect of impressionistic painting was a significant artistic advancement.

Not only does impressionism involve unique subject matter and unique use of color, but most notably it involves unique technique. A third aspect of impressionism that defines it is the technique of using broad, fragmented brush strokes. On canvas, these brush strokes looked a little bit similar to a comma or a semi-colon. Instead of mixing the colors on a palette, or on a plate before putting them on a canvas, impressionists blended them by putting separate flashes of color on some canvas. Their effect was similar in manner to the way a television screen works. When you sit very close to a television screen you see different tiny dots of color and when you move away those tiny dots of color form a solid visual impression. Because of the nature of these fragmented brush strokes the paintings looked very unfinished by conventional standards. They didn't have the sharp clear outline that is characteristic of the painting of the time; nor did they leave a smooth appearance. Again this method was often frowned upon by the critics of the time, but it added to the originality of impressionism and it created a sense of immediacy

Because the definition includes three specific aspects that differentiate impressionism from other painting styles, each main point focuses on one aspect.

This first main point focuses on the use of natural subject matter. In developing the definition, the speaker emphasizes that not only were the subjects natural objects, but that the paintings were done in a natural environment.

This second main point develops the second aspect of impressionism, the use of color.

Notice how the speaker uses clear examples to explain how colors are perceived in shadows.

Notice the good transition that reviews the first two aspects and leads into the third, the use of broad, fragmented brush strokes.

This comparison of the perception of brush strokes and commas is a good one.

Likewise, the comparison to the way we perceive color on a television screen helps the audience to understand the point.

In her conclusion, the speaker reviews the three major parts of her extended definition.

This speech is a good example of using the aspects of a definition as the framework for an entire speech.

and strength of the impressionists, which was the primary goal of their painting.

So, the next time you hear people refer to *impressionistic* painters, you can picture paintings depicting subject matter in its natural setting, painted in vibrant hues of unmixed color, with broad, fragmented brush strokes.

Summary

Defining is giving the meaning of a word or concept.

Definitions in your speeches will be short, stipulated, or extended.

Short definitions are developed through synonym and antonym, classification and differentiation, use and function, and etymology and historical example, and are enhanced with the use of examples and comparisons.

Stipulated definitions are selected or developed to establish a particular line of development in a speech.

Extended definitions are used when a speaker wants to give a comprehensive development of an abstract term.

Notes

1. Richard Weaver, "Language is Sermonic," in Richard L. Johannesen, Rennard Strickland, and Ralph T. Eubanks, *Language is Sermonic* (Baton Rouge: Louisiana State University Press, 1970), 212.
2. Vince Kotny, "Business and Education, A Crucial Connection," *Vital Speeches*, (May 1, 1986), 438.
3. Edward Cornish, "The Family and Its Home in the 1980s," *Vital Speeches*, (December 1, 1980), 120.
4. Delivered in speech class, University of Cincinnati. Used with permission of Wendy Finkleman.

Chapter 13 | Reporting

Last year, a suburban high school instituted a new program designed to cope with increasing substance abuse by high school students. How's the program working?

Several years ago, the city council approved plans for the rehabilitation of Fountain Square West. What's the status of the project?

This fall, the Student Union reopened its main cafeteria with promises of better food, a more congenial atmosphere, and lower prices. How's it doing?

In each of these cases, the speeches that are given to answer these questions are reports.

When *reporting*, you are presenting an audience with news about an event, a place, or a project. Although reporters may turn to written sources for background information, their primary sources of information are likely to be from participation, observation, interviews, and surveys. In this chapter we discuss interviewing for information and conducting surveys and then conclude with a speech assignment and a sample speech.

Interviewing for Information

Much like an effective newspaper reporter, you are likely to get some of your best and most quotable information through interviews. Because good interviews do not "just happen," let us look at the principles that govern interviewing for information. Interviewing involves defining the purpose of the interview, selecting the best person to interview, planning carefully, writing questions, conducting the interview itself, and interpreting the results.

Defining the Purpose of the Interview

Too often interviewers go into an information interview without a clear purpose. Your purpose is clear only when you can write it in one complete sentence. Without such a clear purpose, your list of questions all too likely will have no direction. As a result, you will come out with information that does not fit together well. Suppose you are thinking about getting information about the food service in your dormitory. The following are possible specific purposes for your interview:

1. To get a personal sketch of the person responsible for meal planning
2. To determine the major elements a dietitian must account for in planning dormitory meals
3. To determine how a dietitian can run a cost-effective program that provides good nutrition at a reasonable price

Selecting the Best Person

Somewhere on campus or in the larger community, there are people who have or who can get the information you want. How do you find out whom you should interview? Suppose you are going to discuss a question related to food service in your dormitory. One of the employees can tell you who is in charge of the dining hall. Or you could phone your student center and inquire about who is in charge of food service. When you have decided whom you should interview, make an appointment. You cannot walk into an office and expect the prospective interviewee to drop everything on the spur of the moment.

Before going into the interview, get information on the topic. If, for instance, you are going to interview the dietitian who determines the menus and orders the food, you already should know something about the job of dietitian and something about the problems involved in ordering and preparing institutional food. Interviewees are more likely to talk with you if you appear informed; moreover, familiarity with the subject will enable you to ask better questions. If for some reason you go into an interview uninformed, then at least approach the interviewee with enthusiasm and apparent interest in the job.

You also should be forthright in expressing your reasons for scheduling the interview. Whether your interview is for a class project, a newspaper article on campus food, or something else, say so.

Planning Carefully

Good interviewing results from careful planning. A good plan begins with good questions. Write down all the questions you can think of, revise them until you have worded them clearly and concisely, and put them in the order that seems most appropriate. Your questions should be a mix of open and closed questions and should be neutral rather than leading. Moreover, you should be alert to the need for follow-up questions.

OPEN AND CLOSED QUESTIONS *Open questions* are broad-based. They range from those with virtually no restrictions such as "Will you tell me about yourself?" to those that give some direction such as "Will you tell me about your preparation for this job?" *Closed questions* are those that can be answered yes or no or with only a few words, such as, "Have you had a course in marketing?" or "How many restaurants have you worked in?" Open questions encourage the person to talk; closed questions enable the interviewer to get a lot of information in a short time.

Which type of question is best? The answer depends on what kinds of material you are looking for and how much time you have for the interview. An opinion poll interviewer who wants specific responses to specific questions relies mostly or entirely on closed questions; a person primarily interested in the thoughts and feelings of another person may ask only open questions. In an information-getting interview for a speech, you will want enough closed questions to get the specifics you need and enough open questions to stimulate people to include anecdotes, illustrations, and personal views.

NEUTRAL AND LEADING QUESTIONS *Neutral questions* are those in which the person is free to give an answer without direction from the interviewer; *leading questions* are those in which the interviewer suggests the answer expected or desired. A neutral question would be, "How do you like your new job?" A leading question would be, "You don't like the new job, do you?" In most interviewing situations, leading questions are inappropriate. They try to force the person in one direction and can make the person defensive.

PRIMARY AND FOLLOW-UP QUESTIONS *Primary questions* are planned ahead of time; *follow-up questions* relate to the answers you get to the primary questions. Follow-up questions can encourage the person to continue ("And then?" "Is there more?"), probe into what the person has said ("What does 'frequently' mean?" "What were you thinking at the time?"), and plumb the person's feelings ("How did it feel to get the prize?" "Were you worried when you didn't find her?").

Your effectiveness with follow-up questions may well depend on your skill in asking them. Because probing follow-up questions can alienate the interviewee (especially when the questions are seen as threatening), in-depth probes work best after you have gained the confidence of the person and when the questions are asked in a positive climate.

Writing Questions

When you list your questions, leave enough space between them to fill in the answers as completely as possible. It is just as important to leave enough space for answers to any follow-up questions you decide to ask. Some interviewers try to play the entire interview by ear. Even the most skilled interviewer, however, needs preplanned questions to ensure covering important areas. The order and type of questions depend somewhat upon what you are hoping to achieve in the interview.

INTRODUCTION OF THE INTERVIEW In the opening stages you should, of course, start by thanking the person for taking the time to talk with you. During the opening, try to develop good rapport with your respondent. Start by asking questions that can be answered easily and that will show your respect for the person you are interviewing. For instance, in an interview with the head dietitian you might start with such questions as, "How did you get interested in nutrition?" or "I imagine that working out menus can be a very challenging job in these times of high food costs — is that so?" When the person nods or says "yes," you then can ask about the biggest challenges he or she faces. Your goal is to get the interviewee to feel at ease and to talk freely. Because the most important consideration at this initial stage is to create a climate for positive communication, keep your questions easy to answer, nonthreatening, and encouraging.

BODY OF THE INTERVIEW   The body of the interview includes the major questions you have prepared. A good plan is to group questions so that the easy-to-answer questions come first and hard-hitting questions that require careful thought come later. For instance, the question, "What do you do to try to resolve student complaints?" should be near the end of the interview. You may not ask all the questions that you have planned, but you do not want to end the interview until you have the important information you need.

CONCLUSION OF THE INTERVIEW   As you draw to the end of your planned questions, again thank the person for taking the time to talk with you. If you are going to publish the substance of the interview, it is a courtesy to offer to let the person see a draft of your reporting of the interview before it goes into print. If a person does wish to see what you plan to write, get a draft to that person well before deadline to give the person the opportunity to read it and to give you the opportunity to deal with any suggestions. Although this practice is not followed by many interviewers, it helps to build and maintain your credibility.

Figure 12.1 gives you an idea of the method used to set up a question schedule for an interview.

Conducting the Interview

The best plan in the world will not result in a good interview unless you practice good interpersonal communication skills when conducting the interview. Let us focus on a few of the particularly important elements of good interviewing.

BE COURTEOUS AND LISTEN CAREFULLY   Your job is not to debate or to give your opinion, but to get information from someone who has it. Whether or not you like the person and whether or not you agree with the person, you must respect his or her opinions. After all, you are the one who asked for the interview.

PUT INTO PRACTICE YOUR BEST LISTENING SKILLS   If the person has given a rather long answer to a question, you should paraphrase what he or she has said to make sure your interpretation is correct. A *paraphrase* is a statement of your understanding of what the person has said. After the dietitian answered the question on interest in nutrition, for example, you might paraphrase by saying, "So, if I understand you correctly, you are saying your interest in dietetics came largely by accident." If your impression is correct, the person will let you know. If you have misunderstood, it gives the person a chance to correct your misimpression.

Figure 12.1

*Interview questions for a
school dietitian.*

Background
What kinds of background and training do
you need for the job?
How did you get interested in nutrition?
Have you worked as a dietitian for long?
Have you held any other food-related
positions?

Responsibilities
What are the responsibilities of your job
besides meal planning?
How far in advance do you plan meals?
What factors do you take into account when
you are planning the meals for a given
period?
Do you have a free hand or are constraints
placed upon you?

Procedures
Is there any set ratio for the number of
times you put a given item on the menu?
Do you take individual differences into
account?
How do you determine whether or not you
will give choices for the entree?
How do you try to answer student
complaints?
How do your prices compare with meals at a
commercial cafeteria?

KEEP THE INTERVIEW MOVING   You do not want to rush the person;
but when the allotted time is ending, you should call attention to that fact
and be prepared to conclude.

BE AWARE OF YOUR NONVERBAL IMPRESSION   How you look and act
may well determine whether the person will warm up to you and give you
the kind of information you want. Consider your appearance. You want to
be dressed appropriately for the occasion. Because you are taking the
person's time, you should show an interest in the person and in what he
or she has to say.

Skilled reporters know that attentive listening is essential to good interviewing.

Interpreting the Results

The interview serves no useful purpose until you do something with the material, but you should not do anything with it until you have reviewed it carefully. If you took notes, it is especially important to carefully write complete answers while the information still is fresh in your mind. After you have processed the material from the interview, you may want to show the interviewee a copy of the data that you will use. You do not want to be guilty of misquoting your source.

You also may find it necessary to check out the facts you have been given. If what the person told you differs from material you have from other sources, you should double-check its accuracy.

The most difficult part is interpreting and drawing inferences from the material. Facts by themselves are not nearly as important as the conclusions that may be drawn from those facts. Carefully think through your analysis of the material before you present its substance in a speech or publication.

Conducting Surveys

Interviews are appropriate ways to get information from people who are personally involved with the subject on which you are reporting, but if you want data from those who are most affected by an event or a project, you may want to conduct a survey. As you will recall from our discussion in Chapter 3, a survey involves asking many people the same question or questions. A good survey is a product of a clear research goal, well-constructed questions that are designed to elicit answers that are relevant to the goal, and a representative sample of the population about which you want information.

First, you need a research question or series of questions; second, you must identify the population you want to sample. The actual sample probably will be rather large and will need to be drawn at random. For instance, suppose you wanted to continue your research on food at the university cafeteria. In the last section we saw how we might interview the dietitian who determines the menus and orders the food. Now that you have her insight into the way the cafeteria is run, you might decide that you want to survey student opinion about the cafeteria.

Research Goal

Before you can begin the task of constructing a questionnaire, you must be sure of your goal: What is it that you hope to find out by conducting the survey? Suppose you wanted to continue research on the student union cafeteria that just reopened under new management. To help you develop a good report, you might decide that you want to determine student response to the advertising claims that the cafeteria has been making: better food, more congenial atmosphere, and lower prices. Now that you have a goal in mind, you can begin work on the questionnaire.

Samples

Once you have determined your goal, you consider the question of who you will survey. Suppose you wanted the opinion of the student body to the question, "Should the university require Fundamentals of Effective

Speaking for all students?" Although you could attempt to survey the entire student body (say, 12,000 students), it is far more likely that you would select a sample. At first it would seem that the more people you sample, the smaller the chances of error. And although that is true, most samples that are used for polls are rather small. For instance, to get the opinion of a population of 100 million, a poll of 1,000 to 1,500 will reveal as much as a poll of 10,000 to 50,000.[1] Thus, for a population of 12,000, you would want to survey at least 100 students.

Although you need to poll many people, the size of a poll is less significant than the *type* of sample. You must make sure that your sample is representative in some sense. For instance, for the poll to determine whether Fundamentals of Effective Speaking should be required for all students, you must sample freshmen, sophomores, juniors, and seniors, an equal number of males and females, Greeks and independents, and people of all races.

You also may want to survey only some part of the population. A survey of a part of a total population is called a *stratified survey*. You may wish to stratify by race, age, sex, education, or any other variable. If you are doing a stratified survey, then you must make sure that each person surveyed is within the survey group.

The survey of those students who eat at the student union cafeteria would be a stratified survey. If you gave your questionnaire to every student as he or she entered the cafeteria on one day and collected from as many students as possible as they left, you would have a good sample of the students who eat at the cafeteria.

Questionnaires

For your survey you design a questionnaire that will get the information you need to achieve your goal. If your goal for a survey of students who eat at the student union cafeteria is to get their answers to questions about food quality, atmosphere, and prices, you begin by phrasing your questions. The three kinds of questions that you are most likely to use are called two-sided, multiple-choice, and scaled.

Two-sided questions are simple closed questions that ask for a *yes–no* or *true–false* response. These questions are used most frequently to get easily sorted answers. National polls such as those run by the Gallup Organization often feature two-sided questions. In December 1989, for example, to the question "Was the U.S. justified or not in sending military forces to invade Panama and overthrow Noriega?" 80 percent of respondents answered that it was justified and 13 percent said it was not.[2] For your cafeteria survey questionnaire, you might consider a closed-question phrasing such as, "Do you approve of the quality of the food at the student union cafeteria — Yes or No?"

Despite their popularity, two-sided questions have two major problems. The first is that they do not offer people the opportunity to express their degree of agreement or disagreement. Suppose one person hates the food while another person tolerates it. To the question of "Do you like the food?" you may get one *yes* and one *no* answer. But instead of the two answers balancing each other, because of the respondents' intense feelings, the two together should be weighted toward the negative. A second problem is that yes–no questions multiply the problems of a question with a biased structure. For instance, the yes-or-no question could be phrased, "Do you believe management is doing as good a job as it could in providing the best food for the price at the university cafeteria?" With the inclusion of "best food for the price" you virtually invite a student to say "no."

Multiple-choice questions give respondents alternatives. This type features such variations as checklists and rank ordering. For instance, the *Newsweek* poll conducted by the Gallup Organization after the Panama invasion featured the following multiple-choice questions.[3]

With Noriega ousted, the United States should:

14%   Go ahead with the process to give Panama control of the Panama Canal

39%   Halt the process indefinitely until we are satisfied with the situation there

39%   Halt the process entirely and maintain U.S. control of the canal forever

For your cafeteria survey you might phrase the following question:

I eat at the student union cafeteria
_____ nearly every day
_____ at least three times a week
_____ at least once a week
_____ at least once a month
_____ rarely (less than once a month)

Scaled questions are those that allow a range of responses to a statement. Scaled responses are particularly good for measuring the strength of a person's attitudes toward the subject. If you had decided to use scaled questions for your cafeteria survey, to the statement "I like the food at the university cafeteria," each person would be allowed the choices of *strongly agree, agree somewhat, don't know* (or *aren't sure*), *disagree somewhat,* and *strongly disagree.* For a survey for the student union's cafeteria clientele, you might propose the following:

For each of the following four statements, circle the answer that best represents your opinion:

1. I like the food at the university cafeteria.	Strongly Agree	Agree Somewhat	Don't Know	Disagree Somewhat	Strongly Disagree
2. I believe the food at the university cafeteria is fairly priced.	Strongly Agree	Agree Somewhat	Don't Know	Disagree Somewhat	Strongly Disagree
3. I believe the atmosphere at the university cafeteria is pleasant.	Strongly Agree	Agree Somewhat	Don't Know	Disagree Somewhat	Strongly Disagree

ANALYSIS OF STATISTICS   After you have taken your survey, you are ready to analyze. No matter how you do your survey, it is open to some percentage of statistical error. The only poll that would be without error would be one in which everyone in the population was surveyed and everyone completed the survey. Even then, people's opinions may change somewhat from day to day. If you have a large sample and if there is a clear-cut trend, then you probably can trust your figures. But if the poll is inconclusive, then you will want to be careful and avoid making too much of the results.

Assignment
Using Reporting Techniques

1. Prepare a four- to seven-minute report on an event, place, or project that involves your neighborhood, campus, or city. An outline and a bibliography are required. Significant amounts of information must come from interviews. Use of survey information also is encouraged. Evaluation of the speech will focus on information quality and the clarity of development.

    Some topics that are suitable for reports are

    Status of drug abuse on campus
    Substance-abuse rehabilitation programs
    Adult literacy programs
    Urban renewal

2. Write a critique of at least one report you hear in class. Outline the speech. As you outline, answer the questions in the report checklist.

Checklist	**Report**

Check items that were accomplished effectively.

Specific Goal

_____ 1. Was the specific goal clear?

_____ 2. Was the specific goal designed to increase audience information?

Content

_____ 3. Was the speaker effective in establishing expertise on this topic?

_____ 4. Did the speaker get and maintain audience interest in the information throughout the speech?

_____ 5. Did the speaker use interview material?

_____ 6. If so, was the material informative?

_____ 7. Did the speaker use survey material?

_____ 8. If so, was the material informative?

_____ 9. Did the speaker explain information in a way that helped the audience understand the information?

_____ 10. Did the speaker use _____ repetition? _____ transition? _____ association? _____ humor? _____ visual aids? to help the audience understand and/or retain the information?

Organization

_____ 11. Did the introduction _____ gain attention? _____ gain goodwill for the speaker? _____ lead into the speech?

_____ 12. Did the speech follow a _____ time order? _____ space order? _____ topic order? _____ causal order? _____ problem–solution order?

_____ 13. Was the order appropriate for the intent and content of this speech?

_____ 14. Did the conclusion _____ tie the speech together? _____ leave the speech on a high note?

Language

_____ 15. Was the language _____ clear? _____ vivid? _____ emphatic? _____ appropriate?

Delivery

_____ 16. Was the speech delivered _____ enthusiastically? _____ with good eye contact? _____ spontaneously? _____ with appropriate vocal variety and emphasis? _____ with good pronunciation? _____ with effective bodily action?

Evaluate the speech as (check one) _____ excellent, _____ good, _____ average, _____ fair, _____ poor.

Use the information from your checklist to support your evaluation.

Speech — Cafeteria Food

Specific Goal: I want my audience to understand the three major differences in perception between Service America and University of Cincinnati (UC) students about the food at the university cafeteria.

Introduction
I.   Every year thousands of parents send their children to live in the dorms at the University of Cincinnati.
II.   Are these students getting the same quality food in the UC cafeteria as they did while they were living at home?

Thesis Statement: The three main areas of difference between Service America and the students who use the university cafeteria concern whether the food is fairly priced, whether the students like the food, and whether they are receiving meals that are as nutritious as they would be getting at home.

Body
I.   The first area of difference between Service America and students who eat at the UC cafeteria concerns whether the food is fairly priced.
   A. Clyde Moon, general manager of board operations for Service America, believes that the food is fairly priced.
      1. Students may choose from three separate plans.
      2. The average price per meal for the nineteen-meal per week plan is just $3.20.
   B. The sentiment of the 100 students polled was that the food is not fairly priced.
      1. In addition to the 26 percent who indicated that they strongly disagreed that the food was fairly priced, 50 percent indicated that they somewhat disagreed that the food was fairly priced.
      2. Only 24 percent somewhat agreed that the food was fairly priced — none of these students strongly agreed that the food was priced fairly.
   C. The disparity in attitude about price may come from students who use different criteria for "fairly" priced.
      1. Clyde Moon was figuring fairly priced on the basis of cost of food versus price asked.
      2. Students seemed to be figuring fairly priced on the basis of cost versus their perception of quality.

II. The second area of difference between Service America and the students eating at the UC cafeteria concerns whether the food is liked.

A. Clyde Moon told me that their surveys collected at the "Comments Table" indicated that the students liked the food.

B. Data I received from my survey indicated that students did not like the food.

  1. Seventy-four percent either strongly disagreed (26%) or somewhat disagreed (48%) with the statement that they liked the food.

  2. Although 26 percent somewhat agreed with the statement that they liked the food, none of the students strongly agreed with the statement that they liked the food.

C. The difference in perception may be giving Service America a false sense of student satisfaction with the service.

III. The third area of difference between Service America and students eating at the UC cafeteria concerns whether the food is nutritious.

A. Clyde Moon was able to demonstrate that the food is nutritious.

  1. Service America hires a dietitian to plan the meals.

  2. Students can count on every meal meeting nutritional standards.

B. Yet students do not believe that food is as nutritious as home cooking.

  1. An amazing 90 percent of students either strongly disagreed (52%) or somewhat disagreed (38%) that the food is as nutritious as they get at home.

  2. Only 10 percent somewhat agreed that food was as nutritious as they get at home.

C. In this case Service America and students are looking at nutrition from a totally different standpoint.

  1. Clyde Moon is defining nutrition solely on the basis of total nutritional value of the food prepared.

  2. Students are confusing their perception of taste and looks of food with nutrition.

Conclusion

I. Thousands of parents depend on the UC cafeteria to provide their children with good tasting and nutritious meals at a reasonable price.

II. Although students are receiving food that is nutritious for a very fair price, students disagree, largely on the basis of their dissatisfaction, that the quality of the food is high.

Bibliography

Interview with Clyde Moon, general manager of board operations for
  Service America, Thursday, March 29, 1990.
Survey of 100 students who eat at the university cafeteria.

*As you analyze this speech, judge whether the speaker has gained good
information from both his interview and his poll of students. Then analyze
the way in which he uses the information to develop his three main points.[4]
After you have made your own analysis, study the one provided here.*

Analysis

Although this speech is an investigative report, the speaker has done an excellent job of introducing the speech in a way that is likely to capture and hold audience attention.

His McDonald's allusion is especially creative.

Here the speaker does a good job of explaining the costs of the various meal programs.

Notice how the speaker introduces information that he got through interviewing.

He also does a good job of clarifying what he will do in the speech.

The first main point, price of food, is clearly stated.

Notice the clear explanation of the costs of the meal plans and the good comparison to McDonald's.

SPEECH

Every year thousands of parents send their kids off to live in the dorms here at the University of Cincinnati. Now while these kids can no longer enjoy their mothers' great meals — such as tender, mouth-watering roast beef, light and fluffy mashed potatoes, and steamy fresh vegetables — it doesn't mean that they have to be relegated to McDonald's specialty of two all beef patties, special sauce, lettuce, cheese, pickles, onions, and that all-important sesame seed bun. The university has set up a cafeteria for these students, which is located in Sander Hall and is run by Service America.

Some 3,000 students are on one of three meal plans in which they can either pay 607 dollars a quarter and receive 19 meals a week, 491 dollars in which they would receive 14 meals a week, or the 462-dollar plan in which they would receive 10 meals a week. In addition, the university cafeteria is open to any student on a pay-as-you-eat basis. According to Clyde Moon, general manager of board operations for Service America, their job, as he sees it, is basically to provide the students with the same type of nutritious, great-tasting meals that they are used to receiving at home for the prices they pay. However, Service America's perception of how well they are accomplishing this task does not coincide with those of the students they serve. The three main areas of difference between Service America and the students who use the UC cafeteria are whether the food is fairly priced, whether the students like the food they are being served, and whether the food they are receiving is as nutritious as the food they are used to receiving at home.

The first area of difference between Service America and the students who use the UC cafeteria concerns whether the food is fairly priced. When I asked Clyde Moon about price, he pointed out that the student who buys the 19-meal plan for the quarter — that's 190 meals — pays an average of only $3.20 per day. Even the students who purchase the 10-meal-a-week plan are only paying $4.62 per day, a price far less than they could get at even a fast food place like McDonald's. Nevertheless, the students had a different opinion. In a random survey of 100 students who eat in the UC cafeteria, I found that 76% disagree with the statement that food was fairly priced. Twenty-six percent of the students strongly disagreed, and 50 percent somewhat disagreed. Only 24 percent indicated that they somewhat agreed with the statement. Why so much difference over a question of fact? One possible explanation for this difference is that the students may be equating fair price in terms of perceived quality of the food. If students hate the food, then even $2 a day might be perceived as too much. One student that I interviewed said that the quality of the food just does not match the money that is spent for it.

Notice the good transition that leads into the second contrast.

Notice that the speaker not only gives us the results of his poll, but also interprets the results.

In addition to not agreeing on whether the food is fairly priced, Service America and the students disagree on whether the food is liked. In the interview I had with Clyde Moon, I asked him if he had any information to indicate how much the students liked the food. And he told me that once a month Service America sets up a comments table in which they ask the students what they like and what they dislike about the UC cafeteria. And twice a year they survey all the dorms as well. He says that all the information that they have received from these efforts indicate high student satisfaction with the cafeteria and with the food. The students I surveyed, on the other hand, have a different opinion. Twenty-six percent of those students surveyed indicated that they strongly disagreed, and another 48 percent said they somewhat disagreed with the statement that the food was good. That's 74 percent who say they don't like the food. Once again, none of the students polled indicated that they strongly agreed, and only 26 percent indicated that they even somewhat agreed that they liked the food. Now perhaps we can see why they thought it was overpriced at an average of less than $5 a day for even the most expensive meal plan.

Another good transition leading into the final portion of the speech.

In this section the speaker needed a little more specific explanation of how the dietitian plans meals and determines their nutritional value. In addition he needed to give us information on why students disagreed with the statement that food was nutritious.

He ends the section with a good interpretation.

And as you can imagine by now, not only do Service America and the students disagree on the price and the taste of the food in the cafeteria, they disagree on their nutritious value as well. When I asked Clyde Moon whether students are receiving meals as nutritious as they are used to getting at home, he said, "Definitely." He went on to say that Service America has a dietitian that he works in close coordination with to make sure that students receive well-balanced nutritious meals on a daily basis. Yet, according to my survey, more than 90 percent of the students disagreed with Clyde Moon on this point. Fifty-two percent strongly disagreed with the statement that they were receiving meals as nutritious as they got in their own home and another 38 percent somewhat disagreed. Again we have the question of how there can be such a difference in perception. And again, students' dislike for the food may be affecting their perception. Since some of the food at the cafeteria is made up using some fillers that in no way take away from the nutritional value of the food, but do detract from the taste and looks of the food, students are letting their negative reaction to "taste" affect all of their judgments.

Every year thousands of parents send their children off to live in a dorm at the University of Cincinnati. Each morning when these students wake up, their mothers aren't going to be there to have a hot breakfast for them. And at night when they come home from classes, their moms are not going to be there to have a great tasting, nutritious dinner waiting for them. These students depend on the UC cafeteria to provide these great tasting, nutritious meals for them at a reasonable price. Although Service America is providing nutritious food at a very low price, as a result of student dissatisfaction with quality of the food, they are reporting that they are not satisfied with the prices, the taste, or the nutritional value — and if you ask them about the food, they'll tell you, UC cafeteria food? It's not like what mom used to make.

Summary

When you are *reporting*, you are presenting an audience with news about an event, a place, or a project. Although reporters may turn to written sources for background information, their primary sources of information are likely to come from participation, observation, interviews, and surveys.

When you interview for information, you should define the interview's purpose, select the best person to interview, determine a framework for the interview, and conduct the interview according to the framework.

The key skill of interviewing is using questions effectively. Open questions allow for flexible responses; closed questions require only brief answers. Primary questions stimulate response; secondary questions follow up the primary questions. Neutral questions allow the respondent free choice; leading questions require the person to answer in a particular way.

A survey involves asking many people the same question or questions. A good survey requires a clear research goal. You must be sure that you have determined the kind of information that you want.

Although you can survey the entire population, usually you will question a sample. A sample is made up of enough people to validate the results. More important than the size of the sample is its construction. You must be sure that all segments of the population are sampled proportionately.

Questions can be two-sided, multiple-choice, or scaled. Two-sided questions allow you to tally information quickly. Multiple-choice ques-

A good summary conclusion that refocuses on the three major contrasts.

Speaker does a good job of building a report based on material gained from an interview and a student poll.

tions enable you to sample a variety of responses. Scaled questions allow you to determine respondents' degree of attitude about your subject.

If your results are very close, you must avoid making too much of those results.

Notes

1. Bernard Hennessy. *Public Opinion*, 5th ed. Monterey, Calif.: Brooks/ Cole Publishing Company, 1985, p. 73.
2. "The Panama Invasion: A Newsweek Poll," *Newsweek*, January 1, 1990, p. 22.
3. *Ibid.*
4. Delivered in speech class, University of Cincinnati. Used with permission of Ronald Cushing.

Suggested Readings

Baine, David. *Memory and Instruction* (Englewood Cliffs, N.J.: Educational Technology Publications, 1986). This book on memory has excellent sections on mnemonic strategies.

Biagi, Shirley. *Interviews That Work: A Practical Guide for Journalists*. (Belmont, Calif.: Wadsworth, 1986). An excellent short work that focuses on information interviewing.

Lesgold, Alan, and Robert Glaser (eds.). *Foundations for a Psychology of Education* (Hillsdale, N.J.: Erlbaum, 1989). This book has excellent chapters on learning theory and learning skills that lay a foundation for informative speaking.

Petrie, Charles. "Informative Speaking: A Summary and Bibliography of Related Research." *Speech Monographs* 30 (June 1963), 79–91. This summary still is a useful source.

Rorabacher, Louise. *Assignments in Exposition*, 9th ed. (New York: Harper & Row, 1987). Although this is a book on writing, its chapters on narration, definition, description, and analyses of processes present material that can be adapted to the study of informative speaking.

PART IV

PERSUASIVE SPEAKING

This section discusses the ultimate goal of most public speeches: to change attitudes and bring audiences to action. The discussion in this unit is based on two premises.

First, effective persuasive speaking incorporates all the skills that you have developed thus far. For instance, in addition to applying the steps of preparation that you learned in Part II, Fundamental Principles, you also are likely to use visual aids, demonstration, description, definition, and reporting in your persuasive speeches.

Second, to be effective, persuasive speaking has special responsibilities. This unit thus presents guidelines for your persuasive speech preparation that can ensure that you meet the rational and ethical responsibilities of effective persuasion whenever your goal is to change attitudes or motivate an audience to take action.

Chapter 14, the introduction to the unit, adapts the steps of general speech preparation to speeches designed with persuasive intent. Chapter 14 also stresses the importance of reasons and evidence, motivation, and speaker credibility.

Chapters 15, 16, and 17 develop the specific skills of persuasive speaking that an accomplished speaker should master: argumentation, motivation, and refutation. As with informative speaking, each chapter includes both an assignment that focuses on a specific skill and an example of a speech that models that skill. Whether or not you are required to prepare all the oral assignments for in-class practice, you will want to master each individual skill.

The case study "'If You're Communicating from the Heart, It Will Be Heard'" follows on pages 268 and 269.

Joe Marshall has a compelling reason for mastering the art of persuasive speaking: He wants to change lives.

A teacher and school administrator, Joe has received national recognition as one of the founders of Omega Boys Club, a neighborhood organization established to keep inner-city teenagers from "short-circuiting" their futures by dropping out of school and becoming involved with drugs. Giving persuasive speeches—to audiences as diverse as foundation executives and convicted drug dealers— is a natural outgrowth of his attempts to bring positive change to a world of drugs, dropouts, and gang violence.

While many people begin speaking as part of a job, Joe gained his first experience in public speaking as a student leader at a nearly all-white university. Then, as now, public speaking was "a way of articulating things I feel passionate about. It came from really being concerned about an issue . . . I simply wanted to articulate what was inside of me." Joe's goal, however, is not simply to make a point: He wants to produce results.

"My definition of a good speaker is someone who moves you to think and rearrange the ideas you have about a particular subject. But the best speaker— someone like Martin Luther King, Jr., for example— is someone who moves you to *act*. That's what Dr. King did for me."

In terms of Joe's specific goals, moving an audience to act can mean persuading listeners to become more informed about the problems of black youth or—in the case of some of his most challenging audiences—to choose a better way of life. But whether the desired response is large or small, to reach his listeners' hearts, Joe believes that he must first appeal to their minds.

"Information's first. I have to present information, because people may not have specific knowledge of the problems I'm talking about. So I'll use statistics: The unemployment rate for black teenagers is 50 percent. In some places, 40 percent of black high school students don't graduate; nationally, it's 25 percent. Only 23 out of 100 will go to college, and only 16 will graduate. Fifty percent of the prison population is black. Then I'll say, 'Look, something's wrong with the numbers!'

"I always appeal to people's intelligence, I really do—especially with convicts. I tell convicts, 'I know you've been told that you can run, jump, sing, and dance, but nobody ever told you that you were smart. Well, just listen, and keep what makes sense to you.

"'Now, does it *make sense* to you that only 12 percent of the population accounts for 50 percent of the people in prison? Something's wrong with the numbers! Is it that you had *convict* stamped on you when you came out of the womb? Or are there factors influencing you that you aren't even aware of?'

"You see, I want them to *think* and examine why they're there. And then I've got them, and they're the best audience in the world."

Of course, the choice of information and arguments to present depends on the makeup of the audience. "I'm very conscious of who I'm speaking to," Joe noted. "You have to be." With each audience, he looks for a way to "personalize" his arguments so that they will have visceral as well as rational impact.

"I try to hit a spot with every audience that makes it personal. Then I always want to make them feel something. I try to use examples anyone can understand. For instance, I try to put them in the shoes of the people I'm talking about. I describe what it's like to grow up in an environment where there's no adult guidance, where the father's gone and coke has taken the mother away, and the kids feel the school doesn't care about them, and there's all this easy money from dealing drugs.

"But I also try to show how the problem affects them. Drive-by shootings, for example — they can affect anybody, no matter where they live. So I appeal to people's altruism, but I also try to make it as personal as possible."

Even the most compelling reasoning, however, is only a means to achieving Joe's ultimate goal: getting his audiences to act. For Joe, a persuasive speech about pressing issues is incomplete without a specific recommendation for action.

"I hate speakers who just throw something out and then walk away. If I want someone to learn about black history, I say, 'Read this book.' I try to be very practical, because I want people to take what I've left with them and utilize it in their personal lives. I want them to understand that everybody can play a part in some way. We all can't do the same thing, but we all can do something. If you're not part of the solution, you're part of the problem."

How does a speaker motivate an audience to act? Especially with his prison audiences, one of Joe's favorite ways of motivating change is to create discomfort in his listeners by showing them that their beliefs and their actions are incompatible. (As discussed in Chapter 16, this is the technique of arousing *dissonance*.)

"I don't know what you call it," Joe laughed, "but it works." His speeches to men in jail provide a vivid example:

"I tell convicts, 'What you *want* is to be happy — I *know* you don't want to be *here*. So you may be doing things that you *think* will make you happy, but look at where you are! You *want* to go east, but you're going west! Let's look at why the path you're following isn't going to bring you happiness.'"

As this example shows, part of being persuasive is knowing something about human psychology. But no one listening to Joe can doubt that much of his credibility and persuasive power stems from the sincerity and caring he communicates, including his respect for his audience.

"I really believe in people," he says unabashedly. "Every single person is special and unique. And as a speaker, if you have that attitude in you, you'll talk to everybody directly. People have told me they thought I was talking directly to them, even though I was in a room with 600 people. You see, I acknowledge that humanity all the time. And if I think of great speakers who influenced my life, that's what they did.

"Everybody has a style that's personal, and everybody can communicate. You don't have to speak like Dr. King, or sound like him. If you're communicating from the heart, it will be heard."

| Chapter 14 | Principles of Persuasive Speaking |

erhaps you have imagined yourself giving such a stirring speech that your audience cheers wildly at your persuasive powers. Although everything works well in our fantasies, our real-life attempts at persuading others are not always so successful. *Persuasive speaking* is perhaps the most demanding of speech challenges. Although there is no guaranteed formula for success, by following the guidelines suggested in this chapter you can increase the probability of achieving your specific goal.

In this chapter we define the nature of persuasive speaking, identify the goals of a persuasive speaker, and then stress the principles of persuasive speaking that relate to your specific goals: reasons and evidence, audience perspective, organization, motivation, credibility, and presentation.

Persuasive Speaking Defined

Persuasive speaking is a process in which a speaker presents a message intended to affect an audience in a specific way. Let us see how a persuasive speaker's procedure is contrasted with the informative speaker's.

1. Like informative speakers, persuasive speakers design their speeches to achieve a specific goal. Rather than having the goal of increasing understanding, persuasive speakers design speeches to change beliefs and move audiences to action. Giving a stirring persuasive speech does not simply happen. Yes, there are stories of people who were so moved by a situation that they rose to deliver inspiring, spontaneous orations that brought immediate success. But for every story of spontaneous excellence there are hundreds of stories of long hours of preparation in which people struggled to shape their messages in just the right way to achieve maximum effect.

2. Unlike informative speakers who use material solely to further understanding, persuasive speakers also use their speech material to substantiate a case or appeal to action. In your persuasive speech on secondary education, for example, you would use examples and statistics to support the claim that high school graduates are less prepared to function in a work environment than they were twenty years ago.

3. Like informative speakers, persuasive speakers seek to be perceived by their listeners as having their best interests in mind. Although the members of your audience will recognize that you are trying to influence their attitudes or behavior, they should not perceive you as manipulating or taking advantage of them. All speakers must be sensitive to the legal and ethical considerations that guide effective speaking.

4. Like informative speakers, persuasive speakers assume that listeners have the power to act. Thus, candidates running for office assume that people will act upon their choice at the ballot box. In this sense, persuasive speaking—even the classroom variety—is very "real"; when the speech is given, an audience is present—and that audience can act upon your recommendations.

Factors Involved in Achieving Your Persuasive Speaking Goal

Just as persuasive speaking can be compared to informative speaking on specific goals, so it also can be compared in terms of its interest, understanding, retention, and attitude, all of which are used to achieve specific speaking goals.

1. *Like informative speakers, persuasive speakers must generate enough interest in their information to arouse audience attention.* In any speech people make value judgments about whether they will listen to the material you present. Suppose your specific goal is to

have the audience believe that it should support a tax package for the funding of a program to increase basic skill levels of high school students. If your listeners do not attend to your speech because they are not interested in programs to increase such skill levels, they cannot be persuaded. In your speech, then, you must consider effective means of generating and maintaining interest.

2. *Like informative speakers, persuasive speakers must explain their information in ways that will enable the audience to understand it.* If members of an audience do not truly comprehend the information, it probably will not affect their beliefs or move them to action. In your speech on funding an educational program, for example, your audience will be unmoved if it does not understand the nature of the funding or how this funding will be used to increase skills. In your speech, then, you must clarify the specific ideas and programs that you support.

3. *Like informative speakers, persuasive speakers must discuss information in ways that will enable the audience to remember it.* In your speech on funding an educational program, for example, gaining your audience's belief in the importance of a tax program will be of little value if, after you conclude your speech, the audience cannot remember what it was to believe or why. As in informative speaking, you must use strategies that emphasize ideas and make them vivid.

4. *Unlike informative speakers, persuasive speakers must be aware of and adapt to audience attitudes toward both speakers and their information.* A persuasive speaker must understand where the audience stands on a specific goal so that he or she can develop a speech strategy to adapt to audience attitudes. For instance, in your speech on funding an educational program, if you know the attitude of your audience toward supporting increased high school student skill levels, you can prepare a strategy that addresses that specific attitude.

Now let us turn to detailed and specific principles that you can use to incorporate these factors in your speaking.

Writing a Persuasive Specific Goal

Principle 1

You are more likely to persuade an audience when your specific goal is clearly defined.

How you write your specific goal may well determine the degree of success you attain with the speech. Although any random statement may influence another person's actions (for example, merely saying, "I see the new Penney's store opened in Western Woods" may "persuade" another person to go to Penney's for some clothing need), the successful persuader does not leave the intent of the message to chance.

Wording Goals

In Chapter 2, we discussed five guidelines for writing specific speech goals: (1) continue writing until your tentative specific goal is a complete sentence that states the exact response or behavior you want from your audience; (2) write out three or more different wordings of the goal that reflect your sensitivity to the needs of the audience and the occasion; (3) do not write the goal as a question or capsule statement; (4) write the goal so that it focuses on only one idea; and (5) revise the infinitive until it indicates the specific audience reaction that you desire. Thus, "I want my audience to believe that the City of Cincinnati should build a downtown entertainment center" is a clearly defined persuasive speech goal: It is a complete sentence that clearly states the single response the speaker wants from the audience.

When you are certain that your prospective goal meets the five guidelines, you then write a thesis statement based on that goal. For the goal of getting your audience to believe that air traffic controllers need to be tested for drugs, for instance, your thesis statement might be: "It is necessary to test air traffic controllers for drugs because drug use among air traffic controllers is a problem and because the risks of accidents increase markedly when air traffic controllers use drugs on the job." If you do not have enough information to complete the thesis statement at this time, delay doing so until you have sufficient information.

Kinds of Persuasive Specific Goals

After you have written several persuasive speech goals, you will note that they can be grouped by similarities of general purpose and by subject matter.

CLASSIFICATION BY GENERAL PURPOSE Under the heading of general purpose, speeches can reinforce, establish, or change a belief, or move an audience to action. Let us consider each of these.

1. *Speeches that reinforce an existing belief.* These speeches are given when you believe that your audience has weak commitment to an appropriate belief. For instance, suppose that your audience has

limited faith in its responsibility to vote. With an election upcoming you decide to give a speech designed to strengthen a more positive belief. You might phrase your speech goal as, "I want the audience to reaffirm its belief that every American has a responsibility to vote."

The following are other typical examples of such goals:

I want the audience to reaffirm its belief that America is the land of opportunity.

I want the audience to strengthen its belief in the right of every student to an equal opportunity for education.

I want the audience to reaffirm its belief in our right to freedom of worship.

2. *Speeches that seek to establish a belief.* These speeches are given when you believe that your audience does not hold a clearly articulated belief on an issue. For instance, suppose you strongly believe in the importance of recycling but that your audience has developed no beliefs related to the issue. As a result, you may decide to phrase your speech goal as, "I want the audience to believe that the community should start a recycling program."

The following are other typical examples of speech goals that are designed to establish a belief:

I want the audience to believe that our community should establish an adult literacy program.

I want the audience to believe that the city should build a downtown entertainment center.

I want the audience to believe that small schools are better for insecure students than are large schools.

3. *Speeches that seek to change a belief.* These speeches are given when you believe that your audience holds a belief different from your own. Suppose that after studying the issue of tax deductions, you believe that allowing homeowners to deduct their interest payments discriminates against people who live in apartments by choice or by circumstance. Because Americans may deduct house-payment interest on their federal income tax forms (the current practice) and because most Americans believe that such a deduction is their right (the majority opinion), a speech designed "to have an audience believe that the federal income tax deduction for house-payment interest should be abolished" would seek a change in majority opinion, current practice, or both.

There are times when the belief of the audience is different from the belief of the majority of Americans or from current practice. Current laws, for example, prohibit teenage drinking of alcoholic beverages; moreover, the majority of Americans believe that drinking of alcoholic beverages is bad for teenagers, especially those under age eighteen. Yet you may be speaking to an audience of twelve- to sixteen-year-olds who believe they should be allowed to drink alcohol. In this case, a speech opposing teenage drinking would seek to change the belief of a specific audience.

Notice that in these speeches, the response you want is cognitive support. Although the speech may motivate some members of the audience to seek action, the focus of the speech will be on the belief itself.

The following are typical examples of speech goals that are designed to change a belief:

I want the audience to believe that the speed limit on all interstate highways should be raised to seventy miles per hour.

I want the audience to believe that capital punishment should be abolished in all fifty states.

I want the audience to believe that Social Security benefits should be lowered.

4.   *Speeches that get an audience to take action.* Although a portion of such a speech may be directed to establishing or changing specific audience beliefs, the emphasis of your speech will be on motivating members of the audience to take action. The following are examples of such goals.

I want my audience to donate money to this year's Fine Arts Fund.

I want the members of my audience to write to their congressperson to support legislation in favor of gun control.

I want my audience members to attend the school's production of *A Chorus Line*.

I want my audience members each to donate one hour a month to one of the city's established literacy programs to tutor an adult in reading.

You may have noticed that some of the examples under the same heading (for instance, to change a belief) seem to be of different types. Another way to classify speech goals is by subject matter rather than by general purpose.

CLASSIFICATION BY SUBJECT MATTER   The subject matter of persuasive speeches that affect beliefs may state a fact (past, present, or future); evaluate a person, place, thing, or action; or propose a policy.

1.   *Speeches affecting audience beliefs about statements of fact.* Statements of fact are either true or not true. Many times a speaker's goal

is to reinforce, establish, or change an audience's belief about a statement of fact. Specific goals using statements of fact are a mainstay in courts of law; they also are used in deliberations over politics, education, and the environment, and in other contexts as well. The following are typical speech goals taking positions on statements of fact:

I want the jury to believe that Jones is guilty of murder in the first degree.

I want my audience to believe that the Greenhouse effect is a reality.

I want my audience to believe that SAT tests discriminate against minorities.

2. *Speeches affecting audience beliefs about statements of evaluation.* A speaker's goal may be to reinforce, establish, or change an audience's evaluation of a person, place, thing, or action — that is, show whether the person, place, thing, or action is good or bad. The following are typical speech goals of evaluation:

I want my audience to believe that small schools are better for most students than are large schools.

I want my audience to believe that accounting is the best course to take to prepare for a career in business.

I want my audience to believe that Jones is the best quarterback in the league.

3. *Speeches affecting audience beliefs or actions about statements of policy.* A speaker's goal may be to reinforce, establish, or change an audience's belief about a proposed action or it may be an attempt to move an audience to action. Policy speeches are most likely to be heard in settings in which lawmakers give speeches favoring or opposing suggested legislation. The following are typical speech goals advocating policies:

I want the audience to believe that work on nuclear power plants should be halted.

I want my audience to vote for an increased budget for women's athletics.

I want my audience to believe that Social Security benefits should be lowered.

Notice that both sets of speech goals, by general purpose and by subject matter, meet the same tests of wording. Despite their differences in emphasis, a list of speech goals can be grouped in either way. For example, the speech goal, "I want my audience to believe that Parsons is guilty of robbery" may be listed either as a goal of establishing an audience belief or as a goal of affecting audience belief on a statement of fact. Whether your professor assigns speeches by general purpose or by subject matter, the advice in the remainder of this chapter will help you to prepare a speech that gives you the best possible chances of success.

Skill Development Exercise
Writing Persuasive Specific Goals

Write a persuasive specific goal and then rewrite it two or three times with slightly different wordings. Identify your goal as one reaffirming, establishing, or changing a belief, or as one seeking action. Then identify your goal as one affecting beliefs related to statements of fact, statements of evaluation, or statements of policy. If at this stage you do not know what your audience believes, you may wish to hold final wording of your goal until you have finished the next section on audience attitude.

Analyzing Your Audience

Principle 2

You are more likely to determine the most effective speech strategy when you understand your audience's interest and knowledge levels and attitude toward your goal.

Analyzing Audience Data to Make Assessments

Because much of your success depends on determining how your audience is likely to react to your material, you must analyze audience data carefully to make reasonable assessments.

As we established in Chapter 2, you can make reasonably accurate estimates of audience interest, knowledge, and attitude based on demographic information. The more data you have about your audience and the more experience you have in analyzing audiences, the better are your chances of judging its attitudes with accuracy, although a precise differentiation of opinion is seldom necessary. Knowledge gained from your analysis then is processed in two ways: You assess your audience position and then develop a strategy for adapting to that position.

Interest, Understanding, and Retention

Although the issues of interest, understanding, and retention were discussed fully in Chapter 8, "Principles of Informative Speaking," we will review them here.

AUDIENCE INTEREST   Because persuasion is not likely to take place if you cannot engage audience interest in your speech, you must assess whether the audience is likely to have enough immediate interest in your goal to listen to your information; moreover, you must determine what you can do during the speech to build or maintain such interest.

AUDIENCE UNDERSTANDING   Because persuasion is not likely to take place if your audience is unable to understand your arguments and information, you need to assess whether they *are* likely to be understood; if not, you need to find a way of explaining information and arguments that facilitates audience understanding.

AUDIENCE RETENTION   Persuasion is less likely if your audience is unable to remember what it is supposed to believe or do or why it is supposed to do so. Thus, you must assess the likelihood of audience retention; if it seems unlikely, you need to think about how you can emphasize key points more vividly.

AUDIENCE ATTITUDE   Because persuasion is not likely to take place if your audience has a negative attitude toward your goal, you should assess the direction and strength of audience attitudes about your topic in general and specific goal in particular. What do we mean by an "attitude"? An *attitude* is a predisposition for or against people, places, or things. Your attitude usually is expressed in evaluative terms — you like or dislike something. For instance, in reference to the concept of physical fitness, a person may be predisposed to favor physical fitness, so we could say that the person has a positive attitude toward physical fitness.

The earlier section of this chapter on specific goals discussed persuasive speaking and its effect on beliefs. But how do beliefs relate to attitudes? Most psychologists see a belief as the cognitive aspect of an attitude; that is, we believe something to be true if someone can prove it to our satisfaction. On the subject of physical fitness, I might believe that keeping in good physical condition increases my chances of avoiding heart disease. So if I hold a favorable attitude toward physical fitness in general, it will be easier for me to hold a belief that being in good physical condition lowers the likelihood of my developing heart disease.

Students of persuasion realize that people's expressions of attitudes or beliefs take the form of opinions. An *opinion* is a verbal expression of an attitude. Saying, "I think physical fitness is important" is an opinion reflecting a favorable attitude about physical fitness; saying, "I think keeping in good condition lowers my chances of heart disease," is an opinion reflecting my belief.

Figure 14.1

An opinion continuum.

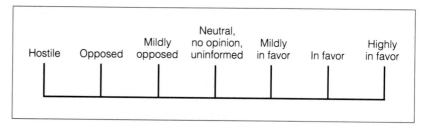

There is a difference between an opinion and a behavior. A *behavior* is an action related to or resulting from an attitude or a belief. As a result of their attitudes or beliefs, people behave in certain ways. For instance, people who believe in the value of physical fitness may work out three or more times a week in order to stay in good physical condition. Exercise is the behavior that results from the attitude.

Often there is harmony among these elements. For instance, a person may have a favorable *attitude* toward physical fitness; the person may then give the *opinion* that good physical conditioning is important; and as a result of this attitude, the person may *work out* at least three times a week. Of course, it is possible for discrepancies to occur: A person may voice the opinion that physical conditioning is important, but then never work out.

Audience attitudes are expressed by opinions, which may be distributed along a continuum from highly favorable to hostile (see Figure 14.1). Even though any given audience may have one or a few individuals' opinions at nearly every point along the distribution, audience opinion tends to cluster at a particular point. That cluster point represents the general audience attitude for that topic. Because it would be impossible to direct your speech to all the various shades of attitudes held by the members of your audience, you must classify audience attitude as predominantly *no opinion* (either no information or no interest), *in favor* (already holding a particular belief), or *opposed* (holding an opposite point of view) so that you can develop a strategy that adapts to that attitude.

Now let us consider specific strategies based on the classifications of no opinion, in favor, or opposed. Suppose your goal is to have your listeners believe that they should alter their intake of saturated fats so as to lower their overall cholesterol levels.

NO OPINION   An audience that has no opinion is either uninformed, neutral, or apathetic. The most appropriate speech goals for audiences with no opinion are goals that establish a belief or goals that move the audience to action.

Regardless of the strength of your case or your conviction, to speak persuasively you need to adapt to your audience's preexisting beliefs and attitudes. Even powerful leaders like the Soviet Union's Mikhail Gorbachev must tailor their persuasive goals and tactics to specific audiences — including hostile ones.

If you believe your audience has no opinion because it is uninformed, your strategy should be to give enough information to help your audience understand the subject before you develop persuasive appeals that are directed toward establishing a belief or that seek to move listeners to action. For instance, if you believe your audience has no opinion about lowering cholesterol levels because it is uninformed, then only a few members of your audience will know what cholesterol is, how it is formed, and what effects it has on blood composition. Even those who know what cholesterol is may not know enough about it to form an opinion about its effects. In the early part of the speech, then, you would define cholesterol, talk about how it is formed, and share medical evidence about its effects on the human body. You must be quite careful about how much time you spend on this informative part of the speech. If it takes more than half of your allotted time to explain what you are talking about, you may not have enough time to do much persuading.

If you believe your audience has no opinion because it is neutral, then you see your audience as being able to reason objectively and accept sound reasoning. In this case, then, your strategy will involve presenting the best possible arguments and supporting them with the best information you can find. If your assessment is correct, then you stand a good chance of success with that strategy.

If you believe your audience members have no opinion because they are apathetic, all of your effort may be directed to moving them out of their apathy. Your audience may know what cholesterol is, how it is formed, and even understand the medical information of negative effects, but it may not seem to care. Instead of emphasizing the information with this audience, you would emphasize motivation. You will need less material that proves the logic of your arguments and more material that is directed to your listeners' personal needs.

You should not expect too much even from a neutral audience. Major attitude change is more likely to come from a series of speeches over a period of time than from a single speech. Because your classroom speaking allows for only one effort, however, you will want to make the most of it.

IN FAVOR If you believe your listeners favor your position, you do not have to convince them of the merits of lowering their fat levels, but you must provide a specific plan of action. The most appropriate speech goal for a favorable audience is to reaffirm a belief, or more likely, to move them to action.

Although this sounds like an ideal situation, it carries many hazards. When an audience already is in favor of your topic, it seldom is interested in a rehash of familiar material. For instance, if members of your audience favor lowering their cholesterol levels, you would make a mistake by staying with the importance of lowering cholesterol levels. What keeps people who have a favorable attitude from acting is their lack of agreement on *what* to do. Your job is to provide a specific course of action around which they can rally. When you believe your listeners are on your side, try to crystallize their attitudes, recommit them to a particular direction, or suggest a specific course of action that will serve as a rallying point. If you can focus the speech on a specific way of reducing saturated fat intake, you can perhaps get audience attitudes going in the same direction. The presentation of a well-thought-out and specific solution increases the likelihood of audience action.

Even when audience members are on your side they may perceive that what you want them to do is impractical. If so, they are likely to ignore your appeal regardless of its merits. For instance, if your goal is to have class members write letters to their congressional representatives, the act of letter writing may seem impractical even to an audience of partisans. If, on the other hand, you suggest writing a short message on a postcard *and* you can give your listeners preaddressed postcards, they may be more inclined to dash off a few lines if they agree with the merits of your appeal.

OPPOSED An audience that is opposed will have attitudes ranging from slightly negative to thoroughly hostile. The most appropriate speech goals for audiences that are opposed are those arguments that change a belief.

If you believe your listeners are slightly opposed to lowering their saturated fat intakes, you can approach them rather directly with your argument, hoping that its weight will swing them to your side.

Another part of your strategy should concern the presentation of arguments in ways that lessen your listeners' negative attitudes without arousing their hostility. With a negative audience you must be careful to be objective with your material and make your case clearly enough that those members who are only mildly negative are more likely to be persuaded and those who are very negative will at least understand your position.

If you believe that your audience is hostile toward your goal, you may want to approach the topic indirectly or you may want to consider a less ambitious goal. To expect a complete shift in attitude or behavior as a result of one speech probably is unrealistic. William Brigance, one of the great speech teachers of this century, used to speak of "planting the seeds of persuasion." If you present a modest proposal that seeks a slight change in attitude, you may be able to get an audience to at least consider the value of your message. Later, when the idea begins to grow, you can ask for a greater change. For instance, the audience may comprise people who are "fed up" with appeals to monitor their diets. Because you believe that your goal is important to them regardless of their negative attitude, then you should develop a strategy that will be more subtle. This will involve recognizing their hostility and talking about the topic in a way that will not arouse that hostility.

This chapter later continues its discussion of strategies by featuring the types of persuasive speech organizations that are appropriate for each type of audience.

In reference to your specific persuasive speech goal, is your audience's attitude likely to be in favor, neutral, or opposed? What speech strategies will you use to adapt to that attitude?

Giving Logical Reasons and Evidence

> **Principle 3**
>
> *You are more likely to persuade an audience when the body of your speech contains logical reasons and good evidence that support your speech goal.*

The main points of a persuasive speech usually are stated as *reasons* — that is, statements that tell *why* a proposition is justified. Human beings take pride in being rational — we seldom do anything without some real or imagined reason. Persuasive speech theory in the 1980s focused sharply on persuasion as a cognitive activity; that is, people learn "by experiencing sudden insights that involve broad reorganization of cognitive structures."[1] One way to reason with your audience is by providing good, well-supported reasons that support your proposition.

Finding Reasons

How do you draw up a list of reasons to consider? You can identify relevant good reasons simply by taking a little time to think about the subject for the speech. Suppose you wanted to persuade your friends to increase their exercise. You might begin by asking yourself, "Why should my friends increase their level of exercise?" You might then think of the following three reasons: (1) To help them control their weight, (2) to help them strengthen their cardiovascular systems, and (3) to help them feel better. For most of your speeches, however, you will need to supplement your own thoughts with reasons you discover through observation, interviewing, and reading. Find as many reasons as you can through research, and then choose the best ones.

For example, for a speech goal phrased "I want the audience to believe that the United States should overhaul its welfare system," you might identify six reasons:

I. The welfare system costs too much.
II. The welfare system is inequitable.
III. The welfare system does not help those who need help the most.
IV. The welfare system has been grossly abused.
V. The welfare system does not encourage its clients to seek work.
VI. The welfare system does not encourage self-support.

Once you have compiled a list of possible reasons, select the best ones (probably no more than three or four) on the basis of the following criteria:

1. *Choose the reasons that best prove the proposition.* Sometimes, statements look like reasons but do not supply much proof. For instance, "The welfare system is supported by socialists" may sound like a reason for overhauling it, but it does not really offer much proof that the system needs overhauling. Who supports a system is not relevant to a decision concerning whether that system should be overhauled.

2. *Choose reasons that can be supported.* Some reasons that sound impressive cannot be supported with facts. A reason that cannot be supported should not be used in the speech. For example, the fourth reason, "The welfare system has been grossly abused," sounds good, but if you cannot find facts that support the statement, you should not use it in your speech. You will be surprised at how many reasons mentioned in various sources must be dropped from inclusion in a speech because they cannot be supported.

3. *Choose reasons that will have an impact on the intended audience.* Suppose that in support of the proposition "Eat at the Sternwheeler" you have a great deal of factual evidence to back up the statement, "The seafood is excellent." Even though you have a good reason and good support, it would be a poor reason to use in the speech if the majority of your listeners did not like seafood! Although you cannot always be sure about the potential impact of a reason, you can make a decent estimate of its possible impact based on your general audience analysis. For a speech on eating out intended for a college audience, for example, the reason "The meals are reasonably

priced," is likely to have greater impact than it would on an audience of business executives.

Finding Evidence to Support Your Reasons

Reasons are only generalizations. Although some are self-explanatory and occasionally even persuasive without further support, most require development before people will either accept or act upon them. Reasons are supported with factual statements and expert opinions. Let us briefly summarize the differences between factual statements and expert opinions, which we discussed in Chapter 3.

FACTUAL   The best support for reasons are factual statements, or statements that can be verified. Statements such as "Alzheimer's is the fourth leading cause of death for adults," "In 1989, the San Francisco Bay Area experienced an earthquake that measured 7.1 on the Richter scale," and "The last half of 1989 saw Eastern bloc countries electing noncommunist rulers" all are factual.

EXPERT OPINIONS   Statements from people who have good reputations for knowledge on the subject represent *expert opinions*. Although factual support is best, there are times when facts are not available or are inconclusive. In these situations you can further support your conclusions by using opinion. "By 2050 Alzheimer's may afflict 14 million people a year" is an expert opinion.

Let us illustrate evidence by supporting a proposition with fact and opinion.

Specific Goal: I want my audience to shop at Schappenhouper's food stores. Why?

Reason 1: Because the prices are lower.

 Evidence by Fact:
 If we look at prices at four major markets for five basic foods — eggs, chopped meat, lettuce, potatoes, and milk — we find the prices are lower on average at Schappenhouper's. Beginning with eggs, at Schappenhouper's they are 93 cents a dozen, at store A they are 96 cents, at B they are 101 cents, and at C they are 97 cents. Next let's look at chopped meat . . . , and so on.

 Evidence by Expert Opinion:
 Mrs. Goody, a fraternity cook who comparison shops every week, says, "I shop at Schappenhouper's because prices are lower for comparable foods."

At this stage your persuasive speech will have a logical structure: a clear speech goal, reasons to support that goal, and support for the reasons.

In this chapter we have defined reasoning as the presentation of reasons and evidence in support of a specific goal. In the next chapter we will continue our discussion by analyzing the different types of reasoning that you will use in your speeches.

Skill Development **Exercise** *Selecting Reasons*	1. Write the specific goal that you will use for your first persuasive speech. 2. Write at least six reasons that support your specific goal. 3. Place stars next to the three or four reasons that you believe are the best.

Organizing Material to Meet Audience Attitudes

Principle 4

You are more likely to persuade an audience when you organize your material according to expected audience reaction.

Although the nature of your material and your own inclination may affect your organization, the most important guideline is expected audience reaction or attitude. As a result, the specific organization you select will depend on whether your audience favors your proposition and, if so, to what degree.

You will recall from Chapter 4 that a reasons order is one of the five common speech organizations. The following organizational methods — statement of reasons, problem–solution, comparative advantages, criteria satisfaction, and negative method — are different examples of reasons order that may prove useful to adopt as stated, or they may suggest an organization that you believe will work for your audience given the material you have to work with. For the purposes of illustrating persuasive organizational patterns, we will use the same specific goal and the same (or similar) arguments. With some topics and some material, one form is likely to be better — the forms are not entirely interchangeable. Nevertheless, by applying each method to essentially the same arguments, you can contrast the forms and better understand their use.

Statement-of-Reasons Method

When you believe your listeners have no opinion on the subject, are apathetic, or are perhaps only mildly in favor or mildly opposed, the straightforward and topical *statement of reasons* may be the best organization. With this pattern each reason is presented as a complete statement justification for the speech goal:

Specific Goal: I want my audience to vote in favor of the school tax levy on the November ballot.

I.   Income will enable the schools to restore vital programs.
II. Income will enable the schools to give teachers the raises they need to keep up with the cost of living.
III. The actual cost to each member of the community will be minimal.

Problem–Solution Method

Recall from Chapter 4 that the *problem–solution* pattern provides a framework for clarifying the nature of the problem and for illustrating why a given proposal is the best one. Usually there are three main points in a problem–solution speech: (1) There is a problem that requires action, (2) the proposal will solve the problem, and (3) the proposal is the best solution to the problem. This pattern may be best for an audience that has no opinion or is mildly pro or con. Now let us see how a problem–solution organization would look for the school tax–levy goal:

Specific Goal: I want my audience to vote in favor of the school tax levy on the November ballot.

I.   The shortage of money is resulting in serious problems for public education.
II. The proposed increase is large enough to solve those problems.
III. For now, a tax levy is the best method of solving the schools' problems.

Comparative-Advantages Method

The *comparative-advantages* pattern focuses on the superiority of your newly proposed course of action. With this pattern you are not trying to solve a problem as much as you are suggesting a better alternative. This pattern can work with any audience attitude except hostility. A comparative-advantages approach to the school tax–levy speech goal would look like this:

Specific Goal: I want my audience to vote in favor of the school tax levy on the November ballot.

    I.   Income from a tax levy will enable schools to raise the standards of their programs.

   II.   Income from a tax levy will enable schools to hire better teachers.

 III.   Income from a tax levy will enable schools to better the educational environment.

Criteria-Satisfaction Method

When you are dealing with audiences that are opposed to your ideas, you need a pattern of organization that will not aggravate hostility. The *criteria-satisfaction* pattern, which first states the objective criteria with which audience members are likely to agree and then shows how the speech goal meets those criteria, is one of two patterns that are particularly effective with hostile audiences. The pattern focuses on developing a "yes" response before you introduce the goal and reasons. A criteria-satisfaction organization for the school tax–levy speech goal would look like this:

Specific Goal: I want my audience to vote in favor of the school tax levy on the November ballot.

    I.   We all want good schools.
       A. Good schools have programs that prepare our youth to function in society.
       B. Good schools are those with the best teachers available.

   II.   Passage of the school tax levy will guarantee good schools.
       A. Passage will enable us to increase the quality of vital programs.
       B. Passage will enable us to hire and keep the best teachers.

Negative Method

The *negative* pattern, the second method that is particularly effective for hostile audiences, focuses on the shortcomings of all solutions except the one offered in the proposition. To persuade a hostile audience to vote for a tax levy, you might use this organizational pattern:

Specific Goal: I want my audience to vote in favor of the school tax levy on the November ballot.

I. Saving money by reducing services and programs will not help the schools.

II. The federal government will not increase its help to the schools.

III. The state government will not increase its help to the schools.

IV. All we have left is to pass the tax levy.

Skill Development Exercise *Organization* Select an organization for your speech. Justify your selection on the basis of your audience analysis.

Using Language to Arouse Emotions

> ### Principle 5
> *You are more likely to persuade your listeners when your language arouses their emotions.*

From the time of Aristotle's *Rhetoric*, the first complete book on persuasion (written more than 2,000 years ago), students of public speaking have been aware of the power of arousing emotions. In the words of Richard Weaver, "A speech intended to persuade achieves little unless it takes into account how people are reacting subjectively to their hopes and fears and their special circumstances."[2] What is an emotion? An *emotion* is subjectively experienced as strong feeling and physiologically involves changes that prepare the body for action. Many of our emotions are triggered by physical happenings. For instance when a dog jumps from behind a tree it frightens us. Emotions are also triggered by words. For instance, when a friend says, "Go to the play—don't worry about me, I'll be all right alone," we may feel guilt. In this section we are interested in the conscious effort of a speaker to phrase ideas in ways that appeal to the emotions of the listeners.

Effective persuasive speech development is logical-emotional. I like to look at logic and emotion as inseparable elements within a speech. Thus, we should not look for additional material that will arouse fear or pity or joy—we should look for good reasons and for support that will, *if properly phrased*, arouse fear or pity or joy.

Suppose you are to give a speech calling for more humane treatment of the elderly in our society. In the speech, you want to make the point that older people often feel alienated from the society that they worked so many years to support and develop. In so doing, you can present facts and figures to show how many older citizens are not employed, how many are relegated to nursing homes, and how many skills and talents are lost. These are all good points. If, in addition, you can cause your listeners to *feel* sad, angry, or guilty about that treatment, you can add affective dimension to the material. The role of emotional appeal is to compel listeners to *feel* as well as to *think* about what is being said. Let us first consider how you create wording that has emotional impact and then let us consider where you should focus emotional appeal in the speech.

Developing Emotional Impact

Emotional appeal grows out of an emotional climate. You are the catalyst in developing that climate.

1. *Clearly identify the emotions you want your listeners to experience.* What emotion or emotions do you want your audience to experience as a result of your speech? If you are giving a speech designed to get the audience's support for more humane treatment of the elderly, you may want your listeners to feel sadness, anger, grief, caring, or, perhaps, guilt. If you are giving a speech designed to get the audience to attend your school's production of a musical, you may want your listeners to feel joy, excitement, or enthusiasm. If you are not sure what it is that you want your audience to feel, any speech effectiveness is likely to be accidental.

2. *Identify the information you have that is likely to stimulate those emotions in your listeners.* Suppose that you have determined that you want your listeners to feel sad about the lack of positive goals or aspirations of the elderly. What information do you have that will *show* the lack of goals or aspirations. Perhaps you have data from interviews with elderly people in which their only talk of the future is the inevitability of death. Perhaps you have accounts of social workers saying that many elderly people live totally in the past — they are reluctant to talk about or even think about the future. Or perhaps you have information to show that many nursing homes do very little to give their clients anything to look forward to. These are all examples of the kinds of information that are likely to cause another person to feel sad.

3. *In practices, replace vague, flat sentences that carry no emotional impact with specific, vivid descriptions and explanations.* It is unlikely that you will use your most specific and vivid language in your

first practice sessions. Your first practices enable you to get the order and logic of your speech in mind. When you are comfortable with *what* points you want to make, you can start working on *how* to make them. And, as the following comparison shows, a situation does not have to be a highly emotional one to develop emotional appeal through specific, vivid language.

In an early practice session, for example, you might make a point about the elderly's lack of goals and aspirations as follows:

> What struck me most about many of the elderly living in nursing homes is their lack of goals. They occupy most of their time watching television, but they don't pay much attention to it. It's as if they're just passing time.

This segment explains the point, but there is little in it that would cause a person to feel the sadness of lack of goals. Now let us see how you could make the same point, but increase its emotional impact.

> What struck me most about many of the elderly living in nursing homes is the emptiness of their lives. They spend much of each day huddled in front of a television set. But they show virtually no involvement and seldom show any change in expression, as if what they see is largely unimportant. Their lives have largely passed — they look forward to nothing. Each day is but a repeat of the past — another hollow experience — that leads inevitably to death.

With just a few changes, mostly the inclusion of phrases that help to create the image of emptiness, you would have a much more powerful statement.

Focus of Emotional Appeals in the Speech

As you practice your speech, you should focus your emotional appeals on major points you are making in the introduction and conclusion.

1. *Rework major points.* If a speech is well designed, the listeners are most likely to remember the main points, for these are the ideas that are expected to provide listeners with the primary reasons for their believing or acting as you wish. If, however, when listeners think of your main points they do not also feel the power of those points, you are losing much of the value of them. Suppose that in your speech in which you want the audience to believe that television commercials are still sending negative messages about women's roles, for example, you want to make the point that "Television commercials still portray women primarily as housewives whose major thoughts are restricted to domestic issues."

Although this is a clear statement that may well be remembered, it has very little emotional power. With just a slight revision you could make the point as follows:

Television commercials still portray women primarily as housewives whose major thoughts are restricted to the comparative cleanliness of their laundry and their floors.

This phrasing has a greater chance of stimulating a sense of outrage because the vague phrase "domestic issues" has been replaced by more vivid images. But with a little more thought you might be able to ridicule the silliness of the premises of such commercials and heighten the sense of outrage:

Tell me, what is a woman's role as seen through the eyes of a television commercial? Primarily as a housewife—a housewife with two deep all-consuming prayers: "Oh, that my clothes will come out white!" and "Oh, that my floors will be spotless!"

Each of the statements makes essentially the same point, but this third example has more staying power because it has more emotional clout.

2. *Put special effort into the introduction and conclusion.* Perhaps your greatest opportunities for meaningful emotional appeal occur in the introduction and conclusion of your speech. As we have said, in the introduction you capture and heighten audience interest and you set the tone for the speech. Then, in the conclusion you try to take advantage of your final moments to so cement the message of the speech in the minds of the listeners that they cannot shake it. Betsy Burke's speech on euthanasia illustrates excellent use of emotional appeal in both her introduction and conclusion.[3] She began her speech as follows:

Let's pretend for a moment. Suppose that on the upper right-hand corner of your desk there is a button. You have the power by pushing that button to quickly and painlessly end the life of one you love: your brother or father. This loved one has terminal cancer and will be confined to a hospital for his remaining days. Would you push the button now? His condition worsens. He is in constant pain and he is hooked up to a life-support machine. He first requests, but as the pain increases he pleads for you to help. Now would you push that button? Each day you watch him deteriorate until he reaches a point where he cannot talk, he cannot see, he cannot hear—he is only alive by that machine. Now would you push that button?

After giving reasons for changing our laws on euthanasia, she concluded her speech as follows:

I ask again, how long could you take walking into that hospital room and looking at your brother or father in a coma, knowing he would rather be allowed to die a natural death than to be kept alive in such a degrading manner? I've crossed that doorstep—I've gone into that hospital room, and let me tell you, it's hell. I think it's time we reconsider our laws concerning euthanasia. Don't you?

Regardless of your beliefs about the subject of euthanasia, I think you will have to agree with me that you would be inclined to experience sadness as you empathize with her feelings.

Skill Development Exercise
Building Emotional Appeals

Identify the three most important points you want to make in your speech.

1. What emotion are you trying to arouse with each?
2. How can you make those points in ways that are most likely to increase the emotional appeal of the points?

Practice the wording of each of the points at least three times. Which expression most clearly and vividly makes the point?

Building Credibility

Principle 6

You are more likely to persuade your listeners when they have faith in your credibility.

In Chapter 8, "Principles of Informative Speaking," we outlined the nature of credibility and the characteristics that you need to develop to be perceived as credible. Credibility is equally important, if not even more so, to persuasive speaking. Almost all studies confirm that speaker credibility has a major effect on audience belief and attitude.[4]

You also will recall that credibility comprises perceived competence, good intentions, character, and personality.

In your persuasive speeches, in addition to being well prepared, emphasizing your interest in the needs of the audience, and looking and sounding enthusiastic, you also must behave ethically to demonstrate credibility.

What are ethics? *Ethics* are the standards of moral conduct that determine our behavior. Ethics include both how we act ourselves and how we expect others to act. How we treat those who fail to meet our standards says a great deal about the importance we assign to ethics. Although ethical codes are personal, our society has a code of ethics that is implicitly understood even if unwritten and that operates on at least a verbal level.

Especially when we believe strongly in the righteousness of our cause, we are faced with the temptation of bowing to the belief that the end justifies the means or, to put it bluntly, that we can do *anything* to achieve our goals. We all are well aware of people who have ridden rough-shod over society's moral or ethical principles.

How you handle ethical questions says a great deal about you as a person. What is your code of ethics? The following five guidelines reflect the standards of hundreds of students whom I have seen in my classes over the past few years. I believe that these five provide an excellent foundation for a set of personal ethical standards.

1. *Lying is unethical.* Of all the attitudes about ethics, this is the one most universally held. When people know they are being lied to, they will usually reject the speaker's ideas; if they find out later they were lied to, they often look for ways to punish the speaker who lied to them.

2. *Name-calling is unethical.* Again, there seems to be an almost universal agreement on this guideline. Even though many people call others names in their interpersonal communication, they say they regard name-calling by public speakers to be unethical.

3. *Grossly exaggerating or distorting facts is unethical.* Although some people seem willing to accept a little exaggeration as an element of human nature, most people consider "gross" or "distorted" exaggeration to be equivalent to lying. Because the line between some exaggeration and gross exaggeration or distortion often is difficult to distinguish, many people see *any* exaggeration as unethical.

4. *Condemning people or ideas without divulging the source of the information is unethical.* Where ideas originate often is as important as the ideas themselves. Although a statement may be true regardless of whether a source is given, people want more than the speaker's word for any damning statement. If you are going to discuss the wrongdoing of a person or the stupidity of an idea by relying on the words or ideas of others, you must be prepared to share the sources of those words or opinions.

5. *Suppression of key information is unethical.* If you have material to support your views, you should present it; if you have a motive that affects your view, you should divulge it. Audience members have the right to make a choice, but they must have full information in order to exercise that right.

Delivering the Speech Convincingly

> **Principle 7**
>
> *You are more likely to persuade an audience if you develop an effective oral presentation style.*

Your presentation style is a composite of your language and your oral delivery. In previous chapters we have presented the characteristics of language and delivery that you must develop to increase your effectiveness. Moreover, in just the last section we reiterated the point that a dynamic speaking style also helps to build your credibility with your audience. Finally, throughout the text we have emphasized the importance of practicing your speech until your presentation (language and delivery) become a positive factor in your speech.

Although I have nothing new to offer in the discussion of this principle, I reemphasize the importance of good delivery to persuasive speaking. As negative examples I am reminded of the 1988 presidential race between Michael Dukakis and George Bush, a race in which neither speaker was able to generate excitement about presidential priorities. At the same time, I am reminded of Democrats Gary Hart and Jesse Jackson and Republican Jack Kemp, each of whom captured the excitement of the electorate even though for a variety of reasons they could not capture their respective nominations. A final plea: If you cannot go into your persuasive speeches with a burning belief in the importance of your ideas to both your specific audience and society in general, then you are not fulfilling your responsibility as the champion of your ideas.

Checklist	**Persuasive Speech**

Check items that were accomplished effectively.

Specific Goal

_____ 1. Was the specific goal clear?

_____ 2. Was the specific goal designed to _____ reinforce a belief?
_____ establish a belief? _____ change a belief? or
_____ move to action?

_____ 3. Was the specific goal adapted to this audience's interests, knowledge, and attitudes?

Content

_____ 4. Did the speaker present clearly stated reasons?

_____ 5. Did the speaker use facts and expert opinions to support these reasons?

_____ 6. Was the speaker effective in establishing his or her credibility on this topic?

_____ 7. Was the speaker ethical in handling material?

Organization

_____ 8. Did the introduction gain attention and good will for the speaker?

_____ 9. Did the speech follow a _____ statement of reasons order?
_____ problem–solution order? _____ comparative advantages order? _____ criteria satisfaction order? _____ negative order?

_____ 10. Was the order appropriate for the type of goal and assumed attitude of the audience?

_____ 11. Did the conclusion further the persuasive effect of the speech?

Language

_____ 12. Was the language _____ clear? _____ vivid? _____ emphatic? _____ appropriate?

_____ 13. Did the speaker use emotional language to motivate the audience?

Delivery

_____ 14. Was the delivery convincing?

Evaluate the speech as (check one) _____ excellent, _____ good, _____ average, _____ fair, _____ poor.

Use the information from your checklist to support your evaluation.

Putting Persuasive Principles into Practice

We conclude this chapter with a typical assignment, a general persuasive-speaking checklist, and an example of a persuasive speech (including an outline) that illustrates the principles discussed in the chapter.

Assignment
Persuasive Speech Goals

1. Prepare a four- to seven-minute persuasive speech that develops a goal that is designed to *change a belief* or *bring an audience to action*. An outline is required.

2. For one or more of the speeches you hear during a round of persuasive speeches, complete the checklist and then write a two- to five-paragraph evaluation of the speech.

Speech — Television and Children

OUTLINE: LIMITING CHILDREN'S TELEVISION VIEWING

Specific Goal: I want my audience to believe that parents should limit the time their children spend viewing television.

Introduction
   I. Television is America's most frequent baby-sitter.
  II. Children watch television an average of more than twenty-five hours per week.
 III. Excessive television viewing can be very harmful to children.

Thesis Statement: Parents should limit the time their children spend viewing television because heavy television viewing desensitizes children to violence and increases violent tendencies in children.

Body
   I. Heavy television viewing leads to major problems for children.
      A. Heavy television viewing desensitizes children to violence.
         1. By age fifteen the average child has seen more than thirteen thousand televised murders.
         2. Some of the most violent television programs are children's cartoons.
      B. Heavy television viewing encourages aggressive traits in children.
         1. Children learn that a violent character is successful.
         2. Children translate violent tendencies into action.

II. The problem can be solved by limiting the number of hours that children watch television.
    A. Many voluntary programs of limiting viewing have been tried.
    B. Children show many improvements even after short periods of time.
       1. Children are more calm and relaxed.
       2. Children play less violently.

III. Limiting the number of hours of television viewing is a good solution.
    A. It does not require formation of regulatory commissions.
    B. It does not involve any programming censorship.

Conclusion

I. Television viewing leads to desensitization toward violence and aggressive tendencies in children.

II. Television, America's most popular baby-sitter, must be controlled.

Bibliography

Friedrich, L. K., and Stein, A. H. "Television Content and Young Children's Behavior," in J. P. Murray, E. A. Rubenstein, and G. A. Comstock, eds., *Television and Social Behavior*, vol. 2. Washington, D.C.: U.S. Government Printing Office, 1972.

Hickey, Neil. "Does Television Violence Affect Our Society? Yes." *TV Guide* (June 14, 1975).

Kiester, Edwin, Jr. "Here's What TV Is Doing to Us." *TV Guide* (December 17, 1977).

Safran, Claire. "Tonight's Assignment: No TV!" *TV Guide* (April 7, 1979).

"What Television Is Doing to Children." *Newsweek* (February 21, 1977).

Read the following speech aloud. Then, analyze it on the basis of organization, reasoning, and evidence, motivation, and speaker credibility. After you have read and analyzed the speech refer to the analysis in the opposite column.[5]

Analysis

The speaker opens with three questions. The reference to the role of television as a baby-sitter adds to the attractiveness of the opening. She gives credit to certain positive effects of television; then she lays the groundwork for the problem.

SPEECH

Do you have a little brother or sister? A niece or nephew? A preschool-age neighbor? Do you know who is their most frequent baby-sitter? If these children are like the average child in the United States, their most frequent and favorite baby-sitter is likely to be a television set! This baby-sitter can take children to faraway places, make them laugh, and teach them many things. Unfortunately some of the things that television teaches are very harmful and need to be stopped.

The speaker continues her opening by clearly documenting exactly how much time the average child watches television.

This statement leads the speaker into the body of the speech. Her wording tells us that she will follow a problem–solution pattern.

Here she stresses the point that heavy television viewing leads to two major problems. She then clearly states the first problem: Heavy television viewing desensitizes children to violence.

She supports her statement with statistics and a quotation. Although these statistics are quite dramatic, she needs to document her source. The emphasis placed on the fact that children's cartoons are even worse than regular programming helps make the point even stronger. The Bombeck quote is a very powerful one. In addition to supporting the reasoning, it adds a strong emotional appeal.

The second problem, that heavy television viewing encourages aggressive traits in children, also is clearly stated.

This is another excellent bit of information, but again the speaker needs to give us specific documentation for the source of this study.

The speaker gives us partial documentation for this study, but she needs to tell us when the study was done.

According to current Nielsen reports, children watch television an average of over twenty-five hours per week. Many children watch television for longer periods of time than they spend in school. They watch television for longer periods of time than they spend with their family or playing with their friends.

Today I want to discuss with you the potential harms of this heavy television viewing to children and how those harms can be controlled.

Let me start by clarifying the problem: Heavy television viewing leads to two major problems for children. The first problem is that heavy television viewing desensitizes children to violence. It does this by exposing children to so much violence that the concept of violence is no longer meaningful. By the time children who watch an average of twenty-five hours of television a week reach the age of fifteen it is estimated that they will have witnessed more than thirteen thousand televised killings! The sad part is that some of the most violent shows are children's programs. Especially cartoons. The average cartoon hour has six times the amount of violence than that which occurs in the average adult drama series. In one of her syndicated columns, Erma Bombeck wrote, "During a single evening, I once saw 12 people shot to death, two people tortured (one a child), one dumped in a swimming pool, two cars explode with people in them, and a man who crawled three blocks with a knife in his stomach. And you know something? I didn't feel shock or horror. I didn't feel excitement or repugnance. The truth is, I didn't feel anything." Children watch television, they see what is happening, but far too often they don't feel anything.

The second problem is that heavy television viewing encourages aggressive traits in children. Children learn from television that a violent character is successful. And they use that violent behavior as a role model. A study was done in which children were shown two different television shows. In these shows the heroes accomplished the same goals but one used violent means and the other one used nonviolent means. What did the study show? The children rated the hero who used the violent means as more successful, as more wonderful — the hero they would want to model themselves after.

In addition, studies have shown that children translate these violent tendencies into action. Friedrich and Stein did a study where three different groups of preschool children were shown three different kinds of programs. One group saw a violent television program, one group saw an educational television program, and one group saw what was basically

This point is developed with a detailed example of a study, a quotation from a psychologist, and the conclusion of both the original surgeon general's report and the follow-up study.

This final sentence is a good strong wrap-up to this reason.

Here the speaker moves from the problem to the solution. The solution to the problem is clearly stated.

Here the speaker shows that the solution does not require legislation or any infringement on programmers' rights. Although this was the third point on her outline, mentioning the point here is all right.

Although the support for how well the solution works is a little skimpy, it is well documented. We would like to see more evidence that such a plan does work. Still, at least the speaker did try to give support for the effectiveness of the plan.

The summary conclusion is satisfactory. Notice how the speaker returns to the theme developed in the opening of the speech.

Throughout the speech, the speaker blends logical information and emotional appeal quite well. Although she has enough evidence to support the statement of the problem, she needs more specific documentation of sources. In all, a good persuasive speech following a problem–solution pattern.

a neutral program. The children were shown these three kinds of television programs for just a half hour three times a week, for a month. It was found that the children who had seen the violent television programs for just those three half-hour episodes for the one-month period actually played more violently and more aggressively with their playmates than those children who had seen either type of the other two programs. Dr. Robert Liebert, a psychologist at the State University of New York, said, "The amount of TV violence a child viewed at age 9 was the single most important determinant of how aggressive he was at age 19." Both the original 1973 surgeon general's report on television violence and children and the 1983 follow-up study confirm that television violence encourages aggressive behavior in children.

So our problem: Television violence has a harmful effect on children's behavior by desensitizing them and by teaching them violent aggressive actions.

But there is a solution to this problem and the solution is basically an easy one. Parents need to limit the number of hours that their children spend watching television. By reducing the total number of hours children watch, we can reduce both the desensitization and the aggressive behavior. This is a simple solution that every family can accomplish. We don't have to create another regulatory commission; we don't have to censor television programmers. All we have to do is to limit the amount of hours that our children spend watching television.

Does such a simple solution work? Yes. A 1979 issue of *TV Guide* reported that at the Horace Mann School for Nursery Years in New York families had begun a voluntary program of limiting the television viewing of their children. After just three weeks, there was a dramatic change at school. In addition to many other benefits such as being more creative in play, all the children were calmer and much more relaxed. Children were no longer recreating the violent behavior in their play that they had earlier.

So we have seen that excessive television viewing on the part of small children leads to desensitization toward violence and aggressive tendencies. Television may be America's most popular baby-sitter. But for the good of our children, it must be controlled.

Summary

Persuasive speaking is perhaps the most demanding of speech challenges. Although there is no guaranteed formula for success, with careful preparation, you can increase the probability of achieving your specific goal.

Persuasive speaking is a process in which a speaker presents a message intended to affect an audience in a specific way. Persuasive speech preparation is similar to informative speech preparation. You will design your speech to achieve a specific goal, but instead of using your information to solely further understanding, you use your material to substantiate a case or appeal to action. Also, like informative speaking, you must generate interest in your information to arouse audience attention, you must explain your information in ways that will enable your audience to understand it, and you must discuss the information in ways that will enable your audience to remember it. The greatest contrast with informative speaking is the need to be aware of and adapt to your listener's attitudes.

The directions for preparing a persuasive speech parallel those for preparing an informative speech.

First, write a clear persuasive speech goal that states what you want your audience to believe or do.

Second, build the body of the speech with good reasons and good evidence. Reasons are statements that answer *why* a proposition is justified; evidence includes both facts and opinion that give support to the reasons. Reasons and evidence form arguments.

Third, create the best organization for the speech. The choice of organizational methods are statement-of-reasons, problem–solution, comparative-advantages, criteria-satisfaction, and negative.

Fourth, word your main points and key ideas with emotional appeal. To develop emotional impact you need to clearly identify the emotions you want your listeners to experience, identify the information you have that is likely to stimulate those emotions, and then in practice, replace vague, flat sentences that carry no emotional impact with specific, vivid descriptions.

Fifth, use your credibility advantageously. Credibility is built on competence, intention, character, and personality. One of the most important ways to build credibility is by behaving in an ethical manner.

Finally, deliver the speech convincingly. Good delivery is especially important in persuasive speaking.

Notes

1. Kay Deaux and Lawrence S. Wrightsman, *Social Psychology*, 5th ed. (Monterey, Calif.: Brooks/Cole, 1988), 21.

2. Richard Weaver, "Language is Sermonic," in Richard L. Johannesen, Rennard Strickland, and Ralph T. Eubanks, *Language is Sermonic* (Baton Rouge: Louisiana State University Press, 1970), 205.

3. Betsy Burke, speech on euthanasia delivered in persuasive speaking class, University of Cincinnati. Portions used with permission of Betsy Burke.

4. Kenneth E. Anderson and Theodore Clevenger, Jr., "A Summary of Experimental Research in Ethos," *Speech Monographs*, 30 (1963), 59–78.

5. Delivered in speech class, University of Cincinnati. Used with permission of Mary Heintz.

Chapter 15 | Reasoning with Audiences

When Lyndon Johnson was president, he often began discussions with his colleagues by saying, "Let's reason together." In public speaking, *reasoning* with an audience means presenting arguments and evidence in support of your speech goal.

In this chapter we will discuss the formulation of arguments that serve as a basis for sound persuasive speaking. We conclude the chapter with a speech assignment and an example of a speech (and its outline) that is designed to illustrate reasoning with audiences.

Reasoning Defined

Reasoning is the process of drawing inferences from facts or proving a proposition with reasons and facts. We thus can reason to arrive at a logical conclusion, and we can reason to prove the validity of our position to others. Let us consider the relationship between drawing inferences and forming arguments.

Drawing Inferences

Suppose you notice that your car is "missing" at slow speeds and stalling at stoplights, that your gas mileage is lower than normal, and that your car is not as "peppy" as it should be. What do these facts mean? If you know anything about cars, you probably will *infer* that your car needs a tune-up.

Forming an Argument

Further suppose that to get the money for a tune-up for your car you must convince your wife, husband, father, mother, or whoever is in charge of the purse strings, that the car does in fact need a tune-up. You will use the same material you used to draw the inference to form the arguments you will use to convince that other person. You start with the conclusion, "The car needs a tune-up." Then you present your observations as four reasons in support of that proposition: (1) The car is missing at slow speeds, (2) it is stalling at lights, (3) it is getting lower than normal gas mileage, and (4) it is not nearly as peppy as usual. In your presentation, you would elaborate the reasons with appropriate details.

The Reasoning Process

Whether you draw inferences from facts or whether you plan to present arguments with supporting facts, you need a method of studying the reasoning process. A good way to do this is by identifying the essentials of the argument and putting them down on paper.

Essentials of Reasoning

Reasoning is a product of three essentials: data, a conclusion, and a warrant for the conclusion.

DATA *Data* are the evidence, assumptions, or assertions that provide the basis for a conclusion. In the car example we used to define reasoning, the data are "missing at slow speeds," "stalling at lights," "lower than normal gas mileage," and "lack of pep."

CONCLUSION The *conclusion* is the inference drawn or the inference to be proven. In our example, the conclusion is, "The car needs a tune-up."

WARRANT A *warrant* is a statement that explains the relationship between the data and the conclusion. It is a verbal statement of the reasoning involved. It shows how the conclusion follows from the data that have been presented. Warrants usually are implied rather than stated. But to test the soundness of the reasoning, a warrant actually must be stated. One way to state the warrant for our car example is to say that missing at slow speeds, stalling at lights, getting lower gas mileage, and being less peppy are all *signs* or *indications* that the car needs a tune-up. The warrant, then, indicates how you arrived at the conclusion from the data supplied. As you will see later in this chapter, after you have phrased a warrant you can decide how good the reasoning is by weighing the strength of the warrant.

DIAGRAMING REASONING To get a visual picture of the reasoning, you can use the diagrammatic method developed by Stephen Toulmin.[1] Let us see how this looks. Using *(D)* for data, stated or observed; *(C)* for conclusion; *(W)* for warrant; and an arrow to show the direction of the reasoning, our example could be written as follows:

(D)   Engine misses at slow speeds.
       Car stalls at lights.
       Gas mileage is lower than usual.   → *(C)*   The car needs
       Car lacks pep.   a tune-up.

         (W) (These occurrences are major signs
                of the need for a tune-up.)

The warrant is written in parentheses because it is implied rather than actually stated.

Turning Reasoning into a Speech Outline

The conclusion you draw becomes the specific goal for your speech, and the data become the reasons and support. The car tune-up speech would be outlined as follows:

Specific Goal: I want the audience to believe that the car needs a tune-up.

   I.   The engine misses at slow speeds.
  II.   The car stalls at lights.
 III.   Gas mileage is lower than usual.
 IV.   The car lacks pep.

Forms of Reasoning: Types of Warrants

After you have written several warrants, you will see that they fall into one of several groups, each having certain clearly defined characteristics. In this section we look at several of the most common warrants or forms of reasoning and group them under their traditional headings of inductive or deductive.

Inductive reasoning means working from specifics to some conclusion. With inductive reasoning you discover what is true or what was true in the past, and then you predict that something is true or will be true in the future. The conclusions of inductive arguments are tested on the basis of probability. That is, we predict that the conclusion will be true most of the time. The higher the probability (the closer to 100 percent), the better the argument. Four common forms of inductive reasoning are generalization, analogy, causation, and sign.

Deductive reasoning is a form that moves from premises to conclusions. If the premises are true, then the conclusion is not just probable, as in an inductive argument, but also *certain*.

Generalization Warrant

In reasoning by generalization, we draw a conclusion based on a series of examples or cases. Suppose that Paula Larson is running for senior class president, and we plan to argue that Paula will win the election. If we found several related items of information, we could use them as the basis for a generalization. For instance, in examining Paula's record as a campaigner, we discover that she was successful in her campaign for treasurer of her high school junior class, for chairperson of her youth group at church, and for president of her sorority. From these three examples of Paula as a candidate for office, we generalize that she will be successful in future campaigns, of which president of the senior class is one. We predict that what was true in several instances is true (or will be true) in all instances (or at least in the instance we are considering).

Let us look at other examples of reasoning by generalization:

Instances: Dan Snider, an Alpha, is editor of the school paper; Paul Dreiser, an Alpha, is president of the Intrafraternity Council; Ken Stewart, an Alpha, is student body president.

Generalization conclusion: Alpha fraternity is an organization of campus leaders.

Instances: Al is a liberal and he votes Democratic; Marge is a liberal and she votes Democratic; Dean is a liberal and he votes Democratic.

Generalization conclusion: Liberals vote Democratic.

Now let us return to the reasoning of the generalization on Paula Larson for president. In diagram form, the argument would look like this:

(D)   Paula was successful in her
campaign for treasurer of her
junior class, in her campaign for
chairperson of her church youth   →   *(C)* Paula will
group, and in her campaign for   be elected
president of her sorority.   president of
                                                                    the senior
                                                                    class.

      (W)   (What is true in representative campaigns
            will be true in this campaign.)

Now suppose we wished to prepare a speech predicting Paula's victory. A speech outline using instances as reasons would look like this:

Specific Goal: I want the audience to believe that Paula Larson will be elected president of the senior class. (Conclusion)

I.   Paula has run successful campaigns in the past.
   A. Paula was successful in her campaign for treasurer of her high school junior class.
   B. Paula was successful in her campaign for chairperson of her church youth group.
   C. Paula was successful in her campaign for president of her sorority.

Analogy Warrant

An *analogy* is a comparative generalization. In reasoning by analogy, what is true of something with one set of circumstances will be true of something else with similar circumstances. Suppose that in trying to predict Paula Larson's success in her candidacy for president we compare her circumstances with Heather Nelson's, who was elected president two years earlier. As we compare the two we find several similarities: Both are very bright, both have a great deal of drive, and both have track records of successful campaigns. Reasoning by analogy, we argue that because Paula is similar to Heather is so many ways and because Heather was elected, Paula also will be elected senior class president.

Let us look at other examples of reasoning by analogy:

Comparable example: The affirmative action program at Carson Limited has increased levels of employment and promotions of women and members of racial minorities.

Analogy conclusion: (Because our company is similar to Carson Limited in so many ways), an affirmative action program will result in increased levels of employment and promotions of women and members of racial minorities here.

Comparable example: New York is making money from off-track betting.

Analogy conclusion: Ohio (which is similar to New York in many ways) would make money from off-track betting.

Now let us return to reasoning by analogy that Paula will be elected president. In diagram form, the argument looks like this:

(D)   Heather who is bright, has a great deal of drive, and has a track record of successful campaigns was elected two years earlier. → (C)   Paula will be elected president of the senior class.

(W)   (Because Paula is similar to Heather in brightness, drive, and track record.)

Now suppose we want to prepare a speech predicting Paula's victory using analogy. A speech outline using this argument would look like this:

Specific Goal: I want the audience to believe that Paula Larson will be elected president of the senior class.

I.   Paula has the same characteristics as Heather Nelson, who was elected two years earlier.
A. Paula and Heather are both bright.
B. Paula and Heather both have a great deal of drive.
C. Paula and Heather have track records of successful campaigns.

Causation

Causation is a form of reasoning that proves a conclusion on the basis of a special connection between the data and the conclusion. When we say that a causal relationship exists, we mean that one or more circumstances cited always (or at least usually) produce a predictable effect or set of effects. In analyzing Paula's campaign for election, you might discover that Paula has campaigned intelligently and has won the endorsements of key campus organizations. If these two items can be seen as causes for victory, then you can argue that Paula will win the election.

Other examples of causal reasoning are the following:

Causal factors: Clark is intelligent, has studied hard, and has a good attitude.

Causal conclusion: (Because intelligence, study, and good attitude are causes of passing grades), Clark will pass the course.

Causal factors: Moose Gordon is back in the lineup at offensive tackle, and Speedy Marshall is fully recovered from his leg injury.

Causal conclusion: (Because the two key players on the team are back at full strength), Stellar University will win the big football game.

Now let us diagram the Paula-will-be-elected argument to test the reasoning involved.

(D) Paula has campaigned intelligently and has won the endorsements of key campus organizations. $\longrightarrow$ *(C)* Paula will be elected president of the senior class.

(W) (Intelligent campaigning and key endorsements are causes of, or result in, winning elections.)

Now suppose we want to prepare a speech predicting Paula's victory using causal reasoning. A speech outline using this argument would look like this:

Specific Goal: I want the audience to believe that Paula Larson will be elected president of the senior class.

I. Paula has engaged in the procedures that result in victory.
   A. Paula has campaigned intelligently.
   B. Paula has key endorsements.

Sign

Sign is a form of reasoning that proves a conclusion on the basis of a connection between the symptoms and the conclusion. Signs are indicators. When certain events, characteristics, or situations always or usually accompany something, we say that these events, characteristics, or situations are *signs*. For instance, leaves turning brown and falling are signs of autumn. A fever, nausea, and blotchy skin are signs of an allergic reaction. Signs are often confused with causes; but signs are indicators, not causes. A fever is a sign of sickness. It occurs when a person is sick, but it does not cause the sickness. If in analyzing Paula's campaign, you notice that Paula has more campaign posters than all other candidates combined and a greater number of students from all segments of the campus are wearing Paula for President buttons, you may argue that these are indicators or signs that Paula may win the election.

The following are other examples of sign reasoning:

Signs: New car sales are skyrocketing. Housing starts are up.

Sign conclusion: (Because car sales and housing starts are signs of a recovery), the recession is over.

Signs: Tom has bleary eyes and a runny nose.

Sign conclusion: (Because bleary eyes and a runny nose are signs of a cold), Tom has a cold.

Now let us return to the Paula-will-win-the-election argument. In diagram form, the argument looks like this:

(D) Paula has more campaign posters than all other candidates combined.

Students from all segments of campus are wearing her campaign buttons.

$\longrightarrow$

(C) Paula will be elected president of the senior class.

(W) (Numbers of campaign posters and buttons are signs of an election victory.)

Now suppose we want to prepare a speech predicting Paula's victory using sign reasoning. A speech outline using this argument would look like this:

Specific Goal: I want the audience to believe that Paula Larson will be elected president of the senior class.

I. The key signs of an election victory are present in Paula's campaign.
   A. Paula has more campaign posters than all other candidates combined.
   B. Students from all segments of the campus are wearing her campaign buttons.

Using Warrants in Combination

A speech may be the product of one or many forms of inductive reasoning. The following is an example of an outline in support of the prediction of Paula's victory that uses all the forms we have discussed. In preparing your speech you might select the arguments from among the four listed that you think would be most persuasive to your audience.

Specific Goal: I want the audience to believe that Paula Larson will be elected president of the senior class.

   I. Paula has run successful campaigns in the past.
       A. Paula was successful in her campaign for treasurer of her high school class.
       B. Paula was successful in her campaign for chairperson of her church youth group.
       C. Paula was successful in her campaign for president of her sorority.
  II. Paula has the same characteristics as Heather, who won two years earlier.
       A. Both are intelligent.
       B. Both have drive.
       C. Both have good track records in campaigns.
 III. Paula has engaged in procedures that result in campaign victory.
       A. Paula has campaigned intelligently.
       B. Paula has key endorsements.
  IV. Paula's campaign has the key signs of an election victory.
       A. Paula has more campaign posters than all other candidates combined.
       B. Students from all segments of the campus are wearing her campaign buttons.

Deduction

As we have mentioned, *deduction* is a form of reasoning that is used in moving from statements that are true to a related statement that must be true. A deductive warrant may be stated: "If two related premises are true, then a conclusion based on those two premises must be true." Suppose that you missed hearing the results of the student election but you hear Paula giving a victory speech to the student body. You might reason as follows: Only winners give victory speeches, Paula is giving a victory speech, so Paula must have won the election.

Now let us diagram the deductive argument about Paula's victory to test the reasoning.

(D) A person must win to give a
       victory speech.
                                             →   *(C)* Paula must have
       Paula is giving a victory   won the election.
       speech.

       (W) (If it is true that a person must win to give a
              victory speech and that Paula is giving a
              victory speech, then it is certain that Paula
              won the election.)

Checklist	**Reasoning**

Check items that were accomplished effectively.

Specific Goal

_____ 1. Was the specific goal clear?

_____ 2. Was the specific goal designed to _____ reinforce a belief? _____ establish a belief? _____ change a belief? or _____ move to action?

_____ 3. Was the specific goal adapted to this audience's interests, knowledge, and attitudes?

Content

_____ 4. Did the speaker present clearly stated reasons?

_____ 5. Did each reason give direct support to the specific goal?

_____ 6. Was each reason important to the audience's acceptance of the goal?

_____ 7. Did the speaker use facts and expert opinions to support these reasons?

_____ 8. Was the evidence for the reasons well documented?

_____ 9. Could the warrant for each of the arguments be easily identified?

Organization

_____ 10. Did the introduction gain attention and good will for the speaker?

_____ 11. Did the speech follow a statement-of-reasons order?

_____ 12. Were the reasons presented in an order that adapted to the audience's attitude toward the goal?

_____ 13. Did the conclusion further the persuasive effect of the speech?

Language

_____ 14. Was the language _____ clear? _____ vivid? _____ emphatic? _____ appropriate?

Delivery

_____ 15. Was the delivery convincing?

Evaluate the speech as (check one) _____ excellent, _____ good, _____ average, _____ fair, _____ poor.

Use the information from your checklist to support your evaluation.

The following are other examples of deductive reasoning:

Premise: All students at State University must have a GPA above 2.2 to compete in intercollegiate athletics.

Premise: Mitchell is on the basketball team.

Deductive conclusion: Mitchell has a GPA above 2.2.

Premise: When total rainfall upriver is more than three inches in a week, Old Coney floods.

Premise: Rainfall upriver the last five days has been a staggering five inches.

Deductive conclusion: Old Coney will flood.

Assignment
Using Reasons to Persuade

1. Prepare a three- to six-minute speech in which the focus or force of your persuasion rests on the presentation and development of two to five reasons.

   Speech Goal: You can, of course, use reasoning as your primary persuasive method whether your goal is to reaffirm, establish, or change a belief, or to move to action. Thus, the emphasis in this assignment is not on the *type* of proposition, but on the *means of supporting* it.

   Content: Each argument you consider for your speech should take the form of a reason and supporting evidence. Each argument is likely to be analyzed as an argument from example, cause, analogy, or sign.

   Speech Organization: Because the emphasis of this assignment is on clarity of reasoning, the main points of your outline should follow a statement-of-reasons organization. You should select your reasons on the basis of soundness of argument and potential impact on the intended audience.

2. Write a critique of one or more of the speeches given to meet this assignment. Because the focus of this assignment is on reasoning, you will want to use the reasoning critique checklist.

Speech — Learn to Speak Spanish

OUTLINE: LEARNING TO SPEAK SPANISH

Specific Goal: I want the members of my audience to believe that they should learn to speak Spanish.

Introduction

I. What if you found yourself all alone in a foreign country, incapable of communicating with those around you, only to learn that the country was the United States?

II. Such a scenario is not that far from reality, for Spanish is the second most popular spoken language in the United States.

Thesis Statement: You should learn to speak Spanish because it will benefit you personally, economically, and practically.

Body

I. Learning to speak Spanish will benefit you personally.
   A. You will be able to learn a great deal about Spanish culture.
   B. You will appreciate the beauty of the language.
   C. You will have fun.

II. Learning to speak Spanish will benefit you economically.
   A. You will be qualified for one of the many jobs available to those who speak Spanish.
      1. Translators are needed in many areas.
      2. Companies are expanding into Spanish-speaking countries.
   B. You will be less likely to be taken advantage of by Spanish-speaking merchants.

III. Learning to speak Spanish will benefit you practically.
   A. You will be better prepared for the future.
      1. The Spanish-speaking population is growing at a phenomenal rate.
      2. By the year 2000 there will be 30 to 35 million Spanish-speaking people in the United States.
   B. You will be better able to communicate with your own neighbors.
      1. Western cities have significant Hispanic populations.
      2. Major cities in other parts of the country have growing Hispanic populations.

Conclusion

I. Spanish is the language of the future.

II. Wake up to reality — learn Spanish while you're still ahead of the game.

Bibliography

Arcienga, Thomas A. "Bilingual Education in the 1980's" *Educational Digest* (September 1982), 8–10.

"Florida's Latin Boom." *Newsweek* (November 11, 1985), 55–56.

Kiddle, M. E., and B. Wegmann, *Perspectivas*. New York: Holt, Rinehart & Winston, 1978.

"Language War in Florida." *Newsweek* (June 30, 1986).

As you analyze this speech of conviction, judge whether each of the reasons is stated clearly in the speech and whether the developmental material supports the reasons clearly, completely, and interestingly.[2] After you have made your own analysis, study the analysis given here.

Analysis

Creation of this hypothetical situation helps the speaker get the audience interested by developing curiosity about the intent of the speech.

Here the speaker tells us that she will try to convince the audience by presenting three major benefits. Her goal is to present three reasons (benefits) that we will find logically compelling enough to convince us that we should learn Spanish. If the audience is convinced of the logic of the development, then they may not only give intellectual agreement to the proposition, but also be moved to action. For the speech to work, the audience will have to see the reasons as compelling and will have to believe that the reasons have been supported strongly enough to be believed. Notice that the first point is clearly stated. Also notice that each of the points are adapted to the audience. The speaker puts the emphasis on "you."

Much of the strength of the proof is through the speaker's own experience. She relies on her experience to carry much of the weight of the support for the first two points in the speech. Although her authority comes through rather strongly, we also could use documented evidence to support a few of the assertions, most notably, "as language experts say." Nevertheless, I like her use of examples to give support to her points.

SPEECH

What if you suddenly found yourself all alone in a foreign country incapable of communicating with those around you? Then what if you found that this foreign country was your own United States? This may sound like an episode from the "Twilight Zone," but it's really not that far from reality, for Spanish is the second most popular spoken language in the United States.

I'd like to convince you why you should start to learn to speak Spanish now. You will benefit from learning to speak Spanish in at least three major ways.

First of all, learning to speak Spanish will benefit you personally. Spanish is educational. You can learn a great deal about the second most dominant culture in the Western hemisphere. If you check our library or the library downtown, you'll find a large section of books written in Spanish about the Spanish culture. And I think that's a very educational experience. Moreover, you will find yourself developing a much greater appreciation of the beauty of the language. According to the authors of *Perspectivas*, a Spanish language book, Spanish poetry is some of the most beautiful poetry you'll ever read. One of my favorites is *Noches Serena*, translated *Night of Stars*. Although it's true that this poem has been translated into English, there's an old saying, "Tradutori, traditori," meaning "the translator is a traitor." As language experts say, you just cannot translate Spanish into English effectively — especially poetry.

On a personal level, learning Spanish will be just plain fun. It's fun to be one of those people who can communicate with someone on your left side when the person on your right side doesn't understand what you are saying. It's also fun because it makes the foreigner in the United States feel very much at home. And I've had a couple of friends who felt really impressed that I went out of my way to learn their language. It made them feel very comfortable, and it was just kind of a neat feeling for me as well.

The speaker's second benefit is clearly stated. Here, particularly, we see the speaker using her own experience to provide support for her point. I think this section shows that a person's direct experience often can carry more support for a reason than a quotation or factual statement from a random source.

"I understand that" is weak. Here is one of the places where documented source material is necessary.

Good use of a hypothetical example to help make the point.

An interesting and rather persuasive section. Her use of Spanish adds to her personal credibility and gives added weight to the example.

Final point is clearly stated. Good use of statistics. I would still like to hear the source for these statistics.

A very good conclusion.

All that this speech lacks to make it superior is more documentation for key points. The reasons are clear, and taken as a group they provide strong support for the need to learn Spanish. Moreover, the use of personal experience and examples gives plenty of support for the reasons. By the end of the speech, the majority of class members did believe that there were benefits to learning Spanish.

Secondly, learning to speak Spanish can benefit you economically. There's an increasing demand for Spanish fluency in the United States today. And translators are needed in literally every area of society — in government, in law, in education, in medicine — you name it, there's a need for it. When I worked at the Cleveland Clinic a couple of years ago, people came in from all over the continent for care at its world-renowned cardiology department. And since so many of the people who came through spoke only Spanish, there was a tremendous need for Spanish translators. One of the jobs of the translator was to make the person feel at home outside of their country, but to do that you had to speak Spanish.

In addition, United States companies are expanding into Spanish-speaking countries and there's a need for workers who know the language. And I understand that for those who are willing to learn Spanish, or who speak it already, the pay package is very good. Also, if you do decide to travel to any Spanish-speaking countries — Spain for its art or culture, Mexico or Peru with their historic monuments, or Central America for its beautiful, sunny beaches — the Spanish people will be less inclined to take advantage of you. They are not going to be able to say, "Hay un americano muy estúpido — no problema, no problema," but the "no problema" will benefit *you* because you can speak Spanish.

Finally, learning to speak Spanish will benefit you practically. By the year 2000 it is estimated that there will be 30 to 35 million Spanish-speaking people in the United States. Right now, all across the United States, and I don't just mean Florida or California, I mean major cities all across the United States, there is a significant population of Spanish-speaking people, so you might need this language just to communicate with your very own neighbor.

Spanish is clearly the language of the future. There is no longer a simple choice to learn that language; there is an urgency brought on by the dramatic growth of this language in our country. So whether you sign up for a course here at the university, take a community education class, or study on your own, wake up to reality and learn to speak Spanish while you still have the advantage.

Summary

One way of achieving your speech goal is to reason with your audience. In public speaking reasoning with an audience means presenting arguments in support of your speech goal.

A speech argument is the product of three essential elements: data, conclusion, and warrant. Data constitute the evidence, the facts and opinion, that provide the basis for a conclusion; a conclusion is the inference drawn or the inference to be proven (in a speech, the inference is usually stated as a reason); and a warrant is a statement that explains the relationship between the evidence (facts and opinion) and the conclusion (the reason).

Warrants are classified as inductive or deductive. *Inductive reasoning* involves the drawing of a conclusion from one or more specifics. The conclusions of inductive arguments are tested on the basis of probability — the higher the probability, the better the argument. Common forms of inductive reasoning are generalization, analogy, causation, and sign. *Deductive reasoning* is a form that moves from premises to conclusion. If the premises are true, then the conclusion is not just probable, but certain.

A speech is likely to be the product of several units of argument in support of the specific goal.

Notes

1. Stephen Toulmin, *The Uses of Argument* (Cambridge: Cambridge University Press, 1958).
2. Delivered in speech class, University of Cincinnati. Used with permission of Mary Jo Cranley.

Chapter 16 | Motivating Audiences

Reasoning provides a solid logical base for persuasion and a sound rationale for changing an audience's attitude. But what if sound reasoning is not enough to bring action? What else can you do to increase the audience's chances of doing or believing what you recommend? The catalyst for firing the imagination, causing commitment, and bringing to action is the psychological aspect of persuasion called *motivation*.

In this chapter we will consider three psychological approaches that will help you to determine your overall strategy. We will conclude the chapter with a speech assignment that enables you to put what you have learned into practice and an example of a speech (and its outline) that is designed to illustrate how to motivate an audience.

Strategies

Through the years many individuals have set forth rhetorical and psychological theories of motivation. Although the following three theories are not the only ones available — and they are not necessarily the only ones that work — they have been selected because they help to explain why people behave as they do; moreover, they provide information that you can apply directly in your speeches.

The following three theoretical guidelines can be used to bring an audience to action:

1. People are more likely to act when the speech goal presents a favorable cost–reward ratio.
2. People are more likely to act when the speech goal creates dissonance.
3. People are more likely to act when the proposition satisfies a strong but unmet need.

Now let us examine the theories behind these statements.

Cost–Reward

People are more likely to act when they see that the suggested proposition presents a favorable cost–reward ratio. John Thibaut and Harold Kelley explain social interactions in terms of rewards received and costs incurred by each member of an interaction.[1] *Rewards* are the benefits received from a behavior. Rewards can be economic gain, good feelings, prestige, or any other positive outcome. *Costs* are units of expenditure. They can be perceived in terms of time, energy, money, or any negative outcome of an interaction.

According to Thibaut and Kelley, each of us seeks situations in which our behavior will yield us rewards in excess of the costs; or, conversely, each of us will continue our present behavior unless we are shown that either lower costs or higher rewards will come from changing a particular behavior. Let us consider an example. Suppose you are asking your audience to give money to a charity. The money you are asking them to give is a negative outcome — a cost; however, giving money can be shown to be rewarding. That is, members of the audience may feel civic-minded, responsible, or helpful as a result of giving. If you can show in the speech that those rewards outweigh the cost, then you can increase the likelihood of the audience's giving.

Strategies growing from this theory are easy for most people to understand because the theory is so easily supported by common-sense observations. What makes this theory work for you is your ability to understand the cost–reward ratios in relation to the specific topic that is operating within your particular audience. Suppose that you are, in fact, trying to motivate the audience to give money to a charity. Assuming that this audience has nothing against this particular charity and assuming that it agrees that giving to this charity has merit, how do you proceed? You could ask each person to give ten cents. Because the cost is very low, you are unlikely to meet much resistance, and you will probably get a high percentage of donations; but you will not be making much money for that charity. What if you decide to ask for a donation of ten dollars from each person? Because ten dollars is likely to represent a lot of money to members of a college audience, they must be shown that it really is not that much money (a difficult point to make for any audience); or they must be shown that the reward for giving ten dollars is worth the gift. For most of your audience, talking about how good giving makes a person feel will not be enough. You will have to show them tangible rewards.

In general, people look at calls for action on the basis of a cost–reward ratio—the higher the cost, the greater the reward. Thus, the higher the perceived cost, the harder you will have to work to achieve your goal. In summary, you must achieve one of the following:

1. You must show that the time, energy, or money investment is small.
2. You must show that the benefits in good feelings, prestige, economic gain, or other possible rewards are high.

In your speech, then, you are looking at ways to minimize cost and maximize gain. The speech at the end of this chapter is an excellent example of this strategy.

Cognitive Dissonance

People are more likely to act when the suggested proposition creates dissonance. A second theory from which your persuasive strategies may be drawn is the theory of cognitive dissonance. *Cognitive dissonance* is an inconsistency that occurs between two or more cognitive elements. A *cognition* is a thought or a piece of knowledge about some situation, person, or behavior. For example, if you worked hard to save thirty-five dollars for a gift for your friend, the amount you saved would be one cognitive element. If you proceeded to spend seventy-five dollars for the gift, the amount you actually spent would be a second cognitive element. The inconsistency between money available and money spent would create a discomfort. This discomfort is what Leon Festinger, the originator of this theory, calls cognitive dissonance.[2]

Festinger holds that whenever you get yourself in one of these states of discomfort (and some of us may find ourselves in this state quite often), you have a great desire to *reduce the discomfort*. The greater the degree of discomfort experienced, the greater the desire to reduce it.

What determines the degree of discomfort? According to Festinger the amount of dissonance you are likely to feel depends on at least two factors.

First is the number of elements in each cognition. You are likely to experience less dissonance if there are only two conflicting cognitions than if there are several. For instance, high pay for a job combined with low prestige for that job may create cognitive dissonance, but the degree will be relatively low because only two cognitions are in competition. On the other hand, if higher pay and a better location are in competition with low prestige, little chance for advancement, and less desirable duties, the degree of dissonance will be considerably greater.

The second factor in determining the degree of discomfort is the importance of the entire issue. For example, a person usually experiences less dissonance after making a decision to buy a certain pair of shoes than after making a decision to buy a new car.

When a person experiences dissonance, what can he or she do to relieve it? Festinger suggests four methods of reducing or relieving dissonance:

1. *A person may change his or her attitude toward the decision.* If you bought your friend a present that cost more than you had planned to pay, you can reduce the dissonance by telling yourself that your friend is worth every penny you spent.

2. *A person can change his or her behavior.* If you smoke excessively and the smoking is hurting your relationship with a friend, you can stop smoking.

3. *A person can change the environment in which the dissonance occurs.* If you are an actor of only average ability, but wish to have major parts in school plays, you can go to a smaller school where it is more likely that you can get better parts.

4. *A person may add new cognitive elements.* If you have paid too much for your friend's gift, you might tell yourself that you can cut expenses by avoiding evening snacks for a month.

Now that you can see what cognitive dissonance is, you may be asking what it has to do with developing a persuasive strategy. As a speaker, you have opportunities to create dissonance in the mind of each person in the audience and then to provide the means of relieving the dissonance you have created.

Consider a situation in which you wish to motivate the audience to stop buying cigarettes and liquor from people who obtain their merchandise from out of state. People may buy these products because they are cheaper; people may know that the reason they are cheaper is because the taxes for those products are lower in another state, and these savings are being passed along to them. How can you create dissonance in the minds of these people? You may develop a line of argument linking trafficking in out-of-state cigarettes and liquor with organized crime. Most people believe that supporting organized crime is wrong. If you can show your audience that what looks like a small savings mounts up to really big business for "smugglers," you may well create dissonance between the cognition of saving money and the cognition of supporting organized crime. Although members of your audience may choose to repress a perception of the information you cite, bury that dissonance, or devalue the issue (three common ways of rationalizing), if you can make the point strongly enough at least some members may feel compelled to do something to relieve that dissonance by not buying the products under the circumstances you describe. In summary:

1. People look for ways to relieve dissonance when confronted with conflicting cognitions.
2. You can create dissonance by presenting conflicting cognitions.
3. Your speech proposition can be perceived as a way of relieving the dissonance you have created.

Basic Needs

Abraham Maslow's hierarchy of needs theory is a third theory from which persuasive strategies may be developed. Persuasion is more likely to occur when the proposition satisfies a strong but unmet need in members of the audience. If people are hungry, their main concern is obtaining food. Thus, if you are able to identify audience needs, you have a good start for planning your persuasive strategy.

Maslow divides basic human needs into five categories:[3]

1. Physiological needs
2. Safety needs
3. Belongingness and love needs
4. Esteem needs
5. Self-actualization needs

Notice that Maslow places these needs in a hierarchy: one set of needs must be met or satisfied before the next set of needs emerges. The physiological needs for food, drink, and life-sustaining temperature are the most basic; they must be satisfied before the body is able to consider any of its other needs. The next level consists of safety needs — security, simple self-preservation, and the like; they emerge after the basic needs have been met, and they hold a paramount place until they, too, have been met. The third level includes the belongingness or love needs: the need to identify with friends, loved ones, and family. In a world of increasing mobility and breakdown of the traditional family, it is becoming increasingly difficult for individuals to satisfy this need. Nonetheless, once the belongingness needs have been met, the esteem needs predominate: the quest for material goods, recognition, and power or influence. Maslow calls the final level the self-actualizing need; this involves developing one's

Motivating listeners involves understanding and appealing to fundamental human needs, from physiological needs to higher motives such as the desire for justice.

self to meet its potential. When all other needs have been met, this need is the one that drives people to their creative heights and urges them to do "what they need to do to fulfill themselves as human beings."

What is the value of this analysis to you as a speaker? First, it provides a framework for and suggests the kinds of needs you may appeal to in your speeches. Second, it allows you to understand why a line of development will work on one audience and fail with another. For instance, if your audience has great physiological needs (if they are hungry), an appeal to the satisfaction of good workmanship, no matter how well done, is unlikely to impress them. Third, and perhaps most crucial, when your proposition conflicts with an operating need, you will have to be prepared with a strong alternative in the same category or in a higher-level category. For instance, if your proposition is going to cost money (if it is going to take money in the form of taxes), you will have to show how the proposal satisfies some other comparable need.

Let us make this discussion more specific by looking at certain traditional motives for action. These motives are not the only ones; we present them to suggest the kind of analysis you should be doing. You have selected a specific goal and have determined reasons for its acceptance. Now try to relate those reasons to basic needs and discover where you may be getting into difficulty by conflicting with other motives or other needs.

WEALTH   The desire for wealth, the acquisition of money and material goods, is a motive that grows out of an esteem need. For example, those who have little money perhaps can be motivated to buy a Ford Escort or a Chevrolet Geo primarily because they get such good gas mileage and are so economical to operate. Those who have a great deal of money can perhaps be motivated to buy a Rolls-Royce or a Cadillac because they are prestigious. Does your proposition affect wealth or material goods in any way? If its effect is positive, you may want to stress it. If your plan calls for giving up money, you will need to be prepared to cope with an audience's natural resistance. You will have to involve another motive from the same category (esteem) or from a higher category to override the loss of any money the audience will have to give up.

POWER   Another esteem need is power. For many people, personal worth depends upon their power over their own destiny, the exercise of power over others, and the recognition and prestige that comes from such recognition of power. If your proposition allows a person, group, or community to exercise power, it may be worth emphasizing. On the other hand, if your speech takes power away from some or all of your listeners, you will need to provide strong compensation to motivate them.

CONFORMITY   Conformity is a major source of motivation for nearly everyone. Conformity grows out of a need for belongingness. People often behave in a given way because a friend, a neighbor, an acquaintance, or a person in the same age bracket behaves that way. Although some people will be more likely to do something if they can be the first to do it or if it makes them appear distinctive, most people feel more secure when they act in ways that conform with others of their kind. The old saying that there is strength in numbers certainly applies to conformity. If you can show that many people similar to the members of your audience favor your plan, that argument may well provide motivation.

PLEASURE   When you are given a choice of actions, you often pick the one that gives you the greatest pleasure, enjoyment, or happiness. On at least one level, pleasure is a self-actualizing need; however, it also operates as an esteem need. If your speech relates to something that is novel, promises excitement, is fun to do, or offers a challenge, you probably can motivate your audience on that basis.

These are only four possible motives for action growing out of basic audience needs. Sex appeal, responsibility, justice, and many others operate within each of us. If you discover that you are not relating your material to basic audience needs, then you probably need to revise your procedure.

But knowing which needs an audience has and appealing to those needs are two different things. To maximize your effectiveness you must understand how to trigger these needs.

What happens when your specific goal does not meet a specific audience need? Either you can change the wording of your goal so that it is in tune with audience needs, or you can work to create or uncover an audience need that the specific goal will meet. For instance, if you are giving a speech intended to motivate the audience to go to dinner at Le Parisien (a very expensive restaurant), your goal may meet a need to eat out occasionally, but it is in opposition to most people's need to eat for a reasonable price. For this speech to be effective, you either must change the specific goal to recommend a more modest restaurant (The River Captain, for instance) or arouse some needs that would be met by going to Le Parisien.

In planning strategy in terms of basic needs, you must find out

1. What needs does the audience have at this time?
2. Can the goal be written to satisfy those needs, and if so, how?
3. If the goal does not meet those needs, how can you change the wording to activate unexpressed and perhaps unrealized needs?

Assignment
Persuading to Action

1. Prepare a four- to seven-minute persuasive speech designed to bring your audience to action.

    Specific Goal: Focus your speech on the action; for instance, "I want my audience to donate money to the United Way" or "I want my audience to volunteer an hour a month to tutor adult readings at an established community adult literacy program."

    Strategic Plan:

    a. Because developing a logical base is prerequisite to any persuasive speech, select four or five reasons that you could use to support your speech goal. Then on the basis of your audience analysis check the reasons that you believe are most likely to be effective with this audience.

    b. Select an organization of main points (comparative advantages, problem solution, criteria satisfaction, negative reasons) that you believe is most likely to increase your chance of motivating this audience. Justify your selection.

    c. An audience is more likely to act on your proposal if it has faith in you as a source, so indicate what you need to do to increase your credibility with this audience.

    d. Select one of the following overall strategies to use in motivating your audience to act:

    Lead the audience to believe that the benefits to be gained from the action far outweigh costs of time, energy, or money invested;

Checklist	**Motivational Speech**

Check items that were accomplished effectively.

Specific Goal

_____ 1. Did the speech goal call for a specific audience action?

_____ 2. Was the specific goal adapted to this audience's interests, knowledge, and attitudes?

Content

_____ 3. Were the reasons stated clearly and vividly?

_____ 4. Were the reasons directed to the needs of this audience?

_____ 5. Did the speaker use facts and expert opinions to support these reasons?

_____ 6. Was the speaker effective in establishing his or her credibility on this topic?

_____ 7. Did the speaker lead the audience to believe that the benefits to be gained from the action far outweigh costs of time, energy, or money invested; *or*

_____ 8. Did the speaker create dissonance in the audience that could only be relieved by the action of the specific goal; *or*

_____ 9. Did the speaker lead the audience to believe that the specific goal satisfies such major needs as wealth, power, conformity, pleasure, and so on?

_____ 10. Was the speaker ethical in handling material?

Organization

_____ 11. Did the introduction gain attention and good will for the speaker?

_____ 12. Did the speech follow a _____ statement-of-reasons order? _____ problem–solution order? _____ comparative-advantages order? _____ criteria-satisfaction order? _____ negative order?

_____ 13. Was the order appropriate for a speech designed to get action?

_____ 14. Was the conclusion designed to heighten the need for action?

Language

_____ 15. Was the language _____ clear? _____ vivid? _____ emphatic? _____ appropriate?

Delivery

_____ 16. Was the delivery motivating?

Evaluate the speech as (check one) _____ excellent, _____ good, _____ average, _____ fair, _____ poor.

Use the information from your checklist to support your evaluation.

create a dissonance in the audience that can be relieved only by the action of the specific goal; or

lead the audience to believe that the specific goal satisfies such major needs as wealth, power, conformity, pleasure, and so on.

  e. Identify the emotions that you want to arouse in your audience. Then determine the places in your speech where you are going to focus your emotional appeals.
  f. Practice until your delivery of the speech adds to your motivational effectiveness.
2. Write a critique of one or more of the motivational speeches that you hear in class. Outline the speech. As you outline, answer the questions in the motivational speech checklist.

Speech — Open Your Eyes

OUTLINE: DONATE EYES TO EYE BANK

Specific Goal: I want my listeners to donate their eyes to an eye bank.

Introduction
I.   Close your eyes and imagine living in a world of darkness.
II.   Millions live in this world.

Thesis Statement: People should donate their eyes to an eye bank because corneas are necessary for sight, because corneas can be transplanted, and because donors know that through a donation a part of them lives on and they can be as useful to humanity in death as in life.

Body
  I. The windows through which we see the world are the corneas.
      A. They are tough, dime-sized, transparent tissues.
      B. Normally they are clear.
      C. When they are distorted, they blot out the light.
  II. Those people with injured corneas have the hope of normal sight through a cornea transplant.
      A. The operation works miracles, but it cannot work without donors.
      B. If eyes are transplanted within seventy-two hours after the death of the donor, the operation can be 100 percent successful.
      C. The operation has turned tragedy into joy.

III. There are many reasons for donating.
   A. The donor knows a part of him goes on living.
   B. The donor knows he can be as useful to humanity in death as in life.
IV. I hope you will consider becoming a donor.
   A. Leaving your desire in your will is not enough — the operation must come within seventy-two hours of death.
   B. Get forms and details from a Cincinnati eye bank.
   C. Then, when you die, someone who needs the chance can see.

Conclusion
I. Close your eyes again — now open them.
II. Won't you give someone else the chance to open theirs?

Read this speech aloud at least once and analyze the use of motivation.[4] What motives is the speaker appealing to? After you have analyzed the speech, read the analysis given here.

Analysis

Much of the strength of this speech is a result of the speaker's ability to involve members of the audience personally and get them to feel what she is saying. This opening is a striking example of audience involvement. She does not just tell the audience what it would be like — she has them experience the feeling. The speaker very successfully lays the emotional groundwork for total audience reception of her words.

Here the speaker begins the body of her speech by telling us about the role of the cornea. Notice throughout the speech the excellent word choice, such as "The bright world we awake to each morning is brought to us through. . . ." Here again she does not just tell us what it is like but asks us to imagine for ourselves what it would be like. The "rain-slashed window pane" is an especially vivid image.

SPEECH

Would all of you close your eyes for just a minute. Close them very tightly so that all the light is blocked out. Imagine what it would be like to always live in a world of total darkness such as you are experiencing right now, though only for a moment. Never to see the flaming colors of the sunset, or the crisp green of the world after the rain — never to see the faces of those you love. Now open your eyes, look all around you, look at all of the things that you couldn't have seen if you couldn't have opened your eyes.

The bright world we awake to each morning is brought to us through two dime-sized pieces of tough, transparent, semielastic tissue; these are the corneas, and it is their function to allow light to enter the lens and the retina. Normally, they are so clear that we don't even know they are there; however, when they are scratched or scarred either by accident or by disease, they tend to blur or blot out the light. Imagine peering through a rain-slashed window pane or trying to see while swimming under water. This is the way the victims of corneal damage often describe their vision.

The speaker continues in a very informative way. After asserting that corneal transplants work, she focuses on the two key points that she wants the audience to work with — the operation works, but it must be done within seventy-two hours. Notice that there is still no apparent direct persuasion. Her method is one of making information available in a way that will lead audience members to think about what effects the information might have on them personally.

In this segment of the speech, she launches into emotional high gear. Still, her approach remains somewhat indirect. Although we stress the importance of directness in language in this speech, the use of "no one" repeatedly throughout the examples is done by design. Although a more direct method might be effective, in this case the indirectness works quite well. The real effectiveness of the section is a result of the parallel structure and repetition of key phrases: "no one who has seen . . . human tragedy . . . great joy . . . can doubt the need or the urgency." As this portion of the speech was delivered, the listeners were deeply touched by both the examples themselves and their own thoughts about the examples. Also note how the examples themselves are ordered. The first two represent a personal effect; the final one a universal effect.

At this point in the speech the audience should be sympathetic with the problem and encouraged by the hope of corneal transplants. Now the speaker must deal with the listener's possible reaction of "that may be a good idea for

"To see the world through another man's eyes." These words are Shakespeare's, yet today it can literally be true. Thanks to the research by medical workers throughout the world, the operation known as a corneal transplant or a corneal graft has become a reality, giving thousands of people the opportunity to see. No other generation has held such a profound legacy in its possession. Yet, the universal ignorance of this subject of cornea donation is appalling. The operation itself is really quite simple; it involves the corneas of the donor being transplanted into the eyes of a recipient. And if this operation takes place within seventy-two hours after the death of the donor, it can be 100 percent effective.

No one who has seen the human tragedy caused solely by corneal disease can doubt the need or the urgency. Take the case of a young woman living in New Jersey who lost her sight to corneal disease. She gave birth to a baby and two years ago, thanks to a corneal transplant, she saw her three-year-old baby girl for the first time. And no one who had seen this woman's human tragedy caused solely by corneal disease nor her great joy at the restoration of her sight can doubt the need or the urgency. Or take the case of the five-year-old boy in California who was playing by a bonfire when a bottle in the fire exploded, flinging bits of glass, which lacerated his corneas. His damaged corneas were replaced with healthy ones in an emergency operation, and no one who had seen this little boy's human tragedy caused solely by corneal laceration nor the great joy to his young life of receiving his sight back again can doubt the need or the urgency. Or take the case of Dr. Beldon H. Scribbner of the University of Washington School of Medicine. Dr. Scribbner's eyesight was damaged by a corneal disease that twisted the normally sphere-shaped corneas into cones. A corneal transplant gave Dr. Scribbner twenty-twenty corrective vision and allowed him to continue work on his invention — the artificial kidney machine. And no one who has seen this man's human tragedy caused solely by corneal disease, nor the great joy brought not only to Dr. Scribbner but to the thousands of people his machine has helped save, can doubt the need or the urgency.

There are many philosophies behind such a gift. One of them was summed up by a minister and his wife who lost their daughter in infancy. They said, "We feel that a part of her goes on living." Or take the case of the young woman who was dying of cancer. She donated her eyes and did so with this explanation: "I want to be useful; being useful brings purpose and meaning into my life." Surely if being useful is important there someone else, but why me?" It is in this section that she offers reasons for our acting. If the speech has a weakness, it may be here. I would have liked a little further development of the reasons or perhaps the statement of an additional reason. Here she brings the audience from "Good idea — I'll do something someday" to "I'd better act now." She reminds them of the critical time period and tells them how they can proceed to make the donation. In this section it might be worth a sentence to stress that the donation costs nothing but a little time.

Here the speaker brings the audience full circle. Although she could have used different images, the repetition of those that began the speech takes the emphasis off the images themselves and places it in what the audience can do about those who are in these circumstances. The last line of the speech is simple, but in the context of the entire speech it is direct and quite moving. This is a superior example of a speech to actuate.

are few better ways than to donate your eyes to someone who lives after you. But no matter which philosophy you do adopt, I hope each of you will consider donating your eyes to another who will live after you and who otherwise would have to survive in the abyss of darkness. It will do you no good to leave your eyes in your regular will if you have one; for as I mentioned earlier, there is a seventy-two-hour critical period. If you wish to donate your eyes, I would suggest you contact Cincinnati Eye Bank for Sight Restoration at 861-3716. They will send you the appropriate donor forms to fill out, which should be witnessed by two of your closest friends or by your next of kin so that they will know your wishes. Then, when you die and no longer have need for your sight someone who desperately wants the chance to see will be able to.

Will all of you close your eyes again for just a moment? Close them very tightly, so that all the light is blocked out. And once more imagine what it would be like to live always in a world of total darkness such as you are experiencing right now, never seeing the flaming colors of a sunset, or the crisp green of the world after a rain — never seeing the faces of those you love. Now open your eyes. . . . Won't you give someone else the chance to open theirs?

Summary

The catalyst for firing the imagination, inspiring commitment, and bringing to action is the psychological aspect of persuasion called *motivation*.

People are more likely to act when the speech goal presents a favorable cost–reward ratio. Costs are units of expenditure; rewards are the benefits received from a behavior. To use a cost–reward strategy in a speech, you must show that the time, energy, or money invested is small; or that the benefits in good feelings, prestige, economic gain, or other possible rewards are high.

People are more likely to act when the speech goal creates dissonance. *Cognitive dissonance* is an inconsistency that occurs between two or more cognitive elements. To use cognitive dissonance in your speech you must present conflicting cognitions and show how the action in your speech goal will relieve the dissonance you have created.

People are more likely to act when the proposition satisfies a strong but unmet need. Maslow divides basic human needs into a hierarchy of psychological needs, safety needs, belongingness and love needs, esteem needs, and self-actualization needs. To use needs strategy in your speech, you must help the audience identify certain unmet needs and then show how acting on the specific speech goal will fulfill those needs.

Notes

1. John W. Thibaut and Harold H. Kelley, *The Social Psychology of Groups* (New York: Wiley, 1959).
2. Leon Festinger, *A Theory of Cognitive Dissonance* (Evanston, Ill.: Row, Peterson, 1957).
3. Abraham H. Maslow, *Motivation and Personality* (New York: Harper & Row, 1954), 80–92.
4. Speech given in speech class, University of Cincinnati. Used with permission of Kathleen Sheldon.

Chapter 17

Critically Evaluating Arguments: Refuting

When you are confronted with a speech that makes a claim, you can accept it, reject it, or perhaps suspend judgment. On what basis do you make such an evaluation? Moreover, if you reject a speech you can sit quietly and fume or you can take issue with the speaker who made the claim. The goal of this chapter is to give you the expertise to evaluate arguments critically and to refute those that you believe are faulty or not in the best interests of the audience.

Refutation is the process of proving that an argument or series of arguments, or the conclusion drawn from that argument or arguments, is false, erroneous, or at least doubtful. Sometimes refutation is only a small segment of a speech. Suppose you were planning a speech in support of donating money to the United Way. To counter an audience belief that the United Way distributes its money to agencies more for political reasons than for need, you might save a small portion of your speaking time to refute that argument. On the other hand, suppose that you have just heard a colleague argue that your company ought to invest a large portion of its pension plan in real estate, a proposal that you think is very risky. You might thus reply to the proposal with an entire speech of refutation. In either case, the ability to refute is an important skill that any responsible citizen should acquire.

The first part of this chapter considers critical evaluation of arguments. The second part shows how to use the results of critical evaluation in refutation. Finally, we conclude the chapter with a speech assignment that enables you to put what you have learned into practice and an example of a speech (and its outline) that illustrates refutation.

Critical Analysis of Speech Arguments

To critically analyze a speech argument, you must have an accurate representation of that argument. When you evaluate written sources, the entire argument should be on paper in front of you. To evaluate an oral argument, however, you must outline it carefully to preserve its essence. After you have outlined an argument or a series of arguments, you then can begin to examine the reasoning used.

Outlining Arguments

Good outlining requires that you get the key material down on paper accurately. Throughout this book you have been working on your outlining skills. Keep in mind that a good outline is not a transcription of the entire argument. For a persuasive argument, an outline will contain the reason or reasons presented in defense of a conclusion or proposition and the data used to support the reason or reasons with notations of whether the data were documented.

Let us look at an abbreviated written version of an oral argument:

> Public schools have been criticized during the past few years, but the results of some schools in the city show that public schools are capable of high levels of achievement. Park Hills, a public school on the west side, is an excellent example. Three years ago Park Hills raised its standards in all academic courses. It forced its students to work much harder to achieve good grades. According to an article in the June 26 issue of the *Post*, in June, Park Hills had three merit scholars, more than any year in its history. Moreover, student SAT scores were up 20 points from student scores just three years ago. Linden, a public school on the east side, is another example. Four years ago, Linden began increasing homework assignments and now requires two hours per evening of homework as well as three major papers a year of all students. According to that same *Post* article, in June, Linden had 85 percent of its graduating class accepted to college, up 30 percent from four years ago.

The following is the kind of outline you would write to analyze the argument.

Outline

I. Public schools are capable of high levels of achievement.
   A. Park Hills
      1. Raised standards in all courses
      2. Forced students to work harder for grades
      3. Three merit scholars (more than ever)
      4. SAT scores up 20 points in three years
   B. Linden
      1. Two hours of homework per night
      2. Three papers a year of all students
      3. 85 percent of graduates accepted to college (up 30 percent in four years)

Testing the Oral Argument

Once you have the substance of the speech (or argument) written in outline form, you then can begin to test the data and the resulting reasoning.

TESTING THE DATA   For a logical conclusion to follow, the data must be sound. For each item, consider the following:

1. *What is the source of the data?* Is the source a newspaper article? a journal article? a government report? Just because something appeared in print does not make it true. If the data comes from a poor source, an unreliable source, or a biased source, no reliable conclusion can be drawn. In the abbreviated version above, one source, the *Post*, was cited. If no sources are cited, you have the right to ask for sources. When you get the sources, you can raise questions about their quality.

2. *Are the data fact or opinion?* Factual data usually are worth more than opinion, and expert opinion is worth more than inexpert opinion. Can we document that Park Hills raised standards, had three merit scholars, and improved SAT scores 20 points in three years? Can we document that Linden increased homework time, required three papers a year, and sent 85 percent of its graduates (up 30 percent) to college?

3. *Are the data recent?* Products, ideas, and statistics may be obsolete as soon as they are produced. You must ask when the data were true. Five-year-old data may not be true today. Furthermore, even a current article from last week's news magazine may be using old data.

4. *Are the data relevant?* You may find that the data have little to do with the point being presented. This question of relevance leads you into an analysis of the reasoning process itself.

If you are satisfied with the quality of the data (that the examples for Park Hills and Linden are accurate), then you can move to the second step.

TESTING THE REASONING (WARRANTS)   To test the reasoning, you must understand the link between the data and the conclusion drawn. In the above example, the speaker presents data from two schools and concludes that public schools are capable of high levels of achievement. In this case, the warrant, or reasoning link, is not stated. Before you can test the warrant, you must write it out. The speaker is saying, "What has been accomplished in two public schools can be accomplished in most or all." To test the warrant, phrase it as a yes-or-no question: "Is it true that the results in these two examples (Park Hills and Linden) are possible in most or all public schools?" If the answer is yes, the reasoning is sound; if the answer is no, the reasoning is fallacious. As you will recall from our discussion of reasoning in Chapter 15, this argument is illustrative of reasoning by example (generalization). In the next section, we look at the specific tests of this and other types of arguments.

Evaluating Reasoning

You will recall that reason is either inductive or deductive. *Inductive reasoning* means working from specifics to some conclusion. In inductive reasoning you discover what is true or what was true in the past, and then you predict that something is true or will be true in the future. The conclusions of inductive arguments are tested on the basis of probability. That is, we predict that the conclusion will be true most of the time. The higher the probability (the closer to 100 percent), the better the argument.

Deductive reasoning is a form that moves from premises to conclusions. If the premises are true, then the conclusion is not just probable, as in an inductive argument, but *certain*.

Now let us consider the evaluation of inductive reasoning (generalization, analogy, causation, and sign) and deductive reasoning. To enable you to build upon what you have learned, in each of the following discussions we refer back to arguments that we used in Chapter 15 in support of the prediction that Paula Larson will win the senior class election.

CRITICALLY EVALUATING GENERALIZATION WARRANTS   Recall that in reasoning by generalization we drew a conclusion based on several related individual items of information. In support of the proposition that Paula Larson will win the senior class election, the speaker based his or her argument on the three examples: "Paula was successful in her campaign for treasurer of her high school junior class, in her campaign for chairperson of her church youth group, and in her campaign for president of her sorority." This is reasoning from example or generalization. The warrant might be phrased, "Her success in three other campaigns may be used to predict her success in this campaign."

A *generalization warrant* (the verbal statement of the reasoning process) may be tested by asking the following questions.

1. *Are enough instances cited?* Are three campaigns (junior class treasurer, youth group chairperson, and sorority president) enough examples? Because the instances cited should represent most to all possibilities, enough must be cited to satisfy the listeners that the instances are not isolated or handpicked.

    One of the most common thinking fallacies is called *hasty generalization*, which results from a shortage of data. Conclusions from hasty generalization fail to meet the test of sufficient instances cited. In real-life situations, we are likely to find people making generalizations based on only one, or at most a few, examples. For instance, in support of the argument that teenagers favor marijuana decriminalization, a person might cite the opinions of two teenagers who live next door. Yet, the cross-section for that sample is neither large enough nor representative enough. In a speech, the argument may sound more impressive than it is, especially if the speaker dramatizes the one example. But you can refute the argument as a hasty generalization.

    Thus, if a speaker presents a generalization with no data, or with extremely little data, you will want to question the reasoning on that basis alone. Although students in a public speaking class should not make the mistake of hasty generalization in a speech, you may find opportunities to refute arguments on that basis.

2. *Are the instances typical?* Are the three instances typical of all of her campaigns for office? *Typical* means that the instances cited must be similar to or representative of most or all within the category. If instances are not typical, they do not support the generalization. For instance, if these three successes came in very small organizations, they would not be typical of all organizations. If you do not believe that three instances are typical, then you would question the logic of the argument on that basis.

3. *Are negative instances accounted for?* In looking at material we may find one or more exceptions to the generalization. If the exceptions

are minor or infrequent, then they do not necessarily invalidate the generalization. For instance, Paula may have run for chairperson of the chess club but was defeated. That one failure does not necessarily invalidate the generalization. If, however, the exceptions prove to be more than rare or isolated instances, the validity of the generalization is open to serious question. For instance, if we found that Paula ran for office twelve times and was successful on only the three occasions cited, then the generalization would be fallacious. If you believe that negative instances were not accounted for, then you would question the logic of the argument on that basis.

CRITICALLY EVALUATING ANALOGY WARRANTS   Recall that an *analogy* is a comparative generalization. In reasoning by analogy, we say that what is true of something with one set of circumstances will be true of something else with a similar set of circumstances. In support of the proposition that Paula Larson will win the senior class election, the speaker based his or her argument on the similarity between Paula and Heather Nelson, who won two years earlier, by showing that "Paula and Heather are both bright, both have a great deal of drive, and both have a track record of successful campaigns." This is reasoning from analogy. The warrant might be phrased, "Paula's similarity to Heather, who was successful two years ago, can be used to predict her success in this campaign."

An *analogy warrant* (the verbal statement of the reasoning process) may be tested by asking these questions.

1. *Are the subjects being compared similar in every important way?* Are Heather and Paula similar in intelligence, drive, and track records in elected offices? If subjects do not have significant similarities, then they are not comparable. If you believe that the subjects being compared are not really similar in important ways, then you can question the reasoning on that basis.

2. *Are any of the ways that the subjects are dissimilar important to the outcome?* Is Paula's dissimilarity in sorority affiliation a factor? Is her dissimilarity in religion a factor? If dissimilarities exist that outweigh the subjects' similarities, then conclusions drawn from the comparisons may be invalid. If you believe that the ways the subjects are dissimilar have not been considered, then you can question the reasoning on that basis.

CRITICALLY EVALUATING CAUSATION WARRANTS   Recall that *causation* is a form of reasoning that proves a conclusion on the basis of a special connection between the data and the conclusion. When we say that a causal relationship exists, we mean that one or more of the circumstances cited always (or at least usually) produces a predictable effect or set of effects. In support of the proposition that Paula Larson will win the senior class election, the speaker based his or her argument on the points that "Paula has campaigned intelligently, and Paula has key endorsements—both of which result in election." This is reasoning from causation. The warrant might be phrased, "Intelligent campaigning and the presence of key endorsements, major causes of success in elections, can be used to predict her success in this campaign."

A *causation warrant* (the verbal statement of the reasoning process) may be tested by asking these questions.

1. *Are the data alone sufficient cause to bring about the particular conclusion?* Are intelligent campaigning and getting key endorsements themselves important enough to result in winning elections? If the data are truly important, it means that if we eliminate the data, we would eliminate the effect. If the effect can occur without the data, then we can question the causal relationship.

   Another common thinking fallacy, *questionable cause*, is marked by the failure to meet this test. It is human nature to look for causes for events. If we are having a drought, we want to know the cause; if the schools are in financial trouble, we want to know the cause; if the crime rate has risen during the year, we want to know the cause. In our haste to discover causes for behavior, we sometimes identify something that happened or existed before the event or at the time of the event, and label that something as the cause of the event. This tendency leads to the fallacy of questionable cause.

   Think of the people who blame loss of money, sickness, and problems at work on black cats that ran in front of them, or mirrors that broke, or ladders they walked under. You recognize these as superstitions. Nevertheless, they are excellent examples of attributing cause to unrelated events.

   Superstitions are not the only examples of questionable cause. Consider a situation that occurs yearly on many college campuses. One year a coach's team has a winning year, and the coach is lauded for his or her expertise. The next year the team does poorly and the coach is fired. Has the coach's skill deteriorated that much in one year? It is quite unlikely. But it is much easier to point the finger at the coach as the cause of the team's failure than to admit that the entire team or the program itself is inferior. The fact is that examples of this kind of argument are frequent.

If you believe that the data alone are not important or significant enough to bring about the conclusion, then you can question the reasoning on that basis.

2. *Do other data that accompany the data cited cause the effect?* Are there other factors (such as luck, drive, friends) that are more important in determining whether a person wins an election? If the accompanying data appear equally or more important in bringing about the effect, then we can question the causal relationship between cited data and conclusion. If you believe that other data really caused the effect, then you can question the reasoning on that basis.

3. *Is the relationship between cause and effect consistent?* Do intelligent campaigning and key endorsements always (or usually) yield winning elections? If there are times when the effect has not followed the cause, then we can question whether a causal relationship exists. If you believe that the relationship between the cause and effect are not consistent, then you can question the reasoning on that basis.

CRITICALLY EVALUATING SIGN WARRANTS   Recall that a *sign* is a form of reasoning that proves a conclusion on the basis of a connection between the symptoms and the conclusion. Signs are indicators. When certain events, characteristics, or situations always or usually accompany something, we say that these events, characteristics, or situations are signs.

In support of the proposition that Paula Larson will win the senior class election, the speaker based his or her argument on the points that "Paula has more campaign posters than all other candidates combined, and students from all segments of campus are wearing her campaign buttons." This is reasoning from signs. The warrant might be phrased, "The presence of campaign posters and the wearing of campaign buttons are signs or indicators of the likelihood of success in this campaign."

A *sign warrant* (the verbal statement of the reasoning) may be tested by these questions.

1. *Do the signs cited always or usually indicate the conclusion drawn?* Do large numbers of posters and campaigns buttons always (or usually) indicate election victory? If the data can occur independently of the conclusion, then they are not necessarily indicators. If you believe that the data cited do not usually indicate the conclusion, then you can question the reasoning on that basis.

2. *Are sufficient signs present?* Are campaign posters and buttons enough to indicate a victory? Events or situations often are indicated by several signs. If enough of them are not present, then the conclusion

may not follow. If you believe there are insufficient signs, then you can question the reasoning on that basis.

3. *Are contradictory signs in evidence?* Are posters being torn down in great numbers? If signs that usually indicate different conclusions are present, then the stated conclusion may not be valid. If you believe that contradictory signs are evident, then you can question the reasoning on that basis.

CRITICALLY EVALUATING DEDUCTIONS   As we have mentioned, *deduction* is a form of reasoning that is used in moving from statements that are true to a related statement that must be true. A deductive warrant may be stated, "If two related premises are true, then a conclusion based on those two premises must be true." If the speaker argued that Paula must have won the election because she is giving a victory speech and only winners are entitled to such speeches, you would identify this as a deductive argument.

A *deduction warrant* (the verbal statement of the reasoning process) may be tested by asking these questions.

1. *Are the premises true?* If it is not true that people must win in order to give a victory speech or if Paula is in fact not giving such a speech, then the conclusion would not be true. A sound conclusion cannot be drawn from untrue premises. If the premises are not true, then you can question the reasoning on that basis.

2. *Is the conclusion based on the premises?* Does the conclusion concern itself with Paula or with the election? If the conclusion is not based on the premises, then you can question the reasoning on that basis.

As you study your outlines of oral arguments, you may discover other ways that speakers have tried to reason. Let us consider three additional common patterns that are considered to be fallacies of reasoning that you must learn to recognize.

Recognizing Fallacies

APPEAL TO AUTHORITY   An *appeal to authority* is a fallacy based on the quality of the data. When people support their arguments with the testimony of an authority, you can refute it as being fallacious if the use of the testimony fails to meet either of two tests: (1) If the source is not really an authority on the issue or (2) if the content of the testimonial is inconsistent with other expert opinion.

Let us consider cases in which the source is not truly an authority. Advertisers are well aware that because the public idolizes athletes, movie stars, and television performers, people are likely to accept their word on subjects they may know little about. So when an athlete tries to get the viewer to purchase perfume, the athlete's argument is a fallacy.

Although the fallacy of authority may be easy to recognize in a television ad, other examples of the fallacy may not be so easy to recognize. Economists, politicians, and scientists often comment on subjects outside their areas of expertise; sometimes neither they nor we realize how unqualified they are to speak on such subjects. A scientist's statement is good evidence only in the science in which he or she is an expert. Thus, a geneticist's views on the subject of the world food supply may or may not be fallacious, depending on the point he or she is trying to make.

The other test is whether the content of the testimonial is contrary to other expert opinion. Even when an authority states an opinion relevant to his or her area of expertise, that opinion may be fallacious if the opinion is one that is not supported by a majority of other authorities in that field. If a space biologist says that there must be life similar to ours on other planets, his or her opinion is no more logical proof than any other opinion; it is not even an authoritative opinion if a majority of other equally qualified space biologists believe otherwise. If you look long enough you can always find someone who has said something in support of even the most foolish statement. Avoid the mistake of accepting any statement as valid support just because some alleged authority is cited as the source.

APPEALS BASED ON STATISTICS   Fallacies in the use of statistics may be based on the quantity of data, quality of data, or reasoning from data. Statistics are nothing more than large numbers of instances; but statistics seem to have a bewitching force — most of us are conditioned to believe that instances cast in statistical form carry the weight of authority. Yet, the potential fallacies from statistics are so numerous that there is no way we can do total justice to the subject in this short analysis. The old saying, "Figures don't lie, but liars figure," is so applicable to the general use of statistics that you must be particularly careful with their use. To be safe, you should look at any statistical proof as potentially fallacious. Even statistics that are used honestly and with the best of motives still may be fallacious, because the clear, logical use of statistics is so difficult.

As you examine arguments supported with statistics, look for the following:

1.   *Statistics that are impossible to verify.* If you are like me, you have read countless startling statements such as, "Fifteen million mosquitoes are hatched each day in the Canadian province of Ontario"

or "One out of every seventeen women in ancient Greece had six fingers." Now, do not quote these—I made them up; but they are no more unlikely than many other examples I have seen. The fact is that we have no way of verifying such statistics. How does anyone count the number of mosquitoes hatched? How can we test whether anyone counted the fingers of ancient Greek women? Statistics of this kind are startling and make interesting conversation, but they are fallacious as support for arguments.

2. *Statistics used alone.* Statistics by themselves do not mean much. For example, "Last season the Cincinnati Reds drew approximately 1.7 million fans to their seventy home games." Although at face value this sounds like (and it is) a lot of people, it does not tell much about the club's attendance. Is this figure good or bad? Was attendance up or down? Statistics often are not meaningful unless they are compared with other data.

3. *Statistics used with unknown comparative bases.* Comparisons of statistics do not mean much if the comparative base is not given. Consider the statement, "While the Zolon growth rate was dawdling along at some 3 percent last year, Allon was growing at a healthy 8 percent." This statement implies that Allon is doing much better than Zolon; however, if Zolon's base was larger, its 3 percent increase could be much better than Allon's 8 percent. We cannot know unless we understand the base from which the statistic was drawn.

AD HOMINEM ARGUMENT   An *ad hominem argument* is a fallacy occurring with an attack on the person making the argument rather than on the argument itself. Literally, *ad hominem* means "to the man." For instance, if Bill Bradley, the highly intelligent and very articulate former New York Knicks basketball player, presented the argument that athletics are important to the development of the total person, the reply, "Great, all we need is some jock justifying his own existence" would be an example of an ad hominem argument.

Such a personal attack often is made as a smokescreen to cover up a lack of good reasons and evidence. Ad hominem name-calling is used to try to encourage the audience to ignore a lack of evidence. Make no mistake, ridicule, name-calling, and other personal attacks are at times highly successful, but they almost always are fallacious.

Although books written about argument list other valid types of reasoning and often discuss ten or twenty common fallacies, we do not have the space to cover them all here. What can you do when you encounter an argument that does not fit one of the patterns we have discussed?

Outline the argument, test the data, and test the reasoning link. Even if you are unable to identify the type of argument, you can probably still judge its relative strength or weakness.

Skill Development Exercise
Evaluating Arguments

For each of the following write the conclusion that the speaker has drawn, write a warrant that explains the link between the data and the conclusion, and identify the type of warrant (generalization, analogy, cause, or sign). The first one is done for you as an example of how you should proceed.

I see that Ohio has stiffened its penalties for drunk driving and has begun applying them uniformly. I don't think there is any doubt that we are going to see instances of drunk driving dropping in Ohio.

1. *Conclusion:* The number of instances of drunk driving in Ohio will drop.

2. *Warrant:* Stiff penalties and uniform application will result in lower numbers of drunk drivers. (Causation)

Now write the conclusion and warrant for each of the following:

Can you imagine that? In New York a teacher required hospitalization after being beaten by a gang. In Chicago a teacher resigned after being terrorized by midnight phone calls and threats against his family.

1.

2.

If you have been watching indicators lately, you'll notice that interest rates have been creeping upward again. During the past two years, interests rates were flat. For each of the last four months, however, we have seen increasingly higher interest rates. Also, according to an article in *Time*, people are keeping more of their money in savings accounts. I hate to say this, but it seems that we are heading for another recession.

1.

2.

I don't think there is any doubt that we will have bumper corn and wheat crops this year. In each of the past several months, rainfall has been plentiful — average or above for each month. In addition, we haven't had any wild fluctuations in temperature. For the most part, temperatures have been near normal.

1.

2.

Refuting Arguments in Speeches

After you have critically evaluated the arguments presented in a speech, you may want, or may be called upon, to refute the argument or arguments you have evaluated. In the chapter opening, *refutation* was defined as the process of proving that an argument or series of arguments, or the conclusion drawn from that argument or arguments, is false, erroneous, or at least doubtful. If, for instance, someone says, "Martina Navratilova will win the match," and you say, "No, she's no longer able to compete at top levels," what you have said in reply is refutation.

Refutation, like all other aspects of speechmaking, can and should be handled systematically.

1. *Prepare with material on both sides of the proposal.* A speech of refutation requires anticipation of what your opponent will say. For any controversial proposal, you should know the material on both sides. If you have an idea of how your opponent will proceed, you will be in a much better position to reply.

2. *Take careful notes of what your opponent says.* The key words, phrases, and ideas should be recorded accurately and as nearly as possible in the actual words used. You do not want to run the risk of being accused of distorting what your opponent actually said.

3. *Note your reactions to what is said.* Thoughts will come to mind as you are outlining. If you sketch your reactions as you listen, you will be in a much better position to respond.

    Divide your note paper in half vertically and outline your opponent's speech in one column. Use the other column to note your refutation of each particular point. Figure 17.1 illustrates notes on one point of the speaker's argument. Notice that the specific goal is written in full, the main point is written as a complete sentence, and the subpoints include enough words to reflect the content. In the comments column, you sketch your thoughts related to each point made.

4. *Plan your procedure.* At this stage you will have a reasonably accurate account of all your opponent has said. Now, how will you reply? You can base your refutation on your opponent's amount of data, quality of data, or reasoning.

    If the opposition's case is built on an assertion with little or no evidence to support the assertion, you can refute the argument on that basis.

    A better procedure is to attack the quality of the material. If sheer amount of evidence were the most important criterion in proving a point, the person with the most material would always

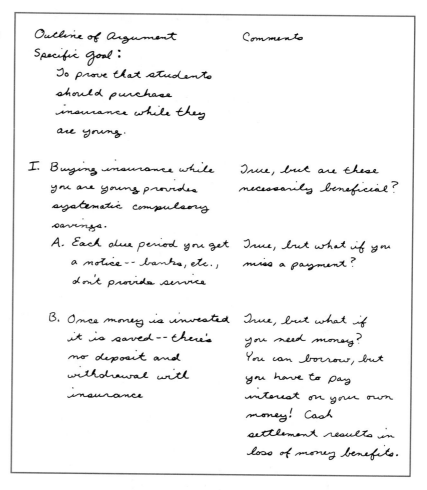

Outline of Argument — Comments

Specific goal:
To prove that students should purchase insurance while they are young.

I. Buying insurance while you are young provides systematic compulsory savings.
True, but are these necessarily beneficial?

  A. Each due period you get a notice -- banks, etc., don't provide service
True, but what if you miss a payment?

  B. Once money is invested it is saved -- there's no deposit and withdrawal with insurance
True, but what if you need money? You can borrow, but you have to pay interest on your own money! Cash settlement results in loss of money benefits.

win — but there is often no direct relationship between amount of material and quality of proof. A statement by a judge who has studied the rights of individual citizens to privacy would be worth far more than several opinions on privacy rights from athletes, musicians, or politicians who have not studied the subject.

For every bit of evidence presented, you should ask the four questions that we outlined earlier (pages 334–335): What is the source? Are the data fact or opinion? Are the data recent? Are the data relevant?

But the best procedure is to refute the reasoning warrants that the speaker has used in the speech. If you identify the primary reasoning as generalization (from example), analogy, causation, sign, or deductive argument, then by asking the questions presented earlier in this chapter you can find the weaknesses of the arguments and attack them directly.

5. *Practice using the four-step method.* Although you do not have as long to consider exactly what you will say, your refutation must be organized nearly as well as your planned speeches. If you think of refutation as units of argument, each organized by following four definite steps, you will learn to prepare and to present refutation effectively.

    a. State the argument you are going to refute clearly and concisely.

    b. State what you will prove; you must tell your listeners how you plan to proceed so that they will be able to follow your thinking.

    c. Present the reasons and data completely and with documentation (a brief reference to source).

    d. Draw a conclusion; do not rely on the audience to draw the proper conclusion for you. Never go on to another argument before you have drawn your conclusion.

To illustrate the process of refutation, let us examine a short unit of refutation directed to one particular argument that is presented in Figure 17.1. In the following abbreviated statement, notice how the four steps of refutation (stating the argument, stating what you will prove, presenting proof, and drawing a conclusion) are incorporated (for purposes of analysis, each of the four steps is enumerated):

> (1) Mr. Horan has said that buying insurance provides systematic, compulsory savings. (2) His assumption is that systematic, compulsory savings is a benefit of buying insurance while you are young. But I believe just the opposite is true; I believe that there are at least two serious disadvantages resulting from this. (3) First, the system is so compulsory that if you miss a payment you stand to lose your entire savings and all benefits. Most insurance contracts include a clause giving you a thirty-day grace period, after which the policy is cancelled (evidence). Second, if you need money desperately, you have to take a loan against your policy. The end result of such a loan is that you have to pay interest in order to borrow your own money (evidence). (4) From this analysis, I think you can see that this systematic, compulsory saving is more disadvantageous than advantageous for people who are trying to save money.

Assignment
Refuting Arguments

1.   Working with a classmate, select a debatable topic and phrase a speech goal that establishes or changes a belief, such as "the United States should establish mandatory, periodic drug tests for all air traffic controllers" or "The United States should withdraw all troops from Europe." Clear the wording with your professor. Phrase the specific goal so that the first speaker is in favor of the proposal. The first speaker then will present a three- to six-minute persuasive speech presenting at least three arguments for the proposal. The second speaker will present a three- to six-minute speech opposing

<table>
<tr><td>Checklist</td><td>Refutation</td></tr>
</table>

Check items that were accomplished effectively.

_____ 1. Did the speaker state the argument to be refuted clearly and concisely?

_____ 2. Did the speaker clearly state his or her position on that argument?

_____ 3. Did the speaker document evidence in support of his or her position?

_____ 4. Did the speaker draw a clear conclusion?

_____ 5. Did the speaker follow these four steps for each unit of refutation?

Evaluate the speech as (check one) _____excellent, _____good, _____average, _____fair, _____poor.

Use the information from your checklist to support your evaluation.

the specific arguments presented by the first speaker. In this one assignment you are provided with an opportunity to cover a persuasive speech emphasizing reasoning and to give a speech of refutation.

2. Write a critique of one or more of the debates you hear in class using the reasoning checklist in Chapter 15 (page 312). Use the questions in this chapter's refutation checklist as a basis for your analysis of the speech of refutation.

Speeches — Lie-Detector Testing

The following two speeches are presented to illustrate a debate format with one supporting a speech goal and the second refuting the arguments presented in the first speech.[1]

Instead of analyzing this first speech on the basis of its effectiveness as a speech, analyze it as if you were to give the speech of refutation. That is, consider its strengths and weaknesses, but do so in a context of how you develop your refutation. After you have determined a strategy for refuting the speech, read the analysis.

Lie detector or polygraph tests used either to screen job applicants or to uncover thefts by employees have become a big business. Hundreds of thousands are given each year, and the number is steadily rising. What I propose to you today is that employers should be prohibited from administering lie detector tests to their employees either as a condition of employment or as a condition of maintaining their job. I support this proposition for two reasons. First, despite technological improvement in equipment, the accuracy of results is open to question; and second, even if the tests are accurate, use of lie detector tests is an invasion of privacy.

First, let's consider their accuracy. Lie detector tests just have not proved to be very accurate. According to Senator Birch Bayh, tests are only about 70 percent accurate. And equally important, even the results of this 70 percent can be misleading. Let's look at two examples of the kinds of harm that come from these misleading results.

One case involves a young girl named Linda Boycose. She was at the time of the incident a bookkeeper for Kresge's. One day she reported $1.50 missing from the previous day's receipts. A few weeks later the store's security man gave her a lie-detector test. He first used the equipment with all its intimidating wiring and then he used persuasion to get information. He accused her of deceiving him and actually stealing the money. After this test, Boycose was so upset she quit her job — she then spent the next two years indulging in valium at an almost suicidal level. Last year a Detroit jury found Boycose's story so convincing that it ordered the department store chain to award her $100,000. Now, almost six years later, she is still afraid to handle the bookkeeping at the doctor's office she manages.

The next example is of a supermarket clerk in Los Angeles. She was fired after an emotional response to the question, "Have you ever given discount groceries to your mother?" It was later discovered that her mother had been dead for five years, thus showing that her response was clearly an emotional one.

Much of the inaccuracy of the tests has to do with the examiner's competence. Jerry Wall, a Los Angeles tester, said that out of an estimated three thousand U.S. examiners, only fifty are competent. Some polygraph operators tell an interviewee that he or she has lied at one point even if the person has not, just to see how the person will handle the stress. This strategy can destroy a person's poise, leading to inaccuracies. With these examples of stress situations and inefficient examiners, the facts point to the inaccuracy of polygraph test results.

Can instances of abuse be admitted without concluding that tests should be abolished? How?

My second reason for abolishing the use of these tests is that they are an invasion of privacy. Examiners can and do ask job applicants about such things as sexual habits and how often they change their underwear. The supposed purpose of lie detector tests is to determine whether an employee is stealing. These irrelevant questions are an invasion of privacy, and not a way to indicate whether someone is breaking the law.

This material demonstrates a threat of government intervention. But has government intervened? Has government determined what constitutes "invasion of privacy"?

Excesses are such that the federal government has been conducting hearings on misuse. Congress is considering ways to curtail their use.

That they are an invasion of privacy seems to be admitted by the companies that use them. Employers are afraid to reveal too much information from tests because they have a fear of being sued. Because of an examiner's prying questions on an employee's background, and because government has shown such a concern about the continued use of polygraphs, we can conclude that they are an invasion of privacy.

Strong emotional appeal in this summary. How can the effect of this be countered?

In conclusion, let me ask you how, as an employee, you would feel taking such a test. You'd probably feel nervous and reluctant to take the test. Couldn't you see yourself stating something that would be misconstrued, not because of the truth, but because of your nervousness? Also, how would you feel about having to answer very personal and intimate questions about yourself in order to get a job.

Because lie detector tests are inaccurate and an invasion of privacy, I believe their use should be prohibited.

In this speech, we would expect the speaker to say something about the two reasons that were presented in the first speech. In your analysis, look to see how the groundwork for refutation is laid; then look for the use of the four-step method of refutation.

Analysis

Good opening. Speaker has clearly stated her position.

SPEECH OF REFUTATION: USING LIE-DETECTOR TESTS

My opponent has stated that the use of lie detector tests by employers should be abolished. I strongly disagree; I believe employers have to use these tests.

Speaker has clearly laid the groundwork for her negative position. This material establishes a need for some measures to be taken against theft. It shows that tests are not being used without good reason.

Before examining the two reasons she presented, I'd like to take a look at why more than 20 percent of the nation's largest businesses feel a need to use these tests and why the number is growing each year. Employers use lie detector tests to help curb employee theft. According to the National Retail Merchants Association, employees steal as much as $40 billion of goods each year. Moreover, the figure increases markedly each year. The average merchant doesn't recognize that he loses more to employees than to outsiders — 50 to 70 percent of theft losses go to employees, not to shoplifters. This use of lie detector tests is a necessity to curb this internal theft.

This represents further clarification of what affirmative has done and what negative proposes to do. It helps to place the affirmative attack in proper perspective.

Good direct attack on level of accuracy. Notice she states opponent's point, states her position on the point, and then presents the evidence. She needs a concluding statement to tie the unit of refutation together.

But why are Kelley's figures better than Bayh's? The speaker needs to show us.

Good job of debating the conclusion to be drawn from the example. Still, I would like to have heard her make a closer examination of the examples themselves.

That businesses use the tests does not prove that businesses are convinced they are accurate. Need more factual data here.

This is a further attempt to put the affirmative argument into proper perspective. Judge's ruling gives strong support to her position.

Good line of argument. Any attempt at refuting alleged abuses would be damaging to the negative position.

Here the speaker does a nice job of bringing emphasis back to the need for the tests.

Now, I do not believe that my opponent ever tried to show that there is not a problem that lie detector testing solves; nor did she try to show that lie detector testing doesn't help to deter internal theft. Notice that the two reasons she presented are both about abuses. Let's take a closer look at those two reasons.

First, my opponent said that the accuracy of results is open to question; in contrast, I would argue that these tests are remarkably accurate. She mentioned that Senator Bayh reported a 70-percent level of accuracy. Yet the literature on these tests as reported by Ty Kelley, vice president of government affairs of the National Association of Chain Drug Stores, argues that the level is around 90 percent, not 70 percent.

She went on to give two examples of people who were intimidated and/or became emotional and upset when subjected to the test. And on this basis she calls for them to be abolished. I would agree that some people do become emotional, but this is hardly reason for stopping their use. Unless she can show a real problem among many people taking the test I think we'll have to go along with the need for the tests.

If these tests are so inaccurate, why are one-fifth of the nation's largest companies using them. According to an article in *Business Week*, "Business Buys the Lie Detector," more and more businesses each year see a necessity for using the tests because they deter crime. These tests are now being used by nearly every type of company—banks, businesses, drug stores, as well as retail department stores.

Her second reason for why the tests should be abolished is that they are an invasion of privacy. I believe, with Mr. Kelley, whom I quoted earlier, that there must be some sort of balance maintained between an individual's right to privacy and an employer's right to protect his property. In Illinois, for instance, a state judge ruled that examiners could ask prying questions—there has yet to be any official ruling that the use is "an invasion of privacy."

My opponent used the example of asking questions about sexual habits and change of underwear. In that regard, I agree with her. I think that a person is probably pretty sick who is asking these kinds of questions—and I think these abuses should be checked. But asking questions to screen out thieves, junkies, liars, alcoholics, and psychotics is necessary. For instance, an Atlanta nursing home uses polygraph tests to screen out potentially sadistic and disturbed nurses and orderlies. Is this an invasion of privacy? I don't think so.

It is obvious to me that some type of lie detector test is needed. Too much theft has gone on and something must be done to curtail this. I say that lie detector tests are the answer. First, they are accurate. Companies have been using them for a long time, and more and more companies are starting to use them. And second, it is only an invasion of privacy when the wrong types of questions are asked. I agree that these abuses should be curbed, but not by doing away with the tests. Employers cannot do away with these tests and control theft; the benefits far outweigh the risks.

Summary

Refutation is the process of proving that an argument or series of arguments, or the conclusion drawn from that argument or arguments, is false, erroneous, or at least doubtful. Sometimes refutation concerns only a small segment of a speech. At that time you reply to the proposal with an entire speech of refutation.

To critically analyze a speech argument, you must have an accurate representation of that argument in outline form. When you have outlined the speech, you can test the data and the reasoning.

You test data by asking questions about source, recency, relevancy, and whether the data were fact or opinion. You test the reasoning by asking questions about the warrant for the particular argument. For arguments from example you question the number and typicality of the instances and whether negative instances were accounted for. For arguments from analogy you question the similarity of the subjects and whether any dissimilarities have been omitted. For arguments from cause you question whether data are sufficient to bring about the effect, whether other data may have caused the effect, and whether the relationship between cause and effect is consistent. For arguments from sign you question the number of signs, the relationship of the signs to the conclusion, and the omission of contradictory signs. For deductive warrants you question whether the premises are true and whether the conclusion is directly related to the premises.

In your analysis you also look for such fallacies as appeal to authority, appeals based on statistics, and ad hominem argument.

Refutation must be handled systematically. You should prepare with material on both sides of the proposal, take careful notes of what your opponent says, note your reaction to each argument, plan your procedure, and present your refutation following the four-step method.

Note

1. These two speeches are based on a debate between Sheila Kohler and Martha Feinberg presented at the University of Cincinnati, and are used here with their permission.

Suggested Readings

Hoyenga, Katharine Blick, and Kermit T. Hoyenga. *Motivational Explanations of Behavior.* Monterey, Calif.: Brooks/Cole, 1984. A comprehensive analysis of motivation with emphasis on social motives for influencing others.

Kahane, Howard. *Logic and Contemporary Rhetoric.* 5th ed. Belmont, Calif.: Wadsworth, 1988 (paperback). This excellent source gives outstanding pointers on the use and development of logical argument and considerable emphasis on identifying and eliminating the fallacies of reasoning.

Larson, Charles U. *Persuasion: Reception and Responsibility.* 5th ed. Belmont, Calif.: Wadsworth, 1989. A solid textbook that places more emphasis on the receiver of the persuasive message than on the persuader.

Moore, Brook Noel, and Richard Parker. *Critical Thinking: Evaluating Claims and Arguments in Everyday Life.* Palo Alto, Calif.: Mayfield, 1986. One of the best of the recent paperback books that focus on evaluating everyday arguments.

Packard, Vance O. *The Hidden Persuaders.* New York: Pocket Books, 1975 (paperback). This popular book, first published in the 1950s, still makes for excellent reading about the problems and excesses of persuasion.

Pratkanis, Anthony R., Steven J. Breckler, and Anthony G. Greenwald, eds. *Attitude Structure and Function.* Hillsdale, N.J.: Lawrence Erlbaum, 1989. A cognitive view of the structure and function of attitude.

Smith, Mary John. *Persuasion and Human Interaction.* Belmont, Calif.: Wadsworth, 1982. An excellent review and critique of theories of persuasion.

PART V

ADAPTING TO OTHER OCCASIONS AND FORMATS

Because at times you will have to apply your skills to ceremonial occasions and group contexts, in this part we discuss information that you will need to meet these goals.

The kinds of special occasion speeches that you are most likely to give are introductions, presentations, acceptances, welcomings, and tributes.

There also will be times when the speech you give will be the presentation of the deliberations of a committee or group that has been assigned the task of solving a problem or making a decision. Chapter 19 on groups discusses both the group problem-solving process and methods of making group discussion public.

| Chapter 18 | Adapting to Special Occasions |

Some of the speaking that you are called upon to do will be under circumstances that are best described as ceremonial. In these speeches, you may give information or you may persuade, but also you must meet the conventions of the particular occasion. So even though the guidelines for speech preparation that we have studied throughout this book will serve you well, you must also be familiar with the needs that these particular ceremonial occasions serve.

Even though no speech can be given by formula, certain occasions require at least the knowledge of conventions that various speakers observe and that audiences may expect. Because speakers should always use their own imagination to determine how to develop the theme, they should never adhere slavishly to those conventions. Still, you must know the conventions before you can decide whether to deviate from or ignore them entirely.

This chapter gives the basics of accomplishing five common types of special speeches: introductions, presentations, acceptances, welcomings, and tributes.

Introductions

This occasion calls for a short but critically important speech.

Purpose

The purpose of this speech is to pave the way for the main speaker. If you make the introduction in such a way that the audience is psychologically ready to listen to the speech, then you have accomplished your purpose.

Procedure

Your listeners want to know who the speaker is, what the person is going to talk about, and why they should listen. Sometime before the speech you should consult with the speaker to ask what he or she prefers to have said. Usually, you want the necessary biographical information that will show who the speaker is and why he or she is qualified to talk on the subject. The better known the person is, the less you need to say about him or her. For instance, the introduction of the president is simply, "Ladies and gentlemen, the president of the United States." Ordinarily, you will want enough information to allow you to talk for at least two or three minutes. Only on rare occasions should a speech of introduction last longer than three or four minutes; the audience is assembled to hear the speaker, not the introducer. During the first sentence or two, then, establish the nature of the occasion; in the body of the speech, establish the speaker's credibility. The conclusion usually should include the name of the speaker and the title of the talk.

Considerations

There are some special cautions concerning the speech of introduction. First, do not overpraise the speaker. If expectations are too high, the speaker will never be able to live up to them. For instance, overzealous introducers may be inclined to say: "This man [woman] is undoubtedly one of the greatest speakers around today. You will, I am sure, agree with me that this will be one of the best speeches you've ever heard." Although this statement may seem complimentary, it does the speaker a disservice by emphasizing comparison rather than speech content.

A second caution is to be familiar with what you have to say. Audiences question sincerity when introducers have to read their praise. Many of us have been present when an introducer said, "And now, it is my great pleasure to present that noted authority . . ." and then had to look at some notes to recall the name. Finally, get your facts straight. The speaker should not have to spend time correcting your mistakes.

Assignment *Speech of Introduction*	Prepare a two- to three-minute speech of introduction. Assume that you are introducing the featured speaker for some specific occasion. Criteria for evaluation will include creativity in establishing speaker credibility and presenting the name of the speaker and the speech title.

Presentations

Next to introductions, presentations are the ceremonial speeches that you are most likely to give.

Purpose

The purpose of a presentation speech is to present an award, prize, or gift to an individual or group. Sometimes, a presentation accompanies a long tribute to an individual. Usually, the speech is a fairly short, formal recognition of some accomplishment.

Procedure

Your speech usually has two goals: (1) to discuss the nature of the award, including its history, donor, or source, and the conditions under which it is made; and (2) to discuss the accomplishments of the recipient. If a competition was held, describe what the person did in the competition. Under other circumstances, discuss how the person has met the criteria for the award.

Obviously, you must learn all you can about the award and about the conditions under which such awards are made. Although the award itself may be a certificate, plaque, or trophy that symbolizes some achievement, the contest may have a long history and tradition that must be mentioned. Because the audience wants to know what the recipient has done, you must know the criteria that were met. For a competition, you must know the number of contestants and the way the contest was judged. If the person earned the award through years of achievement, you should know the particulars of that achievement.

Ordinarily, the speech is organized to show what the award is for, gives the criteria for winning or achieving the award, and states how the person won or achieved the award. If the announcement of the name of the recipient is meant to be a surprise, what is said should build up to the climax, the naming of the winner.

Considerations

For the speech of presentation there are only two special considerations: (1) Avoid overpraising; do not explain everything in such superlatives that the presentation lacks sincerity and honesty. (2) If you are going to hand the award to the recipient, you should be careful to hold the award in your left hand and present it to the left hand of the recipient. At the same time, you want to shake the right hand in congratulations. If you practice, you will find that you can present the award and shake the person's hand smoothly and avoid those embarrassing moments when the recipient does not know quite know what he or she is supposed to do.

Assignment
Speech of Presentation

Prepare a three- to five-minute speech in which you present a gift, plaque, or award to a member of your class. Criteria for evaluation will include showing what the award is for, the criteria for winning, and how the person met the criteria.

Acceptances

When an award is presented, it must be accepted. The acceptance speech is a response to a presentation speech.

Purpose

The purpose of the acceptance speech is to give brief thanks for receiving the award.

Procedure

The speech usually has two parts: (1) a brief thanks to the group, agency, or people responsible for giving the award; and (2) thanks to those who share in the honor if the recipient was aided by others.

Unless the acceptance is the lead-in to a major address, the acceptance should be brief. (A politician accepting a gift from the Chamber of Commerce may launch into a speech on government, but the audience probably will be expecting it.) As the Academy Awards program so graphically illustrates, however, when people are honored, the tendency is to give overly long and occasionally inappropriate speeches. The audience expects you to show your gratitude to the presenter of the award; it does not expect a major address.

Assignment
Speech of Acceptance

This assignment may well go together with the speech-of-presentation assignment. Prepare a one- to two-minute speech of acceptance in response to another speaker's speech of presentation. The criterion for evaluation will be how imaginatively you can respond in a brief speech.

Welcomings

Another common ceremonial speech is the welcoming.

Purpose

The purpose of a speech of welcome is to express pleasure for the presence of a person or organization. In a way, the speech of welcome is a double speech of introduction. You introduce the newcomer to the organization or city, and you introduce the organization to the newcomer.

Procedure

You must be familiar with both the person or organization you are welcoming and with the situation to which you are welcoming the person. It is surprising how little many members of organizations, citizens of a community, and students at a college or university really know about their organization or community. Although you may not have the knowledge on the tip of your tongue, it is inexcusable not to find the material you need to give an appropriate speech. Likewise, you want accurate information about the person or organization you are introducing. Although the speech will be brief, you need accurate and complete information from which to draw.

After expressing pleasure in welcoming the person or organization, give a little information about your guests and about the place or the organization to which the guests are being welcomed. Usually the conclusion is a brief statement of your hope for a pleasant and profitable visit.

Considerations

Again, the special caution is to make sure the speech is brief and honest. Welcoming guests does not require you to gush about them or their accomplishments. The speech of welcome should be an informative speech of praise.

Assignment
Welcoming Speech

Prepare a speech welcoming a specific person to your city, university, or social organization. Criteria for evaluation will include how well you explain the nature of the institution and how well you introduce the person being welcomed.

Tributes

The final ceremonial speech that we will consider is the tribute.

Purpose

The purpose of a speech of tribute is to praise someone's accomplishments. The occasion may be, for example, a birthday, the taking of an office, retirement, or death. A formal speech of tribute given in memory of a deceased person is called a *eulogy*.

Procedure

The key to an effective tribute is sincerity. Although you want the praise to be apparent, you do not want to overdo it.

You must have in-depth biographical information about your subject. Audiences are interested primarily in new information and specifics that characterize your assertions, so you must have a mastery of much detail. You should focus on the person's laudable characteristics and accomplishments. It is especially noteworthy if you find that the person had to overcome some special hardship or meet some particularly trying condition. All in all, you must be prepared to make a sound positive appraisal.

One way to organize a speech of tribute is by focusing on the subject's accomplishments. How detailed you make the speech will depend on whether the person is well known. If the person is well known, be more general in your analysis. If the person is little known, provide many more details so the audience can see the reasons for the praise. In the case of distinctly prominent individuals, you may be able to show their influence on history.

Considerations

Remember, however, that no one is perfect. Although you need not stress a person's less glowing characteristics or failures, some allusion to this kind of information may make the person's positive features even more meaningful. Probably the most important guide is for you to keep your objectivity. Excessive praise is far worse than understatement. Try to give the person his or her due, honestly and sincerely.

Assignment
Speech Paying Tribute

Prepare a four- to six-minute speech paying tribute to some person, living or dead. Criteria for evaluation will include how well you develop the person's laudable characteristics and accomplishments.

Summary

In addition to informative and persuasive speeches, you also are likely to have occasion to give speeches of introduction, presentation, acceptance, welcome, and tribute.

Introductions are speeches that introduce a speaker. A presentation is a speech in which you present an award, prize, or gift to an individual or group. An acceptance is a response to a speech of presentation. A welcome is a speech that expresses pleasure at the presence of a person or an organization. A tribute is a speech that praises someone's accomplishments.

Chapter 19 | Speaking in Problem-Solving Groups

Despite the many jokes about committees and the often justified impatience with them, the committee system and the group discussion it encourages can and should be an effective way of dealing with common problems. For our purposes, *problem-solving group discussion* is defined as a systematic form of speech in which two or more persons meet face to face and interact orally to accomplish a particular task or to arrive at a solution to a common problem. To speak effectively in groups you must prepare carefully and understand the responsibilities of both the leader and the group members.

Preparation for Problem-Solving Discussion

To prepare for either public or private discussion, you will need to state the problem, analyze it, suggest possible solutions, and select the best one.

Stating the Problem

In many groups, the wheel-spinning that takes place during the early discussion stages results from members' questions about the function, purpose, or goal of the group. As soon as possible, the group must clarify its goal. Usually the person, agency, or parent group that forms a particular work group indicates what the group should do. For example, a group may be formed "to determine the nature of the curriculum" or "to prepare a guideline for hiring at a new plant." If the goal is not this clear, it is up to the group leader or representative to find out exactly why the group was formed and what its goals are. If stating the problem is up to the group, then the group should move immediately to commit it to paper; until everyone agrees on what they have to do, they will never agree on how to do it.

Because the goal of discussion is to stimulate group thinking, the discussion problem should be stated as a question. Questions elicit responses. In phrasing a question, make sure that it (1) considers only one subject, (2) is impartially worded, and (3) uses words that can be defined objectively. "Should the United States cut back its foreign aid program and welfare?" considers two different questions; "Should the United States recognize those wretched Palestinians?" would be neither impartial nor definable.

Discussion topics may be stated as questions of fact, value, or policy.

1. *Questions of fact* concern the truth or falsity of an assertion. Implied in such questions is the possibility of determining the facts by direct observation or by spoken or recorded evidence. For instance, "How much rain fell today?" is a question of fact because rain can be measured and recorded. Likewise, "Is Smith guilty of robbing the warehouse?" is also a question of fact. Smith either committed the crime or he did not.

2. *Questions of value* concern subjective judgments of quality. They are characterized by the inclusion of certain evaluative word such as *good, reliable, effective,* or *worthy.* The purpose of questions of value is to compare a subject with one or more members of the same class. "What was the best movie last year?" is a question of value. Although we can set up criteria for "best" and measure our choice against those criteria, there is no way of verifying our findings. The answer still is a matter of judgment, not a matter of fact. Similarly, questions such as, "Is socialism superior to capitalism?" and "Is a small-college education better than a large-college education?" also

are questions of value. Although such questions are widely discussed in social groups, they are less likely to be the ultimate goal of work groups.

3. *Questions of policy* judge whether a future action should be taken. The question is phrased to arrive at a solution or to test a tentative solution to a problem or a felt need. "What should we do to lower the crime rate?" seeks a solution that would best solve the problem of increased crime. "Should the university give equal amounts of money to men's and women's athletics?" provides a tentative solution to the problem of how we can achieve equity in financial support of athletics. The inclusion of the word *should* in all questions of policy makes them the easiest to recognize and the easiest to phrase of all discussion questions.

Analyzing the Problem

Analyzing the problem is the second step in preparation. *Analysis* means determining the nature of the problem: its size, its causes, the forces that create or sustain it, and the criteria for evaluating solutions. Sometimes analysis takes only a few minutes; often it takes much longer. In preparing for problem solving and in the discussion itself, analysis too often is ignored because most groups want to move directly to possible solutions. For instance, if your goal is "to determine what should be done to solve the problem of thefts of library books," the group may want to start by immediately listing possible solutions, although a solution or a plan can work only if it solves the problem at hand. Before you can shape a plan, you must determine what obstacles the solution must overcome and what obstacles the solution must eliminate, as well as whom your plan must satisfy. Before you begin to suggest a solution, you must determine that the following questions about the problem have been answered:

1. What is its size and scope?
   a. What are its symptoms? (What can we identify that shows that something is wrong or needs to be changed?)
   b. What are its causes? (What forces created it, sustain it, or otherwise keep it from being solved?)
2. What criteria should be used to test the solution? Specifically, what checklist must the solution meet to best solve this problem? Must the plan eliminate the symptoms, be implemented within present resources, and so on?

Suggesting Possible Solutions

Most problems have many possible solutions. You should not be content with your work until you have listed as many as you can find.

How do you find solutions? One way is for you or the group to brainstorm. *Brainstorming* is free association; that is, it involves stating ideas in random order as they come to mind until you have compiled a long list. In a good ten- to fifteen-minute brainstorming session, you may think of several solutions by yourself. Depending on the nature of the topic, a group may develop ten, twenty, or more possibilities in a relatively short time. Other possible solutions will come from reading, interviews with authorities, or observations.

If your goal is phrased as a yes-or-no question, suggesting solutions is simplified. For instance, the question, "Should financial support for women's sports be increased?" has only two possible answers.

Selecting the Best Solution

If the group has analyzed the problem carefully and listed several potential solutions, then the final step involves only matching each proposed solution against the criteria. For instance, if you have determined that hiring more patrols, putting in closed-circuit TV, and locking outside doors after 9 P.M. are three possible solutions to the problem of increased crime in dorms, then you can begin to measure each against the criteria. The solution that meets the most criteria or the one that meets several criteria most effectively would be the best selection.

The Outline Agenda

Now let us put together questions with a sample (and somewhat abbreviated) outline agenda that would help the group proceed logically. The group has been convened to discuss "meeting the needs of women on campus."

1. State the problem (suggested wording):
   What should be done to equalize social, athletic, and political opportunities for women on campus? (Assume that the group has agreed upon this wording.)
2. Analyze the problem of meeting the needs of campus women:
   I. What is the size and scope of the problem?
       A. How many women are there on campus?
       B. What is the ratio of females to males on campus?

      C. What opportunities currently are available to women?
         1. What social organizations are available? What is the ratio of women to men who belong?
         2. Are women involved in political organizations on campus? To what extent?
         3. What athletic opportunities are open to women? Are they intramural or intercollegiate?
   II.   What are the causes of the problem?
      A. Do women feel discriminated against?
      B. Does the institution discriminate?
      C. Do societal norms inhibit women's participation?
      D. Do certain groups discriminate against women?
   III.   What criteria should be used to test solutions?
      A. Will women favor the solution?
      B. Will it cope with discrimination if discrimination does exist?
      C. Will it be enforceable?
      D. Will it comply with Title IX?

3. State possible solutions:
(This list can be started only at this point; other possible solutions will be revealed as the discussion progresses.)

Should a women's center be initiated?
Should a special-interest seat on all major committees be given to women?
Should women's and men's athletic teams be combined?
Etc.

4. Determine best solution:
(To be completed during discussion.)

Leadership in Problem-Solving Group Discussion

A problem-solving group discussion will not work well without effective leadership. Ordinarily, we think of an appointed or elected person acting as leader and all others in the group acting as contributors of content. Although it is often done that way, it does not have to be. A group can be organized so that everyone shares leadership. Thus, a group can have leadership regardless of whether it has a designated leader.

What Is Leadership?

Leadership may be defined as exerting influence to help a group achieve a goal. Let us explore the two key ideas in this definition.

1. *Leadership means exerting influence. Influence* is the ability to bring about changes in the attitudes and actions of others. When you influence those in your group, you show them why an idea, a decision, or a means of achieving a goal is superior in such a way that members of the group will follow those ideas of their own free will. Members of your group will continue to be influenced as long as they are convinced that what they have agreed to is right, in their own individual best interest, or in the best interest of the group.

2. *Leadership results in reaching a goal.* In the context of a task or problem-solving discussion, this element of leadership means accomplishing the task or arriving at a solution that tests out to be the best solution available at that time.

Who Will Lead?

Should a group have an appointed or elected leader? Or should everyone in the group share the responsibility for leadership? When someone is appointed or elected leader, the group looks to him or her for leadership. If the individual is a good leader, the group will benefit. Each participant can concentrate on considering the issues being raised, confident that the leader will guide the group justly. The disadvantages of having an appointed or elected leader are seen when the person is so unsure of direction that the group rambles about aimlessly; when the leader is so dominant that participants do not feel free to contribute spontaneously and the discussion follows a path predetermined by the leader; and when the leader is so unskilled that the group flounders and becomes frustrated and short-tempered. Good leadership is a necessity; when the appointed leader cannot provide it, the group suffers.

When the group has no appointed leader, everyone has the right and the obligation to show leadership. Ordinarily, leadership will emerge from one, two, or perhaps three members of the group. Because no one has been given the mantle of leadership, everyone is on an equal footing, and the discussion can be more spontaneous. Disadvantages occur if no one assumes leadership or if a few compete for leadership. In such situations, the discussion becomes "leadershipless." Depending on the qualities of the participants, leaderless discussions can arrive at truly good decisions, or they can be a rambling, meaningless collage of facts and opinions. If you have only one round of discussion, begin with the method in which the group has the most confidence.

Leadership Traits

Numerous researchers have looked for those particular traits that would enable us to predict leadership ability and account for leadership success. Although traits research does not provide the answers, studying traits does give us certain indicators of leadership.

Marvin Shaw, a leading authority in group research, found correlation between individual traits and leadership measures.[1] He cited four traits: ability, sociability, motivation, and communication skills. In group studies, he found that relative to ability, leaders exceed average group members in intelligence, scholarship, insight, and verbal facility. Relative to sociability, leaders exceed group members in such things as dependability, activity, cooperativeness, and popularity. Relative to motivation, leaders exceed group members in initiative, persistence, and enthusiasm. Finally, relative to communication, leaders exceed group members in various communication skills. This does not mean that people with superior intelligence, or those who are most liked, or those with the greatest enthusiasm, or those who are the best communicators will necessarily be leaders. We believe it does mean that people are unlikely to be leaders if they do not exhibit at least some of these traits to a greater degree than those whom they are attempting to lead.

Do you perceive yourself as having any or many of these traits? If you see them in yourself, then you are a potential leader. Because several individuals in almost any group of people have the potential for leadership, determining who ends up actually leading depends on many things other than the possession of these traits.

To some extent, whether you will be permitted to lead again may depend upon how well you lead when you have the opportunity. Leadership requires exerting influence, so how you lead may well depend upon whether this influence is a product of power and persuasion, or some combination of both. In effect, who will lead may be a matter of style.

Leadership Styles

The collection of a person's behaviors is called *style*. A casual examination of groups in operation will reveal a variety of leadership styles. Some leaders give orders directly; others look to the group to decide what to do. Some leaders appear to play no part in what happens in the group; others seem to be in control of every move. Some leaders constantly seek the opinions of group members; other leaders do not seem to care what individuals think. Each person will tend to lead a group with a style that reflects his or her own personality, needs, and inclination. Although people have a right to be themselves, an analysis of operating groups shows

All groups require leadership, but different situations call for different leadership styles.

that they work better and feel better about the work they do depending upon the style of leadership.

What are the major leadership styles? Most recent studies define leadership styles as task-oriented (sometimes called authoritarian) or maintenance (sometimes called democratic).

The *task-oriented* leader exercises more direct control over the group. Task-oriented leaders determine the statement of the question, analyze the procedure, state how the group will proceed to arrive at a decision, and usually outline specific tasks for each group member and suggest the roles they desire members to play.

The *maintenance* leader *suggests* phrasings of the question, procedure, and tasks or roles for individual members. Yet in every facet of the discussion, maintenance leaders encourage group participation to determine what actually will be done. Everyone feels free to offer suggestions to modify the leader's suggestions. What the group eventually does is determined by the group itself. Maintenance leaders listen, encourage, facilitate, clarify, and support. In the final analysis, it is the group that decides.

Which is best? According to the definition of leadership as exerting influence to reach a goal, we can see that, by definition, an effective style is one in which the leader takes an active role in the discussion in order to influence its outcome. If that is the case, then why is the task-oriented style *not* the ultimate leadership form? Although there are situations in

which a task-oriented style may be more desirable, other situations exist in which the maintenance style is preferable.

At times, the maintenance or democratic style is inappropriate and may lead to chaos. Participatory democracy has its limits. For instance, during a closely contested basketball game, coaches who call a timeout have one minute to help their players handle a particular defensive alignment the other team is using. They will not use their minute in democratic processes — asking their players if they have any ideas or suggesting a plan and giving the players the opportunity to evaluate it. They will tell the players how to proceed, make a substitution if necessary, and give the players encouragement. When accomplishment of the task is, or appears to be, more important than the members' feelings, then task-oriented or authoritarian leadership may be appropriate. (This is not to say that basketball coaches or other leaders who adopt this style can disregard group feelings.) Ralph White and Ronald Lippitt have shown that a job gets done as fast or faster and often with fewer errors under the task-oriented or authoritarian leader.[2] Authoritarian leadership also seems to work well when the authority is much superior in knowledge and skill to the participants. Again, the basketball example bears this out. Coaches are coaches because of what they know; as long as players respect their superior knowledge, they will work well under the authoritarian style.

There is at least one other advantage of task-oriented or authoritarian leadership—it is easier. Learning to be a good democratic leader sometimes ends in the frustrations of nonleadership. In other words, some people confuse being a democratic leader with not leading at all. Because there is little ambiguity in authoritarian leadership—the leader gives directions and the group follows them—it is far easier to understand and administer.

If authoritarian leadership appeals to you—and many authoritarian leaders do exist, are effective, and win the approval of their groups— perhaps you should consider one other point. The best authoritarian model seems to be "benevolent dictatorship." If authority arises out of the need to control—and perhaps even to crush dissent—it leads to tyranny.

Examine your style closely. What is your natural inclination? How has it worked in the past? Would it be useful to blend some of the characteristics of another style with what comes naturally to you? Remember, these categories are not necessarily hard and fast. Still, the style you adopt is your own. Once you have determined your approach, you must consider your leadership responsibilities.

Responsibilities of the Leader

Group leadership carries several responsibilities. To be an effective leader, you should learn to accomplish each of the following.

Planning the Agenda

As leader, your first responsibility is to plan the agenda. An *agenda* is an outline of what needs to be accomplished during the meeting. In a problem-solving discussion, the agenda should include a suggested procedure for handling the problem. In essence, it is an outline of the problem-solving steps discussed earlier in this chapter. You may prepare the agenda alone or in consultation with the group. When possible, the agenda should be in the hands of the group several days before the meeting. You cannot expect group members to prepare if they do not have an agenda beforehand. When a group proceeds without an agenda, discussion often is haphazard, frustrating, and unproductive.

If you are leading a discussion on what should be done to better integrate the campus commuter into the social, political, and extracurricular aspects of student life, the following would be a satisfactory agenda:

I.   What is the size and scope of the commuter problem?
II. What are the causes for lack of commuter involvement in social, political, and extracurricular activities?
III. What criteria should be used to test possible solutions to the problem?
IV. What are some of the possible solutions to the problem?
V.   What one solution or combination of solutions will work best to solve the problem?

Establishing a Climate

Before the group begins talking, you will want to set up a comfortable physical environment that will encourage interaction. You are in charge of such physical matters as heat, light, and seating. Make sure the room is at a comfortable temperature, that the room is well lit, and, most important, that the seating arrangement will help lead to spirited interaction.

Too often, seating is too formal or too informal for the best discussion. By "too formal," we mean a board-of-directors style. Imagine the long polished oak table with the chairperson at the head, the leading lieutenants at the right and left, and the rest of the participants seated down the line. Because seating may indicate status, how it is arranged can help or hinder real interaction. In the board-of-directors style, a "boss-and-subordinates" pattern emerges. People are unlikely to speak until they are asked to do so. Moreover, no one has a good view of all the people present. But an excessively informal seating also may limit interaction — especially if people sit together in small groups or behind one another.

The ideal is a circle. Everyone can see everyone else. At least physically, everyone has equal status. If the meeting place does not have a round table, you may be better off with either no table at all or an arrangement of tables to make a square at which the members can come close to the circle arrangement.

Give Everyone an Equal Opportunity to Speak

You must direct the flow of discussion to ensure that everyone has an equal opportunity to speak. Decisions are valid only when they represent the thinking of the entire group. In discussions, however, some people are more likely or more willing to express themselves than others. For instance, if a typical eight-person group is left to its own devices, two or three people may tend to speak as much as the other five or six together; furthermore, one or two members may contribute little if anything. At the beginning of a discussion you must operate under the assumption that every member of the group has something to contribute. To ensure opportunity for equal participation, those who tend to dominate must be held somewhat in check, and those who are content to observe must be brought into the discussion.

Accomplishing this ideal balance is a real test of leadership. If ordinarily reluctant talkers are embarrassed by a member of the group, they may become even more reluctant to participate. Likewise, if talkative yet valuable members are constantly restrained, they may lose their value to the group.

Let us first consider the handling of shy or reluctant speakers. Often, apparently reluctant speakers want to talk but cannot get the floor. As leader you may solve this problem by clearing the road for them. For example, Mary may give visual and verbal clues of her desire to speak; she may move to the edge of her seat, she may look as if she wants to talk, or she may even start to say something but pull back when a more aggressive speaker breaks in. To pave the way for her, you might say, "Just a second, Jim, I think Mary has something she wants to say here."

A second method of drawing out reluctant speakers is to phrase a question that is sure to get some answer and, perhaps, discussion. The most appropriate question is one requiring an opinion rather than a fact. For instance, "Mary, what do you think of the validity of this approach to combating crime?" is much better than, "Mary, do you have any additional statistics?" Not only is it specific, but also it requires more than a yes or no answer. Furthermore, such an opinion question will not embarrass Mary if she has no factual material to contribute. Tactful handling of shy or reluctant persons can pay big dividends. You may get some information that would not have been brought out in any other way; moreover, when Mary contributes a few times, it builds her self-confidence, which in turn makes it easier for her to respond later when she has more to say. Of course, there are times when some members do not have anything worth saying because they simply are not prepared. Under such circumstances, it is best to leave them alone.

As a leader, you must also use tact with overzealous speakers. Remember that talkative Jim may be talkative because he has done his homework—he may have more information than any other member of the group. If you turn him off, the group may suffer immensely. After he has finished talking, try statements such as, "Jim, that's a very valuable bit of material; let's see whether we can get some reactions from other members of the group on this issue." Notice that a statement of this kind does not stop him; it suggests that he should hold off for a while. Participants who are difficult to deal with are those who must be heard regardless of whether they have anything to say. If subtle reminders are ineffective with these individuals, you may have to say, "Jim, I know you want to talk, but you're just not giving anyone else a chance. Would you wait until we've heard everyone else on this point?" Of course, the person who may be the most difficult of all to control is the leader. Leaders often engage in little dialogues with each member of the group. They sometimes exercise so much control that participants believe they can talk only in response to the leader.

There are three common patterns of group communication (see Figure 19.1; the lines represent the flow of discussion among the eight participants). Discussion A represents a leader-dominated group. The lack of interaction often leads to a rigid, formal, and usually poor discussion. Discussion B represents a more spontaneous group. Because three people dominate and two are not heard, however, conclusions will not represent group thinking. Discussion C represents something close to the ideal pattern. It illustrates a great deal of spontaneity, a total group representation, and—theoretically at least—the greatest possibility for reliable conclusions.

Ask Appropriate Questions

Perhaps one of the most effective leadership tools is the ability to question appropriately. You need to know when to ask questions and you need to know the kinds of questions to ask.

Figure 19.1
Patterns of group discussion.

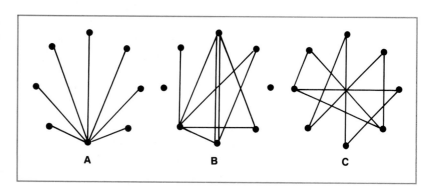

By and large, a leader should refrain from questions that can be answered yes or no. To ask group members whether they are satisfied with a point that was just made will not lead very far; after the yes or no answer, you must either ask another question to draw the members out or change the subject. The two most effective types of questions are those that call for supporting information and completely open-ended questions that give members complete freedom of response. For instance, rather than asking John whether he has had any professors who were particularly good lecturers, you could ask, "John, what are some of the characteristics that made your favorite lecturers particularly effective?"

When to ask questions is particularly important. Although we could list fifteen to twenty circumstances, let us focus on four purposes of questioning.

1.   *To initiate discussion.* At the beginning of the discussion and when each of the individual units of discussion have been resolved, you will need to suggest a starting point for further discussion. For instance, "Okay, we seem to have a pretty good grasp of the nature of the problem, but we haven't looked at any causes yet. What are some of the causes?"

2.   *To probe for information.* Too often group members accept statements without probing further. When an idea seems important, you should see to it that the group does something with it. For instance, on a question of source, you might ask, "Where did you get that information, Jack?" or to develop a point, "That seems pretty important; what do we have that corroborates the point?" To test the strength of a point you might ask, "Does that statement represent the thinking of the group?" or to generate discussion, "That idea sounds rather controversial; should we accept it as stated?"

3.   *To focus discussion.* You can use questions to determine speakers' points or to determine the relationship of the points to the issue or agenda item. For instance, "Are you saying that the instances of marijuana leading to hard-drug use don't indicate a direct causal relationship?" or to what has just been said, "How does that information relate to the point that Mary just made?" or to ask about an issue or an agenda item, "In what way does this information relate to whether or not marijuana is a health hazard?"

4.   *To deal with interpersonal problems that develop.* In any discussion, interpersonal frictions may occur. Sometimes you may need to help members ventilate intensely personal feelings. For instance, "Ted, I've heard you make some strong statements on this point. Would you care to share them with us?" At times, you may need to shield a member from personal attack. Here you can say, "I know Charley

presented the point, but let's look at the merits of the information presented. Do we have any information that counters this point?

Questions by themselves do not make a discussion. In fact, some questions can hurt the discussion that is taking place. An effective leader uses questions sparingly but decisively.

Summarize Frequently

A good problem-solving discussion group should move in an orderly manner toward intermediate conclusions that are represented by summary statements seeking group consensus. For instance, on the question, "What should be done to lower the crime rate on campus?" the group should answer each of the following questions:

1. What is the problem?
2. What are the symptoms of the problem? (Draw intermediate conclusions; ask whether the group agrees.)
3. What are the causes? (Draw an intermediate conclusion on each cause separately or after all causes have been considered; ask whether the group agrees.)
4. What criteria should be used to test the solutions?
5. What is one criterion? (Draw conclusions about each criterion.)
6. What are some of the possible conclusions? (Determine whether all possible solutions have been brought up.)
7. What is the best solution?
8. How does each solution meet the criteria? (Discuss and draw conclusions about each; ask whether the group agrees.)
9. Which solution best meets the criteria? (The conclusion to this final question concludes the discussion; ask whether all agree.)

You need to see to it that the group does not arrive at the final conclusion until each of these subordinate questions are answered to the satisfaction of the entire group.

In addition, you must point out these conclusions by summarizing what has been said and seeking consensus on the wording. If left to its own devices, a group will discuss a point for a while, then move on to another *before a conclusion is drawn*. You must sense when enough has been said to reach a consensus. Then you must phrase the conclusion, ask whether it is correct, and move on to another area. You should become familiar with phrases such as the following that can be used during a discussion:

> "I think most of us are stating the same points. Are we really in agreement that . . . ?" (State the conclusion.)

"We've been discussing this for a while, and I think I sense an agreement. Let me state it, and then we'll see whether it does summarize the group's feelings." (State the conclusion.)

"Now we're getting into another area. Let's make sure that we are really agreed on the point we've just finished." (State the conclusion.)

"Are we ready to summarize our feelings on this point?" (State the conclusion.)

Maintain Necessary Control

Finally, you must maintain control of the discussion. Remember, absence of leadership leads to chaos. Group members need to feel that someone is in charge. If the group has a set of formal rules, be sure that the rules are followed; bending is necessary at times, but a total breakdown does not help the group. As leader, remember that some members will be playing negative roles in the discussion; do not let them spoil the outcome. You are in charge. You are responsible. You have authority. Occasionally, you must exercise it for the benefit of the group. If John is about to talk for the fortieth time, it is up to you to harness him. If Jack and Mary are constantly sparring with each other, it is up to you to harmonize their differences. If something internal or external threatens the group's work, it is up to you to deal with it. And when the group has solved its problem, end the discussion smoothly. Some discussion groups meet by time instead of by problem. Just because you are scheduled to discuss for an hour does not mean that you cannot stop in forty-five minutes if you have done the job.

Responsibilities of Discussants

Although good leadership is essential, a discussion group will fail if its members do not fulfill their responsibilities. Good discussion is characterized by members' accomplishing various task and maintenance roles and avoiding various negative roles.

Fill Positive Roles

Everyone in the group has a responsibility to fill certain roles within the group. A *role* is a behavior that you determine for yourself or that is determined for you by the expectations of the group. Sometimes a person plays only one role throughout the duration of the discussion. At other times, a person may play several roles simultaneously or alternately; and, of course, more than one person can play a given role in a discussion.

Positive group roles fulfill both task and maintenance functions. The *task function* involves those roles that contribute to meeting the group's goal; the *maintenance function* involves those roles that contribute to how well group members handle the way they talk about their tasks, the nature of the interaction, and dealing with the feelings of the group. Thus, when we analyze a discussion, we look first to see how and whether the group solved the problem; second, we look to see how well the group members worked together and whether they liked, respected, and understood one another.

TASK ROLES   In most groups there are at least four major identifiable task roles: the information giver, information seeker, expediter, and analyzer.

1. *The information or opinion giver provides content for the discussion.* Giving information or opinions makes up approximately 50 percent of a work group's comments. Without information and well-considered opinions, the group will not have the material from which to draw its decisions. Probably everyone in the group plays this role during the discussion. Nevertheless, there are usually one or more persons who have really done their homework. As a result of their past experience with this or a related problem, their conversations with people who have worked with similar problems, or a great deal of reading, these people are prepared to provide the facts. In some groups, a designated resource person or consultant is called in solely to fulfill the information-giving role. In most groups, one or more persons take it upon themselves to be especially well prepared.

   To be well prepared, you should have considerably more information than you could get into the discussion. It is not uncommon for discussants to be familiar with information from eight or ten sources. Because you cannot predict all of the ideas that will be covered in the discussion, you cannot prepare speeches ahead of time. Nevertheless, you should be familiar enough with the material that you can find any item you need when you need it. Usually you will bring your sources with you to the discussion.

   In addition to presenting information, you also should be prepared to draw conclusions from information that already has been presented. That information serves as the building blocks for conclusions, and unless you draw conclusions, the information itself will serve little purpose.

To be a valuable contributor, your material must be presented objectively. Let us focus on two recommendations for ensuring objectivity of approach. First, report data—do not associate yourself with it. If you report that crime has risen 33 percent in the past five years, do not feel that because you presented the data you must defend it. An excellent way to present data with a degree of disassociation is illustrated by the following: "According to *U.S. News and World Report*, crime has risen 33 percent in the past five years. That seems like a startling statistic. I wonder whether anyone else found either substantiating or contradictory data?" Presenting data in this way tells the group that you want a discussion and that, whether the data are substantiated or disproven, you have no personal relationship with them.

A second recommendation for ensuring objectivity is to look for material representing different viewpoints. Suppose you were discussing the question, "Should financial support of women's sports be increased?" And suppose that after extensive reading you believed that it should. If in the discussion you spoke only to support your position and took issue with every bit of contrary material, you would not be responding objectively. If during the discussion the group draws a conclusion that corresponds to your tentative conclusion, fine. At least the group has had the opportunity to hear all views. If the group draws the opposite conclusion, you are not put in a defensive position. By being objective, you may find that your views will change many times during the discussion. Remember, if the best answer to the topic question could be found without discussion, the discussion would not be necessary.

Information givers identify themselves by such statements as, "When Jones Corporation considered this problem, they found . . ."; or, "That's a good point you made—just the other day I ran across these figures that substantiate your point"; or, "According to Professor Smith, it doesn't necessarily work that way. He says. . . ."

2. *The information seeker knows when the group needs data to function.* In most groups, more than one person takes this role during the discussion; one or more often are especially perceptive in knowing when more information is needed.

The information seeker raises questions about and probes into the contributions of others. Your obligation does not end with reading items of information into the record. Once an item has been submitted, it is the obligation of the membership to determine whether the item is accurate, typical, consistent, and otherwise valid. Suppose that in a discussion on reducing crime, a person said, "According to *U.S. News and World Report*, crime has risen 33 percent in the past five years." The group should not leave this statement until it has been fully explored. What was the specific source of the data? On what were the data based? What years are being referred to? Is this data consistent with other material? Is any countermaterial available? The purpose of these questions is not to debate the data, but to test them. If the data are partly true, questionable, or relevant only to certain kinds of crime, a different conclusion or set of conclusions would be appropriate.

Information seekers may be identified by such questions as, "What did we say the base numbers were?"; "Have we decided how many people this really affects?"; "Well, what functions does this person serve?"; and "Have we got anything to give us some background on this subject?"

3. *The expediter perceives when the group is going astray.* Whether the group meets once or is an ongoing group, almost invariably some remarks will tend to sidetrack group members from the central point or issue in front of them. Sometimes apparent digressions are necessary to get background, to enlarge the scope, or even to give people an opportunity to get something off their chest. Often in a group these momentary digressions lead to tangents that take the group far afield from its assignment. Because a tangent is sometimes more fun than the task itself, the group often does not realize what it is and discusses it as if it were important to the decision. Expediters are those people who help the group stick to its agenda; they help the group stay with the problem at hand. When the group has strayed, they help lead it back to the mainstream. Expediters are revealed by such statements as, "Say, I'm enjoying this, but I can't quite see what it has to do with whether permissiveness is really a cause"; "Let's see, aren't we still trying to find out whether these are the only criteria that we should be considering?"; "I've got the feeling that this is important to the point we're on now, but I can't quite get hold of the relationship — am I off base?"; and "Say, time is getting away from us and we've only considered two possible solutions. Aren't there some more?"

4. *The analyzer is the master of technique.* Analyzers know the problem-solving method inside out. The analyzer knows when the group has skipped a point, has passed over a point too lightly, or has not taken a look at matters that it should. More than just expediting, analyzers help the group penetrate to the core of the problem it is working on. In addition, analyzers examine the reasoning of various participants. Analyzers may be recognized from such statements as,

"Tom, you're generalizing from only one instance. Can you give us some others?"; "Wait a minute, after symptoms, we have to take a look at causes"; and "I think we're passing over Jones too lightly. There are still criteria we haven't used to measure him by."

MAINTENANCE ROLES   In most discussion groups at least three major maintenance roles help good working relationships: the supporter, the harmonizer, and the gatekeeper.

1. *The supporter rewards members of valuable contributions.* People participating in groups are likely to feel better about their participation when their thoughts and feelings are recognized. Although we expect nearly everyone to be supportive, sometimes people get so wrapped up in their own ideas that they may neglect to reward positive comments. The supporter responds verbally or nonverbally whenever a good point is made. Supporters give such nonverbal cues as a smile, a nod, or a vigorous head shake and make statements like, "Good point, Mel"; "I really like that idea, Susan"; "It's obvious you've really done your homework, Peg"; "That's one of the best ideas we've had today, Al."

2. *The harmonizer brings the group together.* It is a rare group that can expect to accomplish its task without some minor if not major conflict. Even when people get along well, they may become angry over some inconsequential points in heated discussion. Most groups experience classic interpersonal conflicts caused by different personality types. Harmonizers are responsible for reducing and reconciling misunderstandings, disagreements, and conflicts. They are good at pouring oil on troubled waters and encouraging objectivity; and they are especially good as mediators for hostile, aggressively competing sides. A group cannot avoid some conflict, but if there is no one present to harmonize, participation can become an uncomfortable experience. Harmonizers may be recognized by such statements as, "Bill, I don't think you're giving Mary a chance to make her point"; "Tom, Jack, hold it a second. I know you're on opposite sides of this, but let's see where you might have some agreement"; "Lynne, I get the feeling that something Todd said really bugged you, is that right?"; and "Hold it, everybody, we're really coming up with some good stuff; let's not lose our momentum by getting into a name-calling thing."

3. *The gatekeeper helps keep communication channels open.* If a group has seven people in it, the assumption is that all seven have something to contribute. But if all are to feel comfortable contributing,

those who tend to dominate must be held in check and those who tend to be reticent need to be encouraged. The gatekeeper is the one who sees that Jane is on the edge of her chair, ready to talk, but just cannot seem to get in, or that Don is rambling a bit and needs to be directed, or that Tom's need to talk so frequently is causing Cesar to withdraw from the conversation, or that Betty has just lost the thread of discussion. As we said earlier, a characteristic of good group work is interaction. Gatekeepers assume the responsibility for helping interaction. Gatekeepers may be recognized by such statements as, "Joan, I see you've got something to say here"; "You've made a really good point, Todd; I wonder whether we could get some reaction on it"; and "Bill and Marge, it sounds like you're getting into a dialogue here; let's see what other ideas we have."

Avoid Negative Roles

The following are the four most common negative roles that group discussants should avoid.

1. *Aggressors work for their own status by criticizing almost everything or blaming others when things get rough.* An aggressor's main purpose seems to be to deflate the ego or status of others. One way to deal with aggressors is by confronting them. Ask whether they are aware of what they are doing and of the effect it is having on the group.

2. *Jokers clown, mimic, or generally disrupt by making a joke of everything.* Jokers, too, usually are trying to call attention to themselves. They must be the center of attention. A little bit of a joker goes a long way. The group needs to get the jokers to consider the problem seriously, or they will constantly be an irritant to other members. One way to proceed is by encouraging them when tensions need to be released, but to ignore them when there is serious work to be done.

3. *Withdrawers refuse to be part of the group.* Withdrawers are mental dropouts. Sometimes they withdraw from something that is said, and sometimes they simply show their indifference. Try to draw them out with questions. Find out what they are especially good at and rely on them when their skill is required. Sometimes compliments will bring them out.

4. *Monopolizers need to talk all the time.* Usually monopolizers try to impress the group that they are well read, knowledgeable, and valuable to the group. They should, of course, be encouraged when their

comments are helpful, but when they are talking too much or when their comments are not helpful, the leader needs to interrupt them or draw others into the discussion.

When the Group Goes Public

Although most of your group problem solving will be done in private and without the presence of an onlooking or participating audience, occasionally your group will be called upon to go public. At times this means conducting your deliberations in public; at other times this means presenting your group's conclusions to another group. In a public discussion, the group is discussing to provide information for the listening audience as much as analyzing or solving a problem. As such, public discussions have much in common with traditional public speaking. Two common forms of public discussion are the symposium and the panel discussion.

Symposium

A *symposium* is a discussion in which a limited number of participants (usually three to five) present individual speeches of approximately the same length dealing with the same subject. After delivering their planned speeches, the participants in the symposium may discuss their reactions with one another or respond to questions from the audience. Despite the potential for interaction, a symposium often is characterized by long, sometimes unrelated speeches. Moreover, the part designated for questions often is shortened or deleted because "our time is about up." A symposium often omits the interaction necessary for a good discussion. If the participants make their prepared speeches short enough so that at least half of the available time can be spent on real interaction, a symposium can be interesting and stimulating. A good symposium that meets the goals of discussion is much more difficult to present than it appears; as a public speaking assignment, however, the symposium may be beneficial. Rather than solving a problem, a symposium is more effective in shedding light on or explaining various aspects of a problem.

Panel Discussion

A *panel discussion* is one in which usually four to eight participants discuss a topic spontaneously, under the direction of a leader and following a planned agenda. After the formal discussion, the audience often is encouraged to question the participants. The discussion thus can be seen and heard by the audience: The group is seated in a semicircle, with the chairperson in the middle, to get a good view of the audience and the panelists. Because the discussion is for an audience, the panelists are obliged to make good use of traditional public speaking skills. And because a panel discussion encourages spontaneity and interaction, it can be stimulating for both the audience and the participants themselves. The panel works as a form of problem-solving discussion.

Presenting Conclusions

More often than not, after a group has finished its deliberations, the leader is asked to present the group's conclusions in a report or public presentation. The spokesperson for the group reviews the group's goal,

---

Checklist | **Individual Analysis**

For each of the following questions, rate the participant on the basis of 1, excellent; 2, good; 3, average; 4, fair; 5, poor.

Preparation	1	2	3	4	5
Seems to be well prepared	____	____	____	____	____
Is aware of the problem	____	____	____	____	____
Analyzes the problem	____	____	____	____	____
Suggests possible solutions	____	____	____	____	____

Carrying out roles					
As information or opinion giver	____	____	____	____	____
As information or opinion seeker	____	____	____	____	____
As expediter	____	____	____	____	____
As analyzer	____	____	____	____	____
As harmonizer	____	____	____	____	____
As gatekeeper	____	____	____	____	____
As supporter	____	____	____	____	____

Write an analysis of the person's group participation (two to five paragraphs) based upon this checklist.

<table>
<tr><td rowspan="2">**Checklist**</td><td colspan="6">**Leadership**</td></tr>
</table>

Checklist | **Leadership**

For each of the following questions, rate the participant on the basis of 1, excellent; 2, good; 3, average; 4, fair; 5, poor.

	1	2	3	4	5
Creates a good working atmosphere	——	——	——	——	——
Works to develop a cohesive unit	——	——	——	——	——
Has an agenda	——	——	——	——	——
Promotes systematic problem solving	——	——	——	——	——
Asks good questions	——	——	——	——	——
Encourages balanced participation	——	——	——	——	——
Refrains from dominating the group	——	——	——	——	——
Deals with conflict	——	——	——	——	——
Summarizes decisions	——	——	——	——	——

Write an analysis of the person's group participation (two to five paragraphs) based upon this checklist.

discusses the analysis of the problem, mentions potential solutions, gives a summary of strengths and weaknesses of each solution, and then presents the group's conclusion.

Assignment
Group Decision Making

1. Participants select a question of fact, value, or policy for a twenty- to forty-minute discussion. Determine the method of leadership and establish an agenda. Criteria for evaluation of the discussion will include quality of participation, quality of leadership, and ability to arrive at group decisions. Use the individual analysis and leadership checklists in your evaluation.

2. Select a single spokesperson for the group. This person will prepare a five- to seven-minute summary of the group's process to explain how the group conducted its deliberations. Consider the question, the analysis of the question, and your key conclusions.

Part V | Adapting to Other Occasions and Formats

Summary

Problem-solving group discussion is defined as a systematic form of speech in which two or more persons meet face to face and interact orally to accomplish a particular task or to arrive at a solution to a common problem.

To prepare for discussion you must state the problem, analyze it, suggest possible solutions, and select the best one.

Leadership may be defined as exerting influence to help a group achieve a goal. Although groups often have an appointed leader, in many groups a single person emerges to become the actual leader. Leaders often show traits of ability, sociability, motivation, and communication skills. Leaders are likely to assume either an authoritarian or a maintenance style.

The leader plans the agenda, establishes a good working climate, gives everyone an equal opportunity to speak, asks appropriate questions, summarizes frequently, and maintains necessary control over the group.

Participants fill positive task and maintenance roles. The major task roles are information or opinion giving, information seeking, keeping the group on track, and analyzing method and procedure. The major maintenance roles are supporting, harmonizing, and gatekeeping.

Public discussions take place in the form of a symposium or a panel discussion.

Notes

1. Marvin E. Shaw, *Group Dynamics: The Psychology of Small Group Behavior*, 3d ed. (New York: McGraw-Hill, 1981), 325.
2. Ralph White and Ronald Lippitt, "Leader Behavior and Member Reactions in Three Social Climates," reprinted in Dorwin Cartwright and Alan Zander, eds., *Group Dynamics*, 3d ed. (New York: Harper & Row, 1968), 334.

Appendix | Two Contemporary Speeches

The speeches included in the earlier part of this text were given by students. The following speeches illustrate how two contemporary speakers met their challenge of effective speaking. The first is an informative speech; the second is persuasive. Each contains enough examples of the successful application of basic principles to make them worthy of attention. Your goal is not to copy what others have done, but to read and analyze in order to better test the value of what you are planning to do in your own speeches.

Think Strawberries

A speech by James Lavenson, president of the Plaza Hotel, delivered before the American Medical Association, February 7, 1974.[1] I have included this speech in the last six editions of The Challenge of Effective Speaking. *As you read the speech, I believe that you will agree that it is a truly excellent informative speech — one of the best you will find. Notice how Lavenson blends humor, excellent specific instances, informal language, and clear, vivid images to form an extremely interesting informative speech about the hotel business. In addition, notice how he uses the narrative form: He talks about issues that the hotel executive must face by relating his own experiences in changing the operating procedures at the Plaza.*

I came from the balcony of the hotel business. For ten years as a corporate director of Sonesta Hotels with no line responsibility, I had my office in a little building next door to the Plaza. I went to the hotel every day for lunch and often stayed overnight. I was a professional guest. You know nobody knows more about how to run a hotel than a guest. Last year, I suddenly fell out of the corporate balcony and had to put my efforts in the restaurants where my mouth had been, and in the rooms and night-club and theater into which I'd been putting my two cents.

In my ten years of kibitzing, all I had really learned about the hotel business was how to use a guest room toilet without removing the strip of paper that's printed "Sanitized for Your Protection." When the hotel staff found out I'd spent my life as a salesman and that I'd never been a hotelier, never been to Cornell Hotel School, and that I wasn't even the son of a waiter, they were in a state of shock. And Paul Sonnabend, president of Sonesta, didn't help their apprehension much when he introduced me to my executive staff with the following kind words: "The Plaza has been losing money the last several years and we've had the best management in the business. Now we're going to try the worst."

Frankly, I think the hotel business has been one of the most backward in the world. There's been very little change in the attitude of room clerks in the 2,000 years since Joseph arrived in Bethlehem and was told they'd lost his reservation. Why is it that a sales clerk at Woolworth asks your wife, who points to the pantyhose, if she wants three or six pairs — and your wife is all by herself — but the maître d' asks you and your wife, the only human beings within a mile of the restaurant, "How many are you?"

Hotel salesmanship is retailing at its worst. But at the risk of inflicting cardiac arrest on our guests at the Plaza when they first hear shocking expressions like "Good Morning" and "Please" and "Thank you for coming," we started a year ago to see if it was possible to make the 1,400 employees of the Plaza into genuine hosts and hostesses. Or should I say "salesmen"?

A tape recorder attached to my phone proved how far we had to go. "What's the difference between your $85 suite and your $125 suite?" I'd ask our reservationist, disguising my voice over the phone. You guessed it: "$40!"

"What's going on in the Persian Room tonight?" I asked the bell captain. "Some singer" was his answer. "Man or woman?" I persisted. "I'm not sure" he said, which made me wonder if I'd even be safe going there. 6

Why is it, I wondered, that the staff of a hotel doesn't act like a family playing hosts to guests whom they've invited to their house? It didn't take too long after becoming a member of the family myself to understand one of the basic problems. Our 1,400 family members didn't even know each other! With that large a staff, working over eighteen floors, six restaurants, a nightclub, a theater, and three levels of subbasement, including a kitchen, a carpentry shop, plumbing and electrical shops, a full commercial laundry — how would they ever know who was working there, and who was a guest or just a purveyor passing through? Even the old timers who might recognize a face after a couple of years would have no idea of the name connected to it. It struck me that if our own people couldn't call each other by name, smile at each other's familiar face, say good morning *to each other*, how could they be expected to say amazing things like "Good Morning, Mr. Jones" to a guest? A year ago the Plaza name tag was born. The delivery took place on my lapel. And it's now been on 1,400 lapels for over a year. Everyone, from dishwashers to the general manager, wears his name where every other employee, and of course every guest, can see it. Believe it or not, our people say hello to each other — by name — when they pass in the halls and the offices. At first our regular guests thought the Plaza was entertaining some gigantic convention, but now even the old-time Plaza regulars are able to call our bellmen and maids by name. We've begun to build an atmosphere of welcome with the most precious commodity in the world — our names. *And* our guests' names. 7

A number of years ago, I heard Dr. Ernest Dichter, head of the Institute of Motivational Research, talk about restaurant service. He had reached a classic conclusion; when people come to a fine restaurant, they are hungrier for *recognition* than they are for food. It's true. If the maître d' says, "We have your table ready, Mr. Lavenson," then as far as I'm concerned the chef can burn the steak and I'll still be happy. 8

When someone calls you by name and you don't know his, a strange feeling of discomfort comes over you. When he does it twice you *have* to find out *his* name. This we see happening with our Plaza name tags. When a guest calls a waiter by name, the waiter wants to call the guest by name. It will drive him nuts if he doesn't know. He'll ask the maître d', and if he doesn't know he'll ask the bellman, who will ask the front desk . . . calling the guests by name has a big payoff. It's called a *tip*. 9

At first there was resistance to name tags — mostly from the old-   10
time, formally trained European hoteliers. I secretly suspect they liked
being incognito when faced with a guest complaint. We only had one
staff member who said he'd resign before having his dignity destroyed
with a name tag. For sixteen years he'd worn a rosebud in his lapel and
that, he said, was his trademark and everyone knew him by it. His resig-
nation was accepted along with that of the rosebud. Frankly, there are
moments when I regret the whole idea myself. When I get on a Plaza
elevator and all the passengers see my name tag, they know I work there.
Suddenly, I'm the official elevator pilot, the host. I can't hide, so I smile
at everybody, say "good morning" to perfect strangers I'd ordinarily ignore. The ones that don't go into shock, smile back. Actually, they seem
to mind less the fact that a trip on a Plaza elevator, built in 1907, is the
equivalent of commuting to Manhattan from Greenwich.

There are 600 Spanish-speaking employees at The Plaza. They   11
speak Spanish. They don't read English. The employee house magazine
was in English. So was the employee bulletin board. So were the signs
over the urinals in the locker rooms that suggest cigarette butts don't
flush too well. It was a clue as to why some of management's messages
weren't getting through. The employee house magazine is now printed
one side in English, the other in Spanish. The bulletin board and other
staff instructions are in two languages. We have free classes in both languages for departmental supervisors. It's been helping.

With 1,400 people all labeled and smiling we were about ready last   12
June to make salesmen out of them. There was just one more obstacle to
overcome before we started suggesting they "ask for the order." They
had no idea what the product was they would be selling. Not only didn't
they know who was playing in the Persian Room, they didn't know we
had movies — full-length feature films without commercials — on the
closed-circuit TV in the bedrooms. As a matter of fact, most of them
didn't know what a guest room looked like, unless they happened to be a
maid or a bellman.

The reason the reservationists thought $40 was the difference be-   13
tween two suites was because they'd never been in one, much less actually slept there. To say our would-be salesmen lacked product
knowledge would be as much an understatement as the line credited to
President Nixon if he had been the Captain of the Titanic. My son told
me that if Nixon had been Captain of the Titanic, he probably would
have announced to the passengers there was no cause for alarm — they
were just stopping to pick up ice.

Today, if you ask a Plaza bellman who's playing in the Persian Room   14
he'll tell you Ednita Nazzaro. He'll tell you because he's seen her. In the
contract of every Persian Room performer, there's now a clause requir-

ing him to first perform for our employees in the cafeteria before he opens in the Persian Room. Our employees see the star first, before the guests.

And if you ask a room clerk or a telephone operator what's on the TV movies, they'll tell you because they've seen it — on the TV sets running the movies continuously in the employees' cafeteria. 15

Believe me, if you are having your lunch in our cafeteria and watch "Female Response" or "Swedish Fly Girls" on the TV set, you won't forget the film. You might, however, suspect the chef has put Spanish fly in your spaghetti. 16

Our new room clerks now have a week of orientation. It includes spending a night in the hotel and a tour of our 1,000 guest rooms. They can look out the windows and see the $40 difference in suites, since a view of the Park doesn't even closely resemble the back of the Avon building. 17

As I mentioned, about six months ago, we decided it was time to take a hard look at our sales effort. I couldn't find it. The Plaza had three men with the title "salesman" — and they were good men. But they were really sales-*service* people who took the orders for functions or groups who came through the doors and sought us out. Nobody, but nobody, ever left the palace, crossed the moat at Fifth Avenue, and went looking for business. We had no one knocking on doors, no one asking for the order. The Plaza was so dignified it seemed demeaning to admit we needed business. If you didn't ask us we wouldn't ask you. So there! Our three sales-service people were terrific once you voluntarily stepped inside our arena. You had to ring our doorbell. We weren't ringing yours or anyone else's. 18

This condition wasn't unique to our official sales department. It seemed to be a philosophy shared by our entire staff — potentially larger sales staff of waiters, room clerks, bellmen, cashiers, and doormen. If you wanted a second drink in the Oak Bar, you got it by tripping the waiter. You asked for it. If you wanted a room you were quoted the minimum rate. If you wanted something better or larger, you had to ask for it. If you wanted to stay at the hotel an extra night, you had to ask. You were never invited. Sometimes I think there's a secret pact among hotelmen. It's a secret oath you take when you graduate from hotel school. It goes like this: "I promise I will never ask for the order." 19

When you're faced with as old and ingrained a tradition as that, halfway countermeasures don't work. We started a program with all our guest contact people using a new secret oath: "Everybody sells!" And we meant everybody — maids, cashiers, waiters, bellmen — the works. We talked to the maids about suggesting room service, to the doormen about 20 mentioning dinner in our restaurants, to cashiers about suggesting return reservations to departing guests. And we talked to waiters about strawberries.

A waiter at the Plaza makes anywhere from $10,000 to $20,000 a 21 year. The difference between those two figures is, of course, tips. When I was in the advertising agency business, I thought I was fast at computing 15 percent. I'm a moron compared to a waiter. Our suggestions for selling strawberries fell on responsive ears when we described a part of the Everybody Sells program for our Oyster Bar restaurant. We figured, with just the same number of customers in the Oyster Bar, that if the waiters would ask every customer if he'd like a second drink, wine, or beer with the meal, and then dessert—given only one out of four takers we'd increase our sales volume by $364,000 a year. The waiters were way ahead of the lecture—they'd already figured out that was another $50,000 in tips! And since there are ten waiters in the Oyster Bar, even I could figure out it meant five grand more per man in tips. It was at that point I had my toughest decision to make since I've been in this job. I had to choose between staying on as president or becoming an Oyster Bar waiter.

But, while the waiters appreciated this automatic raise in theory, 22 they were quick to call out the traditional negatives. "Nobody eats dessert anymore. Everyone's on a diet. If we served our chocolate cheesecake to everybody in the restaurant, half of them would be dead in a week."

"So sell 'em strawberries!" we said. "But sell 'em." And then we 23 wheeled out our answer to gasoline shortages, the dessert cart. We widened the aisles between the tables and had the waiters wheel the cart up to each and every table at dessert time. Not daunted by the diet protestations of the customer, the waiter then went into raptures about the bowl of fresh strawberries. There was even a bowl of whipped cream for the slightly wicked. By the time our waiters finish extolling the virtues of our fresh strawberries flown in that morning from California, or wherever he thinks strawberries come from, you not only have had an abdominal orgasm but one out of two of you order them. In the last six months we show our waiters every week what's happening to strawberry sales. This month they have doubled again. So have second martinis. And believe me, when you get a customer for a second martini you've got a sitting duck for strawberries—with whipped cream. Our waiters are asking for the order.

"Think Strawberries" is the Plaza's new secret weapon. Our reser- 24 vationists now think strawberries and suggest you'll like a suite overlooking Central Park rather than a twin-bedded room. Our bellmen are thinking strawberries. Each bellman has his own reservation cards, with his name printed as the return addressee, and he asks if you'd like him to make your return reservation as he's checking you out and into your taxi. Our room service order takers are thinking strawberries. They suggest the closed-circuit movie on TV ($3.00 will appear on your bill) as long as you're going to eat in your room. Our telephone operators are even thinking strawberries. They suggest a morning Flying Tray breakfast when you ask for a wake-up call. You just want a light breakfast, no ham and eggs? How about some strawberries?

We figure we've added about three hundred salesmen to the three-man sales-service team we had before. But most important, of course, is that we've added five pure sales people to our sales department. Four of them are out on the street calling — mostly cold — on the prospects to whom they're ready to sell anything from a cocktail in the Oak Bar to a corporate directors meeting to a bar mitzvah. The chewing gum people sell new customers by sampling on street corners. The Plaza has chewing gum licked a mile. Our sales people on the street have one simple objective: get the prospect into the hotel to sample the product. With the Plaza as our product, it isn't too difficult. And once you taste the Plaza, frankly, you're hooked.   25

In analyzing our business at the hotel we found, much to my surprise, that functions — parties, weddings, charity balls, and the like — are just about three times more profitable than all our six restaurants put together. And functions are twice as profitable as selling all 1,000 of our rooms. Before we had this analysis, we were spending all our advertising money on restaurants, our nightclub, and our guest rooms. This year we're spending 80 percent of our advertising money to get function business — weddings instead of honeymoons, banquets instead of meals, annual corporate meetings instead of a clandestine romantic rendezvous for two. We've added a fulltime bridal consultant who can talk wedding language to nervous brides and talk turkey to their mothers. Retailers like Saks and Bonwit's and Bergdorf's have had bridal consultants for years. Hotels have banquet managers. Banquet managers sell wedding dinners. Bridal consultants sell strawberries — everything from the bridal shower, the pictures, the ceremony, the reception, the wedding night, to the honeymoon, to the first anniversary.   26

When you fight a habit as long-standing as the hotel inside salesman, you don't just wave a wand and say, "Presto: now we have four outside salesmen." We want our new salespeople to know how serious we are about going after business. We started an executive sales call program as part of our "Everybody Sells" philosophy. About forty of our top and middle-management executives, ones who traditionally don't   27 ever see a prospect, are assigned days on which they make outside calls with our regular salesmen. People like our personnel director, our executive housekeeper, our purchasing director, and our general manager are on the street every day making calls. Our prospects seem to like it. Our salesmen love it. And our nonsales "salesmen" are getting an education about what's going on in the real world — the one outside the hotel.

As a matter of fact, that's why I'm here today. I made a sales call 28 myself with one of our salespeople. We called on your program chairman and tried to sell him strawberries. He promised that if I showed you a strawberry he'd book your next luncheon at the Plaza. I'm looking forward to waiting on you myself. Thank you very much.

Educating the Black Child: Our Past and Our Future

A speech by Marian Wright Edelman, founder of the Children's Defense Fund, delivered before the Congressional Black Caucus's 17th annual legislative weekend banquet on September 26, 1987.[2] The Congressional Black Caucus is a formal organization of black members of the U.S. House of Representatives. In addition to members of the House, the audience included celebrities such as Jesse Jackson, Coreta Scott King, and Rosa Parks.

This persuasive speech is an excellent example of problem–solution organization, clear reasons, and highly motivational language. But by far the most important reason for including this speech is the way in which the speaker adapts to her audience. The speech is an effort to motivate high-income black leaders to commit themselves to the betterment of the larger segment of the black population that is not so fortunate. As you read the speech, make note of the various means of motivation the speaker uses.

> It was the best of times, it was the worst of times, it was the age of wisdom, it was the age of foolishness, it was the epoch of belief, it was the epoch of incredulity, it was the season of light, it was the season of darkness, it was the spring of hope, it was the winter of despair. (*A Tale of Two Cities*, book 1, chapter 1).

> You have no right to enjoy a child's share in the labors of your fathers unless your children are to be blest by your labors. (Frederick Douglass, "The Meaning of July Fourth for the Negro.")

For many of you sitting in this room, it is the best of times. Black 1
per capita income is at an all-time high and many of you have moved up
the corporate ladder even if the ladders you are on frequently don't
reach toward the pinnacle of corporate power. Black purchasing power,
now at $200 billion, exceeds the gross national product of Australia and
New Zealand combined. But it has not yet been translated into commen-
surate black economic influence and benefit. Black elected officials are
more numerous than ever (6,681 in 1987, a 350 percent increase since
1970). But white economic power still controls our city tax bases. The
amassing of committee and subcommittee chairmanships (8 full House
Committee chairs including the Select Committee, and 18 Subcommittee chairs) by members of this Congressional Black Caucus is impressive
by any standard, although the main political game in town is cutting the
budget deficit. Spelman College, my alma mater, looks towards its future
with a stronger endowment and student body than ever before while
many other black colleges are struggling mightily to survive.

Bill Cosby is America's favorite Daddy and Michael Jackson and 2
Whitney Houston dot the top ten charts. Black leadership has permeated
a range of mainstream institutions. Bill Gray chairs the House Budget
Committee, Frank Thomas heads the Ford Foundation, and Cliff Whar-
ton heads TIAA-CREF. A. Barry Rand is in charge of marketing at Xerox. Anita De Frantz is America's representative to the Olympic
Committee, and Richard Knight is the city manager of Dallas.

I am proud of these and many similar accomplishments and ap- 3
plaud the black middle class for whom the times are good tonight. We've
worked hard to get where we are. However, we have to work harder still
to stay there and to move ahead.

But there is another black community that is not riding high to- 4
night and that is going down and under. If you and I don't build a bridge
back to them and throw out some strong lifelines to our children and
youths and families whom poverty and unemployment and hopelessness
are engulfing, they're going to drown, pull many of us down with them,
and undermine the black future that our forebears dreamed, struggled,
and died for.

I am grateful, therefore, that the Congressional Black Caucus has 5
focused attention this year on Educating the Black Child. Just as Martin
Luther King, Jr., and others accepted the challenge of their time, so the
challenge of our time is educating all of our children in mind, in body,
and in soul if we are to preserve and strengthen the black future.

It is the worst of times for poor black babies born within a mile of 6
this hotel and in many inner cities around the country who have less of a

chance of living to the first year of life than a baby born in Costa Rica. Black babies are still twice as likely to die in the first year of life than white babies.

It is the worst of times for black youth and young adults trying to form families without decent skills or jobs and without a strong value base. Young marriages have essentially stopped in the black community. Sixty percent of all black babies today are born to never married single mothers; 90 percent of those born to black teens are born to unmarried mothers. One out of two children in a female-headed household is poor. Two out of three (67.1 percent) children in black female-headed households are poor. If that household is headed by a mother younger than 25, three out of four are poor. Even when teen pregnancy results in marriage, young two-parent families are almost three times as likely to be poor as those with parents 25 to 44 years of age.

A significant cause of this black family problem lies in young black men's eroding employment and wage base. Only 26.5 percent of all black male teens were employed in 1986 and 61.3 percent of those 20 to 24 years old. And even when they are lucky enough to work they frequently can't earn enough to lift a family out of poverty. Between 1973 and 1984, the average real (inflation-adjusted) annual earnings among males ages 20 through 24 fell by nearly 30 percent (from $11,572 to $8,072 in 1984 dollars). This sharp drop affected virtually all groups of young adult males — whether white, black, or Hispanic — although young black men suffered the most severe losses (nearly 50 percent). So the links between teen pregnancy and poverty are related not just to age and single parenthood but also to the poor skills and employment experience young parents seek to bring to the work force and to the lower wages young workers are paid.

To combat the poverty which is engulfing half of the black babies born today — half of our future as a black community — we must all work to prevent too early sexual activity and pregnancy and encourage our boys and girls to wait until they have the education and economic stability to form lasting families. If the share of single births in the black community grows at the rate of the last decade, by the year 2000, only one black baby in five will be born to a married woman. And if you don't care about these babies unselfishly you'd better care selfishly, for the future black voting and economic base upon which much of our leadership status rests resides in the health and education of the black child and the strength of the black family.

Not only are too many black babies and youths fighting poverty and sickness and homelessness and too little early childhood stimulation and weak basic skills preparation, they are also fighting AIDS and other sexually transmitted diseases; drug, tobacco, and alcohol addiction and crime which hopelessness and the absence of constructive alternatives and support systems in their lives leave them prey to. A black baby is seven or eight times more likely to be an AIDS victim than a white baby and minority teens (15 to 19) are the highest risk group for a range of sexually transmitted diseases. A black youth is five times more likely than a white youth to end up in an institution and is nearly as likely to be in prison as he is to be in college. Between 1979 and 1985 the number of black youth in juvenile detention facilities rose by 40 percent while the number of black youth entering college immediately after high school graduation fell by four percent. More black males go to prison each year than go to college. There are more black drug addicts than there are black doctors or lawyers.

Now some of you sitting here will ask what this has to do with you. 11 You struggled and beat the odds and those folks who haven't made it could do the same. Others of you will rightfully say you're already doing your bit for the race by achieving yourself and by contributing to black organizations. Still others place the blame for growing black family poverty and weakening community bonds and support systems on urbanization and the continuing racial discrimination in national life which devalues black talent and curbs black opportunity.

As many nuggets of truth as each of these views may contain, I will 12 simply say that unless the black middle class begins to exert more effective and sustained leadership with and without the black community on behalf of black children and families both as personal role models and value instillers and as persistent advocates for national, state and local policies — funded policies — that assure our children the health and child care, education, housing, and jobs they need to grow up into self sufficient adults, to form healthy families, and to carry on the black tradition of achievement, then all of our Mercedes and Halston frocks will not hide our essential failure as a generation of black haves who did not protect the black future during our watch.

Just as our nation is committing moral and economic suicide by 13 permitting one in four of its preschool children to be poor, one in five to be at risk of being a teen parent, one in six to have no health insurance, and one in seven to face dropping out of school at a time when the pool of available young people to support an aging population and form a strong workforce is shrinking, so we are committing racial suicide by not sounding the alarm and protecting our own children from the poverty that ravages their dreams. For America will not treat our children fairly unless we make it.

We must recapture and care about our lost children and help them gain the confidence, self-esteem, values, and real world opportunities — education, jobs, and higher education which they need to be strong future guardians of the black community's heritage. 14

How do we do this? There are nine steps we must take if we are to help our children. 15

The first step is to remember and teach them that black folk have never been able to take anything for granted in America and we had better not start in these waning Reagan years of budget deficits and looming economic recession. Frederick Douglass put it bluntly: "Men may not get all they pay for in this world, but they must certainly pay for all they get." So you make sure that you are ready to do your part to help yourself and black children and to hold public and private sector officials accountable for doing their part in fostering health, education, and fair employment policies that are essential to black family survival. 16

Tell our children they're not going to jive their way up the career ladder. They've got to work their way up — hard and continuously. Too many young people want a fast elevator straight to the top floor and resist walking up the stairs or stopping on the floors of achievement between the bottom and top. Tell them to do their homework, pay attention to detail, and take care and pride in their work. People who are sloppy in little things tend to be sloppy in big things. Tell them to be reliable, to stick with something until they finish and resist jumping from pillar to post. And tell them to take the initiative in creating their own opportunity. They can't wait around for other people to discover them or to do them a favor. 17

The second step is to teach them the importance of getting a good education. While not a guarantee of success, education is a precondition to survival in America today. At a time when a smaller proportion of black high school graduates go on to college than ten years ago, we need to tell all of our children that college pays. In 1986, the average unemployment rate among black college graduates under 25 was 13.2 percent — more than one in every eight. Among young black high school graduates, it was 26.6 percent — more than one in four. College doubles their chance of getting a job. And we need to insist that they get a liberal education and learn how to think so that they can navigate an ever changing job market. 18

The third step is to tell them that forming families is serious 19 *business and requires a measure of thoughtful planning and economic stability.* In 1986, one in every five black families with children under 18 had someone unemployed. Of those 44 percent were single parents with no one at work. Among black married couples with children, only 18 percent had no one working.

That is the crucial point. Education alone, although of enormous value in itself, cannot guarantee a young black adult the income needed to raise children in economic safety today. But two black adults, both working, have the safety net of the second income when unemployment strikes. Remember, that's the only safety net President Reagan hasn't found a way to cut yet.   20

All these figures are from 1986, the fourth year of a long period of economic recovery. When the next recession arrives — and it will — the black unemployment rates will soar. Since this recession will come at a time when we have an extraordinary budget deficit, there is a great danger that the American voters will buy the argument that we must cut government spending in order to reduce interest rates and stimulate the economy. If this happens, there will be many unemployed teachers, nurses, employment counselors, and government workers of all sorts.   21

There is a warning here that relates to steps one and two. Just as black penetration into civil and social service professional jobs occurs, the growth and security of such jobs fall. Just as blacks rise to senior ranks in industrial and industrial union jobs, steel and auto manufacturing industries enter a steep decline. The economic goal posts keep shifting. How, then, do we work towards a full share in the power to set the goals in place, and not just the right to run the race?   22

The fourth step is to set goals and work quietly and systematically towards them. So often we feel we have to talk loud rather than act effectively. So often we get bogged down in our ego needs and lose sight of our broader community goals. T. S. Eliot in his play "The Cocktail Party" said that "half the harm that is done in this world is due to people who want to feel important." Wanting to feel important is good, but not at the expense of *doing* important deeds — even if we don't get the credit. You can get a mighty lot done in this world if you don't mind doing the work and letting other people take the credit. You know what you do and the Lord knows what you do and that's all that matters.   23

The fifth step is knowing the difference between substance and style. Too many of us think success is a Saks Fifth Avenue charge card or a "bad" set of wheels or coming to this Black Caucus dinner. Now these are things to enjoy, but they are *not* life goals. I was watching one of President Johnson's inaugural balls on television with a black college president's wife in Mississippi when Mrs. Hamer, that great lady of the   24

Mississippi civil rights movement who lacked a college degree, but certainly not intelligence or clear purpose, came onto the screen. The college president's wife moaned: "Oh my, there's Miz Hamer at the President's ball and she doesn't even have a long dress." My response was: "That's alright. Mrs. Hamer with no long gown is there and you and I with our long gowns are not." So often we miss the real point—we buy BMWs and fur coats before we think about whether where we're going to drive and wear them is worthwhile. Nobody ever asks about what kind of car Ralph Bunche drove or designer suit Martin Luther King, Jr., bought. Don't confuse style with meaning. Get your insides in order and your direction clear first and then worry about your clothes and your wheels. You may need them less.

The sixth step is valuing family life. We must build on the strong 25
black tradition of family and teach our children to delay family formation until they are economically and emotionally stable and ready to raise the new generation of black children and leaders. Black and white men must support their children as best they can and not have them until they are ready to take responsibility for them. We must strengthen family rituals: prayers if we are religious, regular family meals, and participation in school work and in non-school activities. Our children need constructive alternatives to the street. We must *do* things with our children. Listen to them. Be moral examples for them. If we cut corners, they will too. If we lie, they will too. If we spend all our money on our backs and wheels and tithe no portion of it for our colleges, churches, and civic causes, they won't either.

We must join together as an entire community to establish an ethic 26
of achievement and self-esteem in poor and middle class black children. They can do science and math as well as basketball and football, computers as well as cotillions, reading along with reggae. If we expect these accomplishments of them, support them in their learning processes, and help them in setting priorities. They need strong consistent adult buffers to withstand the negative messages of the external world that values them less than white or middle class children.

When I, like many of you, was growing up in my small segregated 27
southern town, the whole outside world, the law of the land, local officials, the media, almost everybody outside our own community told black children we weren't worth much or were second rate. But we didn't believe it because our parents said it wasn't so. Our preachers said it wasn't so. Our caring teachers said it wasn't so. And they nurtured us as a community, shielded us against the constant psychological battery of our daily environment and made us understand that we could make it — had to make it — but in order to do so, we had to struggle to make our

own opportunities in order to help change America. And we went on to college — poor and black — and tried to carry out their other lesson to give some of what they gave us back in service to others left behind. Service, they taught, is the rent you pay for living. Where is our buffer today for the black and poor children who are daily wounded by a national administration who would rather judge than help the poor? Where are the strong local officials and community voices and hands shielding and fighting for the poor children in our city streets against the ravages of drugs and crime? Where are the role modelling, mentoring, and tutoring programs that help black children overcome the pernicious undercurrents of many, even our purported friends, who really think black children lack the potential of other children? What activities are your churches and sororities and fraternities sponsoring to keep children busy and off the streets?

The seventh step is to vote and use our political and economic   28
power. Only 51 percent of all voting age blacks voted in the 1980 election and only 56 percent in the 1984 election. Seventy percent of 18- to 25-year-old black youths did not vote in the last election. People who do not vote have no line of credit with people who are elected and pose no threat to those who act against our interests. Don't even pretend that you care about the black community, about poor children, about your nation, even about your own future, if you don't exercise the political leverage Medgar Evers and others died to make sure we had. And run for political office. And when you win don't forget that you are the means to serve others well and not the end.

No one running for president or any office should get black com-   29
munity support unless they have a well thought-out set of policies designed to lift the black child and family. Similarly, we need to use our economic power for the benefit of black families, particularly in industries where we constitute a large market share.

Two last steps and I'm done.   30

Remember your roots, your history, and the forebears' shoulders on   31
which you stand. And pass them on to your children and to other black children whose parents may not be able to. As a black community today there is no greater priority than assuring the rootedness of all our children — poor, middle class, and Ivy League. Young people who do not know where they come from and the struggle it took to get them where they are now will not know where they are going or what to do for anyone besides themselves if and when they finally arrive somewhere. And if they run into bad weather on the way, they will not have the protective clothing to withstand the wind and the rain, lightning and

thunder that have characterized the black sojourn in America. They need the anchor and rightful pride of a great people that produced a Harriet Tubman and Sojourner Truth and Frederick Douglass from slavery, a Benjamin Mays and Martin Luther King, Jr., and Fannie Lou Hamer from segregation, people second to none in helping transform America from a theoretical to a more living democracy.

The last step is to keep dreaming and aiming high. At a time when   32
so many in public and private life seem to be seeking the lowest common denominator of public and personal conduct, I hope you will dream and set new examples of service and courage.

Dr. Benjamin Mays, a former president of Morehouse College and   33
role model for me said: "It must be borne in mind that the tragedy of life doesn't lie in not reaching your goal. The tragedy lies in having no goal to reach. It is not a calamity to die with dreams unfulfilled, but it is a calamity not to dream. It is not a disaster to be unable to capture your ideal, but it is a disaster to have no ideal to capture. It is not a disgrace not to reach the stars, but it is a disgrace to have no stars to reach for. Not failure, but low aim, is sin." We must aim high for our children and teach them to aim high.

I'd like to end with part of a prayer for children written by Ina   34
Hughes of South Carolina.

> We pray for children
> Who spend all their allowance before Tuesday,
> Who throw tantrums in the grocery store and pick at their food,
> Who like ghost stories,
> Who shove dirty clothes under the bed, and never rinse out the tub,
> Who get visits from the tooth fairy,
> Who don't like to be kissed in front of the carpool,
> Who squirm in church and scream in the phone,
> Whose tears we sometimes laugh at and whose smiles can make us cry.
> And we pray for those
> Whose nightmares come in the daytime,
> Who will eat anything,
> Who have never seen a dentist,
> Who aren't spoiled by anybody,
> Who go to bed hungry and cry themselves to sleep,
> Who live and move, but have no being.
> We pray for children who want to be carried and for those who must,
> For those we never give up on and for those who don't get a second
>   chance.
> For those we smother . . . and for those who will grab the hand of anybody
>   kind enough to offer it.

Please offer your hands to them. Let your Amen be in your committed actions to help black children when you leave here. They desperately need your help on a one-to-one basis and in the political arena. We must all work to redirect the nation's foolish priorities which favor bombs and missiles over babies and mothers upon whom our real national and community security rest.

Notes

1. Reprinted from *Vital Speeches*, March 15, 1974, 346–348. Used with permission.
2. Reprinted from *Congressional Record*, October 7, 1987, Vol. 133, No. 156, S13779–S13781 (Washington, D.C.: Government Printing Office).

Index

speech and analysis, 315–316
  testing, 334–340
Reasons order, 82–83
Reavey, Edward, Jr., 114, 121n
Receiver, 10–11
Recording material, 62–63
Refutation, 344–351
  assignments, 346–347
  checklist, 347
  defined, 332
  fallacies, 336, 338, 340–342
  outlining, 345
  speeches, 347–351
  steps in, 346
Rehearsal, 137–141
Relevance, 188–189
Remembering, 162–165
Repetition, 110–111, 162–163
  in informative speaking, 190–191
Reporting speech, 248–265
  assignment, 258
  checklist, 259
  defined, 248
  and interviewing, 249–255
  outline, 260–262
  and analysis, 262–264
  and surveying, 255–258
Research, 51–62
  citing, 63–64
  recording, 62–63
Resonance, 126
Restatement, 110–111
Rhetorical question, 113–114
Ritchey, G. H., 201, 213n
Roget's Thesaurus, 101
Roles, 378–384
Rorabacher, Louise, 265
Roskens, Ronald W., 121n
Ross, Marion, 91, 97n
Rubin, Alan M., 173
Rubin, Rebecca B., 173

Sampling, for survey, 255–256
Schertz, Robert H., 121n
Sexist language, 117
Shaw, Marvin E., 369, 387n
Sheldon, Kathleen, "Open Your
  Eyes," 328–330
Sign, 309–310
  testing, 339–340
Sikorski, Gerry, 121n
Simile, 107–109
Simple words, 103–104

Sites, James N., 121n
Skimming, 58–59
Slides, 208–209
Smith, Mary John, 353
Social Sciences Index, 55
Source, 7–8
Source material, 51–62
  citing of, 63–64
Space order, 81
  in descriptive speeches, 232–233
Speaker, 7–8
Specific purpose. *See* Speech goal
Specific words, 77, 102–103
Speech goal, 17
  defined, 33
  general, 32–33
  persuasive, 272–277
  specific, 33–35
Spontaneity, 125
  in rehearsal, 139–140
Stage fright, 20–21, 141–144
Startling introduction, 87
Statistical sources, 56
Statistics, 66–67
  fallacies, 341–342
Steil, Lyman K., 171n
Stereotyping, 119–120
Story, 88
Strickland, Rennard, 247n, 302n
Style. *See* Language
Subjects. *See* Topics
Subordination, 75
Summary, 91, 377–378
Superstition, 338
Supporter, 382
Supporting material. *See* Source;
  Source material
Survey, 53–54, 255–258
  questionnaires, 256–258
  samples, 255–256
Suspense, as an introduction, 89
Symposium, 384
Synonym, 239

Tacey, William S., 171n
Task roles, 379–382
"Television and Children," Mary
  Heintz, 298–300
Thesis statement, 35–37
Thibaut, J. W., 319, 331n
"Think Strawberries," James
  Lavenson, 388–395
Time order, 80–81

Titling speeches, 93–94
Topic order, 81–82
Topics, for speeches, 223, 232, 244,
  258
  selecting, 29–32
Toulmin, Stephen, 305, 317n
Transitions, 111–113, 191
Tributes, 361–362

Understanding, 158–160
"Using Lie Detector Tests,"
  Martha Feinberg, 349–351
  Sheila Kohler, 348–349

Value, questions of, 364–365
Variety and expressiveness, 129–130
Visual aids, 71, 192, 194
  chalkboards, 209–210
  charts, 204–208
  computer graphics, 210
  drawings, 203–204
  films, 208
  graphs, 206
  maps, 205
  models, 202
  objects, 201
  pictures, 202–203
  projections, 209
  speaker as, 201
  speech assignment, 212
  use of, 211–212
Vital Speeches, 404n
Vividness, 77–78, 106–109
Vocabulary, and listening, 102,
  158–159
Vocal folds, 127
Vocal interferences, 130–131
Voice, 125–132
  pitch, 127
  production, 126
  quality, 128–129
  rate, 128
  variety and expressiveness,
    129–130
Volume, 127–128

Ware, John E., 150n
Warrants, 303. *See also* Reasoning
Washington Post, 404n
Watson, Kittie W., 171n
Weaver, Richard, 99, 121n, 238,
  247n, 289, 302n
Welcomings, 360–361

Photo Credits